MARY,

TOOK  OUGH
TO WRITE, NUT HERE IT IS.

HOPE YOU ENJOY

is it sisters?

A Lesbian Love Story

Nancy Lehigh

TWO P's PUBLISHING
BAYSIDE, CA

Two P's Publishing
1836 Old Arcata Road, Box 102
Bayside, CA 95524

Printed in the United States of America

This is a memoir. I have tried to recreate events, locales, and conversations from my memories of them. In order to maintain their anonymity, I have changed the names of individuals and some places and some identifying characteristics and details.

ISBN:978-0-98817121-0-4

Library of Congress Catalog Number: 2012948491

Front Cover Art: Les Deux Amies/The Two Friends
1894 Oil on cardboard
Back Cover Art: La Grande Loge/The Large Theatre Box
1896 Lithograph
by Henri de Toulouse-Lautrec (1864-1901 French)
Musée Toulouse-Lautrec, Albi, France

ISBN: 0988172104
ISBN 13: 9780988172104

people, places & purpose

Though this is a memoir based on actual events, the names of the characters, as well as some of the names of places, have been changed to preserve anonymity. Those within my inner circle of friends and family, however, will no doubt call me out on making a thin attempt to shield at all. They will likely recognize many of these accounts, and perhaps even recognize themselves within them. To those who do, I thank them now for enriching my life with their participation, not just within the stories told here, but beyond what is written. For that and more, I truly love you.

Over the years many have supported and encouraged my efforts to complete this remembrance. A family of friends who have been there for me in so many ways: Jim, Tim, Karen, Marge, Lisa, Helen, Vee, Patricia, Hokie, Sue, Mary, Ginger—you form the netting beneath the tightrope of my life which was pretty perilous for a long while. Others likewise furnished friendship, advice, read early efforts, and offered kind words: Judith, Stephanie, Martha, Marita, Linda, Richard, and Nita. Friends also of key significance to me: Virginia, J.O., Jeanne, Beverly, Jon, Gill, Irene, Warren, Marcie, Steve, and EJ.

Inexpressible thanks go to Jessica Taylor Tudzin for her superb editing skills, understanding heart, her encouragement, and friendship—this is finally a book because of her.

These chronicles are documented primarily for my family so they may know about my life with my True Love, an amazing woman named Alice. I also wrote it for our friends, so they may understand how much they mattered in the life we created together. And finally, I wrote it for those who chance upon it, to have a first hand account of the times Alice and I lived in—the turbulent 1970s and the decadent 1980s—and the effect this era had on us.

It is a tale of friends, neighbors, family, mothers, and daughters. A yarn infused with the flavor of California—-piquant and spicy Greater Los Angeles and the invigorating, soul-satisfying redwood country of Humboldt County. Plus a dash of the chili and tang of Texas. And a savory pinch of the East Coast. Ultimately, though, this is a love story ... a story of True Love between two women, Alice and me.

is it sisters?

A Lesbian Love Story

premise & promises

I wager fewer than one in twenty ever finds True Love. Hell, I'll stick my neck out and say fewer than one in two hundred find it. And I'd probably be covered if I upped the odds to one in two thousand.

A wise gambler will pass on the bet.

Sure, many people claim to have met their "soul mate." Yet, for a significant number, divorce statistics are testament to a case of mistaken identity. True Lovers don't divorce or split up. But, as mine did, they can leave in death.

True Love, if it comes at all, seeks *you* out. Some obstinate people stalk it, passing up a lifetime of chances for happiness along the way in search of some overblown notion of perfection.

And others, perhaps more than we would care to imagine, just abandon the idea of True Love altogether. After several tries, they settle instead for the closest resemblance to it, ultimately believing True Love is a myth, a fairy tale, a fool's folly. To them the ideal mate doesn't exist, so they quit looking and choose perhaps someone who makes a decent living or can be a good parent, someone who won't make them want to serve up a strychnine cocktail after a few years.

Well, be warned!

True Love does exist. Though, not decked out in the lace and velvet of courtly manners and medieval tales, nor bestowing gossamer wakeup kisses from Prince Charming. True Love waltzes in, not to troubadour ballads and mincing madrigals, but with all the discord of a dropped piano.

True Love is a lightning strike and nearly as rare. It crashes into your life like a wrecking ball, cracks through the hardpan of your carefully laid plans, and bursts into bloom like a replicating virus. It is messy and ill timed and will not be denied. True Love does not care if you don't believe in it. It thumbs its nose at objections and impediments—such as being already tied to someone else.

Like some joke detective, True Love may even appear in disguise. In my case, materializing as a razor-tongued, tawny blonde: an imposing *woman,* in cowboy boots!

Oh yeah, do be warned.

But if True Love finds you—once the scourging winds sigh away and the scouring dust settles—you will dwell in the true north of your life, aligned with your destiny. By the transforming alchemy of True Love, all there is of real magic in this world, your soul shall be replete, your heart will awake to its song.

a blonde in boots

"**I**'ve been in love with you since the moment you walked into my lab."

I don't know exactly what I expected Alice to say, but that sure wasn't it.

We are in my living room, pretty much bare of everything but towering stacks of packing boxes filled with all my worldly possessions. I have my third tumbler of wine in hand, having gulped down two in a row and still I remain sober as a hangman. Trying to drink myself calm. Hoping to stop the fluttering of my hands and the quivering in the cold core of my gut. Trembling from the icy chill I feel in my bones, which has nothing to do with the cozy temperature of the room and everything to do with my out-of-control emotions.

The light from the fire roars high, painting soft shadows on her sweet face and highlighting her short, softly curled, blond hair with golden glints—the same gold sheen as on my wedding band.

"I've been in love with you since the moment you walked into my lab."

This was her shocking reply to what I just told her a minute ago. Well, first I blathered on for two hours, at long last to convey that I worked these last several months in her company every day, falling slowly and inexorably in love with her.

"I'm in love with you, Alice." There. I said it to her, flat out. Finally.

I never had romantic feelings for a woman before in all my thirty-one years. There is no explanation for it. Nothing she's ever done or said has led me here; Alice never indicated in any way that she has anything like this kind of feeling for me.

Till now.

She's just been herself. Apparently that's been plenty enough—just being herself—and I am thoroughly seduced, wild and shaking with need.

I think I vainly hoped when I confessed my love that she might merely laugh and pat me on the head and tell me, "Poor dear. Relax. You'll get over it." When I dared allow myself a fleeting thought of how she might react to my feelings about her, it was with mortal fear that she'd be stiffly offended, or distressingly embarrassed, or painfully discomfited. Still, I knew I must not go away, cannot leave her without telling her how I feel. Without saying, "I love you." Or I would forever regret it.

But it's all so hopeless anyhow. I leave California in five days to join my husband in Texas. Yes, my husband—a man I love very much. And how can I possibly have fallen in love with anyone else, let alone a woman, when I am married? Committed.

"I've been in love with you since the moment you walked into my lab."

These words are still ringing in my ears, and Alice is quietly gazing at me with heated eyes, smoky blue and brimming with love. I am lost in those expressive eyes as the memory slowly unfolds of the day we met. Those blue eyes come into sharp focus as I first saw them eight months earlier, on a winter morning in 1972.

We were to argue about it much later, about what happened in that moment of meeting. Alice contends I blurted out, "I'm Nancy, and who in the hell are you?"

Of course, I didn't. I wouldn't. Would I? I think I was raised better than that.

I had already been at my job as an X-ray tech for a couple of months, at a small family medical practice in Southern California, when Alice Joan Quincy, the clinic's new lab tech, arrived on the scene. A co-worker prefaced my first encounter with this new person by describing her as "a real character ... and wearing cowboy boots, no less." Not exactly medi-cal footwear I thought, even by California standards. Tennis shoes, per-haps. Birkenstocks with socks, possibly. But cowboy boots?

I went about my morning routine on that day and finishing that, strolled down the hall from my two small X-ray rooms to the tiny galley-shaped lab, two doors down. I rounded in the doorway and there she was: a tall, solidly built, short-haired blonde in her late thirties, under her white lab coat wearing a Western-cut shirt tucked into neatly pressed khakis. And sure enough—on her feet, dark-brown smooth leather cow-boy boots, with ornate spiral stitching, round-point toes, and under-slung walking heels. I could not have known it at the time, but Alice had a surgically fused ankle, for which she needed at least one and a half inch height in her shoes. Boots gave her the support she needed. Plus, as an added benefit, they looked just damn cool.

Then there were those riveting eyes of hers. I would learn that they were capable of changing color with her mood—ranging from ice blue with anger or intensity, to azure most of the time, to smoky blue in pas-sion, and even sometimes, when in private thought, to a faded, bluish-green, like the color of worn-out dollar bills. She had been a tow-headed kid, as I later saw in pictures. The bright sunlight coming in the lab window this day discovered a few remaining natural platinum strands amid the darker blond.

Alice said much later that meeting me hit her like a lightning bolt. I can't vouch for that. But I can tell you that for me the air became sud-denly charged, and I felt like a sparkler had gone off inside me. All my senses heightened, with objects suddenly appearing in sharp relief with highly defined edges. My ears rang and I felt dizzy. I felt as if I had been pole-axed.

I was merely puzzled by these sensations and at the time shook it off, too dumb to know what it meant until many months later. Until that time though, I woke every morning, for the first time in my adult life, anxious to go to work. Walking around all day cuddling a bubble of joy in my gut, laughing more than I had in years. We were to infect everyone we worked with, Alice and I, with our foolishness and play.

A no-nonsense nurse in her mid-forties managed our clinic. A tall, lean redhead, speaking with a slight drawl left over from her Tennessee upbringing, she'd run the place like a tight ship for some twenty years. We dubbed her Big Red. Not because she's big, understand, but that she's mighty. Funny thing though, under all that discipline she was about as playful as they come. I think Alice had much to do with setting the tone in the clinic. I suppose I had no small hand in it either, but for the most part, Alice was the one who orchestrated the merriment while the rest of us happily followed suit. Under her sway—and Big Red's watchful eye—our small staff treated patients with good-humored respect, and turned the work out like it was greased.

Alice's wit was so dry, I heard cracking laughter coming all day long from her lab, some of it from pretty sick patients who were dispensed a little therapeutic humor along with their blood sampling or urine collection. Everyone in the clinic managed to darken her door a couple times a day, and all went away lighter, including Jane, the clinic orderly and all around office gopher.

Jane worked for each one of the clinic's six physicians. Her ability was to appear out of thin air the very instant any one of them happened to need her. She had a knack for it, a true talent. And she moved! One day, she swept into the lab with a request slip for Alice to do a glucose tolerance on Mrs. Alderdice, a regular patient.

"Here's the slip, Alice. Can she come in tomorrow for it?"

"On one condition," answered Alice.

"What's that?"

"That you sit down in that chair there, right now."

Puzzled, Jane followed the strange directive. Alice sat in the blood-draw chair facing Jane and scooted back a little.

"Put your foot up on my knee here,"

"Wh-what?"

"Foot! Up here," insisted Alice.

Looking down at her untied shoe, Jane broke into a sunny smile and lifted her foot onto Alice's knee. Calmly, Alice tied the shoelace that had been trailing behind Jane as she hurried about the clinic.

From that point on, a couple of times a week, Jane would dash up to the lab door, swoop in, drop into the chair, lift her foot—shoelaces dangling—and Alice would whirl around from whatever she was doing to fix Jane up. And with a big smile and a "thanks!" Jane would dash out the door on her way to the next errand.

Even double-knotted, Jane's shoelaces came undone with regularity. It went along with her uncanny ability to speed unbidden where required in this busy medical clinic.

"She just spins out of her shoes," Alice explained.

One time, Big Red was in the doorway delivering instructions to Alice regarding a patient. Jane flew in, dropped into the chair, hung her foot in the air and Alice, not missing a beat as she replied to Big Red, tied the unruly laces, and patted Jane's foot in dismissal. Big Red's eyes followed Jane's hurrying form down the hall, then turned back to Alice with a look of approval spreading across her face. Alice, paying no mind, continued on with their discussion.

One of my fondest memories at the clinic happened on a Wednesday afternoon, on the doctors' golf day, a day we would typically close the office early. Alice and I had just finished our morning routine and were on a coffee break before leaving. It turned out that this would be no ordinary Wednesday. Instead it became the day we would later refer to as the Great Cleanout. Jane popped into the lab, shoes tied for once, to make the pronouncement:

"Come on! Everybody's enlisted to help in the Great Cleanout. You don't want to miss it. Jackie's been bitching about having to do it for days, and we're all gonna show up and spoil her martyrdom. Come on!"

Big Red had issued the order to have the long-neglected storeroom cleaned out and organized. She delegated the task to Jackie, one of the clinic's back-office nurses. Thin and wiry, fast-spoken Jackie had minor delusions of grandeur and a healthy chip on the shoulder. She could be a huge pain in the ass, often bitching and acting put upon, the cause of much eye rolling amongst the staff. To be fair, she was in the process of a divorce, after long years of a childless marriage to a real dork. Even so, it was not uncommon to hear mutterings by the crew, something to the effect of "suited to each other" and "now they'll likely find two other people to make miserable."

"The Dork and the Bitch," Ella the bookkeeper once quipped. "Sounds like an Irish pub." This statement out of the mouth of a woman who was never malicious. Well, unless she was speaking of Jackie, that is.

So, partly to help out, and mostly in self-defense—else we would hear about it for days—we all pitched in. Many hands do make light work; the storeroom was emptying quickly, and Jackie was in her glory, controlling the show and issuing orders officiously. She took it so seriously you'd have thought it was wartime triage for the wounded.

"Put the toilet riser in this corner!" she barked. "That one's for crutches and wheelchair parts—ambulation, not elimination!"

7

Jackie ordered Sally the front-office clerk to throw out a box of toys and stuffed animals. "They're too old and dirty to fool with," she declared as she turned away from Sally to find another order to issue.

It was then that Alice snatched a plushy something from atop the pile Sally was balancing and clutched it under her lab coat, close to her bosom.

"No! Not this one!" shouted Alice. "This one gets to live!"

And abruptly, Alice turned on her boot heel and smartly marched back to the lab with the saved thing, half the staff trailing behind her.

The Great Cleanout was nearly done now anyway. Fortunate, too, 'cause Birdie, another sweet-natured nurse, was beginning to look murderous. I don't think she could have held out much longer before she crowned Jackie, the Great-Cleanout Nazi, with the aforementioned toilet riser.

Alice turned the corner of her lab, shielding the salvaged toy against her body as though someone was about to wrest it from her.

"Mine! Mine, I tell you! Back, back!" she cried. With all the drama of a third-rate actor, Alice peered under beetled brow at the four of us—Jane, Big Red, Birdie, and myself—all crammed into the little lab galley.

"Give it over," Big Red demanded, beckoning Alice with her fingers.

"We just want to see it," Birdie chimed conciliatorily, a disposition much improved since leaving Jackie's presence.

"What is it? Let me see!" Jane pleaded, trying to peer inside Alice's lab coat for a better look.

Alice's eyes caught with mine. She was making quite the show, regarding us all as callous villains out to kidnap her progeny.

I cocked an eyebrow at her and held out my hand, and Alice instantly straightened up and handed me ... a teddy bear. A small, dirty-white teddy bear. Just a common toy bear, nothing fancy—only about a foot tall. And very grimy, with the fur worn off in spots and a large hole worn into the bottom of a back paw. But for all that, it had the sweetest expression.

We all gushed at once. Oohing and aahing and tsk-tsking. Grown women. Such a fuss.

I was certain the little guy could be salvaged and volunteered to take him home and clean him up. "I'll bring him back to you tomorrow," I promised, catching Alice's eye first, then looking pointedly at Big Red for assurances.

"Mine?" asked Alice to Big Red.

Big Red sighed hugely, dramatically. "Yours," she conceded, adding with a pretend threat, "I won't let the big bad nursie take it from you and throw it away. If ... you promise to behave."

Alice agreed, nodding in mock eagerness.

The teddy bear cleaned up nicely. I rolled it in the dryer a few times first, then scrubbed it with foamy detergent, taking care not to loosen the seams, and dried it with a hair dryer. I also dusted it with baking soda to freshen it up and fluffed the worn fur lightly with a hairbrush.

The bear had floppy shoulders and hips. He was comfortingly soft all over, as a matter of fact. Worn spots ranged along the edges of his little ears, and he had a nearly bald patch on his belly, but otherwise he was beginning to look pretty good, bearing some semblance of his original creamy whiteness, which contrasted nicely with his black button eyes and black-thread nose and mouth. The inner part of the ears still had some peachy color.

Altogether, he had metamorphosed into a fine-looking fellow. While darning the hole in his foot with white embroidery thread, I had a light-bulb moment of inspiration and headed for my medicine chest.

As usual, the next morning I came in to work earlier than everyone else. I placed the teddy bear prominently on top of the specimen refrigerator, right inside the door of the lab. He looked quite dapper, sitting on the round-cornered, vintage fridge—a wounded and worn survivor of pediatric examining rooms.

A band-aid covered the hole I darned on his foot. One of his arms was bound in a narrow Ace wrap, with a handkerchief for a sling. I thread-tied a tongue depressor upright to the stubby end of the other arm and wound several strips of gauze in figure-eights around the top of his head, leaving his ears protruding. He seemed to peer out from under the dressing's edge. And to top it off, I fashioned a small red cross in felt and centered it on his gauzy forehead. Utterly charming.

When I emerged a couple hours later from my early morning fluoroscopes, in time for my mid-morning coffee break, a small crowd had gathered around the lab door. The crowd parted as I came closer. Alice was standing in the far corner of the lab where the counters met, and the look in her eyes lit a fiery radiance in the pit of my stomach that quickly spread to my face in a huge blush.

"He says his name is Theodore Von Bear," she announced. "And he's very glad to be home."

Everyone laughed and chattered, stroking my arm and patting my back, voicing their approval before melting away, one by one, going back about their business.

Alice dropped her eyes finally, but the warm smile on her face remained. And for some reason, I couldn't catch my breath.

To properly put my relationship with Alice in full perspective, allow me to rewind nine years, back to 1963, just after John F. Kennedy's assassination. It was then that I joined the Army. I was twenty-two years old and the world was upside down, with real and perceived enemies lurking at every corner of the globe. My personal life seemed stuck in limbo, and my country needed me, so I had been told at the recruiting center.

I don't mean to make light of it. The violent shooting death of our youngest, most forward-thinking president was a life-altering experience for those of us who watched the tragedy unfold in the media. It really was the impetus for my decision to enlist. It was the impetus for a generation of young people—my generation—to call many things into question, when the scales of complacency fell off our eyes. In 1963, our involvement in Vietnam was, for the most part, overlooked by most Americans; the issue had not yet approached the boiling point. However, the next ten years would see the escalation of all this, as fighting raged, as news of atrocities and cover ups surfaced. People would question our government, and opinion throughout the country would be strongly divided.

After finishing my hitch in late 1966, I continued living where I landed, in San Antonio, Texas. I wasn't looking for love when Don asked me out; I was still shaking off the residual effects of a disastrous two-year affair. Don was divorced, retired Air Force, a father of four, and, at age thirty-eight, twelve years my senior. In truth, he was a sweet guy, bright and hard working. Not handsome, but pleasant looking and cheerful, with blue eyes. Although he kept himself fairly fit, he carried a slight paunch. His buzz cut was consistent with his age and retired military status. I remember him for his trusting nature. More trusting than mine, actually.

Don loved his kids, but didn't connect with them in any meaningful way, leaving that chore to his ex-wife, their mother. He willingly paid child support every month; his entire retirement pay went to them. While his kids seemed to love him, I think they feared him, too. Don could be strict and distant. At times, he spoke in platitudes, and often was just plain awkward.

We dated for a while, and in time, Don moved in with me, and that is how it was for two years. I kept Don uncomfortably "living in sin"—people still thought of it like that at the end of the sixties. Only the flower children were sexually liberated in these times. I was totally cool with living together, but Don's Catholic upbringing, our twelve-year age difference, and his need for conformity prompted his pressure to marry. So we did. Though I wasn't *in love*, I did love him. And anyway, unlike the me of today, I was then too cynical to believe in a soul mate. I had known pitifully few relationships that worked, which certainly did not include my parents'. Although I knew some reasonably happily marrieds, they did not seem, any of them, to share True Love.

I waited until I was twenty-eight years old to marry. I can't say I was unhappily married, just not ever really in sync with it. Things changed between Don and me after we stood at the altar. Subtle things. Undisclosed expectations, for instance, which seemed to go with his notion of marriage, but not mine. Unvoiced role assignments and vague assumptions of male-female capabilities. A set of proprieties he deemed suitable to married couples. Perhaps Don brought ideas from his previous failed marriage into ours.

Naïvely, I thought everything would be the same as when we'd been living together; the only difference would be the framed license on the wall. Wrong! After three years of it, I knew that somehow I had settled, and the realization filled me with a vague sense of loss.

I had never known a drinker before, either. Well, not this intimately. Don wasn't an abusive drunk, nor even a daily drunk. He tended to binge drink, so I learned to avoid public situations with him when the binge was on. But we were both so busy it didn't happen that often anyway.

11

Don worked as a fulltime lab tech in San Antonio, at the same hospital where I, too, was employed. He attended college evenings and Saturdays, carrying a full course load in business. For my part, I worked fulltime at the hospital and sold jewelry on the side at house parties. Minimal contact seems to keep a lot of married couples together.

We moved to Los Angeles when Don accepted a job selling lab equipment. It was then that I took the X-ray technician job at the clinic where I met Alice, where my story begins.

Don's territory was the entire state of California. His job called him out of town, driving all over the Golden State, no less than three weeks out of the month. Weekends he spent at home—when he would drink. I didn't mind him being gone, but I began to detest his crawling into a bottle whenever he returned.

Shortly after Alice's arrival to the clinic, Peanuts cartoon strips began to appear on the top of my film processor, a "good-morning" gift from her to me. They had originally been sent to her by her mother. Alice didn't take the paper, getting most of her news from the radio, so her mother supplied the cartoons in weekly letters from Northern California. Alice quietly dropped one outside my door every morning when she came in. Now, looking back on it, they were like receiving a morning kiss.

Exams were conducted the old-fashioned way in this small clinic, with a fluoroscope machine in a room of total darkness. The MD and I wore red-tinted goggles to maintain night vision whenever we left the dark into the stark light of day. In the photographic darkroom, I sent the films through the processor to come out "magically" transformed as X-rays.

Upon my arrival to work each morning at seven-thirty, before anyone else got there, I mixed up the barium solutions for that day's scheduled upper GI's, barium swallows, and barium enemas. Barium is a white, chalky, inert element, used internally in medicine to outline the gastric organs so they can be seen under fluoroscope and on X-ray film. In those years, it came in powder form and had to be blended with water into different consistencies for the exams. Even when highly diluted, barium dries with a pernicious white film over every surface it touches. Bottom line, it's a messy substance to work with.

Since my tiny X-ray department didn't include a sink, I used the one in Alice's lab to mix the barium solutions and I tried to clean up after myself—truly, I did. Wiping down as best I could the shiny stainless steel sink, back splash, and counter, before I took my mixes into the X-ray room. Invariably, some chalky residue from this dirty task was always left behind. Always. By the time the lousy stuff dried, I would be in the examination room with the radiologist. And Alice would arrive at work to a dirty sink.

My daily routine was a juggling act, starting with fluoroscopic exams at eight o'clock. By nine-thirty or ten, after the fluoros, the radiologist would then read the films, plus all the X-rays I had done the previous day, and dictate his findings before leaving the clinic around eleven o'clock. Throughout the afternoon, I would transcribe and type his dictated results, in between taking the routine patient X-rays of chests, abdomens, heads, joints, bones. So, while the doctor read the films each morning, I tidied the darkroom and film processor, and straightened the X-ray room, the dressing room, and the restrooms, before going into the lab to clean up any mess I may have left behind in Alice's sink.

One morning in particular I didn't get off so easy. I found Alice standing at her counter, meticulously pipetting urine into test tubes, her back to the door ... and to me.

"Good Morning," I greeted her cheerily.

"Harrumph!"

"Harrumph?" I questioned, speaking to her back.

"Harrumph!" she repeated. "And ... bother!"

"What? I practically warble 'good morning' and in return all I get is a 'harrumph' and a 'bother'?"

"Harrumph! And bother! ... And *tarnation*!" She took a moment to glance over her shoulder at me, with a small smile to soften the tiny edge of challenge in her voice.

"That bad, huh? Whatsa matter?"

"My sink." She had turned back to the counter, resuming her precise lab tests.

13

"What about it?"

"It's got white film all over it. Again."

"So it has. It's called barium and you know I come back and clean it up every morning. It has to dry in order to see where any splashes are," I replied reasonably.

"Yeah. So ... harrumph."

"And bother. And tarnation," I finished for her.

"Yeah."

"Okay. Duly noted. Not much I can change about it, however."

She laid the glass pipette carefully on a towel-lined lab tray, put the rack of tubes into the centrifuge, closed the lid, flipped the toggle, and set the timer.

"Well, I don't have to like it," she said with a grumble.

"No, you don't ... but you'd be happier if you just ignored it."

Alice finally turned to face me, leaned into the corner of the counter, casually crossed one leg over the other, and replied: "Just so long as you know I'm simply ignoring it and not that I'm actually liking it."

"Well ..." I paused a moment. "I imagine a 'harrumph' now and again will remind me."

"Yeah," she said with a twitch of her lips. "That's what I thought."

In our conversations, which were daily, I learned that Alice was as voracious and eclectic a reader as I was, and, like book-lovers everywhere, we had much to chew on. Fellow readers can forage together for years. We talked about authors and various genres, from history, religion, art, and music, to science, medicine, and astronomy. Fiction and poetry were among our favorites.

We also talked critters. My Brittany Spaniel, Cherub—my first dog and companion for six years—was the little love of my life. And Alice, well, she had a lifetime of experience with dogs, cats, horses, farm animals, and whatnot (a bugger to care for, those what-not.)

It never occurred to me to assign our chats real importance, not in the romantic sense anyway. First of all, I was a married woman. And we are talking about another woman here. And this was 1972. Oh, it was obvious to me that Alice was not your average bear. But at this point I only suspected Alice's sexual orientation, though not from anything overt on her part. It was merely apparent in her demeanor. She knew who she was, and there wasn't much of anything she seemed scared of. She had a very matter-of-fact, "take-me or leave-me" attitude, with an easy natural confidence and self-assurance. Alice fell within the discreet parameters that we recognize today with so-called "gaydar," though not for any conscious telegraphing on her part. She was private and contained and circumspect. And I certainly never picked up on any flirtatiousness from her. If it was there, it was too subtle for me to catch.

Homosexuality, I would read soon enough, had long been considered not only a deviance within the realm of human norm, but a psychiatric disorder. People could be (and very often were) institutionalized, for one reason only—that they were gay!

It was not until the next year, 1973, that homosexuality would be removed from the official list of psychiatric pathology. And not until two years after that, in 1975, would American psychologists strike it from their list of disorders.

This decision—based largely on the life work of Dr. Edith Hooker, a psychologist whose extensive and definitive research focused on male homosexuality—resulted in new psychiatric and psychological assessments and conclusions.

As for me, well, I wasn't a *complete* idiot. I had been in the Army and seen some things. I presumed homosexuals hit their teens, found themselves in some strange, sexually reversed polarity of humanity, and made the best of it. The poor unfortunates.

Dumb. I was Dumb.

And here I was, nearly thirty-one years of age and straight as a string. Only experiencing the usual childhood fumblings, a crush on the seventh-grade English teacher, and that sort of thing. But I was never boy crazy, and I *never* considered girls. I basically had my fair share of men and never questioned my proclivities.

Of course, I had read James Baldwin and Tennessee Williams, and I knew what "gay" meant. However, how they came to be that way and what else about it, up until I met Alice, had been only of passing interest to me.

I was ignorant. But I was about to get a schooling.

DATELINE, 1972—Congress passes Title IX, prohibiting sex discrimination in schools receiving federal funds, thereby boosting girls' participation in school sports as well as encouraging athletics among adult women.

National Organization for Women (NOW) and other feminist organizations take on AT&T for practices of sex discrimination. Senate passes the Equal Rights Amendment (ERA) by an 84 to 8 majority, sending it to the House for ratification.

The Equal Employment Opportunity Act (EEOC) is passed, further empowering the Civil Rights Act of 1964. Shirley Chisholm, a Democrat, becomes the first black woman to run for presidency in a major party. New York Times wins a Pulitzer for The Pentagon Papers, a study consisting of classified material on the expansion of the war in Vietnam.

day by day

At home I began to fill my conversation with Alice references till, naturally, Don wanted to meet her. The opportunity presented itself when my old army friend Naomi was in town on leave. Don and Naomi and I made a date with Alice for dinner at a nearby Italian restaurant, and she showed up with her friend Betty. We ordered drinks at the bar while waiting for a table. Don and Betty both had two drinks to the one each we three ordered, and they kept up the liquid pace throughout dinner. Don and Alice seemed to hit it off, and Naomi and Alice appeared to like each other, too.

Still, at times things felt tense.

"… and Nancy and I wound up trying to explain it to Big Red," Alice finished telling an anecdote.

" 'Nancy and I' … 'Nancy and I' … that's all I ever hear anymore. 'Nancy and I,' " Betty, a little tipsy, complained to the table at large.

I saw Naomi's antennae go up. But Don was oblivious to the subtext of the comment, or too much into the booze to catch it. Alice was observably uncomfortable, and I was merely puzzled that Betty seemed … well, jealous. And I wondered why.

I guess I really can't fault Don. I mean, what's worse: his obliviousness or my naïveté?

At any rate, the evening ended without incident, and the next day at work, Alice appeared casual and commented favorably about Naomi and Don. And we both left it at that.

Don and I knew only two people when we landed in L.A.—Dick and Sarah. Dick was a friend of ours in San Antonio, a fellow X-ray tech: he in the Air Force, me the Army; we'd met at several workshops. Dick was posted on loan for some isotope training to Brooke Army Hospital in San Antone, where I was stationed, and soon he married his longtime sweetheart, Sarah, bringing her to Texas a few months before his tour was up.

Don and I often socialized with them. We included them in our holiday celebrations, and had great fun with them while they honeymooned. When Dick was discharged, they returned to their home in Southern California. Now, two years later when we arrived in L.A., Sarah was very pregnant and due in a month. Dick was responsible for getting me the job at the clinic, and I owed him much for it. I really needed the work and, as it would turn out, it would become the greatest job I ever had.

Dick was easily one of the funniest people I knew, and Sarah was a lovely, pragmatic woman, as calm and unflappable as Dick was excitable and rollicking. As natives of Southern California, a rare breed at the time, they served as our personal tour guides, taking us to all the charming places, costing little or no money. The tide pools at Leo Carrillo State Park in Malibu, named for the actor and conservationist who played Pancho in *The Cisco Kid,* will long stay in my memory. They were the first tide pools I had ever seen. We went often because I was so crazy about them.

On one occasion, Sarah took charge of finding us a nice spot to have our picnic while Don, Dick, and I climbed all over the rocks exploring the pools for sea life—anemones, crabs, clams, sand dollars. We all took turns helping Sarah haul her bulk up from the sand when she got uncomfortable, which was often in her advanced state of pregnancy.

Dick and Sarah had just bought a new house in a brand new development, a cow pasture mere weeks before, and the soil still retained the bovine ammonia to prove it. The housing tract was bare of all but little box houses on empty wide streets, absent tree or bush—one, growing anywhere in the ex-pastureland. It was fun helping them get settled into their new home and planting their first trees and flowers. And a pure delight to see them bring their new baby son, Billy, home from the hospital.

They both met Alice when she came to my thirty-first birthday party in August, hitting it off like they'd all been friends forever.

It's exceedingly gratifying when friends of yours form friendships with each other. It is a validation of your good taste in people, and so entertaining as they show themselves off to each other and display those qualities that make you love them all. This is one of my favorite things to happen, and weaves intricacy into the tapestry of your life in those lovely combined patterns, tracing the shape of your destiny.

Don did his usual pre-party bar preparation for my party, sampling the liquid wares while laying out glasses, ice buckets, and citrus twists. So by the time our guests arrived, he was already three sheets to the wind. I knew he wouldn't be long for it.

Had Dick not helped Don barbecue the steaks, we still might be there waiting for our dinner. By the time Don got to preparing Alice's steak, he did a very odd thing. He tossed it on the grill, grabbed it with the tongs, flipped it over, and in a heartbeat, flung it on a plate and handed it to her.

"Rare enough for you?" he asked.

Alice accepted the plate from him, eye-balling him all the while.

"Jesus, Don!" remarked Dick. "Wipe its nose and run it by the coals once, why don't you? That steak's barely cooked!"

"No, it's all right," Alice said.

Again, I knew I missed something, some subtle byplay.

Don was well into the booze, yet still he managed to toss back a couple more drinks before he said, "Okay, it's time for everyone to leave, isn't it? The party's about over."

Dick and Sarah looked up startled, forks at their mouths, plates still full. Alice was politely trying to saw through a hunk of raw meat on her plate.

"Just ignore him," I instructed. It wasn't even 7:30 pm. "Don, behave yourself! It isn't even dark yet. We've barely begun our dinner," I chided.

"Oh. Oh. Sorry."

"Don, honey, let me fix you a plate; you need something to eat," I said, reaching for a platter.

"Hell no! It'll spoil a good buzz-on." He scooped a few ice cubes into his glass, and poured it full of gin.

Eyes caught eyes all around the table, and everyone calmly went about enjoying their dinner, as Don drank his. I had seen him do this before; I recognized this for a binge and knew it would end soon with him tottering off to bed. Like I said, he wasn't a bad drunk, just a complete one. And it made me angry to be left in social circumstances like this.

This time, however, I wasn't so perturbed. Alice was there, and I was enjoying myself.

Sure enough, not ten minutes later, Don stood up and announced, "Well, goodnight all. I think I'll go to bed now," and staggered off into the house.

With Don now gone, Dick asked Alice for her plate, and slid the bloody steak back on the grill. "Let's give that cow a few more minutes, shall we?"

Alice smiled and lit a cigarette, and conversation continued to flow.

Darkness fell on our backyard, creating yet another soft summer evening for which Southern California is so well known. We had finished our dinner and were into coffee and birthday cake while Don's snore, muffled in his bedclothes, resonated distantly from within. Dick and Sarah took that as their cue, and picked up sleeping Billy, rounded up the endless baby gear it takes to travel with one, and bid their farewell.

After they left, Alice and I remained in the yard, poured some more wine, and settled in the lawn chairs and talked. And talked. And talked. We talked of mothers and families. Friends. Pets. Loved ones. Life forces and dreams. Pain and suicide. We talked till dawn. She was relaxed and confident in herself, her abilities, her intelligence, her womanhood, in her right to be alive, and to make her way—her own way—in this world. Daily, in the smallest, least-noticed areas, she had opened new vistas of thought for me. Her approach to life virtually infected me with some welcome, miracle, live-vaccine, and revitalized my concepts.

A particular fragment of that conversation remains in my memory. We were discussing our outlook on life, and, of all random things, what it must have been like to be a Jew during the Second World War, imprisoned in one of Hitler's concentration camps.

"I couldn't have stood it," I said. "It simply would not have been worth it to me to try to stay alive. I mean, you'd never know, of course, unless it really happens to you, but I feel sure I'd have been one of those people who curls up and dies, or gets herself shot. I have real 'quality of life' issues and I just wouldn't want to live any longer in a world where such a horror could happen to me or anyone around me."

"Really?" asked Alice.

"Yes. Would you? What would you have done?"

"Well, I wouldn't want to live like that either, but I wouldn't just roll over and let them win. I'd probably have tried to grab a gun and take a few of the sons-of-bitches with me."

"Would you?" I asked. But I knew Alice was capable of it. I had already witnessed a small sample of her righteous anger at the clinic. It was no huge stretch to imagine her going into 'Avenging Angel' mode and mowing down a few Nazis. "Well, in any event," I added, "I wouldn't struggle to survive, I don't think."

"No," she backtracked, "neither would I. But not for that reason, exactly. More because I'm probably going to have to come back and do it all over again, so there's no point in hanging on to a lost cause."

She referred to her long-ago car accident, and this time elaborated on the beliefs and values she adopted out of that experience. I found them close to my own, formed from reading books on religion and philosophy, with the usual minor, brief foray into witchcraft, the occult, and the like, and back out again. (If you investigate Christianity at any length, you come full circle, analyzing the motives behind the Inquisition and the witch hunts, which lead you into the ancient origins of paganism and Goddess worship, and back again to its suppression by the Church, who linked these nature-based ideas to their concept of Satan.)

At any rate, I had spent years delving into various spiritual issues. Though Alice had taken her own path, we both came pretty close to the same basic conclusions.

We talked till the early morning dew fell on us. Shortly after we retreated indoors to escape the chill, Alice decided to call it a night and drove home. And I retired to the bedroom, crawling in next to Don, still snoring in his drunken stupor.

❈

In May 1972, the US Navy had mined Haiphong Harbor in Vietnam and commenced bombing in response to the Viet Cong crossing the demilitarized zone (DMZ.) With the mining of the harbor, TV broadcasters reported the news with great alarm, more strident, more apocalyptic in their assessment of the potential results of our aggressive military action. The nation went on high alert. The war in Vietnam raged. The US was committed with unnumbered troops, armament, ships, and planes. And North Vietnam had acquired their weaponry from the Soviets and Chinese. In essence, the world's superpowers—the US and the USSR— were in vicarious conflict with each other in that remote little country. And the move by our Navy against them breaching the DMZ looked like it might escalate it further.

Don and I were following the newscasters' assessments, when he hatched an emergency plan: "Okay, here's what we'll do. We'll agree on a place to meet somewhere in the state. You take Cherub to work with you in the car for the first few days. We'll both pack water and supplies. Take a pistol with you, too, in the trunk. You keep the radio on, and if you feel this is going to get worse, I want you to leave work, get on the road, and meet me where we will agree. Okay?"

"What? You can't be serious?" I protested.

"Of course I'm serious, Nancy. This is really alarming, and L.A. is a prime target for attack. So, I want us to be prepared."

"Oh, Don. I'm not going to do that. If things get worse, the last thing I will do is get out on the highway with six million other crazies all trying to leave the city at the same time, all panicky. No way!"

"Now, Nancy, don't joke about this."

"Don, I am completely serious. I won't even consider it." I was adamant.

"Well, what will you do, then?" asked Don, stunned.

"Listen, if I get any warning of it all going bad, I will drive home by all the back roads, light a fire in the fireplace, open a bottle of wine, take my dog on my lap, and pray to be at Ground Zero."

He was horrified. "You can't mean that!"

"I mean every word. I have no wish whatsoever to survive a nuclear attack, or a Third World War fought right here—killing, raping, thieving, looting, violence in every neighborhood—and that's just the locals taking it out on each other in panic! Half of us would be dead at the hands of the other half before a foreign boot even touches our soil. I don't wish to physically fight for survival. I simply don't have the gumption for it," I declared with all the sincerity I could muster. This was the stuff of nightmares, and given the choice, I would sooner die.

"I can't believe it. Not trying, not wanting to stay alive?" he said. It made him angry. "It's a basic instinct. How can you think this way?"

"Well, I do. And I always have, Don. It would be more than I can tolerate. Survival to me means a reasonable quality of life, and I can't think of a worse scenario than what we're talking about."

We stared at each other for a long moment before Don stood up and left the room. We never spoke of it again.

Interesting how a core philosophy of life, so basic, so fundamental, goes for years without surfacing in relationships. I guess we all draw our personal line in the sand and make assumptions that those we love feel the same way.

Certainly, as our world changes and circumstances alter, we re-evaluate. We move that line for ourselves, estimating new dangers and threats, determining what we will and won't put up with, can and cannot do, if faced with life-threatening sickness or circumstance, and what steps we'll take to protect ourselves, our loved ones, home, life. How we actually react, if put to the test, might surprise us. But underneath it all, some final, personal, moral determination is made. And it is almost never stated before then. I had done exactly that in the space of four months with two key players in my life.

In the end, Don and I had a poles-apart response to dealing with a grave crisis. And Alice and I also came away a bit astonished at each other's solution to a hypothetical life or death situation. Rather amazing.

DATELINE, 1972— **Richard Nixon** becomes the first US president to enter the People's Republic of China and meet with Chairman Mao Zedong. **Five intruders** are arrested trying to bug the headquarters of the Democratic National Committee, initiating the **Watergate scandal. President Nixon** makes a secret agreement to sell wheat at a discount to the Soviet Union, enraging American farmers to call it the "Great Train Robbery."

Congress passes the Clean Water Act; Oregon passes the country's first bottle recycling law; **EPA bars DDT** on the grounds that it accumulates in the food chain.

Britain takes over Northern Ireland in direct rule. **Governor George Wallace** of Alabama is shot and left paralyzed while stumping for his presidential bid. **Arab terrorists kill** 11 Israeli athletes in Olympic Village in Munich, Germany. **Mark Spitz** sets the Olympic record for gold medals, winning seven. **Carlton Fisk** is named American League Rookie of the Year.

The **Supreme Court rules** the death penalty as unconstitutional. **Roberta Flack** wins a Grammy for *The First Time Ever I Saw Your Face*, winning Best Song as well as **Best Writer for Ewan McColl**. Best female vocal performance goes to **Helen Reddy** for *I Am Woman*, which becomes the **unofficial anthem** for the women's movement (70 percent of song purchasers are women.)

sea change

Full fathom five thy father lies;
Of his bones are coral made;
Those are pearls that were his eyes:
Nothing of him that doth fade,
But doth suffer a sea-change
Into something rich and strange.

The Tempest, William Shakespeare

Over the first several months of our budding friendship, Alice and I shared our lives' history with each other. But I knew she was leaving blank areas—big blank areas. She was private, and I was disinclined to pry.

She did, however, relay the story of her auto accident in 1961, when she was twenty-seven years old—riding as a passenger, not driving. It had nearly killed her, and practically crippled her permanently. Almost every bone on the right side of her body had suffered a break or displacement. Her injuries included a dislocated shoulder, a snapped collarbone, two breaks in her upper right arm, three broken ribs, a dislocated hip posteriorly, and a crushed ankle.

After the accident, her family rallied around. Her mother and stepfather rented a house in the Los Angeles area, one with large doorways to accommodate a hospital bed, and later a wheelchair, and they moved

Alice in. To help with finances, her stepbrother Tony also moved in, along with his best buddy, both paying room and board.

Alice's mother, Nora, tended to Alice throughout the ordeal, plus fed and cared for everybody else—all of them working various shifts, with no duplications. The beleaguered woman cooked and fed round the clock, in addition to caring for Alice, who was totally bedfast for the best part of a year in a heavy plaster body cast from armpit to buttock, with a separate leg cast, plus an arm cast held out from her body by a wire armature. Just managing the bedpan must have been an engineering feat for them both. Nora later acknowledged it was the most challenging—and selflessly rewarding—time of her life.

Early on, of course, Alice was heavily sedated for the pain. But ultimately it was nine months to lie abed with nothing to do but think. And till then, she told me, she had avoided thinking about her life. She considered it a waste of time when there was partying to be done, taking life all quite for granted, a trait of the young and reckless.

She never said so, but I think Alice must have been a very angry young woman. And speculating on it later, I'm sure she had a lot to be angry about, in view of the unpopularity of her life choices then. Well-meaning matchmakers constantly hounded a woman who took too long to marry. And lesbians ... well, they took a lot of flack. That holds true today, too, of course, but, at the same time, now there is also wider support and acceptance. Back then, most gay people tried to keep it secret. For someone as straightforward as Alice, this presented problems, I'm certain.

She told me she was constitutionally incapable of lying, and this always got her into a lot of trouble. When asked for her opinion, I once heard her warn, "Don't ask me if you don't really want to know." Her sister-in-law didn't speak to her for six months after asking Alice's estimation of a newly purchased dress.

Alice was indeed a wild child. Too smart for her own good. Society wasn't too keen on smart women back then either, let alone smart, gay women. On paper, she may have appeared under-educated and working class, but in reality, she was refined, over-read, and more intelligent than anyone she ever worked for, or with. A lethal combination, to say the least. So, a rebel, and a party animal, and reckless as they come—till the car wreck.

26

It was a sea change. She came out of the plaster cast a totally different person. Friends before had faded away. New people entered her life, people she wouldn't have glanced at earlier. Life had taken on new meaning. She had acquired a calm nucleus, and she lived more in the moment than anyone I had ever known.

I'll let her tell you for herself in this letter sent me much later:

October 25, 1973

Hi Lovely Lady,

Have given thought to what you asked me ~ thumb-nail sketch of what I want in life ~ will try to explain. Thirteen yrs. ago I wanted everything in the world w/ moon and stars thrown in. Big house, huge stereo, new car, money, over-much booze. Was really gung-ho for trying everything, doing everything I hadn't done. I was so busy trying to grab everything that I couldn't see anything. There wasn't much I didn't have or try ~ there was nothing I couldn't do ~ there still isn't, it just isn't so important anymore.

When I woke up in the hospital I knew I wasn't going to die, no one else did tho'. I also knew if I wasn't going to die (I really didn't care if I did @ that moment) something was going to have to change ~ I didn't want things the way they were before. So when I finally got to take my ton of plaster home I couldn't do much except look, listen + be ~ Started to look around, had my mother open all of the windows so I could see the trees + sky, hear the birds + crickets, feel the wind + cold. All of a sudden there was a world there which I'd never seen before, there were flowers growing, kids playing, people ~ not just other beings, but real people w/

real feelings, wants + needs. There had always been people there, but only to give me a place to go or have around to fill up the hrs. Understand? Now I listened to them, saw them, + even talked to them once in a while. It was a new + exciting thing.

Now what I want in life is pretty simple. Some people say it shows a decided lack of ambition ~ I disagree. I want a home, not an elaborate house ~ a comfortable home. Food + wine, enough, not too much. Books + good company (friends to know, talk to, be with). Time ~ life is so short. I want time to stop + listen to the ocean, sit + watch the seagulls, walk in the forest + hear the wind in the trees, feel the silence. To sit in front of the fireplace + hear + see the fire. Never be in such a hurry I can't stop and watch puppies playing. Make any sense? And most important ~ someone to love. Someone to share the things that are important ~ even things that aren't important like dirty coffee cups. That, my love, is you. Hope you can decipher this + it answers the question ~ if not, ask me more. Will stop now ~

Take care, my love. I love you, Nancy.

Alice

This was Alice, during our writing phase. From the moment I met her, it was pretty obvious she knew who she was, confident and unafraid, meeting life on its own terms. Likely this was residual from the accident, part of the sea change.

Even in most of her later letters, she tended to be a woman of few words—a few pithy words. At all times she was direct, which she called a failing as well as a virtue, declaring this a trait of Archers, the Sagittarian sign she was born under.

Alice wasn't a towering woman, but she could be imposing. She was solid at 5 feet 10 inches and 180 pounds when I met her (she would gain about twenty more pounds over later years.) Above and beyond her physicality, she projected strength and could be formidable. It wasn't anything she strove for, it was just who she was; moreover, the few times I saw her angry, it felt like she brought down the skies. Few would ever cross her. I told her once, early on in our relationship, that if she ever got truly mad at me, I'd probably wither up and blow away. Mostly because, though rare to see, I knew her anger never to be anything but righteous.

Couple this with the fact that when she chose to, she could see into your soul. And that was scary to a lot of people. She readily saw through masks and pretenses, though if she liked someone enough, she could actually draw them out from behind their pose till they were comfortable just being themselves. Alice didn't easily suffer fools.

And she never did get angry with me. The few times in our life that I vexed her or got on her nerves with something, she just said, "Nancy, that's enough." And it immediately made me stop and examine what I had been doing. With me, she always was a big softie.

However, I ventured very much ahead of myself here with these few things. So allow me to backtrack.

On this particular day, we are in deep conversation in the lab and she finishes a thought, "… in the long run, it doesn't really matter," says Alice.

"What doesn't?"

"Everything, nothing. Almost everything we worry about, that drives us nuts, that we fuss about … it doesn't really matter."

"Then what does?" I ask.

She looks at me for a long moment. "Well, exactly! That's exactly what matters."

"What? What matters? Are you deliberately being obtuse?"

"I've never been so accused in all my life!" She goes wide-eyed and slaps her chest dramatically, putting the lie to actually being indignant.

I sigh. "Well, are you going to tell me what you mean, or are you going to sit there and play Zen Master with me?"

"What I mean is," she says patiently, "knowing the only things that matter is all that really matters."

"You are, aren't you?" I whine. "You are gonna sit there and play Zen Master with me."

"Lady, it's simple. Most of what we think is important doesn't amount to a tinker's dam in the end. And it's up to you to learn what does."

I am quiet for a minute, looking into her deep blue eyes. Thinking. She really does look like a Zen Master. She has a sweet, soft face, and those brilliant eyes of hers reflect her intelligence. And then there is the quiet core of her, evident in this moment, which is so seductive.

"Well," I say finally, "we get out of here—out of this life I mean—with only two things that I can think of: what we learn and how we love."

It is her turn to be quiet, to look full at me. I see a play of thoughts go through her eyes in flashes. And the pull gets stronger.

"And that's all," she says. "That's what really matters."

Again her eyes flash. There is a heart-stopping moment, and then the corner of her mouth tugs up. "The trick, of course, is to keep that uppermost in your mind when the shit piles on."

I laugh. "Well, I can tell you what matters right now. I've just smoked my last ciggie. I'm out."

It is Alice's turn to chuckle, and she picks up her pack of Marlboros and shakes out a cigarette for me.

On another day, a drizzly, chilly day in early June—June gloom in Southern California—the type of day that begs for the consolation of a wee bit of the Irish, I prop myself in the doorway of Alice's lab. "You know what I wish I had on a dreary day like this?" I ask. "An Irish coffee."

"God, that sounds like a little bit of heaven, if e'er I heard it," says Alice, in a deplorable Irish brogue while removing blood specimens from the refrigerator. More complex lab panels and analyses than the routine need to be done in the main laboratory, and this small physicians' lab is only an outreach of that.

The main lab's courier, Josie, transports samples and supplies back and forth between the two labs, and she overhears all this as she packs the specimens in a portable cooler. "Well, hey," Josie interjects, "there's an Irish pub just up the street called The Harp. And it's lunchtime." We exchange looks all around, and off we go with a casual, "Be back soon!" tossed off in Big Red's direction.

The Harp is indeed Irish, with a real Irishman at the taps who introduces himself as Paddy, and maps of Auld Erin festooned the walls, along with shamrocks and harps everywhere hanging, and two tipplers at the bar, named O'Leary and Faye. They are all friendly without being intrusive. The coffee is fresh, the cream real and thick and laced with Irish whiskey that you would swear is distilled from the breath of the gods. And the pours are generous.

We each have two.

Josie, or "Jo" as we call her, is a young, longhaired, hippie-type, who possesses a bright and refreshing outlook, working that dead-end job of running errands for the lab, transporting specimens back and forth. She's also learning metalwork and jewelry making on the side. She will go on to become a wonderfully talented custom jeweler, and a friend for life, both to Alice and me. But today, over our Irish coffee, she regales us with an entertaining tale.

"So there I was," Josie relates, "not even stoned, not even drunk, just out before dawn with Norman, the guy who's been teaching me to work jewelry. We'd been working real hard all through the night on a piece of intricate casting, which we had to do three times over, till the cast was right. It was critical to finish, and we couldn't just leave it. So now we were just taking a break, walking around Belmont Shores, and we came to that big, old pond there; you know the one? It's full of ducks, hungry ducks. So Norman and I went in and found some old, dry bread at his place, and his roommate and girlfriend were just getting up, so we made some coffee, and all four of us went back to the pond to feed the ducks as the sun came up. Pretty soon, here come a couple of policemen, acting really belligerent."

Josie tells the story in character, doing all the voices for us. She does it well.

" 'What's going on here, then?' one of the cops asked.

" 'What do you mean, officer?' Norman said, politely.

" 'Where have you been this last hour?' Chimed in the other cop.

" 'Casting a ring and bracelet,' " I told them. " 'We were working on some jewelry. We just came out for a walk, and we're feeding the ducks, that's all.'

" 'We're gonna have to take you in,' said the first cop.

"We thought he was kidding, and Norm and I both laughed." Josie sips her Irish coffee, a wry expression on her face. "We shouldn't have done that 'cause both the cops got real irked.

" 'Turn around and face the car, and spread your legs,' " Josie says, back in her cop character voice.

" 'Hey, officer, officer!' Norman protested, trying to make nice. 'What's wrong? We didn't do anything.'

" 'Well, that remains to be seen,' the first cop said. 'We're placing you all under arrest for suspicion of robbery.'

"Seems while we were feeding the ducks, some guy was robbing the Xerox machines in the library," she tells us. "The janitor called the cops, and my friends and I were picked up, fingerprinted, and put in jail before the librarian found the true bad guy hiding in the restroom. I'm sure they were hassling us 'cause those *pigs* figured a few longhaired hippies had to be guilty of something, right?" She takes a last swig of her drink and continues. "Man, I can tell you I don't have much use for cops since then, either."

Alice and I are sympathetic, drinking to her in support and solidarity.

"Can you beat that?" Josie ends. "Of all the possible scofflaw acts and civil disobedience I might have been caught in, I get busted for 'felony' duck feeding. *Shit*!"

After two Irish coffees, this strikes all three of us hysterically funny, and we laugh our way out the pub door.

"You gels be sure to bring yerselves back again, now won'tcha. 'T'was a pleasure to have such lovely lassies gracin' the place, 'n all." An Irishman for sure, that bartender.

Jo departs to run her errands, leaving me and Alice still laughing when we come bursting through the door of the clinic. Big Red is waiting for us. She looks intently at us for a moment, then down at her watch.

"A late lunch, then?" she asks, pointedly.

"Two, actually," replies Alice. "Bushmills and coffee at The Harp."

I warned you: Alice is nothing if not honest.

"Hmmph," Big Red responds. "You both think you can work this afternoon?"

"Please," Alice says, "you wound me to the quick, woman! I'll suck a peppermint drop if you insist, but I'm on the job."

"Me, too, ma'am," I say.

"Hmmph," she says again, but the corner of her mouth is twitching. "That's a pretty rough place, I hear. You girls should be careful."

"Point noted," Alice acknowledges, and we both wheel around and scurry off to our respective workstations, applying ourselves to our chores with all the circumspection and inordinate care of the slightly inebriated. Fortunately, we both have some non-essential chores to take care of for nearly an hour before patient care resumes.

We won't make a habit of it, but on an occasional Friday thereafter, Alice and I, and sometimes Josie, will go take a "music lesson" at The Harp, making sure we order something to eat from the grill, along with our *single* Irish coffee.

DATELINE, 1972—Henry Kissinger announces, "peace is at hand" in Vietnam, in time for President Nixon to take 49 states in his re-election. **US troop numbers fall** to 69,000 in Vietnam, just as Nixon orders the military to resume heavy bombing in North Vietnam.

Bob Fosse, Liza Minnelli, and Joel Grey win Oscars for Best Director, Best Actress, and Best Supporting Actor respectively, for *Cabaret*, which explores bisexuality among its themes.

All In The Family and *The Mary Tyler Moore Show* make their television debuts. *The Flip Wilson Show* and *Marcus Welby M.D.* are among the top-rated shows on the three networks.

lone star state again

It's late September 1972, and Don has left for Austin, Texas to begin a new job. Over the next four weeks that ensue, it is my task to give the clinic my two-week's notice, pack up our two-bedroom house, arrange for movers, shut off the utilities, close the bank accounts, and head back to Texas in my little 1969 VW Fastback with my dog Cherub. Everything is planned and organized, right down to the packing tape. Everything, that is, but the affair I will have with Alice. Goddammit! It will change everything!

D on got the call on a Sunday morning. It was a friend in Texas who had recommended him for a sales position. "Report for the interview in Austin by tomorrow afternoon," says his friend, and within a matter of hours, Don's off to the airport.

The next day, Monday morning, I breeze into work, finish my early morning barium exams, clean up my X-ray rooms, and pop into the lab where Alice has just completed her fasting blood draws. It is our usual time for mutual, midmorning coffee. I conscientiously swab out the barium-splattered sink, pour a cup for us both, plop down in the blood-draw chair as I have every other workday morning before.

"Guess what? Don flew to Texas yesterday, he interviews today, and if he gets the job, I'll be ... leaving ... in a couple weeks."

That's when it hits me.

I'm leaving. Leaving *her*.

A huge wave of sorrow washes over me, and Alice looks like a horse has kicked her.

Our coffee break is short this morning. I suddenly realize I have a lot to do, trying somehow to cover my confusion. I feel as sick to my stomach as Alice appears.

She has been there with me, alongside me, yet ephemeral like a fleeting ghost ship—the Flying Dutchman gliding full and free and flying—while I doggedly maneuver oars in a wooden dinghy, adrift on the surface of a vast, eternal, dead sea, en route to nowhere. Alice, in these few brief months has shown me how bogged down and becalmed my life is, and how it could potentially be different. And now I am setting a course right out of her life.

Sure enough, Don is hired on the spot. And wouldn't you know, his new boss immediately wants Don to drive with him up to Dallas for a week to start learning the ropes. Then directly after, hop a plane to the company headquarters in Albany, N.Y., for three weeks of training and orientation. Once again, I am on my own.

"Two weeks, huh?" Alice asks guardedly the next day.

"Well, I'm giving two weeks notice today, which I hope is time enough to get somebody else here, but I'll need at least another week after that to get my own show on the road. Dammit, the same thing happened when we moved out here, too. Don gets a job, they start him immediately, and I'm left to pack up a whole household by myself, and move 1,400 miles. Like it's a snap. Like all you have to do is piss on the fire and call the dogs. I swear he is never around when I need him most."

I am stressed, distressed, and conflicted. Half of which I don't understand.

Later in the week, I make arrangements to disconnect the utilities, along with other various closures. I sort, toss, and pack in a flurry. This time isn't as bad as the last, since Don and I had already put quite a bit of our possessions in storage before we left Texas last year. That had been a major job, deciding what to leave and what to take, and then packing it all up. Since then, we have been living pretty much in representational mode, with just enough towels and linens and kitchen supplies to get by, knowing at some point we either will go back to Texas, or haul all our stuff out to the coast and settle here. I'd have preferred the latter, it being my fondest dream all along. I love California.

On Thursday morning, at coffee break in her lab, Alice asks, "While you've been here these last months, did you ever have a chance to go to Ports O'Call?"

"Ports O'Call? Where's that?"

"It's way down at the end of San Pedro, near Terminal Island in Long Beach. It's a little tourist harbor village with shops full of curiosities from all around the world."

"No, I never even heard of it. What's it cost to get in?"

"Nothing, just parking. The merchants are all hoping to entice your money out of your pockets with their exotic wares."

Laughing, I say, "I see. No, I'll be sorry to have missed that. Sounds like a rather quaint and proper fleecing could be had there."

Alice's mouth quirks up. "Well, if you'd like to go, I'm free tomorrow night. I promise to slap your hands anytime I see you reach for your wallet."

"Well, what's to keep *you* safe from temptation?" I'm teasing, of course, but she seems to take it another way.

She catches her breath, and stands up suddenly. "Um ... I forgot I have a Stat urine to do," she explains, but she avoids looking at me and starts setting up her pipettes.

"Okay, then. I'll leave you to it," I reply, walking to the doorway. "So what time tomorrow night?"

She pauses, looks at me over her shoulder, urine sample held midair, "Uh ... you'll go?"

"Sure. I've got a standing date with packing tape and cardboard boxes, but I'd love to break it. Sounds like it would be fun."

She nods, looking back at her test tubes and body fluids. "Pick you up at six o'clock. Bring a sweater, it gets cold down along the water in the evening."

"You got a date, then."

is it sisters?

"Yep," she acknowledges, and for a moment before I turn I think I see her hand shaking.

It turns out to be a lovely balmy evening. We drive over a bridge—Alice behind the wheel and me in the passenger seat of her car—into the extensive and massive Port of Los Angeles. A sight unto itself, with great cargo ships at dock, cranes and gantries dangling high in the air, and stack after stack of cargo containers lined along the piers, and boarded on freighters. It's a crazy quilt of corrugated colors in neat, precise blocks, piled so high that from a distance you forget the individual size and weight of each. All heavily packed with manufacturing and goods, soon either to be transported by truck or train domestically, or set out to sea, bound for distant ports.

Alice parks the car, and we head to the entrance; *Ports O'Call* it reads in an arching sign overhead.[†] It's a magical place, with couples and families strolling alongside us, on the herringboned, brick-lined walks that lazily meander along sinuous lanes designed to lead you inevitably past every shop in the village. Tiny twinkling lights outline the various shop windows displaying clothing, trinkets, gifts, exotic imports from far away. We see brass Buddhas and ivory chess sets, knitted wools, glittering jewelry, sandals and bags, watches and clocks. A feast for the eyes. And other senses, too, with tantalizing perfumeries and incense boutiques, tea and coffee shops, ice cream parlors, candy stores with imported chocolates and salt-water taffies. A reggae store and a tobacconist. And the seafood restaurants that overlook the lights of the harbor, and serve up skewered shrimp and oyster shooters. But it's the soft pretzel vendor with a paint-box red, wheeled cart at the corner of a tiny lane that absolutely surprises me, and I am irresistibly drawn.

"Ohmigod! Soft pretzels! I haven't seen any since the last time I was in Pennsylvania," I exclaim.

"Soft pretzel?"

[†] I warn you not to try such a visit today. The shiny, clean charm and sparkling shops of 1972 is no more. Oh, the bones are still there, in a dirty, smelly carcass that still bears the name of the place. Sadly, it has become a hangout for gangs, a noisy crush of polyglot people amid rundown, crass, junky stores, and unsanitary vendors of shrimp and seafood, much of it suspiciously less than fresh, if not deadly.

"If you have to ask, you are in for a treat, m'dear. There's nothing like them."

And these are the real thing, just as I remember them growing up. The cart holds long baked rows of the twisted treats, visible through a front window bordered by a bright-red frame, and gold letters on the top edge proclaiming, GENUINE SOFT PRETZELS and WARM AND GOOD.

"I never heard of them before," Alice says, pulling out a couple of dollars.

"They are a favorite in Philly. And these look and smell like home." The pretzels are shiny, golden, and about four inches tall and three inches wide, baked together in a long, side-by-side string. The vendor pulls off two and separates them, one for each of us. They are fat and puffy, salted with coarse grains, and guaranteed to be warm and chewy.

"Now, Alice, to eat these properly, you have to put mustard on them." I pick up both, one in each hand, leaving behind the waxed paper that the vendor used to pull them off the baked row.

"Mustard?"

"Sure," chimes in the vendor as he hands Alice her change. "That's the way to enjoy them. Mustard." He pauses, and with a laugh adds, "But they're better with beer."

Alice smiles, and picks up the big yellow mustard squeeze bottle, aiming the nozzle at the pretzel in my left hand. "Hold still," she says, "I don't want to miss."

Deliberately and expertly, as if she has done this a thousand times, she lays a wide stripe of yellow hot dog mustard in a continuous line along every twist and turn of the oversized pretzel.

"You do that very well," I comment. "I bet you're the one everyone pleads with to write Happy Birthday on the cake."

"Yep. I never waiver and I never miss a spot," she says, and with that she runs the mustard along the bottom of the pretzel. I gasp with shock, gaping at the wide streak of yellow ooze trailing in an unbroken line from one side of the pretzel, *across* my thumb, onto the pretzel again. I whoop out a sharp laugh, and Alice puts one hand on my shoulder to steady me as I shake with escalating mirth, and she swiftly traces along the pretzel in my other hand, topping it with a stripe of mustard. Again, she follows the twists and turns, and completes the pretzel's pattern unbroken, right up over my thumb with a fat squirt of mustard.

I am weak with merriment. Hysterical. Nearly bent over double, all the while clutching on to both pretzels.

"Don't you drop them, or we'll have to buy two more, and do it all over again," Alice threatens, handing the mustard bottle back to our amused vendor.

"Here, here," she says, and tsk-tsks in mock reproach. "Better let me take them from you." She takes a big bite from one as she rescues both pretzels from my limp hands. "Hmm, you're right. They *are* good with mustard."

I am helpless with laughter, holding my mustard-adorned thumbs out in front of me, tears leaking from my eyes.

"You want to be careful not to get any of that on your clothes," Alice cautions, chewing on pretzel. "That stuff stains, you know."

My howls renew, and I back up against the pretzel cart so I will be less likely to fall down.

"Here now, take this," she hands me my pretzel. "Hold onto it, Nancy." She takes hold of my other thumb at the base and draws it up toward my mouth. "Lick that off now, before it gets on everything," chiding, as if I am a wayward child who has made a mess.

Trying to catch my breath, I suck the mustard off my thumb, and, still huffing with hilarity, I transfer the pretzel, and lick off the opposite thumb. "I can't believe you did that," and I crack up again.

"Did what?" she asks innocently, taking another bite from her pretzel. "Yours is gonna get cold if you don't stop laughing and eat up." Every time I begin to wind down, she keeps the joke going.

"Stop! You've gotta stop before I wet myself, Alice."

"Okay. We'll walk over to this little place I know for some shrimp to go with our pretzels. They have a restroom."

After we finish our seafood and pretzel meal, we wander the winding streets of shops back to the car. It has been a great night: perfect California waterfront, perfectly enchanting village, perfect fun.

She drives me home and into my driveway. "Well, that was really something else, Alice. Thank you so much for thinking to take me there. I wouldn't have wanted to miss it. It'll be another great California memory for me."

She nods as I get out of her car and walk in front of it, taking the path to the house, before she calls out, "Nancy, c'mere a minute."

"What?" I walk back over to the driver's side.

"There's something I've wanted to mention all night."

"What is it?"

She reaches out the window, palm up, and I give her my hand. She pulls it up into the dim light from the car, and turns it in my direction, so I can see. "You're apparently unaware of it, but just so you know … you seem to have these really strange, yellow thumbs."

She drops my hand as I rear backwards, laughing raucously, slammed by the full force of a good running gag pulled off by a clever comedienne with wry wit and timing, and belatedly I muffle my mouth with that hand, sporting its mustard-stained thumb. Having cracked herself up, she throws the car in reverse, backs out and drives off, waving and laughing—cackling like a maniac—as she goes.

The clinic doesn't find a replacement for me right away, so I work an additional week, three total since Don had left. By my last day of work, I had already returned all our rented furniture, and all our possessions were packed in boxes, all but a coffeepot, an ashtray, our bed, and two folding lawn chairs in the living room. I have never been more distressed than during these three weeks.

I plow into the moving details as if pursued by the Furies, hoping to use up the jittery energy. My insides are fluttering all the time, as though the bubble of joy is now a wildly frightened creature. My midsection trembles visibly, and I am constantly light-headed. The countdown is on.

My last day at the clinic falls on a Tuesday. It has finally come—and gone. There was a mixed air of celebration and sadness all day, people coming in and out of the lab and X-ray rooms wanting to know more of the details of what my life will be like from here on; they wish me well, tell me they will miss me, give me small gifts, and serve up cake and coffee.

Theodore Von Bear sits atop his refrigerator with a large blue teardrop pasted to his face, a hanky in his hand, and a black mourning armband on his furry little arm. A small sign propped between his legs reads,

41

"Bye-Bye." Jane and Sally decorated him very early this morning, before Alice or I came in.

The next day, Wednesday, Alice calls me at home. "I can get tomorrow afternoon off, if you can stop long enough. Want to go to Lion Country Safari?"

It turns out to be a truly magical day. For the first time in three weeks, I feel calm. Maybe it's Alice and her remarkable tranquility. Maybe it's just getting away from it all. Maybe it's the wide, open space of the free-range animal preserve, cleverly designed to keep the predators from the prey, but so disguised as to make you think you are indeed on the African veldt, with giraffes, eland, rhinos, dik-bik, and cheetahs, and brilliant, pink flamingos in the park's manmade wetlands.

We drive through the park in Alice's station wagon and are cautioned at each new area we enter to stay in the car, keep on the dirt track, and keep the car windows rolled up as we continue from one wild animal habitat to another.

As we enter one area, a blue VW Bug is in front of us … at a dead stop, held at bay by a resident lioness. The big cat, tired of merely leaning on the little car, hops up on the convex hood of the Beetle. We hear a *Boing!* as the hood indents with the lion's weight.

The couple in the car—hysterical, red-faced, and hollering—begin to madly beat on their horn. Being helpful, Alice blasts hers, too, hoping to attract the attention of one of the patrolling keepers in their Land Rovers.

The lioness, however, simply ignores all the hubbub, and calmly and systematically surveys the landscape from the elevated perch of the blue VW hood, taking her time, no doubt planning how to overcome the elaborate divisions of the cleverly architectured terrain, and bring down some real meat for a change. In her own sweet time, the magnificent beast makes an easy, fluid leap to the ground. With a *BOP!*, the hood of the VW pops back into shape.

As the lioness saunters off, the shaken couple lets out the clutch and drives off. At the next rise they meet with a ranger in a Land Rover. Watching that frightened couple in the blue Bug point and gesture and tell their tale to the Ranger makes Alice and me grin at each other in this shared moment as we roll by. You know, the funny thing is I truly do not remember a word exchanged between us the whole time we are together this day. The afternoon passes like a lovely dream, sweet and satisfying, but slightly surreal.[†]

And I am to spend another restless, sleepless night, trying to figure out what the hell is going on with me.

Suddenly it is Friday night, and Alice, Josie, and Dick and Sarah meet me at The Harp. The folks at the bar decided to make my last stand here an event, complete with a farewell cake and a complimentary Irish coffee. Anything for a party must be the bar mantra, since the five of us are far from being regulars.

After a few drinks, Josie leaves to meet a date. Much later, after putting a big dent in The Harps' supply of Jameson and Bushmills, Dick and Sarah declare they tied one on enough, and go on their way as well. Alice and I soon after decide to call it quits, too.

"Can you drive?" I ask, "I think I'm too bombed." (The irresponsible days before designated drivers.)

"Yeah, I can," Alice answers. "You just wanna leave the Big Bug here, then?"

"I'll get a ride tomorrow, and come back and pick it up. So, will you take me home?"

I never ask her afterwards, but I am sure she has a lot of anxiety about how things are unfolding. All I know is I am instantly sober (I'm sure she is, too), and by the time we get home, I know I could have driven myself, after all. Since this is to be goodbye, I am flooded with very sobering emotions—sadness, fear, longing, regret, and every other sorrow you can think of.

When we enter the house, Cherub meets us with her usual combination of wild greeting and general bent-out-of-shape rebuke because she has been left alone. After the dog leaps in the air, whimpers, and turns

---

[†] Sadly, this amazing Park will close a decade later, in 1984, evidently sacrificed to turn this valuable Southern California land into yet more tedious tracts of banal homes and prosaic shopping malls. I do know that on more than one occasion, idiotic assholes, despite all instructions to the contrary, actually were known to *get out* of their cars to see the animals closer, even *leaving their cars* in the middle of the free-range Wildlife Preserve stocked with lions, cheetahs, rhinos and the like, to take pictures or some damn dumb thing. Don't know if there were any actual injuries as a result, but those morons certainly did deserve to be take-away dinner. Disney has had a park in Florida since 1967, I hear, with a similar concept, but evidently considerably less visitor freedom.

herself inside out with joy to see me, she sits in the middle of the living room and pointedly gives me the back of her head.

"Cherub," I call her softly. After a moment, she turns her head to look at me, radiating disapproval and reproach. Then, deliberately, she turns her head away again, sending her censure through a wide penumbra from the back of her skull. Alice and I snicker behind our hands at the dog's dramatics, momentarily dispelling the anguish of this, our leave-taking.

The house is stacked high with boxes everywhere, and the two rickety lawn chairs in the living room are the only seating available. I percolate some coffee, and we drink our way through two pots before we decide to cook some eggs. We talk and talk, into the wee small hours of the night. When we finally get past the evasive conversation, about everything except us, Alice finally asks if I knew.

"Did you figure out yet that I'm kinda strange?"

"Always knew that," I answer.

"No ... I mean, that I'm ... gay." We are not nearly so direct in these days about such matters; the word "gay" is still, for the most part, a code word.

"Yes, I think I've known that pretty much all along," I say. "I was in the Army, you know. There were a lot of those people there—gay people."

I'm sure she laughs to herself at this.

I did have a gay friend in the Army. For about a year, I worked with a guy named Steve in the X-ray clinic. He had confided in me that he lived in dire fear of being discovered, and dishonorably discharged before his hitch was up. Steve's lover, a schoolteacher, was a thoroughly sweet and decent young man. A couple of times, to keep up the necessary pretenses in those years, I acted as the heterosexual cover-girl, the "beard," for each one of them at their individual family gatherings. My brief stint as a fag-hag.

I had supper at their place a few times. Once, a really fun guy was among the guests in attendance—a drag queen and gay as pink ink. He left early to perform at a club in town. And get this! He carried his huge array of beauty products and makeup in a fishing tackle box. A big, battered, orange metal, tackle box.

Truly cool!

"Well, what do you think about it?" Alice pursues the topic.

"About you? Well, I'm curious about how it affects your life, how you manage to live as you want to, with the rest of us pretty much disapproving. But now I feel suddenly like I don't know anything about you."

"You know *everything* about me, lady. Everything that matters. The fact that I like girls is just a small part of who I am. The essential things about me you already know—better than anybody else."

Her words alarm me. "How can that be, Alice? I don't know *anything* about you, your personal life, who you've loved, lived with, what your life is about?"

"I tell you, you know me better than anyone alive, lady. I don't open up to anyone the way I have to you."

"But look at what I *don't* know about you. This can't be true!"

"Yes, it is ... What do you want to know?"

I am not at all clear what I *do* want to know about her. Alice always has a barrier there, a place where I am reluctant to press. Perhaps it is a thinner shield for me than the brick wall she puts up for most people. Still, she is quite simply very private, by nature and by necessity, and most people who approach too close are just instinctively warned away.

"Tell me where you are now. Are you with anyone?" I ask, timidly.

She takes her time, gathers her thoughts, then describes her last relationship, with Betty. They have lived together for about six years, but haven't really "been together" for the last four. Betty drinks, drugs, and sleeps around. She is an unhappy person, and seems hell-bent on staying that way.

Two years prior to this, when Alice went up north to take care of her mother who'd had a heart attack, Betty tagged along. She got a job cracking crab at a cannery and spent her nights in the bars. Alice went to work at the county hospital and spent her nights at home with her mother. When Alice moved back down to L.A., so did Betty.

She doesn't really want Alice, but doesn't want anyone else to have her either. Just one month ago, Alice finally asked Betty to leave. Alice tells me she left with reluctance and some unpleasant drama. This happened only about three weeks after that uncomfortable dinner at the restaurant with Don and Naomi.

Alice shakes her head ruefully, "Well, anyway, after the turbulence of my life the last few years, I came to the conclusion that I was gonna just stay by myself and not get involved with anyone unless it was the real thing. Unless it was the love I've been waiting for all my life."

Alice pauses a moment, her eyes focused far away. "I like my own company," she continues, "and if it means I live alone for the rest of my life, so be it. It would be better than what I've had, better than what I've done till now. Just sort of wandering into relationships, and then spending the next few years trying to extricate myself from something I wasn't all that involved in. Trying to disengage from someone I didn't care *nearly enough* about in the first place."

"Well, being alone isn't the worst thing you can be," I concur. "I lived alone for four years before I joined the Army, and I highly recommend it for everyone. As a matter of fact, I think much of people's problems stems from just that, not being able to be alone, not finding out who they are before they foist themselves off on somebody else. But there's nothing worse than being in a relationship with somebody and still being alone," I finish.

And in so saying, I realize I am speaking firsthand. Don is in one marriage, and I am in another. I am his wife and a full participant in *his* marriage, but I am pretty much adrift and alone in mine. I earn a paycheck, cook, clean, do laundry, willingly share his bed, keep his social life running, and take care of his emotional life. Like most wives at this time.

He cares about me; it isn't that. Don is dear, and by the standards of the day is a "good husband." He works, he is faithful, he is mild-mannered, and he means well. But he isn't really there; he doesn't seem to feel required to be, and I doubt it is in his makeup to be more. Not that he is withholding, or deliberately emotionally unavailable. Just clueless. Ours is pretty typical of most marriages, here in 1972.

Perhaps my own expectations about marriage are too much. I want intimacy. Closeness of the soul. Sharing of the heart. A partnership in spirit. True Love.

"But there's nothing worse than being in a relationship with somebody and still being alone." My statement is still hanging in the air like it has a balloon around it. The echoes of it are in my ears, and we both are taking our time to digest it.

She says, "Well, I'm probably gonna be alone for the rest of my life, because I'm hopelessly and completely in love with a woman who is not available. She's married."

And what I'm going to tell you now, you will not believe. Here, the most remarkable thing happens. Across the distance between us, from those facing lawn chairs in that empty living room, something opens in the air, and a shaft of clear, emerald-green light travels from her eyes to mine, riveting and connecting. A green light so pure and vibrant, so *greenly* shimmering and lovely....

And so quickly gone. Dimness lags behind after the visitation of the light. Then, the room slowly brightens again. And I am completely rattled, trembling. Unable to speak. At a loss to explain what I have seen. *If I truly have seen what I think I've seen.*

I'm not aware of much else after this, except dawn is breaking, and she takes me to get my car, still at the Harp. We each go our separate ways, presumably to sleep the Saturday away. Except sleep won't come, and I pace the house all day. And tread the rooms most of the night, trying to sort it out, find the source of my confusion, my agitation.

I encountered lesbians for the first time in the Army. (Well, first that I knew of, anyway. Probably I had been in the company of dozens of gay women I never knew about, since we are everywhere, you know.) I had thought they were poor wretches who were destined to live unhappy, abnormal lives. And they deserved our tolerance and pity. There, but for the grace of God, go I.

So much for grace. God must have a spectacularly twisted sense of humor.

My vibratory state has intensified since the green light. I feel shaken and chilled. And would you believe ... I *still* don't get it? I still don't get what Alice was driving at. Dense! Really dense, I am!

Chalk it up to stupidity. Chalk it up that I am unaccustomed to applying female-to-female connections to the context of romantic love. Chalk it up to befuddlement at being with Don for five years, loving Don, and suddenly overcome with feeling like I'm in love with someone else. That's what it comes down to. I have finally identified it and what it means. I am in love with Alice. I've fallen in love with her.

Her!

I call her on Sunday morning, and ask her to come over—and bring a jug of wine. I have to talk to her.

Alice arrives about four hours later with a jug of wine ... and reinforcements. She has brought along Fran, her blind friend. Alice must be petrified, now that I think of it. To need protection like that. Or assurance that nothing will happen.

Well, it won't work.

I build a fire in the fireplace in an attempt to shake the chill in my bones, pour a goblet of wine, and commence to beat around the barn for a couple hours. Meanwhile, Fran lies down on the floor near the fire, puts the stereo headphones on, pulls Cherub up close to pet her, and gives us all the privacy a blind and, for all intents and purposes, deaf woman can provide.

I ramble on forever, and finally I take a deep breath and brave it. "Alice, I don't know at all what you feel. And I'm not expecting anything from you. It's just…"

Alice looks at me steadily, not giving anything away.

In for a penny, in for a pound.

"I— " I start again. "Even if this embarrasses us both, even though I want to cringe from mortification at what you might think about this.…" I take another deep breath and plunge on, "I just can't leave … I can't leave *you* … without telling you … without saying … I'm in love with you, Alice. And I never before entertained even the possibility of loving a woman."

Alice takes my hand then, strokes the back of it as if to stop my trembling. Fat chance.

"I was literally thunderstruck when we met," she says softly, voice husky with emotion. "I've been in love with you since the moment you walked into my lab and announced, 'I'm Nancy and who in the *hell* are you.' "

I start to protest the quote but before I can, I recall the meeting with sudden clarity: the heart-stopping, head-whacking feeling I had, but never really examined. Then it registers.

"You've been in love with me?"

"Since the moment I saw you," she says, her blue eyes are smoky, warm, and unguarded. I get lost in them for a long time.

I can't quite believe it. I have been so wrapped up in my own feelings, in the expectation that with my pronouncement she would be horrified, discomfited, awkwardly retreating, trying to let me down easy—take your pick.

"But you said you were destined to be alone because you loved a … Oh!" Well, what can I say? When the electricity is turned on, even a dim bulb lights up. "Oh," I repeat, softly.

"Yes—you!" she says, eyes sparkling, radiating. As if everything is all right.

It isn't. The big issue is I am married, and plan to stay married, plan to leave for Texas to join my husband in five days. There is no future for this, no future in this lifeline for this drama to play out. This is all there is, this moment, and whatever moments can be stolen in the next five days. I tell her this in front of witnesses—her blind protector, Fran (still behind headphones) and my faithful dog, Cherub.

The firelight caresses the gentle planes of her face, plays on her blond hair. Like the color of her eyes, the color of Alice's hair is changeable, not with her mood, but with the lighting. In shadow it appears dirty blond, tawny. In daylight it is a paler ash blond. By lamplight, her hair has auburn undertones where it curls under against her neck. And by light of the fire, her hair appears burnished gold ... burnished like my very present wedding ring on the hand that Alice is stroking; my hand, which is still trembling out of control.

"If this is all there is," she says, gazing deeply into my eyes, "if this is all there can be, Nancy, I'll take it. Whatever it is, however much, I'll take it. Whatever you can give me. And I'll accept it."

I sit up straighter, looking at her head on, seeing the truth of this in her eyes.

"Alice, I know I'm going to have some soul-searching to do about this. Major soul-searching. But not now. Not this minute. Now...." And I lean into her, my cheek close to hers and whisper, "Now ... I want you to take me to bed."

The day has transformed to dusk, and we take Fran home to Fullerton. Then go to Alice's apartment nearby. Her schnauzer Patrick, barking wildly, greets us at the door. Her schizoid poodle, Pepé, greets us with spinning circles, and her cat, Rion-kitty rubs figure-eights around her legs.

Her apartment is sparse, home to the few sorry remnants of her recently broken relationship, but hers alone. In the kitchen, a table and single chair, and in the bedroom, a dresser, three bookcases full of books. And an old, miserable, hand-me-down of a bed, with a wretchedly uncomfortable mattress, so impossibly lumpy it should be stuffed with greenback dollars, else there simply is no excuse for it.

Movie kisses used to be chaste and dry, like the Doris Day and Rock Hudson kind. Or sudden and hard like Clark Gable's Rhett Butler in the staircase scene. Or the beach kiss in *From Here To Eternity,* which was really hot stuff in the 1950s.

Alice doesn't kiss anything like that. She doesn't kiss like anyone I have ever kissed before. She takes her time, waits, her mouth close to mine, until I feel the brush of her aura, the tickling electric of her body's field. Her breath mingles with mine; I breathe her in, and our lips meet lightly. Brush apart. Meet again. Mouth warm, soft, gentle. Sweet. Her kisses have a buildup, start leisurely and soft, intensify. She kisses slow, kisses long, kisses deep. She makes me wild.

"Are you okay?" she asks.

"Yes. No. What?"

She chuckles. "You're shivering. Are you okay?"

"Oh, God. I don't know."

"We can stop, you know. If you want to, we don't have to go any further."

"We can? I mean … do you want to?"

"No, fool. I just mean this doesn't have to go any further if you don't want it to. There's no harm done, I mean, if you … "

"Oh, God! Please!" I pull her to me, hungrily meet her mouth with mine.

We undress with the blithe assurance of the young, and I am introduced to the wonder of a woman's body for the first time … and the wonder is, the body is mine! With each trace of her hands on my skin, I feel I am fleshing out, am becoming. As if all along I have occupied space, but never had form. This isn't just sex. I've had sex with men, good sex. I have had generous lovers, and been sexually satisfied. This isn't that. This is the ultimate self-discovery.

Then—as if this isn't revolutionary enough—I encounter the mystery and secrets of another woman's body and realize for the first time why it is men love us so. How can they help it? I truly understand at last what the attraction is. What they need from us. The feel of that lush softness, the comfort. The enveloping warmth, the enfolding embrace. The pliant heat. The enclosure.

Something mysterious opens in me, as if a key has turned, and magically, hidden chambers appear, exposing me to myself. This is a completion like I have never known before, a connection that will bind us for eternity.

And Alice is ... well, she is an uncharted land, and I have never wanted to explore anything so much in my life.

Oh, my. I am in real trouble.

And I only have five days.

"Are you cold?" she asks, when she has enough breath to talk.

"No, I've been shaking like this for days now. You caused it, and I hope it goes away soon, but it could be a condition that lasts a lifetime. I feel like I'm shimmying inside myself, only I can't figure out if it's joy or fear."

"Don't be afraid, lady, I won't ever hurt you," she says, pushing my hair back from my face, kissing me.

"That's the very least of my worries. What I'm afraid of is that I'll hurt you! It's almost inevitable that I will. I'm sorry I let you in for this. I ..."

She stops my words with her fingers on my mouth. "Let me worry about that, love. I'm a big girl. I know what I've gotten myself in for. And I'll tell you again: I love you, and that's all there is to it."

She looks at me earnestly, holds my face in her hands, making me pay close attention. "I will always love you. Period. Whether I can have you or not. And since I *can't* have you the way I want you, with me always, living with me, sharing my life, I'll take what I can get."

"Oh God, that's so unfair." I pull out of her grasp. "What have I done here?" I wail miserably.

"You didn't do it, lady. I did. And what's happening here tonight doesn't have anything really to do with it. The damage has long been done, Nancy."

She traces my brow with her thumb as she speaks, the swell of my cheekbone, the line of my jaw. "I've been in love with you every day for the last eight months. This, tonight, is more than I'd ever dared hope for.

I thought I was going to have to live the rest of my life being in love with someone who didn't love me back, who couldn't love me back, who didn't *even know* it was possible. This for me is like a dream come true, my love."

Her thumbs are on my chin and she runs them back along my jaw, her fingers caressing my neck, the base of my skull. It is impossible for us to speak without touching each other.

"But Alice, it can't go on. This is all there *can* be. There's no future for us." I slump against her, my head in the hollow of her shoulder, and tears well up and spill over. It moves in then—moves in and sets up house-keeping. It will become my sidekick for the next three years. She feels it, feels the despair take up residence in me. Knows she can't prevent it. She cups my chin in her hand, traces her thumb over my bottom lip.

"Lady," she says, quietly, "we'll both live the future one day at a time, anyway. I want to enjoy this moment, love." She kisses me again. "Make it last as long as I can."

We have just finished lovemaking for yet another time this long night, and she is holding me against her, as the pleasurable set of tremors stop, and these wildly tremulous ones come on me once again. "Alice, I need to tell you something."

"What, my love?"

"You may learn to hate me for this, and I may come to hate myself for the hurt I cause, but even so, I swear I will never regret this. Any of this."

"I could never hate you, lady," she says as she kisses my temple, brow, and the frown lines between my eyes.

"And ... there's something else"

"What else, love?" She pulls back a bit to better look at me.

"Alice ... I do believe this is the God-awfullest, boney-est bed I've ever been on in my life."

The next few days are a blur. Alice calls the clinic Monday morning and says she has some personal business to take care of and needs the next few days off. It isn't a total fabrication. Rion-kitty has an early-morning appointment to be neutered. We are out amongst the mass of humanity, driving to Brea in the Monday morning traffic.

We talk and make love all day before picking up the neutered kitty, who is, when we pick him up, wild and freaked instead of sedated. He defies gravity, running the windows inside the car like a centrifuge. Nothing we can do about it but get him home as fast as we can.

Truth be known, it seems like we are the ones in the centrifuge, spinning around an empty center. Certainly we are on the road quite a bit for these five days, from my house to Alice's apartment, she whisking me back and forth in her station wagon to feed and walk Cherub. (It would be too much, too soon, to expect her kids and mine to meet and greet and be okay together.) My little dog is already a space cadet, what with Don gone, boxes stacked all around her, and me twittering all over the place. Poor thing no doubt senses an uncertain future on top of it all. Alice's furry kids are equally shook up, their mom as emotionally edgy as I am.

And somewhere in there, the movers come and empty the house while I spend the day trying to keep Cherub from traumatic shock.

But in between the madness, when Alice and I are together, we live as much in the moment as we can, staving off thoughts of the leaving that looms. We eat and drink and smoke, shower, sleep, and love.

Oh, God, I have never before needed anyone like this, wanted anyone to be so close. Her body is a marvel, a realm of softness and heat and lust. I am crazy to learn it. Taking all I can get of her. Giving her all I can summon up. And playing, too, laughing in the middle of it. Loving it. Loving her.

"I have a bone to pick with you," I announce, breaking the silence as we lie facing each other. She is stroking the round of my hip, tracing the line of it.

"You want to pick the bones out of this boney bed with me?" she teases.

"No. I'm serious. I want to know why you made me go through all that?"

"All what?"

"All that agony. All that long, prolonged, *goddamned,* ever-long agony of confession and—if you loved me all this time—why did you make me struggle with all that? Make me pick my way through that minefield of humiliation to declare my love for you. To get you to go to bed with me."

"Those are two different things, my love."

"Would you have gone to bed with me if I hadn't said 'I love you?'"

"If you asked me to," she pauses, "yes, likely I would have. I don't think I could have helped myself. I'm crazy about you, you know?" She smiles at me.

I kiss her. I can't help myself. Still, I am not about to be put off. "But why did you let me go through all that, then?"

"Well, two things," she answers, rubbing into the dip of my waist. She props her head up on her hand to look at me. "First of all, I really wanted to know what you had to say. I needed to know how you felt and thought. Secondly—actually, I guess there are three things—but secondly, *you* needed to say it. You needed to phrase it, and speak it, and hear it. And I saw that, and waited for you to get it said."

"Yeah, sorry 'bout that. It took me a long time to get to it, I know. It's only ... well, you weren't much help, dammit." I am petulant about it again. "You might have interrupted me somewhere along the line and made it easier, you know."

Her hand broadens as it takes the rise of my hip, and I almost lose my place again.

"Well?" I push.

"Well, no. I couldn't. You needed to say all that, and I needed to hear it." She leans in to kiss me, making me groan.

I break the kiss, breathless. "What's the third thing?"

"Hmm?" She is kissing my collarbone.

"Third thing," I insist, taking her head in my hands to look in her eyes.

She turns serious, brushing her lips across the palm of my hand before taking it in hers. "Oh, well, y'see. There's a rule," she says. "A straight woman has to make the first move."

"What? There's a Dyke Handbook somewhere with this in it?"

She smiles again. "A true gentle-person never makes a pass at a straight lady, except by explicit invitation. She has to make the move. It's her choice. She is the one crossing the imaginary line, not you—not I, that is. You were the one who was making the decision to do this. It had to be clearly and completely your choice."

"Well, you could at least have given me some encouragement."

"Oh, lady," she breathes. Her eyes are full of stars. "I was encouraging you like crazy!"

Later we are still again, the sweat drying from our bodies, and I remember something else. "You know, Alice, I've never been asked that before."

"What, love?"

"Asked if I wanted to stop … you know, given the choice not to go further."

"Hmm?" She asks, carefully noncommittal.

"I mean there are such differences—with a man and with a woman. I'm gonna be thinking about this for a long time, I know. Sorting this out."

I roll over toward her, laying my head on her shoulder and taking her hand. She has such great hands. They are not "pretty," feminine hands; they are strong. Square. With long supple fingers coming to rounded ends, finger pads softly visible beyond neatly kept, short nails. Her thumbs are gnarly at the base, and jut from a sideways, 90-degree joint to rise tall alongside her hand. Competent hands. And she uses them without extraneous motion or ado. Sure and capable. I realize how I have loved to watch her hands … back in the lab when she was pipetting, tagging specimens. Lighting her cigarette. When she picked up her book to find her place. The way she holds the wheel when she drives. I have taken little mental snapshots of her hands doing all this and more, without knowing it.

I come back to topic. "It's just that—I don't know, there is always a power thing with a man. And you walk such a fine line of consent. And once you've given it, you are committed, and the race has started, you know? I've never been asked before if I was sure I wanted to go through with it, especially once it began. I've never been told before, that I could change my mind if I wanted to, when we were that far into it."

She takes her time in responding, probably going through a range of feelings she is reluctant to express at this point. "How did it make you feel?" she asks.

After a minute, I reply, "Safe." I grin, a little ruefully, "And responsible."

We are both quiet for a moment, and close.

"And something else," I add. "I felt respected." Then I start to cry.

We never really sleep—just doze until the first one to open her eyes starts us off on the journey again. Even in sleep we stroke and nuzzle each other. Sleep in a tangle.

One time we both awake and we are already in the middle of love-making, like our bodies just go on without us, knowing we will catch up when we can. As if our bodies know the timetable we are on, and don't want to waste a minute of it, know we have to fill up with enough of each other's love to live on.

For a long, long while.

As foretold, the time has come—I have to go. I can't postpone it. I can't ignore it. I can't stay.

I kiss her goodbye in her kitchen, where she stands with her coffee. Neither of us says a word. There is nothing that can be said. She holds me in her arms for a long time. I break away, and our eyes hold; I turn, walk out the door, sit in the car, and turn the key. I can't look back as I drive away.

I finally find the freeway, after passing it twice, getting lost and doubling back. It takes, through the blur of tears, almost an hour in the early-morning traffic just to find the on-ramp.

I have a serious urge to just get on the damn road, and keep going east till I come to the end of it, probably somewhere in Savannah, Georgia, maybe just drive into the Atlantic. I can't stay with Alice. I can't leave Don. And I can't deal with any of it.

So I just drive.

DATELINE, 1973—The conflict in Vietnam ends with peace pacts. The Watergate trial reveals conspiracy to conceal White House involvement. Top presidential aides—John Ehrlichman, H.R. Haldeman, John Dean, and Attorney General Richard Kleindienst—resign amid charges of White House cover up.

The American thoroughbred Secretariat wins the Triple Crown Championship. Billie Jean King wins Wimbledon again for the second year in row. She previously won in '66, '67, and '68. She also defeats Bobby Riggs in "The Battle of the Sexes" tennis match.

Nixon fires special Watergate prosecutor and the Deputy Attorney General; newly appointed Attorney General Elliot Richardson resigns after only a few months. Nixon turns over first White House tapes, which include a mysterious 18.5-minute gap, later determined deliberately erased. Vice President Spiro Agnew resigns under threat of indictment for charges of income tax invasion. He is fined $10,000 and three years probation. After Agnew's resignation, Gerald R. Ford is sworn in as first-ever Vice President chosen under 25th Amendment.

The *Washington Post* wins the Pulitzer Prize for Journalism for their investigation of Watergate; Carl Bernstein and Bob Woodward's coverage breaks open misdeeds and cover up at the highest level of government, leading to the resignation of the President of the United States.

Egypt and Israel sign a cease-fire. Gasoline prices skyrocket due to Arab nation embargo of oil exports, citing US aid to Israel in Yom Kippur War. Chilean president Salvadore Allende is overthrown. Egypt and Syria attack Israel.

Eight more states ratify the Equal Rights Amendment (ERA), bringing the total to 30 states. The Supreme Court rules on Roe vs. Wade and makes abortion legal; Texas Attorney Sarah Weddington of Austin, Texas argues in favor of the case, and Nixon-appointed Justice Harry Blackmun writes the decision.

bridging the distance

My Letters to you
Are greater and more important than both of us
Light is more important than the Lantern
The poem more important than the notebook
And the kiss more important than the lips.

My Letters to you
Are greater and more important than both of us.
They are the only documents
Where people will discover
Your beauty
And my madness.

Nizar Kabbani, *Syrian poet*

October 13, 1972

Hi lady,

You were so right ~ all is well + life goes on. How's the Lone Star Beer supply? Holding up well I hope ~ or did Don leave you dry?

Everyone here is asking if you arrived in Texas okay + how you're doing ~ so being the helpful soul that I am, I told them you found out you were lost when you had to float the Big Bug over Lake Superior.

How come you didn't mail postcards to Dick + Sarah? Sure glad I didn't expect to hear you made it okay.

Hope you don't mind my talking to you, it's a hard habit to break. Kind of got used to trying to solve the problems of the world everyday. Somehow Teddy just doesn't fill the bill ~ he listens pretty good, but he doesn't have much to say.

You know how I hate to write ~ but don't have a mike for my cassette recorder, and having trouble finding one that fits.

Write if you feel so inclined and drink a case of Lone Star for me. Much love to all,

Alice

Tues, Oct 24

Alice,

The trip went fairly well, the first day out was really pretty, through those clouds of introspection - the sunset was beautiful beyond belief — no sky like a desert sky, is there? Made it to Casa Grande, then to Van Horn, Tx the next night.

The next day, I had a blowout 13 miles outside of Sonora. It was an area of cross-current winds and I'd been hit by a few of them before it happened — thought it was just another bad gust till I went skidding all over the road — saw the edge of the mountain coming at me and pulled hard on the wheel, wound up crossing the two lanes and skidding sideways in the gravel median — ended up in the gravel, completely turned around and heading back West. Figured for a minute, I was done for — I really did. Got out to survey the damage — the right rear tire was smoking — smoking!! It had been ripped clean away at the whitewall for almost half around, radial steel clearly visible in the gap. A mechanic in Sonora had tried to sell me shocks, which I politely declined. I'm suspicious he may have shoved a knife in the tire or something. Goddamn near got me killed, if he did, the dirty sonuvabitch...

Cherub was unperturbed, in the back seat, watching me struggle with that tiny VW jack in all that unstable gravel. A sweet, buck-toothed cowboy driving a truck that said "Sonora Sorghum Co." stopped and changed my tire for me (he had a heavy-duty jack). It was just past dawn on a fairly untraveled stretch of Hwy 10, and I was very thankful for the help. Car feels like it's sashaying all over the road since then. Don says I'm just snake-bit. Maybe he's right, I honestly don't care if I ever drive another mile.

Tell the busybodies I think the water in Lake Superior is unfit for man or beast, let alone the itty bitty fishies, and those folks up there are not a bit hospitable to wayfaring strangers or motherless children. Tell the loved ones that I never thought I would miss work, but I do — wouldn't help to go find some, cause there'll never be another like our Clinic — did they get my thank you note?

Miss you, my love — we really connect with very few people in this world who understand what we're talking about — rare birds indeed.

Mostly I've been rattled ... and pissed ... and blue. (Sounds like a Law Firm — "Good Morning, Rattled & Pissed & Blue!") Rattled still from my last three weeks there; rattled from you; rattled from what I'm feeling, from nearly being killed on a lonesome mountain road in Texas. Pissed that I had such a close call, which was actually my initial reaction at the time. I was mad as hell that I had gone through all that packing and leave-taking, if I was just gonna get killed all alone 800 miles into nowhere — that the Fates had waited till almost the end of my life to dole me out a dollop of true bliss. I'm pissed at how life gives and takes away at the same time. And I'm pissed at myself for just about everything.

You know why I'm blue, of course. But, was unpacking on Wednesday after Don left and found a 2/3 empty bottle of Irish Mist — got a bit wiped on it, I did. No harm done, just a good Irish drunk, laced with lots of melancholy. Had a good cry listening to Streisand. Better now. And better go.

All my love, lady,

Nancy

P.S. I did send those postcards to Dick & Sarah, including my new address, but would you believe there is not a mailbox from Long Beach to Austin? Nary a one I tell you, nor much else, for that matter — except saguaro cacti — I do remember them — but I am partial to them anyway. Ever seen them?

Of course, that last one was me—the wordy one.

Looking back at it now, forty years later, at the three long years when Alice and I were apart, from when I left California in late 1972 to 1975—I realize how different the times were then. Nixon was President, the war in Vietnam was still in full career, abortion was illegal everywhere in America, and a woman's rights—regardless of her marital status—were limited in every state. Kennedy was dead only nine years and controversy over his assassination continued actively. Man had stepped on the surface of the moon just three years prior, forever changing how we perceive ourselves as we marvel from the vantage point of space itself at our beautiful blue planet.

After eight months of daily conversations, followed by one week of lovemaking, I was hopelessly in love with Alice, and had only just realized it. But here, at this juncture, is where the real romance began. With our letters.

Of course it was all via what we now call snail mail—except, even then, there were grades of slowness. We always paid the extra postage for Air Mail (a postal distinction: price and delivery time between first class and the "faster" Air Mail,) And, indeed, most of our letters voice our frustration with the days it took to get messages to each other, and, as our comments crossed each other in the mail, it was always a game of catch up.

In today's age of Facebook, live chat, texting, and instantaneous email, all of this seems quite antiquated and awkward, and unnecessarily agonizing. But it's all we had at the time. The telephone was difficult, given the nature of our clandestine love affair, and the two-hour difference between California and Texas. Phone calls are mentioned frequently in our letters, as well as their expense in those days (with the monopoly of Ma Bell—properly known as Bell Telephone), though that was the least of our worries. Still, it has to be put in its context: our long distance phone calls averaged $10.50 an hour (a single call ranged up to $31.50 since we talked on several occasions for three hours because the opportunities to do so were so infrequent.)

Now measure that against the fact that in 1972, you could buy 5 pounds of flour for 59 cents, a good loaf of bread for 25 cents, round steak for $1.30 a pound, bacon for 95 cents a whole pound, eggs for 62 cents a dozen, milk for 66 cents a half gallon, 10 pounds of potatoes for 90 cents, coffee for 91 cents a pound, sugar for 65 cents a pound, and oranges for 84 cents a dozen.

I won't try your patience too long with our letters, but I will spend this chapter on those earliest ones in late 1972, some of the first ones we wrote to each other, because I want you to come to know her a bit more as she expresses herself in her own words. And I will share portions of other letters in the next few chapters as well, when I was coming to grips with falling in love with her, with what it meant in terms of my marriage. And how Alice, throughout my struggle, did her best to stay supportive, allowing me to find my own answers.

Oct 25 '72

Hi lady,

Well X-ray has a new tech. - male - Steffen ~Already he's upset because he doesn't have a phone in X-ray. And he has much sympathy for the 'poor, hard-working Jackie' ~ she's already taken him under her wing + convinced him she is the be-all and end-all of the Clinic ~ I snirk a lot (cross between sneer + smirk).

Poor Steffen. Mary came over from the main clinic to show him how to mix Barium + he's moved everything around but the X-ray table + processor, then it turned out to be a typical Mon w/ the usual amt. of phone calls, etc. ~ Now his eyes are beginning to glaze. There being nothing I can do to help + not inclined to be helpful (as I are) I just sit + grin alot.

(Wed) You'd never believe Terrible Tuesday ~ the lab is fine ~ X-ray is hysterical. Came to work + found out you are not the sloppiest Barium mixer in the world ~ he works here now. Even had it all over my centrifuge + floor. The Radiologist was still working at 10:30 | am. Steffen still typing dictation at 4:30 | pm + insists he's going to have his own phone + disposable utility syringes (the glass ones aren't good enough). How did you ever manage to get by w/ using my phone? He really gets spastic about it ~ maybe it's just insecurity.

Chance of rain today so I have writer's thumb already ~ shouldn't be rambling on anyway ~ don't want you to think I miss your company or anything ~ it's just that Teddy has his hat down over his eyes + his hands over his ears, so am having trouble communicating w/ him. After Mon, + Tues. he's probably bothered by battle fatigue.

Everyone asks daily if I'm still taking music lessons at The Harp ~ not being the one to disillusion them, I told them I had increased to nightly sessions.

Love,

Alice

Thurs, Oct. the something

Alice,

Only just wrote to you a day or so ago, but as you mentioned, it's a hard habit to break. Don is on the road for a few days. It's raining, and bloody cold! Maybe I did take a wrong turn and am really in the Klondike — freezing my navel off.

Apartment is rather nice, Don did good. There is a long narrow window by the door and Cherub learned immediately to push aside the curtain and rest her chin on the sill.

Don's been very occupied with the job, and seems to be doing rather well at it. Not that occupied that he hasn't noticed a certain moodiness, but he's got the good sense to let sleeping dogs lie — or lying dogs, sleep — which I've been doing a fair amount of - my escape mechanism.

Miss our Teddy quite a bit, too — Sorry he's not more communica-tive, and after the talk I gave him, too — Maybe it's just all too much for him as well. Take care and write when your writer's thumb clears up.

All my love, lady

Nancy

Oct 30, 1972

Hi Lady :-

Steffen can't spell shit — well maybe shit, but little else — and keeps coming down to ask questions, then locks himself in w/ his typewriter all afternoon + gets upset if you open the door to tell him he has an X-ray. This place sure isn't the same as it was last month.

64

My Librium is fighting with my Pro-banthine while my pyloric valve just sits there all curled up and watches the action ~ or lack of it, whichever. Last Sun. if someone had said vagotomy to me, I'd have bought two of them.

Lay off the Irish Mist, kid, you're supposed to be taking on enough Lone Star for both of us. Besides Irish Mist is my favorite ~ sharing a small space I leave for Irish Coffee. Haven't had a "music lesson" since you left, no big thing I guess ~ never was very talented in that area. Very few other areas, now that I come to think of it.

Guess I'd better stop for a while ~ now I have writer's wrist + it's time to split the scene.

Love you,

Alice

Just for reference: Librium was the Prozac of the day. Pro-banthine was for stomach ulcers, and a vagotomy is a rather grim stomach surgery. Her bum thumb, called a "gamekeeper's thumb," was also giving her fits—from writing to me. It takes its colorful name from the condition that evidently was common to gamekeepers on estates, produced by the repetitive trauma injury to the thumb of wringing the necks of rabbits. (And we think carpal tunnel's a big deal!) Hers had more to do with her accident years before, since I don't think she ever wrung anything's neck in her life, though some people might have tempted her, once or twice. The condition caused her thumb joint alignment to jut out sideways, and it was painful.

Don's new job took him traveling much of each week, bringing him home on the weekends. For the first time since I was fifteen years old, I did not have a job. Even at the beginning, Don's new position paid more than we both made in California, although in Texas income levels were considerably less than California. A full-time, experienced X-ray

65

technician in Texas earned a gross income of just over $8,000 a year in 1972 (in Houston and Dallas wages were only a bit higher.) I had been making $11,000 a year in higher-paying California (which translates to about $35,000 in today's buying power.) If I had worked, the tax bracket for us would have cut everything I earned in half. Working forty hours a week for $4,000 a year was unappealing to me.

Though the tax bite was one consideration in my opting not to get a job, it was just one consideration. Don was quite happy not to have me work. He was a transitional man, from an era where men provided the sole income in the household, just as he had for most of his former married life. But 1972 and '73 pretty much marked the end of an era in which the paradigm consisted of the breadwinning husband and his (assumed) traditional American homemaking wife.

The truth, which I could not divulge to Don, was that I was incapable of working at this point in my life, since I was indulging in a total meltdown. The only difference between me and my certifiably nutty mother was that my nervous breakdown was silent, self-contained, and very private.

On the surface I was learning, in 1972 corporate society, what was expected from the model wife: to be a gracious hostess and wifely asset to her career husband. To be perfectly groomed, well-spoken (when and if she opened her mouth), and neither required nor encouraged to hold or express opinions of anything relative to life issues. I never really succeeded. I was too prideful, too independent, too opinionated, and too convinced I was entitled to own and voice my convictions. Even in my numbed, detached state, I was incapable of being a Stepford Wife.

So, on the outside I pretended to be the perfect company wife, keeping the home fires burning while Don was on the road throughout the week, three weeks out of four (a blessing really, looking back on it.) While he was gone, I wandered the house, kept all odd hours, slept a lot, and vacillated back and forth, from resolve to end it with Alice, to imagining how life would be with her. Wondering how life would be if I stayed with Don, the husband I still loved, but was not in love with. Should I forfeit a future that included Alice, and cut her off, cut her out of my life? I worried what would happen to her if I did. I hoped that some miracle would occur to show me which way to go. I wondered if Don knew, sensed it, felt it, and if he did, was he just waiting it out to see what would happen? I wallowed in guilt about it all.

Thurs, Nov 2

Alice,

Hey buddy, I really hope my letters haven't been giving you a bad way to go - That last one I regretted having sent. It's just the boiler was on overload, needle in the red, and there are no safety valves at this end, so the pressure kinda backed up the pipes to the source. You are okay, aren't you? And you'd tell me true, wouldn't you?

Anyhow, am better now - I have a stiff upper lip, nose to the grindstone, hand on the plow, shoulder to the wheel, and back to the wall - resemble Quasimodo in this position and find it impossible to accomplish anything - besides I have a cramp in my style - hell of a place for a cramp, eh lady?

Met Don's plane at the Austin Municipal Airport last week (he spent week in Dallas with his boss). Admittedly the airport is not the "park bench out in nowhere with a bare light on a pole" that you say Eureka's airport is, but it runs a close second.

I have, in my vast travels, seen a few Dairy Queen stands larger than the terminal building. The airstrip itself would rival many grammar schoolyards. There are 6 Gates in all and #3 thru #6 are to either side of a block long, open-air, glorified carport, which must be a beaut when its raining.

Three airlines are serviced by this edifice: Continental, Braniff, and the newly named Texas International. It was formerly Trans-Texas Airlines, or TTA (dubbed Tree-Top Airlines by the locals). And only the name has changed. Two-thirds of the flights are to Dallas or Houston, and the rest are to such exotic locales as Laredo, Midland-Odessa, or Corpus Christi. If the truth be known - you can't get there from here. From here you can get to Dallas. You can get there from there - but you can't get there from here.

The baggage claim is the height of insouciance - a half hour after you've landed two guys on a tandem bike pulling a little red wagon ride up to the baggage drop and deposit your suitcase on a PERMANENTLY DISABLED conveyor belt - just pick up your bag, podner, and git on home.

67

is it sisters?

Well ... cheered up yet? More later.
Love,

Nancy

Tues AM

Hi, luv,

~ Rage, unrestrained anger + generally pissed off. Can't get my
patients in the lab since our esteemed X-ray tech has decided I can
wait while he mixes up his crap for Barium enemas ~ he comes to
work around eight + by 9:30 is in a big rush. Miss you like crazy,
lady. Do believe I'm having my three o'clock hot flash this morning
~ Now everyone wants to know what's wrong w/ me? May tell them
this afternoon.

You were right ~ you never could find another Clinic ~ Jane just
came in to get her shoes tied. Happy Halloween!

After much wailing + gnashing of teeth I've decided I'm not really
being fair to Steffen ~ he is new around here + you're a hard act to follow ~ Everyone tells him that's not the way Nancy did it, Nancy always
wrote appointments in the lil' book, Nancy always put the patient's age
on stuff, Nancy always wrote the charges so we could read them + etc,
etc, etc.

Always,

Alice

Nov 5, 72

Hi Lady:~

Big Red just caught me and dragged me down to see the Doctor-Man about my nu-moanya. Feel so much better now that I have some more pills to forget to take. Birdie just dashed in the door + and fell into the chair, said, "At last I can sit in the shrine" ~ got up + left. These people sure act funny 'round here. Good thing you left ~ might be contagious.

Your lil' man you used to see walk by the Clinic w/ the pool (que) (cue) stick in lieu of a cane just passed by + waved his stick @ me. Where does he go w/ it?

No sweat lady ~ there's a safety valve here so rave on, maniac. And I only get blue for half the day now ~ the other half I'm too sleepy (mellow) from all the pills to bother with it.

Just got word from my landlady ~ have to get rid of one of my dogs. Fat chance, but didn't tell her that yet. Don't really feel up to the hassle today. Guess they get to barking when I'm not home, which is mostly, it seems.

Love,

Alice

From this outspoken age today, I cannot emphasize enough how different things were in 1972. Today in most places in the civilized world, a woman coming to terms with her homosexual tendencies, or ambiguous proclivities, is not all that rare. And it is generally understood to be a possible choice for some, perhaps even considered no big deal. And among those who deplore it as a human failing, they reject it vociferously. I assure you, back in '72, homosexuality was no topic of everyday conversation, no acknowledged way of life. There was seldom a homosexual portrayed in film or novel unless they were tragic, suicidal, or an embarrassing stereotype held up for ridicule—or comeuppance. Certainly no sit-com contained today's common gay character. Homosexuals were hidden for the most part, shadow people in our midst.

It had been as recent as 1969—three years before I met Alice—that the Stonewall Riots occurred in New York City, the Mecca and American model of sophistication and urbanity, then and now, where one might expect more tolerance. Gay men stood up for their rights against police harassing them in a gay bar called Stonewall in Greenwich Village. They refused to be hassled, ridiculed, arrested, or bashed. In-the-closet homosexuals all over the country heard the rallying cry. It was a landmark uprising; in its own small way the linchpin for gay rights that Rosa Parks' refusal to be moved on a bus had been a turning point for black rights. And this event brought to light, and to the attention of many Americans, the common humiliation and repression of gay life.

San Francisco in the early seventies was synonymous with hippies, flower children, Haight Ashbury, Jack Kerouac, and the beatnik generation. It would be a full decade later before San Francisco came to be more widely known as the Home of the Queers. Armistead Maupin would begin publishing his daily installments of *Tales of the City* in *The San Francisco Chronicle* in 1976. Meanwhile, in Los Angeles and New York City, the women's movement began burgeoning, not yet creeping into the bedroom communities of suburbia. It was indeed a far cry from sweeping the country.

And throughout all this, I was quietly freaking out in Texas. Alice, for her part, was trying to hold it together in California. We were both in pretty bad shape.

Fri, Nov 3

Alice,

Well, get out your translator - am in San Antonio at Naomi's today and no typewriter here. Been rather down about it all — some qualities seem missing in me - and elements in my situation missing for a long time now are suddenly glaringly evident for their lack, and for their comparison with you.

My problem is not with that. My problem is with me — my discontent, which is mostly with myself. I feel caught and trapped and boxed in by my own conflicting emotions. I really did entertain the notion to head for places far away while I was driving here — the urge to be neither there nor here was very strong. Just run away.

God, I miss talking to you. But I shouldn't be talking about this to you even in a letter — you've got your own side of it to deal with, let alone mine. Don't know whether I'll even send this or not. (But I dug it out from under the mattress and decided to send it anyhow. You need to know what a quandary I'm in, even if I don't expect you to do anything about it, not even comment on it if you don't choose.)

Love,

Me.

Mon 11/6/72

Hi lady: ~

Translation was no problem ~ easier than I expected. Lady, things will probably never be the same around here ~ there's nothing to be done for it ~ and no resolutions for me ~ I'm the world's lousiest resolution keeper.

Why are you discontent with you? Why not try being mad @ me, it will give you something to do.

I'm gonna make this short, the pooches & kitty are driving me nuts. Will write again very soon. Needs to talk to you so I know you're there ~ no one else understands my foreign language ~ talk about glaringly apparent.

Write soon.

With much love,

Alice & the furry boys

11/7/72

Alice,

It is Tuesday morning — about one hour before the mail comes — hope there is a letter from you.

Had a terrific storm on Sunday night - water was coming in over the top & under the front door — as you might surmise, the door's fit is a bit off, enough space all around to sling a cat through — Clear and fine since - and freezing (about 50 or 60 degrees) — yeah I know, but am beginning to give up hope that I will ever be warm again — this nervous breakdown has messed with my internal thermostat.

You were right, the whole letter from the Clinic was concerned with your evil ways — I know it's not easy for you there, however you must stay till after your birthday. I have it on the best authority that they are planning a really terrific present for you. Everybody is saving urine bottles like mad.

The mailman hasn't come yet — gets later every day. Think I'll just stop this and concentrate on waiting for a letter. More at the end of the week.

All my love, lady

Nancy

11/11/72

Hi ya all:~

Guess by the time you get this you will have received your letter from work. By the way, they speak with spooned tongue ~ would I talk about an X-ray tech? Especially a sloppy one? Never.

Reckon I'm going to have to look for a place to live since my landlady gave me an "order" to get rid of one of my dogs. Life is so simple if people would just stay out of my world. Meanwhile, I've taken Patrick over to my friends, Mary and Chuck, to foster for a while.

You would never believe how many mikes I've tried on my recorder. Guess when I get rich I'll have to invest in one. Then instead of writer's wrist I would have talker's t'roat, right? You'd never understand me anyway with this rotten cold.

Will stop now, my elbow is wearing thru to the bone. Write when you get time.

Love,

Alice

The winter of 1972–73 in Austin, Texas was very harsh. While normally fairly temperate, that year saw incredible ice and snow. I, of course, was undergoing my own sea change, and the chemistry of my body reflected it. I couldn't seem to get warm; at least, several areas of my body couldn't seem to get warm. The letters between Alice and me hold many references to my ice-cold belly button.

Anytime I thought of Alice for any length of time, I began to tremble again, just as I had in those last days with her. The very thought of her gave me the shaking shivers. It had taken me thirty-one years to make the discovery that I was capable of falling in love with a woman, and the intensity of what I felt was shocking to me. I had no reference for it. Did it mean loving any woman would feel this way? Could this overwhelming passion have been an inherent consequence of any lesbian relationship I might have entered? Would I now be attracted to other women? Had I always been attracted to other women, and rationalized those relationships as close friendships? Or did my overpowering love have only to do with this one woman, Alice? And regardless of the answers, what would ultimately be the ramifications? What of

Don, of our marriage? If I rolled the bowling ball down this alley, how many pins was I gonna knock over?

Alice developed an ulcer trying to cope, first, with my presence in her life, and then, with my absence from it—apart from the letters. No doubt she was wondering how she had gotten herself into this pretty pickle. So much for her resolution to stay out of dramas caused by the people she paired with. Her future hung in the balance with a married madwoman, who was silently coming apart some 1,400 miles away, trying to figure how to—or whether to—save her marriage.

And I was trying to be there for Don, to help him during this crucial period, as he learned the ropes at a new job that could potentially open new doors to a very lucrative career.

Inside, however, all I really wanted to do was pull the covers over my head, curl up in a ball, and sleep for a hundred years while the briar bushes grew all 'round.

Thursday 9th

Alice,

We haven't made any plans for Thanksgiving yet — better get cracking — it's been too damn cold to plan anything outdoors — it was 39 degrees last night and going to 34 tonite - Kkkeerist! and me with lockjaw of the thermostat!

Well nothing in the mail today - disappointment.

There's a scroungy old boy dog hanging around outside the window - he and Cherub whine at each other - she has the windowpane all slobbered up. He doesn't look so sexy to me, but what do I know? Guess I'll have to chase him away. More again soon,

Love,

Nancy

Nov. 13

Hi lady:

It's getting ready to drop some rain on us poor depraved/deprived Californians ~ Wrote you a note Wed but didn't mail it ~ was pretty bad ~ that's why this is in a mangled envelope ~ so I wouldn't waste a perfectly good stamp. Getting pretty good @ saving money huh? That's 8 cents in only 37 years.

Do you realize I hate to write letters? Then suddenly I catch myself sitting rattling on like I didn't have two Stat urines on the counter to do ~ Don't go away.

How's that for a fast Stat? I'm so swift I almost have them done before I get the specimen.

Jane & Sally are having a hoppin' battle w/ Steffen ~ he won't even pull X-rays for them unless the mood strikes him. And this wk the mood hasn't stuck him very often.

Well, guess I'll stop this for now + may even put a Big stamp on it since I'm solvent now.

With much love,
Alice + Boys + orphaned Patrick

Friday, 8:35 PM

Alice,

Just spent 35 minutes on phone with you. You know, at Bell Telephone prices, it would almost be cheaper to fly, considering the time spent and what little gets said. Think I'll start another piggy bank collection - maybe see you in 103 years or so.

Lonely, lonely — even more so after I put down the receiver. Oh lady, whatever shall I do? I love you so much — and if it's possible, I miss you even more. This living in two places has me schizoid, and getting more split all the time. If that damned operator hadn't been in the way — I'd have pulled you through 1400 miles of telephone wire — but I was afraid I'd get that humorless bitch, too.

None of this makes any sense at all, but I'm putting it down anyway — creek of consciousness. God knows I say more than I should — if truth be known, I shouldn't be saying anything at all (why can't I ask you not to write?) It isn't helping any, we both agree on that - Love you, miss you, need you, want you — hell, I even LIKE you — how's that for a kicker?

I love you

Me

PS. Before you get panicky - yes, I want you to keep writing. No, I don't want you to stop — and God, it would be so much easier to keep things right here if you did. But don't know if I could take it and don't want to think about trying.

Nov 16

Hi lady: ~

Tired of sand in my shoes + everytime the moon is full I have to chain my foot to the bed so I don't wake up in the morning in some foreign country like Tennessee, Texas, or Indiana.

By the way, the operator lady apologized & told me it was the rules. She didn't like to interrupt. Anyway, she wasn't bad. Just in the way.

Started to work this morning in the deluge ~ Blew my radiator, so was stranded w/ H2O lapping @ the top of my boots. This weather is getting to be a bit irritating ~ besides I can't swim + I panic when I see more than a cup of H2O all at once.

These people @ work seem to think I'm here to do stuff for them ~ Lil' do they know I only come down here 'cause the counter's just the right height so I can write letters. By the way, don't be an idiot, keep talking ~ I'm a good listener even if I can't be of any help. I'd much rather you used me for a sounding board than to see you build up such a head of steam that the explosion would cover the plains of Texas. Only one request, don't try to put me on with your cheerfulness. I know you better than that.

Am supposed to translate a cookbook for our blind friend ~ that should keep me busy for a yr. or 2. These things are written in a foreign language ~ tsp., pinch, blend, mix, stir ~ easier to just broil steaks or eat plastic fast food.

Haven't talked to Dick since he called for your address last mo. Never called them back. Don't want to talk to any more people about you ~ I can just manage the ones @ work. Amazing, I have to try not to talk now. Used to have to force myself to talk to people.

Got to stop this. Be of good cheer ~ only 6 more wks of 1972. You can make it ~ have great confidence in you.
Much love,

Alice

Mon, Nov 28 '72

Excerpt (from Nancy):

Glad to hear about your cookbook project — if you think the language in them is slightly foreign, you should try following those recipes ... did you know that when they say "Wash turkey thoroughly before stuffing" they do not mean on the Permanent Press Cycle. One time a candy recipe said, "cook until candy forms a soft ball when dropped in water" and I cooked that candy all day, testing all the while — it just lay there. Had to use a chisel to get it off the bottom of the pot, but it never did form a soft ball, hard ball, or badminton birdie, for that matter.

These letters just don't cut it do they? I found the tape very difficult to make — have to get my courage up real high for that, even though you said you enjoyed it. As inadequate as letters are - they are better than nothing, I guess

Miss you very much, lady.

Nancy

11/29

Hi Luv :~

You should be here! Overmuch has happened since Fri. It would be easier to talk than try to write.

Birdie is retiring Dec 1st. Says this part time is too much work. Sure going to miss her around here 5 days a wk. This is a neat place to work but I'm getting an ulcer trying to cheer people up. Came in this beautiful

Fri + said Good Morning! got two "mornings," 3 grunts - ½ moan + large amounts of dead silence.

A lil ol (88yrs) lady came in Wed - name's Hartman - Had a sawed off pool cue for a cane. Guess I'm going to have to get one. They seem to be pretty popular.

Thanksgiving was fantastic. The turkey was cooking in Brea, the rolls were cooking in Anaheim. The salads + pies arrived from LA + San Diego ~ everyone was starved in Fullerton. Everything was fine after the runners rounded up the food.

Best get all of this in the mail. No letter from you in ages.
Take care.

Alice

Monday, 12/4/72

Excerpt (from Alice):

Thank you for all of your unsolicited help for birthday presents ~ I'm going to hit you, lady. Sure hope Dr. T. finds someone else to sing Happy Birthday to after the 10th.

Jane just came in to tell me she saw a cow with two udders over the wkend ~ you can imagine her description. Received tape + letter yesterday ~ thanx much ~ was beginning to think you'd broken your typing finger.

You're rite ~ need a COF2E2 break with you. Have much of no particular importance to say. Was almost afraid to open the pkg you sent~ but then decided even in Texas they don't make urine bottles that big.

Monday Dec 11

Alice,

You wouldn't believe this weather - had hard rain all day yesterday and temperatures hit 30 by about noon — kept raining & icing all night - was 28 degrees when I went to bed.

Wish I had my camera loaded with film - I'd take a picture of this — icicles are hanging all over the cars — ice on streets everywhere, walking and driving precarious — the field in back of us has ice on every blade of long grass — it is fantastic.

Don left for Corpus Christi this AM; said he'd try it, if it got too bad, he'd turn back. Hope he thinks to call me tonite; I don't worry about his driving, he was stationed in Alaska & North Dakota long enough to learn how to manage in this stuff, but Texans don't even know how to drive in rain - accidents by the score on radio.

Just heard the temp is 30 and it's 2:00 in afternoon — with wind chill factor it's 12 degrees! K-K-K-K-Jeepers! So, I don't wanna hear about your 42 degrees last night, that's downright tropical.

Mail hasn't come yet, and won't be surprised if it doesn't — do they still believe "neither rain, nor sleet nor snow, etc"? Don't envy the mailmen today.

Just took Cherub out — I made it to a car door and hung on while she maneuvered the icy grass — you should have seen the accusing looks she gave me — took her forever — she kept searching for a dry warm spot. I made it back to the front door, but she got a little too eager and damn near took a flyer — would have been funny to see, her legs were going everywhere — but was afraid she'd break a bone & I'd have to thaw the car out fast & skate to a vet somewhere.

Hope your birthday was nice and not traumatic like mine are - did you celebrate? Any lil' bottles from the clinic?

Got Xmas card from Dick & Sarah - first I'd heard in so long. Last letter I wrote to baby Billy alone & threatened not to speak to his parents again if they didn't write. Sarah hasn't been feeling too well, female stuff. Dick has joined the ranks of our other Thespian friends (that's Th-thu-Thespian), got shanghaied into helping a bunch of kids put on a ballet - The Nutcracker Suite. Donna said it was wild — he's such a ham, she says (as if we didn't know) he kept following the spotlight around. He was in tails + a false mustache — would have given a lot to see that. Don't know if Dick ballet'd himself - but wouldn't doubt it — good thing I wasn't there, they'd have had to carry me out. If you see him mention it, want him to know his fame has spread far and wide.

Billy is fine - doesn't crawl - he rolls!! - Donna says he follows her down the hall that way and everything - also he has developed a penchant for toilet water — not the bottled kind ... the real stuff. Billy is still cool!

Hallelujah! The mail comes despite weather. Please do send pix of Teddy in his get-up.

In their Christmas card Dick & Sarah sent me the pictures of The Harp, but no negatives. One is of the cake, one of Dick & Sarah, and another is the one Paddy took- he had us all squished together so we'd all be in the picture - Dick is standing on the rungs of the bar stools behind us and looks like he's about to go over backwards - I am grinning glassy-eyed into the camera and it appears my left tit is in the cake. Josie is smiling as usual, but seems to be leaning in to get a closer look at the icing on my tit, and you look positively bombed! It's awful. Call them for Christmas and ask for your own set, but you'll be sorry.

Want to hear more about Jane's two-uddered cow ... where did she see that? Leave it to Jane! (Notice how I refrained from saying, "how udderly fascinating!")

More later and much, much love,

Nancy

Dec 11, '72

Hi, lady :~

Came home tonite + found long letter, so decided since I haven't written since yesterday, would answer it tonite.

Are you ready for Christmas? Ho-ho-ho + all that garbage. Ask me what I want for Christmas. Really want to know? Oct 1st - 12th ~ how 'bout that? Could throw in Aug + Sept for good measure ~ much prefer that time of year w/ daylite saving time. It's dark so soon now. Also too cold to sit in yard til 4/am.

Good skiing in the Mts. Want to go? Do you know how to ski or do you prefer Hot Buttered Rum in front of a roaring fire? Come to think of it, that sounds better than breaking a leg against a tree.

More later if I can think of anything to say (that's dumb, never do say much).
With love,

Alice

Dec 11 & Dec 13

Alice,

Got my Christmas cards all made out — have to stamp & mail them if I can get the Big Bug out of the ice. Tues they predicted more ice & snow, but it didn't happen... Temp stayed above freezing and the sun acted like it had good sense for a change. It was really gorgeous and by noon all the ice in the streets and grass had melted — but it took a half hour to chop the ice off the car — it was really thick in some places. I was so happy about the weather (temp stayed above 50 all day) I was out and traipsing all day. Didn't get much done, but was just good to be OUT.

Today is Dec 13 - Wednesday - and by the calendar, exactly 2 months since I left Calif - hahahahahahaha, makes me hysterical - 2 months!! Some people reckon time funny, you know, they use calendars. Anyhow — looks like I may make it to see 1973 after all — maybe.

Will get this off in mail now and another Friday — it's hard 'cause I answer your letter all at once and then have a long dry spell till next Monday.

All my love,

Nancy

Dec 13, Wed 2/pm

Alice,

Do you feel deluged by mail? I do - and it's glorious !!! I got 2 letters this week- two- 2- 2 - two- too- to- 2- TWO!!! Terr-iff-iccc!!

No I'm not ready for Christmas - solvency is not yet upon us - only potentially so - will be short shrift again this year — My wants are much more ambitious than yours. Want total freedom to have what I really want — without guilt or recriminations or hurt to anyone. See how impossible it is? When I want something I go whole hog — or did you notice? I believe in Santa Claus, but I'm afraid he doesn't believe in me.

I are lonesome, too. All my blond, blue-eyed (sometimes smoky green- eyed) friends are someplace else. Enough rambling — see, I answered in one fell swoop and now don't have anything more to say till next week.

Talk at you later, love.

Nancy

12/14/72

Hi Love:~

60 days, I don't believe it ~ how time crawls. Can't seem to get my head on straight. 24 hrs is 24 hrs, not 426 yrs, 3 hrs + 17 minutes.

  Things at work go on as usual ~ now not only Dr. T, but Big Red says happy birthday every day + you wouldn't believe the urine specimens she has dug up this week. I could float the Spanish Armada.

  Teddy is sitting up there collecting Christmas candy ~ a big grin on his face.

  Fran's Aunt Clare got us tickets to the New Year's Eve party at the pub, so you may not hear from me til around the 2nd wk in Jan. Also have to get moved around the 1st. And I can get my baby boy, Patrick back from his foster parents. Sure hate to move, but Fran and I are pretty compatible and it'll certainly save us both money. Her aunt and mother both cornered me separately to say they are relieved Fran has proven her point that she's capable of living alone, tho' blind, and has opted now for a roommate – they are thrilled I'm it. Anyway I'm about ready to stay in one place forever. Well @ least 6 mo. On 2nd idea, will write 1st + then do other stuff.

  Enough rambling ~ more later ~ Take care, lady.
Much love,

Alice

  I don't know how it happened, or what magic occurred, but with Alice my heart had opened fully for the first time. All my guards and wards were cast aside, and part of my quandary had to do with no longer having my defenses. The shields had dropped; the walls had been breached. Scary.

But I loved the feeling, the notion, of someone willing to look at me directly—be as open to me as I was to her, and love me despite all she saw. This was the true seduction of it. Not the fact that she was a woman, or that sexually this was new territory, or that it was a clandestine affair. The fact was, I was experiencing love in a new dimension. Getting back as much as I gave. More.

Compatibility in people has less to do with what they like, what they believe, or what they hold dear, than it has to do with how equally the energy of their love is matched. One person who withholds or pulls back while the other extends, constitutes a situation badly weighted. Unless the parties take pains to balance it, it will fail despite other areas of similarity.

Always in relationships, especially when they are new, there is the exploring of each other, feeling each other out. No one wants to have her love rebuffed, or blocked, or absorbed by the other, and not returned. But there was no pussyfooting with this. Love was coming from Alice in a steady, open-wide stream, and matched in me fully, very nearly without any ability on my part to modify it in any way. My open heart had a mind of its own, and the rest of me, my brain, body, even my better sense, was along for the ride.

I don't mean to imply I had no control—we all do. It is just that I knew this to be unlike any love ever before directed at me. And my impulse was to knock aside any blockades or barriers, and match it with all the force and fury I could employ.

My response scared the hell out of me.

Notwithstanding, something in me knew to trust my heart. Knew to trust the love Alice was giving, knew it came directly from her heart's core, uncensored and unmetered. I positively knew I could trust her, trust her with knowing—and loving—all of me. All of my strengths, weaknesses, fears, doubts, insanity, vulnerabilities. I could trust that she would never use them against me, never hurt me. Ever.

It was already proved, wasn't it? Alice told me over and over that all she wanted was my happiness. Her hope was that it would include her. Her desire was that my happiness painted her in the picture, but she was also very clear it might not be so, that I might decide to put a stop to it.

She knew that I might come to believe that she should not be in my life. "Then, so be it," she said. And I felt guilty that she was hanging around waiting for me to make up my mind, foregoing any other opportunities at her own happiness.

April 6, 1973

Excerpt (from Alice):

As for encouraging me in what might ultimately be hopeless in the outcome & feeling guilty, that's a bunch of hogwash. You really got your head warped, love. You can't be responsible for my hangup, you know. And you sure as hell can't do anything to change anything ~ it's all up to me, like I told you. It's my problem, love & I have to handle it in my own way.

So no matter what you do or how guilty you feel, it's not going to do any good. You should know Archers are a stubborn lot & it will work out in its own time, in its own way. I never got much done by pushing or trying to work things out my own way ~ usually just mess things up good. So the best way for me is to move slowly & things always turn out for the best w/o my help. In a hundred yrs., who's going to know the difference? Don't worry; it will be okay & no guilt needed since it's not due to anything you are doing or not doing ~ even if you never wrote again I would still have to stumble my way thru it. Also being a stubborn Dutchman, am not one to rule out anything that may occur in the future ~ Never give up hope, you know. As for making a commitment, I've never been one to commit much of myself to anyone. In your case I got a bit carried away ~ but never before & probably never again. So you see, you can't

86

be responsible for keeping me from doing something I wouldn't do any-way. 'Nuff said, I'm sure, but never 'enough to relieve a chronic worrier (tha's you.)

Alice exerted no pressure—in fact took pains not to. She made no demands. She took only what I was willing to give, never reached for more. And all the while her love radiated in a steady, warm effusion that bathed me in a comfort and acceptance unlike anything I had ever experienced, unless perhaps an infant straight from my mother's womb to her maternal arms.

But there was nothing motherly about this. Only that it encompassed the same surety, openness, and fullness, without claim or ownership. Alice's love embraced me without enveloping; there was utter freedom in it. It offered protection without restriction. And it came flowing from her no matter what I did or didn't do about it. In other words, freely given and unconditional.

And it was passionate and pleasurable and sexual and sensual and steamy.

I knew I was being offered a once-in-a-lifetime grant from the gods. To be given what my heart had always sought, to have what every heart desires, what we all seek to find. Just that it came at a time when I was already committed to another, was already launched on another life path.

And it could be fulfilled only at the expense, heartbreak, and pain of another—a person I also loved. Don was sure to be very badly hurt. (A double-edged sword—the surefire trademark of a gift from the gods.)

No, I didn't love him with the same force or intensity. Nor was I loved back anywhere near the same way as Alice loved me, but I knew Don loved me to the fullest he was able. It was simply a candle up against a furnace, that's all.

And I had to bear in mind that in accepting her love, I needed to take a truer leap of faith than is more commonly needed—it was to embark on a life with a woman, living as lovers (because neither she nor I was capable of much subterfuge.) It meant to fly in the face of convention, defy the accepted norms, and carve out a path for ourselves through … what? And to what?

Then again, what if I didn't do it?

Yes, that was the other consideration on the table.

Whenever I thought of turning her away and ending this romance, a cold knot formed in my chest. In those thoughts, a feeling of deadness or dullness came over me that I knew represented the blanket of repression, the muffling I would need, to be able to live without her. I couldn't face that yet. I might have to, if I decided to stay married, to keep living the life I had set up.

And how bad would that be?

I have a loving, faithful husband, even if flawed. But who wasn't? Alice was, too, and that is what I needed to look for. Yes, I needed to wipe the stardust from my eyes, and look at her critically. Find the flaws in her, in the life that would result of loving her, and really see them, see what it might be to live with them.

With Don, I was living with his alcoholism, which he denied. And it was rubbing on me hard. It wasn't the drinking that hurt me; it was his shutting me out. I questioned if he had changed, expanded his drinking, perhaps subliminally aware that my heart, like a football, was in play.

No, Don's habits had not changed. He retreated behind the drink, no different than he's always done. And just as I had always done, I took pains to encourage, comfort, and bolster him. I knew some inner dissatisfaction haunted him that he was unwilling to confront. My comforting may have reinforced him, shored him up, and sent him out into the world knowing a safe, warm home waited for him to return to. But it never really touched his deep-seated insecurities and the demons of doubt within; those could only be routed by his own effort. He chose to drink them down.

Don needed to be loved more than I could give him, perhaps—but there you go, with those incompatibilities again. And he was incapable of matching more love than this ... or at least with me.

And, of course, part of what we all must go through is confronting whether, at the core, we really are loveable, worthy to be loved with someone's whole heart.

I liked myself, initially only for the courage to have dug through all the dirt in younger years, sorting through self-esteem and traumatic family issues. But then gradually coming to terms with myself, imperfections and all. I was pretty much at home in my skin when Alice came into my life.

So, I lived in a land of inner contrasts, with a physically present husband and lover on one hand, who drank himself into a stupor every weekend, all the while professing I was the most important thing in his life. And on the other, a physically absent lover whose presence I felt like a warm velvet bunting, even across the distance of 1,400 miles, who professed to love me enough to allow me whatever time and space I needed to work it out, even if it came to pass that I rejected her.

My own heart opened and closed like a bivalve as I weighed each option, whether to go or stay.

July 12 '73

Hi, luv:~

Dr. C just came by & said good morning to Theodore.

Guess the Post Office would cut back on letter carriers if it wasn't for one Texan & one Calif person. They probably keep one aircraft busy just running back & forth ~ are you a good stowaway? I'm not~ I get airsick, seasick, and scared sick.

Just decided I'd like to take you away to my mountain retreat ~ the fire is laid, the kitchen & bar stocked. Only one problem, with my usual foresight have only one boney bed in the whole place ~ think that would be okay?

This writing has shown me one thing, how very much I love you & want to be w/ you, how much I miss you & how much I miss talking to you ~ I must say, when you sneak in under someone's guard, you really do strike a telling blow w/ long lasting results.

No, you didn't tell me about your 60 minute wrong turn the day you left~ you will never know how hard it was to walk out the door & go to work knowing you'd be gone when I got back. It was even worse when I got back & realized you were really gone ~ I listened for your footstep for days (still do). Also check every BIG Bug for a Tex. plate ~ how 'bout that for slipping the track?

Do you realize in just a short time it will be 1yr since I've seen you, yet so much has been packed into that time. But not enough.

Alice

July 23 '73

Excerpt (from Alice):

I've been giving a lot of thought to this not writing thing, & am about convinced I should take the initiative & stop ~ but then I suddenly find myself filling pages w/ nonsense & kernels of truth & tell self not to mail it as I stand in the P.O. dropping it in the slot. Then when there is no mail I really begin to come apart. You have really become a very important part of my life in such a short time & I'm afraid you would leave a huge vacancy if you ever left it. I find it impossible to imagine life without you. Even letters are good to fill a small corner of the void you left in Fullerton. Nuff said.

Aug 7 '73

Excerpt (from Alice):

Had a really neat dream. Seems I got a phone call from this really neat lady from Texas ~ she said, would you pick me up at the airport if I came out on a vacation. I said, "When?" She said, "As soon as you can get to the airport." Was there in 20min. You looked beautiful. Asked how long you were going to stay (was afraid you were going to catch the next plane home.) You said, "As long as you want me to." You know how long that would be. Was a beautiful dream, but was let down when I woke up, reached for you & you weren't there anymore. Oh well ~ at least you would have liked the rest of the dream.

Aug 14 '73

Excerpt (from Nancy):

Alice,
    Oh, I almost forgot- speaking of dreams, had a dream about you on Friday night- what I remember of it: I was in a brightly lit movie theater, where I met you when I came out to Calif — hardly recognized you — you had been living with Josie and you had dyed your hair black and were wearing eye makeup - real theatrical, like for the ballet — and you had quit smoking — you could only talk to me for 5 minutes because you had things to do — was panicky when I woke up — dream wasn't all bad tho — you leaned over and kissed my neck — of course the whole movie theater saw and they all knew Dick and Sarah and whispered they were gonna tell them—

August 20

Excerpt (from Alice): You really have nite-horses don't you? Never fear, my gray hairs are intact + eye makeup is not for me ~ as for only having 5 min to talk to you, ridiculous! You really must be sweating a meeting w/ me if you are dreaming about brightly lit movie theatres w/

91

everyone in the world looking at us. Best meet me at the Harp. It's pretty dark there. At least until you walk in, then the whole world lites up.

21 Aug 73

Excerpt (from Alice):

So you're really going to make it out to the Late Great State, are you? Can I have an hour of your undivided attention? Would prefer a wk. Or a lifetime? But will have to settle for less, I'm sure.

I think I can handle the eye makeup, but can't get anyone to dye my hair black, so reckon you'll have to settle for me the way I am. Think you can manage that? Am really looking forward to seeing you. Also am afraid to see you. Does that make sense? Anyhow, this Archer promises to remain cool + you know how cool this Archer can be.

Called Billy the other day + Sarah wouldn't let me talk to him. Says it give him ideas + then he calls people while she's not looking. Good kid, that one.

Sept 6 1973

Excerpt (from Nancy):

Yes, lady, you are scheduled for several hours of my undivided attention — matter of fact, hope to spend a whole day in your company that week, more if it can be arranged. And stop teasing me about the eye makeup and dye job — still haven't gotten over the uneasiness of that dream — much prefer you as I remember you - no extra added attractions necessary.

I don't quite believe it- that I'll be seeing you soon. Not hearing you, reading you, but seeing you! Soon.

Me

alice, the kinfolk, and a calling

In Depression-Era Idaho—on the private island where Alice and her grandparents lived—horses and shanks' mare (old-fashioned for "hoofing it") were the sole means of transportation. Accordingly, Alice learned to ride as soon as she perfected her first baby steps.

The family actually did own a car, though they kept it in town on the mainland. Alice's grandfather farmed the island, located in the middle of the Boise River, a much tamer cousin of the infamous Snake River, which flows further to the south. The Boise, however, did have its share of flooding and watery rage.

One favorite family story involves an especially damaging flood amid the many yearly ones. I'll let Alice tell it as she first told it to me—in a letter.

Dec 17, '72

Excerpt (From Alice)

Saw in the paper they were evacuating the old hometown in Idyho. Reminds me of all the fun we used to have when we lived on the island ~ Got to stay up all nite & sandbag the dam ~ so we could have time to get everything important across the river in row boats. Did you ever try to get a cow in a row boat? That's only half the fun. Then you try to keep her in there while you cross the raging river ~ Above the roar you hear this wee small voice in the distance & look back. There stands grandmother on the front porch w/ water lapping around her ankles ~ suddenly you realize you forgot something. She never did believe it was an accident ~ always thought my grandfather felt the cows were more important. Got her out before the dam broke anyway ~ there was so much ice packed in the river you could almost walk over, 'cept me, I'm chicken. Sure ruined our fun when grandfather told us what good work we did ~ we thought we were playing.

Work indeed! What an ugly word.

These solid, salt-of-the-earth people had great influence on Alice's young life. Her grandmother Bessie was a reserved, stern, unyielding woman. But it was her grandfather George who taught her a love of nature, instilled authentic values, and encouraged her independent spirit, much as he had with his daughter Nora, Alice's mother.

Nora married young—bore a son named Lester, then summarily divorced the father. Details are vague, but in those early days of the Great Depression this was surely scandalous. Nora charted her own course, and a year later married Olson Quincy, who lived in a nearby town. She gave birth to Alice in December 1934, according to Alice's birth certificate, although Nora always contended it was actually December 1935. Perhaps the proximity of the December birth to the New Year was what caused the confusion.

During those hard times, Olson and Nora jumped from job site to job site, which necessitated that the couple leave the children with George and Bessie, the grandparents. Olson worked for the government as a field surveyor, and Nora found whatever jobs were available in the nearby factories. The money the couple sent home was a boon.

Nora was not the only unconventional woman in her family. That distinction goes to Mame, Nora's paternal aunt. Mame was a member of the requisite number of church groups, clubs, and lodges to keep her in good standing within the community. But she also was a virtual fixture at every funeral at the local undertaking parlor during her lifetime of eighty-five years. In fact, the discreet signal to begin any funeral service was her arrival, wearing her distinctive black faille picture hat atop her lean, tall form. It was not as if she knew all those people who died; nor was she the town's official weeping mourner. On the contrary, she had a cheery and bright manner, and greeted those she knew at the solemn affairs with warm words and smiles. She just attended for the flowers, she said. Mame had a deep and abiding love of flowers.

Funerals, however, were merely her quirkiness. Her notoriety came from the fact that she lived openly for fifty years with her husband, Sherman, as well as the handyman, Harry—in the same house. It was assumed by the rumormongers that Harry was Mame's lover. Today we might question if Harry was Sherman's lover instead. Or if this was a tidy, little, Idaho ménage à trois? Most people in those years were more naïve, and embellishments like that were not likely to have been considered, even though humans have indulged in such variations since God made dirt.

In any event, both husband and lover attended all social and family functions with Mame, and nothing public was said about it, though it can be certain tongues wagged behind many a white-net, gloved hand. Or exchanged with some behind-the-barn homebrew by the menfolk. Or perhaps the situation had been hashed over long before, and somewhere along the way it became a fact of life, and was simply ignored.

By contrast, Alice's grandparents were upstanding Christian folk who went to church on Sunday, believed in the Golden Rule, and lived the life of country people everywhere. They toiled hard: he digging their living out of the soil, and she digging the soil out of their home and clothes. Bessie, of course, did not approve of George's sister, Mame, but was too Christian a woman to speak of it. She just got stiffer and colder than usual when in Mame's presence, a distasteful event she avoided whenever she could. Bessie also avoided her by attending as few flower-filled funerals as possible.

Growing up, little Alice spent just about all of her time with George, realizing early on that the domestic life of her grandmother was boring, stultifying, and took place indoors. Her grandfather, on the other hand, taught Alice about livestock, the responsibility to them and other creatures, and the interdependence of all living things. Alice rode with him up on the disc, the thresher, and the baler. She also learned from him how things basically worked, how to fix them when they broke, and how the land offered itself under a determined hand. George spoke little, in the taciturn way of people who live in their thoughts all day, but his influence was valued by his family and community alike. Alice never heard him use profanity, even under the greatest duress. However, he occasionally uttered the dreaded words, "By Thunder!" The imprecation was enough to send small children scurrying for cover.

George finally got a gut-full of farms, floods, and frustration, and sold the island. He moved his household into the mainland town where he certainly made a better, if not lucrative living in real estate. But not before Alice, and her half brother and nemesis Lester, enjoyed an idyllic early childhood in this setting.

For eight years on the island, Alice attended a one-room school. With less than twenty students total—she, her half brother, and the children of the island's sharecroppers—all the grades were intermingled. Incredibly, Alice began her education at the age of three—at the same time six-year-old Lester started his. It wasn't at her grandparents' insistence so much as her own. Refusing to be left out of anything her half brother was permitted to do, Alice tagged along with him each morning to the schoolhouse. Day after day, she pressed her face against one of the school's window-panes, spellbound by the class events within. Young Alice gradually wore the teacher down, until, much to her delight, she was invited inside, and handed a *McGuffey's Reader*.

It was then that precocious Alice, at just three years of age, discovered the first of her true passions in life—reading. When we met many years later, this triggered an immediate strong attraction between us, as we played "Have you read ...?" The game of all devout readers.

Alice also learned a strangely bizarre mathematical method in that island schoolhouse. She was always a whiz at figures, including all systems of higher computation (she was never wrong), but her written calculations resembled some quirky formula I never could decipher, and I teased her about it.

Oct 31, 1972

Excerpt (From Alice)

Leave us not pick on my Idaho 'rithmetic ~ you know how sensitive I are. Besides it really doesn't matter how you work out the problem just so you come up w/ the rite ans.

Alice grew up with dogs and cats by the number, the recitation of whose names and histories boggled the mind. Of the few scattered "little kid" pictures Alice had of herself, all but one shows her mounted on her horse, or holding some variety of dog, cat, or creature of some sort. The only snapshot of her alone captures a solidly built, blond girl about ten years old, dressed in a light-colored jacket and skirt, stretched in odd creases across her square little body, as if she had been tugging on the tails of the jacket just moments before the picture was shot, twisting back and forth inside the garment, trying to relieve herself of its constrictions. She wears stretched out socks that slouch down the back of the heel inside her scuffed and dusty, round-toed shoes, and squints defiantly into the camera and sun with a sullen scowl, her white-blond hair circling her head and fluffed to a fare-thee-well. Not an aspiring beauty queen here.

After moving with Olson and Nora to Benicia outside of San Francisco in early 1945, Alice was permitted to continue at her advanced grade level, despite being three years younger than her classmates; her education and natural brilliance simply could not be faulted or denied. The family migrated further south to Orange County, and she graduated from Fullerton High School in Southern California at age sixteen. Initially the school administration held her back a year for being too young, but she made up for it by taking all elective subjects in her senior year, including photography, tennis, calculus, metal and wood shop, mechanical drawing, and even aerodynamics (California schools really did offer these courses back then.) Not because she challenged these subjects on a gender basis, but because, by then, she had taken every academic class the school offered. And she was truant so often they despaired of her. Alice had already learned everything the school board required (and maxed the grades.) So, the administration gave up and shoved her into any damn class she wanted if it kept her in school. But by sixteen, she balked and insisted to be graduated. By then the administration probably felt well shed of her.

Alice later declared that her mother went to her high school more days than she did, just bailing her daughter out of trouble. There was one particularly hairy incident when a tennis teacher, no doubt having had enough of Alice's lip, swatted her rump with a racket as Alice sauntered past, whereupon Alice wheeled around and decked the teacher, knocking her cold. Summoned by the indignant school board, Nora calmly asked Alice what had happened.

"She hit me, so I hit her back," Alice said.

"My daughter doesn't lie," Nora addressed the officials. "Make any more of this, and I'll sue you for assault on a child." With that, she turned her back on them all, and led Alice out of the room.

Most of Alice's high school friends lived on the farms and orchards that proliferated mile across mile of sunny farmland. After school, she and her girlfriends rode horses by the hour through bean fields and eucalyptus groves, breathing air made heady with the seductive scent of orange blossoms.

Decades later on the freeway, speeding by a huge shopping mall, Alice pointed the area out to me, saying, "Geraldine used to live in a large farmhouse between those two trees."

The trees she indicated bore a sorry, choked look from everlasting car exhaust, and were boxed in by concrete sidewalks. And the ghostly, long-gone and forgotten farmhouse in Alice's vision was backed by current-day cinderblock department stores lit with neon signs.

Also in that same area, Alice said something like, "Madge's family had a huge bean field here."

"Where? Which part?" I questioned, looking at the succession of ugly industrial buildings, and auto body shops we were passing.

"All of it. From Western Avenue to Beach Boulevard. We used to make money working in the hot sun with the itinerant pickers here, when the beans were coming on."

Phantoms. People who live in one location for a long time always see phantoms of what used to be.

Alice's first long-term romantic relationship was with Carla, a married woman with four children. Her husband was a philanderer, and she finally got fed up with him and fell in love with Alice, who eventually moved in with her and all the kids. Carla was sweet and warm; she was also an alcoholic. Both Alice and Carla did hospital shift work, and Carla was usually drunk in between, so Alice ended up caring for the kids much of the time. A couple of years later, the philandering husband got a girl pregnant and needed a divorce from Carla to marry her.

That's when Alice's mother Nora got a phone call.

"Hello, who is this?" snarled the male voice over the phone.

"Who wants to know?" Nora demanded.

"I want to speak to Alice."

"So, who is calling?" Like daughter, like mother; Nora wasn't easily pushed.

"Well, this is Mark, Carla's husband, and I want to talk to Alice."

"What about? She's not here. I'm her mother."

"Her mother, huh? Well, your daughter has been having an unnatural sexual relationship with my wife, and I'm naming her co-respondent in my divorce case. You can tell her that."

"Oh, is that so? Well, let me tell you something—you'd better have goddamned good proof of your accusation, because if you take my daughter into court and smear her good name, I will sue you for every cent you have, or ever hope to make. Now, do *you* understand *me*?"

That was the last of the co-respondent business. These were the days before no-fault divorces, when one party had to be the one sued and held to blame. Carla got the divorce; he paid for it. On the grounds of his unfaithfulness.

Alice stayed with Carla for nine years, till the kids were raised and gone. The youngest girl kept in touch with Alice for years afterwards.

Another thing about Alice's family: they all seemed to have interesting occupations. She had an uncle who once played piano for the bandleader, Frankie Carle. And a cousin who retired from a plant in Central California after thirty-six years of packing olives.

Feb 13, '73

Excerpt (From Alice)

Also had a great aunt who made fish flies in some plant for 40 years ~ finally retired at 82; said she wanted to try something else for a while.

She's the one whose boyfriend (the town drunk) lived with her & her husband for 50 years. Quite an old lady, she was.

That was Mame, of course.

During WWII, Alice's mother, Nora, worked as a forklift driver in a defense factory, and earned top prize one year in a forklift competition for all of Northern California, competing with forklift drivers, nearly all of them male, from a variety of factories. I never appreciated this art until I worked in a lumber mill in Humboldt County, and watched them stack units of finished redwood, weighing two-to-three thousand pounds each. The forklift driver layered them twenty-five feet high, with no more than six inches between, row upon row. Astounding!

Alice herself had held a variety of jobs, starting right after she graduated high school. She did piece work in a coat factory making button-holes, and in a Levi factory riveting pockets. She also worked in the vat room of a catsup manufacturer. She refused to consume the company's product, and cautioned all others against it, too. She never explained, and nobody really wanted to know.

When her folks were partners in a travel lodge, she changed linens in guest rooms for a few months. ("Ecchh!" she used to say.) She also peeled and cut potatoes by the hour for french fries, which she deemed a thoroughly miserable chore.

The most unusual job she got after her accident was as an egg candler.

"The doctors told me I'd never be able to work again, so of course I had to prove them wrong," she smirked. "So I took the job."

Candles aren't used anymore to illuminate the eggs to check for fertilization. It's all done with electric light bulbs now, but the concept is still much the same.

"There was a kind of pneumatic rack, which you lowered over the eggs coming up the conveyor belt in the soft baffles which held them," she explained, "and you hit the button with your thumb to apply suction to the soft rubber cups on the rack, allowing you to lift eighteen eggs at a time up to eye level, where you could rotate them and see the light shine through them, revealing any fertilized egg. You lowered the rack back down to the belt baffles and removed your thumb from the button, gently releasing the eggs."

She'd pick out any fertile eggs she had identified, and slip them onto the cross belt where they were packaged for bakeries and food manufacturers and the like. The unfertile eggs were boxed for supermarket consumers.

"The problem was remembering to keep your thumb on the button while you held the eggs up in the air," she recalled. "I dropped a fair share of eggs before I got the hang of it.

"But," she continued, "I always got a seat on the bus after work. People gave me a real wide berth—I stunk so bad. Anyway, after all those uncertain months of recovering from the accident, and doctors telling me I'd never be able to work again, I stood for a week at a conveyor belt, and proved I could do it. So then I went out, and got me a real job." She meant a job in medicine.

The first one was at Rancho Los Amigos National Rehabilitation Center in southeast Los Angeles, when it was, as Alice referred to it, a "cripple hospital."

"It was before physical therapy was much of a vocation," she said. "Sister Kenny, the Australian nurse, had been doing some revolutionary work there, and later in the States with polio victims. A few of us tracked down everything we could read on the subject, and started working with our crippled patients using her techniques. Of course, after a while it became clear Sister Kenny was on to something, and physical therapy, just in its infancy, developed into a separate occupation. But for a couple years there, we were experimenting with any paralyzed patient who was willing, and getting some pretty damned good results, too." Alice spoke proudly of the work done there.

For a little over a year she worked in the Iron Lung Ward at Rancho, and showed me a photo of her favorite patient. In the photo, Alice is standing beside an iron lung. The occupying woman is lying horizontally within it, her face reflected in the mirror mounted above the "lung." The photo of Alice alongside the mirrored image of her patient's face gives the illusion that their faces are practically side-by-side.

For anyone too young to remember polio, or infantile paralysis, it was a scourge that could paralyze the limbs as well as the lungs. By way of an alternating pressure system, the iron lung forced air in and out of the patient's actual lungs, essentially doing the work of breathing for them. The massive respirator looked like a steel drum turned on its side and mounted around a gurney. The patient lay completely inside the metal encasement with only their head sticking out at one end. Padding at the neck maintained an airtight seal, and the patient had to be hand fed. A large mirror was mounted on the front of the lung, so the patient could see who was coming and going around them, and you could talk to their reflection in the mirror without having to lean over them. Caretakers accessed the patient's body through hand ports, or by opening the contraption for very brief moments. Some patients lived in their iron lung for years.[†]

In the early years of her medical career, Alice dabbled in a multitude of jobs: in the medical surgical wards of several hospitals as a nurse's aide; in a hospital surgical and central supply, sterilizing and autoclaving surgical instruments; in a locked-down psychiatric unit; as a morgue tech; and a couple of years in OB-GYN labor and delivery. After years exploring the field, she finally became a lab tech and phlebotomist (one who draws blood.)

"Phle-bot-o-mist," she had remarked. "Sounds like somebody who traffics in tropical plants."

"Jesus, Alice!" I commented when she first recited this litany to me, "why didn't you just go to medical school?"

"Didn't have to," she shrugged. "I got my degree the real way—hands on."

Her bookshelves were lined with such riveting titles as *Principles of Molecular Virology* and *Emerging Bacteriological Pathogens*, and *Textbook of Pathology*, *Bacteriology*, and *Parasitology*. Clearly her vast medical knowledge was more than just hands on. She really did know as much as most doctors, and could have successfully challenged their boards, if such a thing were possible.

As it was, she was everybody's medical consultant within her sphere of influence. When people needed clarification of medical terms or procedures, had questions about symptoms or medication, whether to take their ailment to a doctor or not, what to do about a sick kid in the middle of the night (or a sick dog or cat, for that matter), they asked Alice. She had a phantom shingle hung over her door, and a twenty-four hour telephone available to anyone in need.

[†] Ventilators that force air through hoses hooked up to a patient's mouth or tracheotomy later replaced the iron lung.

She also had a couple of great MD friends, close friends—the kind who invited her to Thanksgiving dinner with their families, or met her for a beer after work. She passed along quite a few consults to these guys, mostly poor folk whom the doctors examined and treated, often for nothing, as a favor to her. One young doctor friend was killed when his plane crashed, just a year or so after I met her. Dean left behind a wife and child, and a brilliant and promising career. Alice was bereft when he died.

And she told the story of working in the psychiatric unit presided over by a real-life Nurse Ratched.

Tues, 8PM

Excerpt (From Alice)

That Charge Nurse was bitter and cruel and sadistic ~ she wielded her puny power over those helpless patients (and us, come to that) without mercy or restraint ~ I think there are certain occupations, like prison guards and psychiatric personnel ~ and maybe even policemen ~ which should require that people rotate out of those jobs every three years and work in some ancillary department or occupation for a while. Three years on those jobs, there often ceases to be any difference between them and the people they are hired to enforce ~

She may be right.

On one telling occasion, while the patients were gathered in the dayroom, the malicious "Nurse Ratched" sent Alice and another aide into the empty ward with orders to collect all the personal items of the patients, because "Ratched" had decided all of the patients were guilty of some infraction of her arbitrary rules. Alice and the other aide gathered bits of string, buttons, checkers, and whatever little, bitty junk the patients had in their nightstands or hidden under their pillows.

All their treasures. Their *only* treasures.

Just as Alice and the other aide were finished, the patients charged the doors of the ward, converged on the two of them, and demanded clangorously to return all the items. Alice and her colleague, holding boxes of the patients' possessions in their arms, walked backwards further into the ward, fronted by the mental patients yelling, waving their arms, threatening, and advancing on them. At the last rank of beds, Alice hollered, "Dump it!" to her co-worker, and the two emptied the boxes of all those personal bits on the last bed on each side of the aisle. They pushed past the hollering, manic patients, massing at the beds, reaching over each other, trying to grab back their worldly goods. Alice and the aide made a beeline to the door, locking the door behind them.

The Charge Nurse "Ratched" stood there outside the ward, smiling evilly, then turned without a word, and walked back to the station.

Alice's experience in obstetrics was of another sort. A nurse known by all as Granny managed that unit. She came from the Ozarks somewhere, and spoke in the rhythms and vernacular of hill people. With her thin, gray hair rolled in a bun, and round, wire glasses perched on her nose, she looked for all the world like one of the Beverly Hillbillies.

Granny was "right smart" and "purely kind," Alice used to say, adding that she also knew all there was to know about "cotching babies."

Granny took to Alice as if she were kin.

She told Alice, "My Mam was midwife on our mountain, and I went to birthin's with her, up hill and down holler, from the time I was old 'nuff to walk alone. Mam was a great healer, and she brung more babies into this world than all these here doctors put together."

Granny finished high school at her mother's insistence, then went into nursing school on a scholarship, graduated top of her class, and later went back for her bachelor's degree in nursing. Her Mam lived long enough to see her earn her nurse's cap.

Granny gravitated across the country, following two husbands—the first died in Korea, and the last she divorced. Despite her country speech, Granny was a damned fine nurse, and a good administrator. She gave all the credit to her mother.

"Mam worked clean, and she tried to teach those poor women all she knew about hygiene and good nutrition. She showed them—and me—about plants for good health, vitamins and such, and plants for healing."

Granny paused as she told this to Alice, glancing right and left before continuing, "And Mam knew the special plants that can slip a babe, or the ones to keep it planted. And there's one or two can be took for staying barren as well. But they're not easy to come by in the city," she finished, her eyes sparkling.

Granny was unconventional, fierce in her devotion to mother and child, and practiced innovative techniques long before their time, and now proven. Like getting laboring women up and walking them, and rubbing their bellies at the right times in labor. Effective midwife techniques, lost for years in "proper medicine"—ruled almost entirely by male doctors.

Once, Alice caught her doing something odd: With her back turned away from the doctors and the other nurses in the delivery room, Granny lifted a newborn up to her mouth. "Granny, what on earth are you doing?" Alice whispered to her. "I saw you actually lick that newborn's foot? What are you doing?"

"Shush, girl!" Granny looked around quickly, relaxing when she saw that she and Alice were unnoticed.

"Listen now, a baby's skin will taste salty if they have what my Mam used to call 'sick salty babe.' I find a way to lick every baby's foot I help deliver, and if I taste salt, I make sure the Doctor orders the tests for it."

Granny was actually referring to cystic fibrosis, which can be recessive in families, as we now know. The tests she sometimes guaranteed to be ordered were not done routinely at that time.

Granny was sorry when Alice quit the hospital, but knew a restless mind was driving Alice into another discipline. "You're a great healer, and you need to keep on a-learning all you ken. But you sure got the gift, girl. I'll miss ya, right 'nuff," were Granny's parting words. Alice never forgot them—or her.

Alice finally took a tangent into pathology in the course of acquiring her empirical medical degree, and there found her true calling. If she'd started sooner, had more education, she probably would have made a career of medical research or forensics. As it was, she got in on the ground floor of early computerization of laboratory testing procedures and autoanalysis. Alice found the combination incredibly satisfying.

Early computers were ponderous and complex and took up space. But they were able to do multiple tests with single samples, and combine multipart procedures impossible in a single manual pass. Alice learned the capability and operation of this pioneering technology, and was really in her glory with this new state-of-the-art science. By this stage in her long career, she truly loved her work.

DATELINE, 1973—**Gerald Ford** meets Soviet Premier Leonid Brezhnev in Vladivostok, Russia to approve the **Strategic Arms Limitation Treaty (SALT.) FBI and CIA efforts** to subvert civil rights and antiwar movements in 1960s are exposed.

Scientists coin the term "global warming" when they determine that chlorofluorocarbons (CFCs) from aerosol spray cans, air conditioners, and other emitters adds chlorine to the atmosphere, upsets the ozone balance, increases harmful UV, and contributes to the **greenhouse effect.**

Patty Hearst, the 19-year-old daughter of newspaper mogul Randolph Hearst, is **kidnapped** by the Symbionese Liberation Army, which extorts $2 million in food for the needy.

Whistle-blower Karen Silkwood is killed in a suspicious car accident on her way to meet a *New York Times* reporter. She was **bringing documents** that ostensibly would **implicate her employer**—a manufacturer of plutonium fuel for nuclear reactors—in alleged safety violations, contamination, and substantial missing nuclear inventory. The **documents are never found.**

Helen Thomas, after covering Washington for 30 years, **is first woman** to be named White House reporter for UPI. **US steel** companies settle for $56 million in back pay and wage adjustments to 386,000 workers for race and sex discrimination. **Women's Studies** is offered in about 1,000 US colleges and universities.

Little League Baseball, Inc., after 57 suits, announces that girls are eligible to compete alongside boys in 9,000 of its leagues. Multiple **women's groups** file a class action suit against the **US government** for withholding millions of dollars in federal funds to colleges, universities, and public schools, due to **failure to enforce** federal law banning sex discrimination in education.

The **Episcopal Church** breaks tradition and **ordains 11 women** as priests. **Bank of America** agrees to pay $10 million in compensatory salary increases to female employees, and increase women's management positions.

All in the Family, *The Waltons*, and *Sanford and Son* earn the top three spots for the fall lineup. *M*A*S*H** begins its long run. *Kojak* and *Cannon* are in the top ten, and the *Sonny and Cher Comedy Hour* is popular. A **controversial episode of *Maude*,** in which **she chooses an abortion,** captures 41 percent of the viewing audience (approximately 65 million people), and **sparks controversy** and protest; sponsors dump the show, and 39 CBS stations refuse to carry the re-run.

and where she stops
nobody knows

It's autumn 1973, one month shy of a year since I had last seen Alice. And as sometimes occurs in life, happenstance intervenes. That welcome force comes by way of Don's company, which called upon him to attend a weeklong product orientation at their West Coast headquarters in San Francisco. Don and I plan the trip west with the notion that we would both fly together into Los Angeles and stay with our friends, Dick and Sarah. Don would then fly on ahead to San Francisco while I stay behind and spend a few days with Alice, before rejoining him on the tail end of his trip.

Admittedly, I am nervous about meeting with Alice after nearly a year, aware it is apt to have one of two outcomes. The first: that this had all been a mere infatuation, blown up all out of proportion—I would realize this once I see her and will have to find a way to resolve a dreadful situation that I encouraged. The second possibility: that after a year apart, I am still deeply and truly in love, perhaps even more so. Neither consequence is remotely reassuring. There is, of course, the chance that Alice will discover that she no longer has the same feelings for me, but somehow I don't set much store by that happening. I trust she knows her feelings more than I do my own.

Our reunion is public, as expected. Dick and Sarah drive Don and me over to Alice's, who is now room-mating in a rental house with her blind friend, Little Fran. Alice has prepared an early supper, and the plan is that the six of us will spend the afternoon together before Don departs for his evening flight to San Francisco.

When I see Alice I know immediately I am in even worse trouble than before. The inner jolt is palpable and unmistakable this time; I recognize the sensation, as if I suddenly shift within myself, come into sharp alignment inside. My heart nearly leaps out of my chest, and my head feels rattled. I can barely look at her; she seems to glow. I am trembling visibly, and she doesn't appear in much better shape as she hugs me, trying to remain casual about it.

We all go into her house to settle down with some beer, booze, and conversation. This works fairly well, until Alice makes the mistake of looking at me in the midst of telling a story.

"So the old lady with the sawed-off pool cue told me that her son had cut the stick exactly to her height, 'cause she really is a teeny, wee bit of a ..." Alice looks at me, falls into my eyes ... and comes to a grinding halt in her storytelling.

Time stands still in the room with everyone witness to it. Alice and I are aswim in each other. After what seems like eons, Alice summons the strength to break the contact.

"I, uh ... uh ... I ... I seem to have lost my place. Sorry!" she stammers. She can't remember where she had been. Well, she remembers where she was in my eyes, but not where she had been in the story that she was just telling a millennium ago.

With our momentary spell broken, I drop my gaze, not daring to look at anyone. The awkward silence spins out for another century or two. Don, in his typical fashion, turns away and goes for another drink. When I muster up the courage to briefly glance up, Dick and Sarah are amused and shaking their heads. Alice just shrugs, her mouth curled into a wry smile.

As supper approaches, we all convene around the grill. Alice is flipping the steaks, and just as she picks Don's steak off the grill, it slips off the tongs and right into the ashes of the fire. Karma has come to bite Don square on the rump for the raw steak stunt he pulled on Alice the year prior.

"Ooops! Oh, Don, I'm sorry," apologizes Alice, graciously offering him her own steak still grilling over the fire. "What a klutz! Here! Why don't you take mine."

"Nope. Nope. Just give me that one," Don says, pointing to the ashes his steak fell in. "That one. It's okay. Put it on the plate, right there."

109

Without further hesitation, Alice fishes the gritty steak from the bottom of the grill, rinses it off under some hot water, and serves it up on Don's plate. I guess on that score, at least, they are now even.

I can't attest to the mood of anyone else through the rest of the dinner. I am in such inner turmoil and hard pressed just trying to get food down. It's all I can do to act normally and hold it together. Finally, the evening breaks up, and Don leaves for the airport and San Francisco, and Dick and Sarah go home. And Alice and I check into a nearby motel.

By now I am shaking and trembling as I had done the year before under similar circumstances. We slide into each other's arms and make love all night. In the morning I wake up cuddled by her, and weep with pure happiness—then sob in pure misery, then cry for all the sorrows of the world. My face is so puffy at the end of it that I have to beg Alice to go out and bring breakfast back rather than face anyone.

For the next couple of days, we travel back and forth between the house she shares with Little Fran and the motel. By the end, both of us are in a sorry state. Totally in love and completely mesmerized with each other. Nearly sated with lovemaking—nearly—and utterly miserable.

And then we must separate—once again.

Of all the world cities I've seen, San Francisco is my favorite, but it is no pleasure this time. Don is edgy and irritable, and so am I. We never discuss our visit back to Southern California, and return to Austin to behave as we always had, resuming the life we've been living for the last twelve months.

9/17/73

Excerpt (From Alice)

Bad news, you've been away from me for five days now & I want you to come home!! I miss you, lady. 'Nuff said ~ just wanted you to know how I feel.

Have been making you a tape ~ already have 25 minutes of listening to the garden grow + another 30 of sitting in front of the burning fireplace ~ all I need is 5min of something else. Any ideas?

Wed night , 6:30

Excerpt (From Nancy)
  Really miss you again - I mean MISS -hurts. Didn't do as good a job at memorizing every last detail. At least, I don't think I did, then every few minutes something comes back to me with startling clarity. And warmth. Can be embarrassing. I've done a lot of squirming around the last few days.
  Amazing how we seem to have a thing for the 13th of the month, isn't? Seems one of us is always disappearing from sight on that day. Never had any trouble with the date before. Beginning to wonder now.

11/7/73

Nancy, love

I need to see you, talk to you, be w/you ~ this is a long nite. Do you realize how very much I love you? How empty I feel without you? How much I would give to be w/you? How much I need you?

Sometimes it scares me to know someone can know so much about the way I think + still more frightening, how I feel. Where went the wall I so painstakingly built up and kept in good repair these many yrs? Along comes this fantastic lady who removed that one brick that held it all up. Can only conclude she's the best wall destroyer or I'm the worst wall builder in the world.

Do you begin to fear for my sanity? Me too. Guess I'd best get out of myself ~ have been trying but everything leads back to you – and then me. Seems you are here everyway but physically ~ can feel your presence. Even on occasion smell your perfume in the nite. I love you lady. I want to spend every minute of the rest of my life with you.

111

Was going to call you tomorrow, but have set up a series of obstacles ~ chain myself to the chair, tie the key across the room, nail the chair to the floor. Hope it works. Sure would like to talk to you tho.

Love,

Alice

Dec 24, 1973

Alice,

Christmas Eve here—there, too, I suppose—that's a brilliant statement to start off a letter, isn't I?

Glad you got the Christmas package—you just seemed like the Brazil nut and Crackerjack type (whatever that means)—you mean you really didn't suspect I was an old stocking stuffer? I am also an Easter Basket maker—but sometimes manage to control that—however I hear one jingle bell and something inside me snaps and I compulsively stuff stockings—one of my many faults.

Don is okay—a model host the night of the tree party—I hate it when he gets drunk when we are entertaining, but he was drinking sanely and was reasonably sober at party's end.

Well love, one night (maybe tonight) build a fire, make a long tall toddy, put on some Christmas music and sit down and send me a nice warm thought—I love you—I wish you a very nice Christmas and a better year for us both and all concerned in 74—be good, lady—take the best care—don't let anything happen to you.

More when I can—but all the love thoughts I can fling out at you in the meantime.

Love,

Me.

Excerpt (From Nancy)

Re Anatomical inequality: Thou are not lop-sided! Truly??? Never noticed, so it can't be much of a lop. Might be a case of exaggerated imagination or some kinda bizarre astigmatism.

Anyhow, Alice, my sweet love, that's it for now. Miss you—wish I could talk to you. Have a whole lot of nothing to say again. —wish I could check out that lop-sided business—don't believe you—although love you, whether I believe you or not—I'd love you if you were flat—I just flat love you.

More later, if you can stand it.

Me

Excerpt (From Alice)

Yes, I art. It is not imagination. It's hard to find a bra in a 38 A+B or B+C or whatever, so I am sure.

Excerpt (From Nancy)

Okay must add that to the list, let's see: taste your chin (preferably before Rion kitty has been there.) Examine uneven distribution, topside—close range. Receive navel warmer demonstration promised one year ago. Point out my 2-mile long hysterectomy scar (forgot to do that. Damn! Had an excellent opportunity but it never came to mind. Oh dear, now I'm thinking about what did come to mind.)

Excerpt (From Alice)

You are a yeller, huh? Only when you get angry? Do you get angry often? No, I'm not a walker-outer ~ can yell if necessary to be heard. It makes me furious to have someone walk out or ignore me while I'm fighting.

Excerpt (From Nancy)

Yes, I'm a yeller—though not necessarily in anger—more to blow off steam— Glad you are not a walker-outer. Furious is not the word for it. Red-spotted insanity is the word. Also am impatient with pouters. Have been known to throw things—usually food since it's often handy. (Remind me to tell you how I threw the cooked fish through the window screen and then had to scrub it off after it had dried). Would prefer a nice heartfelt toe-to-toe, tit-to-lop-sided-tit confrontation (by the way, I never give handicaps for—uh, handicaps ... lop-sided or no.)

Don and I move again. The mobile home that we bought new when we first married sat vacant in San Antonio during our California sojourn. When we moved back to Texas, it sat a little longer while we decided whether to sell it or move it up to north Austin. Eventually we opted for the latter and moved the mobile home nearly a hundred miles. It's good to be out of the temporary apartment and back into our own place again. I spent hours schlepping boxes from the storage rental and unpacking our household items, which I hadn't seen in the year and a half since we had moved to California.

My books! I have all my books again, like long-lost children come home! And I need new shelves for the newly acquired—a perennial problem with me.

The mobile park where we now live is in a rural area, very bucolic and restful, and basically a nice place. Just what I need to help calm my emotional turbulence.

Excerpt (From Nancy)

We decided while we were at it to finally buy the color TV that we have promised ourselves for 4 years. So we did. A 17" and is it ever beautiful! Haven't seen too much of it since we picked it up on Monday, but the little I have seen has spoiled me forevermore.

Oh, and by the way, since acquisition of color TV, all three stations are reviving old black and white movies, just to further piss me off.

It happened quite by accident that I discovered the condoms. I never went into Don's things, just as he never bothered mine. But one morning, a telephone call delayed him, and with 200 miles to travel, was apt to be late for an appointment scheduled later in the day. So he asked me to help gather some things for him to pack. He showered while I pulled together four sets of underwear, four pairs of socks, four shirts and matching ties, and a set of pajamas, and folded them into his open suitcase. I moved his unzipped ditty bag to make room, and two foil-wrapped condoms inside caught my eye. I was stunned and flooded with a mixed bag of emotions.

Deciding I better get myself under control and evaluate the possible meaning of this, and of my reactions, I kept still about it, kissed him goodbye, and settled into a day of thought.

I wrestled with my feelings—anger, disappointment, betrayal—coupled with thankfulness that at least with Don wearing a condom, he wasn't apt to bring anything contagious home to me.

Listen, the moral high ground I stood on was so scant I barely balanced on tiptoe while it wobbled beneath me like a wigwam in a whirlwind.

I had long been acutely conscious of my loss of integrity, my violated promises and broken vows, and I beat myself up daily for it. I could only imagine and dread Don's pain and heartbreak when I ultimately would confess my infidelity to him, let alone his low regard of me. And his shock when he learned the exact nature of it.

When your own sins are so significant, it tends to make you more tolerant and understanding of someone else's failings. I realized with chagrin, however, that if I had found condoms in his bag a few years earlier, my reaction would have been that of righteous outrage and condemnation—perhaps even to the point of irrevocable loss of trust in him. That was how it would have played out, back before my own faithless behavior.

Instead, I was humbled and shamed.

I always considered myself freethinking and tolerant about sexual expression, but when I took my wedding vows, I took them seriously, and obviously expected Don to do the same. Until I met and fell in love with Alice, I never would have thought myself capable of cheating on my husband. Yet, so powerful and compelling were my feelings for her, I acted on them despite my guilt, acted in conscious and deliberate betrayal of myself, Don, and our marriage.

Clearly, I had my own guilt, my own remorse, my own secrets, but I couldn't help wondering about Don's. I played through scenarios in my mind.

Did he have a woman whom he saw regularly, someone he cared about? Did he indulge in casual sex with one or more women on each of his travels out of town? Were these different people, or repeated dalliances? Or did he keep prophylactics just to be prepared for whatever opportunity came his way, the occasional chance he couldn't pass up? And I couldn't help but wonder how long he had those two particular condoms in his suitcase, how frequently he needed to replace them. If at all.

I was angry, sharply angry, but it was mitigated by the glass house I was living in, knowing I had absolutely no right to lob any boulders. And, in both cases, whatever the departures from marital fidelity might have been, each of us had come home to the other, out of genuine caring. For whatever it was worth.

In my resentment, I couldn't help but feel a tiny dollop of relief. I don't mean it assuaged in any way my own guilt, but I knew when the time inevitably came and we discussed my cheating and my relationship with Alice, the reminder of these condoms would prove, if nothing else, that we were both equally human and full of flaws. I felt great sorrow for what I had done to Don, even though he didn't yet know about it.

No, finding those condoms did not relieve me of my guilt. But they did bring much into question: Which is the greater betrayal? The casual sexual escapade, callous for its disregard of sacred oaths, but without consequences of its own (which is what I suspected with Don)? Or the love affair I am having with a woman? Which was the greater transgression? Or is faithlessness just that, no matter the circumstances?

When Don came home on Friday, he settled in with a martini, and I brought up the topic. "Don, you know I never go into your things; I respect your privacy and your possessions, but when you left this week, you asked me to help you pack. Your ditty bag was open and I saw the two condoms you had in there."

The rapid play of emotions crossing his face was so swift they barely could be identified: fear and guilt, remorse and anger, horror and shame, defensiveness. And whatever that "Oh, shit!" feeling is called that goes along with the words, caught, caught, caught.

After a long, pregnant pause, he said, "I just carry them in case, you know?"

"In case! In case? In case of what?" I asked, my voice rising.

"Well, I mean ... I mean," he stammered. "Well, it isn't anything I ... I ever think would happen, but, you know ... in case!"

"No. I'm afraid I don't know. In case of what?"

"Well, just if anything like that ever happened, I'd want to be sure to be protected."

"Well, I really must thank you for the courtesy of not causing a pregnancy out there, or bringing anything home to me," I said sarcastically.

"You know I would never do that." I knew he referred to the numerous times in his career as a lab tech that a doctor received Don's lab results, and had to break the news to the unsuspecting wife that she was infected with gonorrhea, transmitted to her by her own philandering husband.

"Actually, I would never think you'd feel the need to ever have a condom at the ready at all. I think the point is, under what possible circumstances would you be having intercourse with someone else?"

"No. Well, I wouldn't."

"You wouldn't or you haven't?"

"I haven't and I wouldn't."

"But you carry condoms with you just in case, in the off chance you should need them so you can have sex."

"Dammit, Nancy, it's not like that."

"Well, dammit, Don, I wish you would tell me what it is like."

"I just have 'em, that's all."

"What? In case you have a sexual accident, is that it? In case you accidentally want to stick your dick in another woman?"

"Don't get snotty."

"God forbid I should get snotty about the fact that my faithful husband carries condoms with him when he goes out of town."

"Look, there's nothing to it. I have never done anything, and I won't do it. I'll get rid of them."

"No, by all means don't get rid of them. I really would prefer you have them if you think there's a likelihood this could occur, in what? Some moment of weakness? Like a night you'd do something unusual, something out of the ordinary, like have too much to drink—something we both know you never do, right? And if you find yourself about to fuck somebody? I'd just as soon you wear a rubber when you do."

He was silent.

"I think you'd do well to examine your motives. Being well intentioned doesn't quite cover this one. I'm going to bed. Don't bother me when you come in."

❈

Since most things written in those years on lesbianism also touched on (or touted) the subject of feminism, along with my search for answers to my personal dilemma, I got a healthy indoctrination in the women's movement. I had subscribed to *Ms. Magazine* since its inception in late 1972, and more and more the issues raised in its pages began to inflame me.

Like many women of the time (and since), when I began to realize how many instances of my life were the result of a pervasive system of sexism and prejudice against women, I grew angry. Really angry.

So many times I simply wrote things off: the promotion passed-over, the assumption of gender-specific abilities, the need to be three times better than any man doing the same work, the general assumption that women were all emotionally unstable and not too clear thinking. I wrote these things off without analyzing. They were puzzling closed doors, blank walls, low ceilings, or business as usual, and I internalized these things as my individual fault, my failing, my inadequacy.

Moreover, I couldn't account for the fact that when I got married, all of my creditors responded to my notice of a name change with the ultimatum that my husband apply for credit to transfer my account into his name; otherwise, my balances would become immediately due and payable in full. Don had lousy credit; so even with my good job and excellent credit, I wound up losing my accounts—now denied—forced to pay off my balances (luckily small) in full, and immediately. I was no longer considered a safe credit risk.

It seems minor, but I resented my mail suddenly being addressed to Mr. and Mrs. Donald Hammond, as if I had abruptly ceased to exist as an individual. I was now just a wife, a shadow to my husband. It would be the women's movement that would make it commonly accepted for a woman to choose to keep her own name after marriage.

And even my car! I bought it before I met Don and financed it through my own account at the credit union—the loan and the account was solely in my name. When I paid this car off, the State of Texas sent the pink slip to me in his name—his name! Not mine. I had to pay a transfer fee to have him sign over my own car to me.

In those days, a married woman could not have credit in her own name, even if she worked, even if her income was higher than her husband's. For instance, when it came to buying a house, the loan officer said my income (larger than Don's) could not be counted in the loan application. Because we were newly married and I was of childbearing age, the bank assumed that I would quit my job to have children. I argued that we already had four kids to support and I never intended to have children. My assertion fell on deaf ears. I hadn't yet had my hysterectomy (for ovarian cysts.) No matter, it still would have been a moot point. In nearly every state in the country, a woman's earnings in a marriage simply didn't count. A steady, well-paid woman living on her own might qualify for a home loan in a progressive place like Los Angeles or New York City. But Don's income was the sole allowable criterion for our eligibility to buy a house.

No wonder I decided to investigate the women's movement in Austin; I was motivated, and I had the time. And what an eye opener!

In Austin, we had a small women's center of sorts in a house rented by several women. An active Women's Political Caucus existed in Austin with such notable feminists as Ann Richards, who went on to be Governor of Texas; Sarah Weddington, the youngest attorney to ever win a Supreme Court case (Roe v. Wade); and Sissy Farenthold, an attorney and educator and a Democratic State House Representative. Though they held their meetings elsewhere, the members of the political caucus often were present and showed support for our community there.

Before long I was "volunteered" as Director of the Women's Center. As our good luck would have it, we were offered a sizeable assembly hall free of charge, which was attached to a large, elegant residence and meeting facility of the Texas Women's Clubs, an established—and generally considered to be conservative—women's organization. This was very progressive and a generous gesture from such a group. As soon as we moved in, we began to get organized.

Along with two other women, I started consciousness-raising (commonly known as "rap") groups—signing women up, taking them through training, and turning them loose to begin their personal explorations. We were to organize about twenty such groups in the course of two years. We held workshops about alternate lifestyles, which delved into such topics as the career single, celibacy, communes, homosexuality, etc., and another we titled A Woman's Body that provided education in female sexuality, reproduction, STDs, lactation, menopause, complete with breast exams and personal plastic speculums. The Austin Chapter of NOW held its meetings at the Center, and the first Rape Crisis Center in Austin got its start there.

Poor Don didn't know what to make of it. As I realized the extent to which women were considered second-class citizens in our society, it hit me hard, and my activism began to consume my time, energy, and interest, as I took up the fight for social change. He was at a loss, as were most men whose women were beginning to realize truly how they were viewed in our male dominated society, and reacting explosively in consequence.

I was reading all I could find on the subject: Robin Morgan's *Sisterhood is Powerful*; Simone De Beauvoir's *The Second Sex*; Betty Friedan's *The Feminine Mystique*; Germaine Greer's *The Female Eunuch*, and so many more. The book that offered the most help for my personal predicament was Del Martin and Phyllis Lyon's book, *Lesbian/Woman*. It was a primer for any woman considering a life with another woman. Vastly reassuring, and it validated much of what Alice had been telling me.

I learned that there were women out there living happy, normal, productive lives together as couples, absent the drama, depression, or decline so often insinuated in novels. These were women who made lives together, had friends, family, raised children, worked, paid taxes, bought houses, contributed to their communities, some even devout churchgoers … and all of them lesbians.

Now well into 1974 and fueled with many new revelations, it seems like an ideal time to visit Alice. Just before Labor Day, I make excuses to Don, pack the VW Fastback, and hit the road with Cherub in tow. I want to see for myself what Alice's life is, this lesbian life, and how she fits into this world. Her new job is going well; they like her and she, them. Plus, they plan to install that new computerized analyzer, and she is very excited about being the technician designated to learn and operate it.

Alice has extended the long weekend by taking a couple days off, and on my request, takes me to meet some of her friends. I meet Ronnie, who works for the post office and is, at this time, in a relationship with Barb. And then there's Justine, nicknamed Justy, who makes her living as a street singer and studio musician. And Annie and Yvonne (nicknamed Cisco by Alice), who live together in a very charming home and are hospitable and welcoming.[†]

I have a grand time with all of them, and come away with a new understanding of how Alice has set up her life, and more about some of her friends, among those who matter to her the most. There are other friends, family, and people I still need to meet, but this gets me started.

I see firsthand that it is possible to live with a woman partner in a happy, stable, loving environment (at least in California), and not have to resort to subterfuge and misdirection to do it. Not that I wasn't still confused, emotionally torn, still fundamentally undecided. But by now, I am able to lay to rest some misgivings about what life with Alice would be like. And, as you do, I knew her even better now through her friendships. I liked them all and they were obviously devoted to her. Alice knew how to be a good friend, and that goes a long way in my book.

[†] Ronnie later meets Tess and spends the next thirty-seven years up to the present with her. Yvonne and Annie stay together for forty-six years, until Yvonne passes away in 2007.

DATELINE, 1975—John Mitchell, Harry R. Haldeman, and John D. Ehrlichman are found guilty of the Watergate cover up. The Senate Committee investigates illegal FBI and CIA activities and learns of the CIA's role in helping to overthrow Chile's Salvadore Allende as well as a plot to assassinate Fidel Castro.

The last American soldiers evacuate from Saigon as South Vietnam falls to the North Vietnamese invasion. After 14 years, America's Vietnam War ends, leaving 56,559 Americans dead. Communist revolutionary Pol Pot and the Communist party Khmer Rouge take over Cambodia. Cambodia seizes USS Mayaguez and President Gerald Ford orders a rescue operation.

US and Soviet spacecrafts Apollo and Soyuz link up in space. Billie Jean King wins Wimbledon again. O.J. Simpson is NFL Player of the Year for second time. President Ford escapes two separate assassination attempts within 17 days, each by a different woman: Lynette "Squeaky" Fromme and Sarah Jane Moore. IBM introduces the first commercial laser printer. Jimmy Hoffa disappears. Congress votes to admit women to all military academies. First attempt to stop Medicaid abortion funding is defeated.

Supreme Court rules married women do not need their husband's permission and unmarried minors do not need parental consent to obtain an abortion. Freedom of Information Act becomes law. US Circuit Court of Appeals in D.C. orders the FCC, after delaying for 2.5 years, to act within 60 days on claims of sex discrimination in programming and employment by stations in New York City and the District of Columbia.

The Catholic Bishop of the San Diego diocese states that any of its 512,000 members will be denied communion for being members of National Organization for Women (NOW), which it considers a pro-abortion group. Parishioners demonstrate and picket in opposition.

The **Archdiocese of Philadelphia cuts support** of 8,000 church-sponsored **Girl Scouts** who plan a series of sex education workshops in which birth control and abortion would be discussed.

Survey **reveals 70 percent of women** have experienced **sexual harassment** in the workplace; 56 percent say it was physical, and one-third say they experienced negative repercussions upon reporting the abuses.

More than **7,000 women attend** the U.N. World Conference for International Women's Year in Mexico City. **AT&T is ordered to pay** an additional $2.5 million to 2,500 employees for failure to meet intermediate deadline to end job discrimination.

Kiwanis vote for third year **to ban women** from its organization, and revoked two chapters that had admitted women. The National Organization for Women (NOW) establishes the **Task Force for Battered Women and Domestic Violence.**

Rich Man, Poor Man takes second place to *All in the Family*. *Laverne and Shirley* and *Phyllis* are added to the lineup. And *The Bionic Woman* and *The Six Million Dollar Man* bring high tech to the screen.

the road less traveled

Excerpt (From Nancy):

Been sunny, but cold again—not COLD!!—but cold enough. Have the heat on in the house and it feels glorious. Don is out of town or he'd be saying dumb things like "it's just brisk" or "a fine bracing chill" or some idiocy that only means you're not entirely frostbitten yet—all the while in the distance you hear the mournful baying of the St. Bernards, so who's kidding who? Winter, my love, is almost upon us, and the folks in Washington are telling us with the oil shortages we'd better break out sweaters. So I spent the day airing out my mukluks, attaching my zip-out lining to my leggings, and tomorrow I'm adding thermal insulation to my favorite pj's—the ones with the feet and the powder puff tail.

Alice is coming to see me! It's been nearly four months since I last visited her in California, and we are both consumed with yearning and the need to see each other and getting a dose of reality again. Letter writing keeps the contact, but people can change, circumstances chafe, patience wears thin, situations stagnate, and it's possible to just get worn out with it all and want to quit. It hasn't happened yet, in fact each of our meetings reinforces our feelings for each other, makes the need to be together more intense, more necessary. But in my cynicism, I am never

124

sure it will last, or continue to be so. I need reassurances about my own feelings as well as hers.

Her visit feels surreal. I had imagined Alice in my environment for so long, her actual presence takes on a dream-like quality. We spend several days visiting some of my favorite places in the state. The reality of her at my side is too good to believe. We drive outside San Antonio to New Braunfels, a small town that has retained much of its German essence since its founding in the mid-nineteenth century by German immigrants. Here, we eat sauerbraten and schnitz pie in a German beergarten. Then we go back to the motel and make love.

We visit Seguin, one of the oldest settlements in the area, already a thriving community before the Civil War, and eat barbeque. Then we go back to the motel and make love. In San Marcos, we tour the picturesque wetlands of Aquarena in glass-bottom boats, and eat chicken-fried steak at a little country café. Then we head back to the motel and ... you know. And talk. And talk. And talk.

On Alice's last day in Texas, I sit in our room, hold my head in my hands, and let my emotions overflow, weeping for the outcome, what is inevitably to happen. Weeping for the loss—of him or of her. Weeping for the future, with one of them, but not the other. Weeping for the unfairness of it all—and for the incredible miracle of feeling this deep love for two different people. I weep for futility ... and fulfillment.

Alice's plane barely climbs the sky when I am finally honest with Don about her. I tell him I am in love with her, that I have lived with the secret about the extent of our involvement for two long years while I tried to figure out what it meant. I tell him how I feel about her, and about him, and that I've been unfaithful to him with a woman. And sadly, that I am not much further ahead with my understanding of all this than I had been two years before when we moved back to Texas from California.

The first thing he says is, "Oh, Nancy, you mean you've been dealing with this all alone? Oh, I'm sorry, honey; I'm so sorry." And he takes me in his arms and holds me.

This is what I love about him. This right here and right now is who he really is inside, a sweet man who I occasionally glimpsed underneath the repression, the programming, and the protective camouflage. But the words he utters in this moment will be the last nice thing he will have to say about the situation, the last time he will speak about what this means to me—and understandably so.

That he'd think of me at all after such a bombshell is a tribute to the remarkably decent man he is—and to his love for me. It would be over-shadowed by the depth of the pain he will experience at my hand. For after this tender moment, Don justifiably will go on to relate my affair with Alice to how it affects him. But it's much to his credit, this initial generous, unselfish response. Very much to his credit.

My confession hits him hard, as I knew that it would. I have betrayed him, betrayed him in what to him is an especially ego-devastating blow. I had taken a woman as my lover—such an altogether shocking notion in 1975. To Don this is shameful, and he assumes the shame to be his. His take on it is that he has not satisfied me, primarily in the sexual sense, which is not true. And he fears that others who find out about my infidelity with a lesbian will perceive him as a man incapable of satisfying a woman; given the warped thinking of our culture, his fears are probably justified.

He doesn't know how to relate to this situation that threatens our marriage. "How can I hope to compete with that?" is all he can ask.

That night, in our bed, I hold his head in my lap and rub his forehead as he cries. He is inconsolable.

We argue. We fight. We make love. And we talk. And the days and weeks pass by as he and I both live in pain.

I drive to and from California several times before it is all said and done. The trip each way takes two days, driving fourteen-hour days. The southern route through the western states is a fairly easy drive, mostly straight ribbons of road with uninhabited, wide expanses of buttes, pla-teaus, and rocky outcroppings on a distant and ever receding horizon. By night the sky is a twinkling bowl of stars overhead. It is during these drives that I discover a love for solitary trips—and the opportunity it provides to just think.

After about six months of this, Don and I decide to separate. He needs to get away from me for a while and try to sort things out, he says. He found an apartment nearby and soon moves his things out. I stock him with the basic kitchen and linens and such to help him set up. Other than Don no longer being home on weekends, things seem much the same in our home. He calls when he is away, though not often, but I always know where he is. He calls when he's in town, and sometimes he comes over, and we eat together and talk about our situation. Or not, and just pretend it isn't there between us.

Alice and I continue writing through it all. We are still learning about one another, delving into each other's past, exploring each other's opinions, foibles, needs, and desires.

(Excerpt from Nancy):

Everyone (in answer to your question) always wants to feed you because you look as though you would rather starve than bother to fix anything for yourself. You also give the impression (erroneous, I am sure) that you would burn Jell-O—and eat it anyway.

Excerpt (From Alice):

Regarding ruined images: so I'd cook, if it came to that ~ don't care for John in the Bag and such ~ Besides I'm not really too good at role-playing anyway. Am just me and do whatever seems rite or fair or fun. Just don't let all the Big Bad Butches know it ~ they say all of a sudden their friend expects them to do such stuff, too.

Excerpt (From Alice):

Re: books on being gay. May have to talk to you yet ~ my head is a bit different than most books. Besides, to complete your research, feel it's only rite for you to get some information from one who has been there. Right? On the job training is an even better idea.

Oh, an optimist, yes, always & most probably cockeyed as well. However, everything I have ever really wanted has always gotten to me eventually, so I'm not one to rule out any possibility ~ also am the world's most patient person when necessary (I have learned to be) ~ everything happens for the best, you know. The only way I could circumvent what I want is to crawl into a hole or ditch & you know how I feel about crawling into ditches, so you are doomed to letters, phone calls & etc. until you specify a definite wish to be free from them. Even then I'm not sure you wouldn't get a sneaky unsigned card every few days ~ And you couldn't ask me not to write to Cherub, could you? Or possibly write to Cherub for Patrick & 7500 other ways to get around it.

In these months, Don and I toss around different scenarios, different solutions, different living arrangements—me going back and forth between Texas and California. Alice moving to Texas, and me living back and forth between them. None of it is workable.

I know Don could never live with anything other than the traditional marriage. And I'm not so sure Alice could live that way, either. But I'm desperate not to lose either one of them before we considered all of the options. I love them both. It's obvious they both love me, too.

Excerpt (From Alice):

Well, my love, I've been thinking again ~ I have finally come to the conclusion after two years, eight months and 13 days that I don't really think it's going to be a cinch to get over you. Matter of fact don't think I'll ever get over you. Even worse, don't want to. How about that? You are constantly with me, I talk to you in my head about some of the damndest things, would much rather talk to you in person as you know. I seem to be completely dependent on being able to communicate with you. If anything *happened to you I'm sure they would hear me cracking up all of the way to Philadelphia. Then again, I'm not sure I can keep things up like this indefinitely either ~ to never be with you leaves a large vacant area. To realize I may live the rest of my life without you makes everything pretty dull, dreary & hopeless. Know what I mean? Does this make any sense? Never was any good thinking on paper. I love you very much Nancy. It seems like you've always been a part of my life ~ You've always been here. Strange?*

Don't worry ~ am not depressed love, just lonely for the sound of your voice. To see you wondering ~ or just hold you and talk to you. The lonely never goes away either. The sharp edges are slightly dulled by a letter from you or to talk to you on the phone, but the lonely is still there.

As Don and I continue to hash things out, the situation gradually takes a toll on both of us. It soon becomes obvious how affected he is. He suddenly becomes very sick, requiring major surgery for an abscessed bowel and some extended after-care, and another future surgery. Before he is discharged from the hospital, I pack the few items in his apartment and move him back home.

He recovers slowly over the next six weeks. I spend my time cooking and caring for him. Part of the after-care involves a daily sterile dressing change of his extensive, deep surgical wound. We haven't touched in several months, and this forced intimacy heals some of that discomfort, and accents subtle shifts in others. Wordlessly, he lies watching me every day as I remove his bandages, set up the sterile field, cleanse, and re-dress his long, deep, abdominal incision. I concentrate on the procedure, focusing on task, taking care not to contaminate anything. It's been a while since I last worked with sterile technique, and I need to pay strict attention to every detail of the ritual. This daily physical contact is professionally aloof, but also tender and gentle and mute. It gradually does much to restore a kind of peace between us.

Some choices have as little effect on our lives as dandelion fuzz wafting on the breeze, while others take hold and uproot our entire existence. Some decisions may even surprise us, even as we make them.

I'd been raised by two people who viewed life as a constant struggle, and for them it had been, never knowing abundance, only want, deprivation, and hardship. My parents viewed money as elusive and unattainable. Money—or the lack of it—underscored every single aspect of their lives. Coming from that lifelong emphasis on striving to survive, money and the security it represented had long dictated my ambitions as well.

I was married to a man who wore silk suits, Italian shoes, a Rolex watch, and drove a new Mercury Marquee Brougham. I wore a fringe leather jacket, cowboy boots, love beads, and drove a six-year-old VW Bug. We had grown hopelessly out of sync with each other. But it was I who shifted position.

We had a longtime financial goal that together we achieved. As we planned, I worked two jobs while Don worked fulltime and carried a full load in college for two years. I earned most of the money during the year in California while he wet his feet in the sales game, gaining the experience that made him eligible for his current job. And for three years I supported his efforts and enabled his attention to this new job, taking care of all distractions and responsibilities to keep him focused, encouraging him, and advising him, playing the corporate wife.

By 1975, Don's income hit $50,000—a great deal of money for the time, comparable to about $165,000 in today's coin, and up from his income of $8,000 three years prior (comparable to $26,000 in 2012.) His increased income put us into the upper middle class, and we were both free from debt for the first time in either of our lives. The cars were paid off, home paid for, and we had no credit debt. We were at the beginning of prosperity, reaping the fruits of our mutual efforts. And I was about to walk away from it.

Actually I wouldn't walk—I'd leap. Leap in the dark, into the expanse of the unknown, propelled by a decision finally reached after the angst and hesitation that had consumed me for three long years. Though a silly part of me still dithered irrationally, pestered by the unknowns to come. An unknown financial future, except for the certainty I'd be working for the rest of my life. An unknown social future—life as a lesbian, whatever that brought in the way of society's reinforcement or censure. Would I have regrets somewhere down the line? Would I later be conflicted? And would I ever lament leaving the traditional, acceptable man-woman marriage, even loving Alice the way I did?

Don said he was willing to just continue on as if nothing had happened, return to our former lives, if I would just make Alice go away. I don't know if he could have forgiven me, but I know he would have been more than willing to try, just erase it from our lives and carry on. He was very good at drowning out the uncomfortable with liquor whenever it reared its ugly head.

I realized I could have stayed married to Don and reaped the benefits of his earning power, the financial result of my participation along with his. Easily stayed married with one hand tied behind my back; all I needed to do was keep house, occupy his bed, make the requisite public appearances, play the perfect wife. A lot of women do. They settle for less, trading their own life's adventure in the process. Many do it for the sake of the children, sustained by their role, then lost and adrift in midlife when the children leave the nest.

Don required little enough. His emotional life was so contained, so unexamined, so repressed that he seemed not to notice if I failed to show up in our marriage. Or perhaps he didn't want to notice, proven in these last three years by his not discerning any hint of my personal dilemma. Though, admittedly, I had tried to conceal it. And yet, something about me must have been different, one would think; something he should have felt. And his solid and continuous need to drink was doubtless an indication of his own dissatisfaction with himself, or our life together. In truth, life with me was often painful for him long before this, before I met Alice. My demands on him to participate wholly, to strive for inner growth, to meet me in the quest for self-knowledge, made him at times noticeably uncomfortable. I had pressured him in areas he'd sooner leave alone. Yet, he endured it because he, in his own way, loved me.

I knew to stay in that life with Don required that I play-act a role, shut down parts of who I was, what I had become, and who I was becoming. It would be necessary to stifle my ever-growing feminist concerns for the state of women in the world, and my own role as a woman. To deny the depth of my need to fully share who I was with someone who reciprocated with the whole gift of themselves. To stay with Don, I would have had to sell myself out.

But I wanted to live an authentic life.

131

Of course, I weighed all this before considering Alice, and the cardinal fact of my deep love for her, of her love for me. I was, above all else, enthralled by the promise of the power to grow, the hint of the joy of shared hearts, the glimpse of the fulfillment of True Love. In the end, I knew in my heart my future lay with Alice. I couldn't let her go, and didn't want to. The price was too great. I must take the leap and live with my one True Love, and boldly greet whatever came of it.

Don's final surgery is successful. He is well again, and we are done. There's nothing left of obligations, nothing left of the marriage. In the hospital, he asked me not to be home when he gets released. I packed my household things, my personals, my books, left him with household basics, with the house itself, the furniture, his car, the money, and called the movers.

Alice flew out to meet me and drive back with me to California. I was none too steady, after all. Besides, it was a chance for Alice to be in Texas again, to sightsee a bit of San Antonio this time, and to re-acquaint with Naomi, who, since that night Alice first met her at the Italian restaurant in California, has retired and settled in San Antonio where she had been stationed.

Our visit is a marker, a holiday interlude before we drive off into the sunset together.

I need this time to get stabilized, and let the past fall away. With Alice's presence, I begin to feel the relief that my old life is over, that there is no more opportunity for pain with Don, and I cheer up and enjoy myself.

I suppose it is my official "coming out" as I introduce Alice to a few Austin friends, women in my rap consciousness-raising group who know about her and have been supportive of me all along. We stay a day or two in Austin with another good friend, Selene, who extends her hospitality to us as a couple before we head south to San Antonio.

There, we sightsee, visit the Alamo and other local landmarks like the Lone Star Brewery, Fort Sam Houston, and Brooke Army Medical Center, where I trained and worked while in the Army. Alice, Naomi, and I stroll the famed River Walk on one steamy afternoon, past the shops, restaurants, amphitheater, stopping in at Durty Nelly's (we seem destined to gravitate to Irish pubs) for a refreshing Lone Star beer, known in these parts as simply "Star."

After a brew or two, we leave the pub to carry on our exploration of the historic city, ambling along the river with the tourists and the locals, past booths and tables of vendors selling T-shirts, jewelry, Texas souvenirs, watching river boats glide by.

A patch of deserted vendors' tables line the Walk, tables vacant probably till the weekend. Posted on the bare wall, behind one plain table, is a leftover sign, reading: *Ask us about our 18-carat gold.*

Alice veers off from us and walks straight over to the unoccupied table, faces the blank wall and speaks aloud into the empty air. "Your sign says to ask, so what can you tell me about your 18-carat gold? Just what form does that come in? Is it bullion? Or nuggets? I'm curious, so I'm asking."

As she fires off a barrage of questions to the vacant space, to the inert and unresponsive wall as if she were consulting an oracle, I crack up so hard that I double over and step backwards with each wave of laughter that takes me. Naomi catches me before I back off the walkway into the river.

I'm such a sucker for a fool.

A day or so later, on the thirteenth (again) of October, Alice and I load the car, gather up Cherub and her blanket, hug Naomi goodbye, and head west to begin our new life together.

DATELINE, 1976—Romanian gymnast Nadia Comaneci takes seven Olympic medals, three of them gold. The 14-year-old, at 4' 10" and 86 pounds, earns the **first perfect 10 score in Olympic history**. Scoreboards, unequipped to show double-digits, display 1.00. She follows with **six more perfect scores**, winning hearts worldwide. **Dorothy Hamill** wins the gold for figure skating.

Mysterious Legionaire's Disease appears, claiming 29 victims in a Philadelphia hotel. **Patty Hearst** is convicted of armed robbery. Hundreds of **West Point cadets** are discovered **cheating on exams**. **Nobel Peace Prize** is awarded to Mairead Corrigan and Betty Williams, both of Northern Ireland. **Jimmy Carter is elected President.** *Happy Days* and *Laverne and Shirley* hold the two top television spots. *Charlie's Angels* hits #5, *Baretta* #9, and *One Day at a Time* is #10.

Supreme Court rules that the death penalty is not inherently cruel or unusual, and as a form of punishment, is constitutionally acceptable, **reversing its opinion** of four years prior. **Bicentennial celebrations** are held throughout the nation. **Congress passes** Toxic Substances Control Act to control harmful industrial chemicals. **Congress repeatedly overrides** President Ford's vetoes of bills that provide for jobs, health, education, and welfare programs. Viking I and Viking II **space probes land on Mars** and transmit color photographs and data back to Earth.

shifting gears

1976 and the tumblers of our lives are turning, turning, turning.

Alice and I came to know Solange through her volunteer efforts. Two years ago, she dialed the local Braille Institute in Fountain Valley, California and offered her free services as a licensed hairdresser to any blind women who lived near her. And so our blind friend, Little Fran, became her client. By the time we moved to the area and met Solange, she had been cutting Fran's hair every month since.

An incredibly beautiful French woman, Solange had previously spent eight years as a skater in the Ice Follies. She possesses an impossibly narrow body, with an ample bosom and not an ounce of excess fat on her tall and willowy frame, only lean mass.

And parenthetically, she is the first woman I ever met who works out in a gym. In these days, gyms for women are virtually non-existent. Gyms, in fact, are the embodiment of testes and testosterone—a true male bastion.

Solange ignores it all and paces right in and works out. I'm sure she has a regular audience, but I'm equally sure the boys are respectful, if not awed by her determination and concentration.

Her husband, Hugh, is a sweet, refined Englishman, formerly a Queen's Guard—one of those tall, very impressive, palace guards with a great black hat and an absolutely unflappable demeanor. His passion is combustion engines, motorbikes, cycles, and Jaguars, of which he personally owns two vintage models. As an advance man for a motorcycle company, Hugh

135

organizes sponsored races, now assigned to travel from country to country in Europe for a minimum of six-month long stretches at a time.

They are good people, Hugh and Solange, unquestionably an unusual and striking couple, and very much in love. Solange earnestly wants to join Hugh in Europe, now that his job is firm and his assignments clear-cut for the next eighteen months abroad. But that would mean leaving the plant shop she established only a year ago. It is already becoming well known for its exquisite arrangements, consisting primarily of live plants mounted on driftwood with various ferns and bromeliads.

Solange and Hugh also own a four-bedroom house, complete with a pool, a garden, and a garage that houses two prized Jags. The home also serves as the residence for Daisy, a springer spaniel, and Twiggy, a St. Bernard.

The tumblers align.

At the same time, Little Fran's mother—Big Fran—faces imminent danger of losing her job. A laborer for about fifteen years at a local factory, she suffered a long list of job-related maladies and arthritic changes that necessitated that she take a medical leave of absence.[†] But it's become clear by now that she's unable to do the physical labor of factory work any longer.

Meanwhile, Alice and I are dissatisfied with our current living situation and have enlisted Solange's help in looking for another place to rent. In addition to her plant shop, her cosmetology training, and her ice-skating, Solange recently completed a real estate course and earned her license. She's been scouting to find us a place we could afford to buy, but I'm doubtful she'll find something that we can afford in our current financial condition.

And in one fell swoop we all solve our problems.
The tumblers drop, the lock activates and cracks open. And all our lives take a turn as we enter a new era.

Considering the predicaments of all parties, Alice and I call a "family meeting." We hatched a plan and decided to host a Sunday barbeque to present our Big Idea to everybody. Big Fran and Solange hit it off immediately, and thus are receptive to our notion of entering a partnership

---

[†] Such conditions in 1976 were not considered as compensable as they would be today.

with each other. Big Fran agrees to take over the plant shop when Solange leaves for Europe to be with Hugh. Alice and I propose renting Solange's lovely home while we caretake her extensive garden, the pool, and the two vintage Jags in the garage. And of course, the two dogs, Daisy and Twiggy. One bedroom of the four would be used as storage and repository of all their possessions. And Alice and I would try to save up a little to be able to buy a place when Solange and Hugh return to the States in a year and a half.

Well, I guess it wasn't all a bed of roses ... Little Fran has to find a new hairdresser.

When we move into Solange and Hugh's house, Alice is less than thrilled that, since we cannot afford a service, we must keep up the pool ourselves. She has a morbid fear of water and drowning, a holdover from the time her half brother, Lester, pushed her off a ferry into the San Francisco Bay when she was nine years old. An alarm had sounded, life preservers were tossed in, and the Sea Scouts sped through the choppy Bay to rescue her.

She has never trusted water again. Nor Lester, for that matter.

But it is a mark of her trust in me that she is willing to try to overcome her fear of water and learn to swim. She is scared but determined, her jaw set firmly, eyes steely, knees trembling.

"Yes, now, Alice, in order to swim you actually have to get in the pool," I tell her.

"Oh. Yeah. Okay," she answers. From the edge of the shallow end she sits, wobbling knees bent under chin, toes hanging-ten on the lip of the pool. She takes a deep, brave breath and scoots her bottom closer to the underwater steps that lead into the pool, and comes down onto the first one.

"Good," I reassure her as I take her hand. "Now take the next step down, and you will actually be on the pool bottom." She tenses and goes down one more. The water laps just above her knees.

"How're you doing?" I ask.

"Okay, if I don't look out there." She points shakily at the length of the pool, to the deep end, where the water turns ominously blue, and the bottom sinks to unfathomable depths. It would be funny if she weren't so obviously petrified with fear.

"Alice, you have ten feet or more to walk on the flat before the bottom slopes downward. Nothing falls away under you, I promise. There are no surprises. Just a gentle grade for ten feet, at which time the water will be at your chest. Then the bottom descends easily and gently until it reaches the deepest part. See, watch me!" I demonstrate, treading through the pool towards the deeper end. "Walking, walking ... and now I'm on tip-toe, but still touching bottom. See how far out I got before it gets deep?"

"Yeah. About fifteen feet."

I plod back through the water to her. She hasn't budged, her heels backed up smack against the bottom step the whole time we talk.

"And at the deepest part, this pool is how deep?" I ask.

"Eight feet."

"Right, eight feet. But that doesn't *even begin* to happen until about fifteen feet out from where your feet are currently suckered fast to the bottom." She is planted so firmly where she stands I fear we'll have to rock her to break the suction.

"I'm five foot ten."

"Yes, you are."

"The pool is eight feet deep."

"Not today, Alice. Today the pool is only going to be chest deep. Because you and I are going to walk forward now till we get to just that depth."

"Eight feet deep means the water is two feet, two inches above my head."

"Not today, Alice," I say patiently. "Now I'm going to walk backwards in front of you, facing you, and I will keep my feet flat on the bottom. And you just walk with me."

I take hold of her hands, and her grip clamps mine like iron tongs. Trying not to wince, I back up one step, coaxing her to come along with a gentle pull. "That's it," I say, taking another step backwards while she advances one jerky step forward, and then another, and another, looking for all the world like Frankenstein slogging through a bog. The water is now up to our chests, about fourteen feet out from the steps, where the pool bottom is still unmistakably flat underfoot.

"Good. Here we are now. Are you okay?"

"Yes," she answers, slightly breathless. "But I don't want to go any farther." The water is calm, no ripples, no undercurrents, and no concealed sharks lurking beneath.

"Fine. We'll stay here and walk to the side, and then walk across to the other side, so you can see it stays at this depth. Okay?" And together, her hand clutching mine till our fingers are white, squeezed of all blood, we slowly walk across the width of the pool, the depth of the water coming in at a level just below her boobs, leaving them, plus her head and shoulders in the sunshine and fresh air.

"Okay. I believe you," she says with a sigh of relief as she reaches the safety of the pool's edge again. "As long as I can walk upright in the baby part of the pool, I shouldn't drown."

"Right. Now, we're going to go back to the steps." Alice seems comforted to turn her back on those unplumbed depths and return to the shallower waters. "But first squat down and get your shoulders wet." She follows my directive, less scared now than earlier. "Good! Now lie back over my arm and practice floating."

Her eyes widen in alarm, the whites of them visible all the way around. "You mean take my feet off the bottom?" It clearly has not occurred to her that this action is necessary in order to ... uh, in fact ... uh ... swim.

"Yep, right here in three feet of water, and you can keep your fingers on the pool edge." She takes my instruction to mean "grip the edge of the pool for dear life." Seizing like that, her fingertips will bear imprints for another hour of the tiny pebbles imbedded in the pool's bull-nosed lip. And if her grip is any more crushing, I fear she may actually crimp the concrete like pie dough.

"No, don't clutch. Just touch the edge of the pool," I direct, and then move on with the lesson. "Lie back on my arm. Now, the trick is, do not bend your waist! Just stay flat and keep your back straight. If you bend your waist, it causes your butt to drop and you will fold up and sink down."

"I'm afraid my big butt will sink me whether I bend my waist or not!" This last fear she voices cracks me up.

"Alice, you and I couldn't sink unless somebody anchored us to a Chevy." We are two hefty, pneumatic women with all the buoyancy of party balloons.

"This is not a laughing matter. I be a big chicken!" she complains.

"And you won't sink. Relax now. Let your feet float. That's it. Touch the side there if you feel uneasy."

My arm is still supporting her stiff and rigid body on the surface of the water. She's afraid to move or turn her head or even search for the poolside with her fingers, as if the slightest action on her part could generate a rogue wave to bear her under, so she simply stares straight up at the sky.

"Am I floating?"

"You are floating."

"Don't leave me," she pleads, rising terror in her voice.

"Not even if you throw me out on my ear," I tease.

"No, dummy. I mean, keep hold of me." She's exasperated at my failure to address the gravity (so to speak) of her position.

"I am, and you are floating," I assure her.

"How do I get up?" She's had enough.

I instruct her to pull her feet down easy in the water, touch bottom, and then bend at the waist. Of course, she bends first at the waist, forgets to pull her feet down, and her butt drops, causing her to kick out sideways frantically. With a mighty shove I push up under her shoulders and down on her leg.

"Oww! I hit my heel on the bottom!" she whines.

"How'd you do that? For a minute there you were convinced there was no bottom."

"Yeah," she admits, sheepishly. "What did I do wrong?"

"You didn't lower your legs before you bent your waist. Want to try again?"

She takes a deep breath and resigns herself. "One more time, and then I'm done for today."

"Fine. Lie back on my arm. Good, lift your feet. Good. Relax there a minute. Comfy?" Alice is once again too frightened to talk, situated as she is unpredictably on top of perilous waters. She just grunts, and moves her head in a short nod with extreme care.

"Okay. I'm just going to walk across the pool sideways right here in three feet of water, and you keep floating along with only my hand in the small of your back." I slowly slide my arm out, keeping my hand splayed under her waist.

"Ooh." She is one heartbeat from launching up and flinging herself into a mighty flail of panic.

In my drill sergeant voice I bellow, "Don't be scared!" Then more soothingly, I instruct her, "Turn your head and watch the side. See, it's easy." She relaxes only slightly from total rigidity, with this reference point for her eyes. "Now I'll walk across to the other side again and you relax as we go; you're too tense." She relaxes a bit more as I slowly move through the water. "Good."

We are close now to the steps at the baby end of the pool. "Okay, now first lower your feet in the water. Good! Now bend your waist, and up! There you go."

She is solidly on her feet, albeit still in knee-high water. "Okay. I floated," she says, without any triumph in the deed, just the flat inflection one gives to a grim chore finally completed.

We are out of the pool by now and toweling off as I continue, "And tomorrow I will stand up against the side, and you'll float by yourself and hold onto my hand while you do."

She freezes. Her face appears from behind the towel she is using to dry her hair, her expression incredulous. "Without your arm under me?"

"I wasn't holding you up, Alice; the water was. You were floating on it. My arm under you was just to give you a sense of security."

"And you intend to remove that security from me tomorrow?" Her voice is filled with utter disbelief that I would be so callous.

"I won't let you drown, Alice. And in three feet of water you stick out two feet, ten inches higher than the water is." She isn't the only one who can do math.

She mutters, grudgingly, "Only if I remember how to stand up." We walk the little path along the garden to the house.

I am determined to cheer her, to make her feel good about her accomplishment. "Well, it might tax your brain a bit, but I have faith in you. Actually, if you don't think about it at all, you'll do better. You're trying too hard."

Obviously still unconvinced all this is worth her while, she grumbles, "Remind me again why I'm doing this."

"Because you are brave and fearless. A hero in battle, a conqueror of fine women, a prodigious intellect, an undefeatable tiddly-wink player …! "

"Yeah, yeah, yeah, smartass," she interrupts, popping me on the butt playfully. "But I'm still scared of water."

"Not as much as you were yesterday."

is it sisters?

Her lips curve in a smile as she gathers me in her arms. "No, you're right. Not as much. You're a good teacher." She kisses me.

"Mmm. And a willing student."

"Oh? Really? Well, let's just see about that."

And pretty soon I am the one floating.

DATELINE, 1977—For the **first time** in history, a **woman is ordained** an Episcopalian priest. **President Carter pardons** Vietnam draft evaders, threatens reduction in aid to foreign countries violating human rights, calls for "moral equivalent of war" in energy conservation, and signs **Panama Canal Treaty**. US Senate votes to turn Panama Canal over to Panama by the year 2000.

Scientists use bacteria to create insulin. **Supreme Court rules** Medicare funds not be used for elective abortions. US declares **200-mile sovereignty zone** in Atlantic and Pacific to exclude foreign vessels.

Seattle Slew, a 3-year-old American thoroughbred, wins the **Triple Crown**. The **Nuclear Proliferation Pact** is signed by 15 countries, including the US and USSR. Oil begins to flow through the **Alaskan pipeline**.

Apple Computers market the Apple II, the first mass-produced personal computer. A **young Bill Gates founds Microsoft** in Seattle, Wash.

Three's Company, *Little House on the Prairie,* and *Alice* are added to television's perennial favorites list. The **miniseries** *Roots* draws 130 million viewers.

Severe drought prompts the West Coast to begin water rationing. **Californians vote on Proposition 13**, which cuts property taxes and establishes cap of 1.5 percent a year and sets off a national taxpayer's revolt.

Pope Paul VI dies at age 80; the new Pope, **John Paul I, 65, dies** only 34 days into his pontificate; **John Paul II** of Poland succeeds him.

no place like home

Change is in our lives again. Only a scant year has passed since we presented our Big Idea, a plan we had envisioned would last at least eighteen months. But the dollar is falling, devalued terribly overseas, and Hugh's earnings, when converted into European currencies, proved no longer adequate to either his title or work load, nor to his and Solange's monthly expenses.

So the two are now back in the States. Hugh opened a mechanic shop, specializing in British motors, and Solange works weekdays, plus shows homes on the weekends for a realty firm. Big Fran, just a month ago, closed the plant shop with Solange's assent when the landlord took their success as a signal to double the rent. The small business could not support the rent increase, and the landlord would not reconsider a lower offer. As he deserves for his greed, the landlord would sit on the space empty without a tenant for several years.

Solange and Hugh live for the time being with her parents because our rent keeps the mortgage going. Solange, however, has been scouting around for a house for Alice and me to buy on my GI bill.

She eventually finds one in Costa Mesa. It is a modest, three-bedroom, one-bath tract house on a cul-de-sac with a long pie-shaped backyard. The house inside is neat and clean, and the exterior landscaped simply yet appealingly, with green lawns front and back, and many small shrubs and bushes planted throughout. The best part is the price falls within our budget.

Shortly after our offer is accepted, the woman selling it moves out, leaving the house to stand vacant during much of the ninety days that it takes to process my GI loan. Alice and I are both in a state of high anxiety during this time. This is the first house either of us has ever bought, and a debt larger than we'd ever shouldered before. All the red tape of completing the deal wears on our nerves, each stage demanding documentation and resulting in subsequent bureaucratic delays.

Finally the house is within a few days of closing. It's summer hiatus from my regular sales job, and I'm working as a telemarketer to fill in the gap when Alice calls me with the unexpected news that her stepfather Bud has just died. We need to make a trip up the California coast to Humboldt County in the next day or two.

Alice then calls Solange with this bulletin, and, as luck would have it, our walk-through inspection is scheduled for the next day, our closing papers prepared and ready for us to sign.

We haven't seen the house, of course, since we placed our offer three months ago. The dried up lawn and shriveled shrubbery attest to the length of time it has been vacant. But when Solange turns the key in the front door, the real nightmare begins.

The woman who sold us the house, we discover, had bought it with divorce money a few years before, and since then she's taken up with a motorcycle crowd. The neighbors later would tell us horror stories of biker gangs hanging out every weekend on the home's front lawn, sporting tattoos and spiked leather, drinking beer, smoking cigarettes, toking weed, laughing, swearing, tinkering with the cycles, and revving motors from dawn to dusk.

When the woman vacated the house and took to the road with her new biker daddy, she left an invitation to the rest of the gang to use the house—*our house*—as a crash pad.

She had turned the power and gas off. So, of course, the bikers resorted to the living room fireplace to do their cooking, charring the decorative brickwork all the way up to the ceiling. The water stayed in service, and the shower stall, used and never cleaned, became a study in evil green fungus and odious black mold, grown wildly up the walls. Black streaks and pockmarks bear evidence of someone whipping the walls with chains, and decomposed garbage fills the kitchen sink. Outside the backdoor, broken beer and wine bottles strewn a full thirty feet—throwing distance—form a solid ring of glittering glass shards. A final insult: The carpets are now alive with fleas, attaching themselves to our pant legs as we walk through what was to have been our dream house.

While Alice and Solange stand in shock, I burst into tears. "I refuse to sign the papers on this. I can't believe the state of this place. I'm ready to default on the deal and just walk away—just walk away!" I wail.

"Okay, okay, I know it's awful, Nancy," says Solange. "But let me handle it. Let me see what I can get done here. We'll contact the owner and make her give some concessions. We'll get everything fixed. Give me a few days to deal with it."

"You'll have more than a few days, Solange. Alice and I are driving up north in the morning. That's a twelve-hour drive tomorrow, and the funeral is set for the next day. We'll stay a day or two to help her mother, and then, it's twelve hours on the road to come back. But I don't know. I don't know about this. It looks hopeless to me."

"It'll be okay, Nancy," Alice says in a comforting tone. "However it works out, it'll be okay."

"You guys just go up north, and we'll see how it is when you get back, okay?" adds Solange, consoling us with a hug.

The next week, we concentrate on the more immediate problems. Alice's mother Nora is grieving and exhausted, especially from the ordeal before Bud's death, involving several frightening medical emergencies. Nora's health isn't tip-top either; her blood pressure is acting up, plus she's an insulin-dependent diabetic with a heart condition and prior heart attack.

Nora and Bud actually own very little: A small mobile home (mortgaged to the bank), the third-of-an-acre parcel of land it sits on, and a 1968 gold-colored Ranchero with about 80,000 miles on it. That's about it. They both lived on Social Security, and their total cash assets amounted to under two thousand dollars. Still, there are unending details with which the survivor must be concerned. Alice tries to help her mother with the endless errands and issues dealing with their affairs.

Friends and neighbors keep up a steady stream of visits, condolences, and gifts of food. We never cooked a thing while we are here, feasting most of the time on succulent roasts, hearty casseroles, garden vegetables, and homemade pies and cakes.

In between greeting drop-in neighbors, I work to get Nora's place in order. I mow the lawn, do laundry, and clean house. Nora is limited in what she can do in housework, not able to reach over her head or bend down below her knees with her blood pressure problems, so I always make it a point to wash down cupboards, shampoo carpets, take down drapes and blinds and such, whenever Alice and I come up here.

I'm grateful this time for the activity. It keeps me occupied and my mind off the derelict, vandalized house I would be mortgaged to for the next thirty years.

"Okay. Here's what's happened," Solange tells us on our return. "The owner has agreed to make the repairs and clean up. We brought in a crew to clean the house and garage, plus some day laborers to get all the glass up and plant some new bushes and salvage what we could. We changed the locks, had the house fumigated for fleas, carpets shampooed, and the rooms repainted throughout. It actually looks pretty good. Do you want to go see it?"

True enough, the cleaning crew did a reasonably good job, and it now somewhat resembles the house we originally intended to buy. But the gouge marks in the walls remain, (they were painted, but not spackled beforehand), and the carpet looks wretchedly scabrous, much the worse for wear than three months earlier. The backyard is nothing but a vacant lot with patchy tufts of bleached dead grass, but at least it's divested of broken glass. We'll have to take care for foxtails and burrs with the dogs. The front yard is brown and sere; a few new bushes replaced the landscape of tinder brush we'd seen a week ago, but a far cry from the original abundance of plantings. Overall, it's passable, but projects a faint impression of shabbiness now. It feels like a blowsy, sorry, old barfly in full Friday-night makeup and best dress, her ill-used life still showing through, smelling of stale hopes and bitter disappointment.

"Take the house," Solange advises. "Even if you put it right on the market again, we're just at the start of a real estate boom, and the house has appreciated almost $3,000 in the last three months. Take it, and if you want to, we'll list it right away and look for another one for you."

So I sign the papers. But it's not over yet.

The gasman has come out to the house and rings the bell to tell me he can't turn on the gas. He has kind eyes, and his voice conveys apology. "We have to test the lines for pressure when gas service has been turned off, and your pipes fail the test. We're not allowed to turn the gas on with a pressure test this low."

"What? I don't understand. The gas was running fine three months ago."

"Well, that's just it, you see. An old system will run fine when the pressure is steady, but if you turn it off and go to turn it on again, the surge of the pressure in any weak or leaking lines will blow something and make it unsafe." He slouches, slightly turned away from me, tapping his clipboard restlessly against his thigh. "The pressure test is too low, showing that you have a leak somewhere."

"Oh God. Well, what happens now?"

"Well," he says, reluctantly delivering the final blow, "you'll need to call some residential gas or furnace repair companies, and get estimates for locating the leaking place and fixing it. We only repair our outside supply lines."

Three estimates later, ranging from $1,600 to $3,600 (which equals three to six months of mortgage payments), we learn that the house is built on a slab foundation, back in an era when it was legal to lay pipes right in the foundation and pour the concrete in around them. How dumb is that? The only way we can locate the leak is to randomly jackhammer through the floors in the house.

Don't tempt me.

The other option is to re-pipe. Luckily, in this mild So Cal climate, the city's building code allows for this to be done along the eaves under the roofline. The former owner has refused any responsibility for this, so we are stuck with paying it ourselves. Within the first week of occupation, what with the trip north, time lost at work, the cost of moving, and now these repairs, we've spent the entirety of our small emergency cushion.

This marks just the beginning of some hard times for Alice and me.

Nothing more with the house. That had shot its wad at the outset and, once we settled in, we had no further problems with it. As a matter of fact, we would move away in two years' time, and Solange's market boom prediction would be borne out. We ended up making $18,000, after costs, when it sold twenty-six months later.

For now, we made the best of it, moving in, hanging pictures, filling closets, arranging furniture. Our new dog, Brandy, loved her backyard and it was big enough to afford this year-old Great Dane some exercise. She was a stray—gentle, eager to please, performed well in obedience school, and got along with Patrick, Cherub, and Rion-kitty. She's the outside dog, patrolling the backyard and giving us a measure of security, considering the recent history of the house.

Our neighbors, likewise, feel safer with Brandy to alert us all to any intruders. And speaking of the neighbors, any apprehension I had about being the "lesbians on the block" disappears when our neighbors express their relief that "decent people" at last have moved into the house. We could have been green with pink polka dots for all they cared. We aren't Hell's Angels—and we respect peace.

Our first Christmas in the house, and Alice's mother has come to visit for two weeks. It's Nora's first Christmas newly widowed, and Alice feels a little anxious for her. Nora spent a day or so in an outskirt community of Los Angeles with Alice's half brother, Lester, and we all visited Alice's two stepbrothers in Santa Fe Springs for a big family dinner. Nora seemed okay through it all; however, within a week she declared she was missing her home.

Up north a huge storm had hit, knocking power out for three days. Her neighbor, Mattie, called to say her own shed roof had blown completely off. The really bad news was it had landed up the street onto Nora's porch and taken that porch roof down with it. This accounted quite a bit for Nora's sense of urgency to return home. But Alice is secretly glad her mother missed the catastrophe; otherwise she'd have weathered it alone in a dark and empty house, with wind, rain, and shed roofs crashing all around her.

Nora's a very short, round woman, built solid, with a strong barrel shape, and only a little over five feet tall, though she has such a presence she always seems a good deal taller. I often tease her about her short stature.

Sass just comes naturally to me with Nora; she brings it out in me, probably because I delight so much in her droll, mostly understated, put-downs of it.

One time I went a little too far for comfort. "Nora, you're so short, you'd prob'ly have to leap up to kick me in the ass," I sassed loftily, turning as I spoke.

And you know what? She did! She actually landed the side of her foot square in my butt. And yeah, leapt up to do it, too!

The startled look on my face cracked up both her and Alice, doubled them over, and after I recovered from my shock, I laughed till I cried right along with them.

In another silly incident, I was cooking dinner, talking to Alice and Nora as I picked up the bag of frozen corn. I was on some rant or another, and rather emphatically slapped the frozen bag against the counter to break up the clumped contents.

I slapped too hard, jerking the package in the upswing. The bag had already busted and frozen kernels of corn hung in the air momentarily in a golden arc before dropping to the counter and floor, bouncing all over, like some new variety of popping corn.

It struck me as hugely funny, and all the dogs, opportunists that they are, immediately dashed in and began scarfing up the frozen corn from all surfaces as fast as they could.

Alice came to the rescue as I was too helpless from the hilarity of it all, bent over the counter, unable to do anything but laugh—broken up so hard I couldn't begin to catch my breath. Warnings began to blink inside like: beware of a stroke; beware of peeing; ooh, beware of a fart; all of which makes you tighten what sphincters you have, only to boost your runaway mirth that much more.

Weak from laughing, I finally had enough presence of mind to turn off all the fires on the stove and stagger over to plop at the table where Nora sat calmly watching the whole show. Alice managed to clear up enough of the corn to avert a vet bill and joined us both at the table.

"I think you'll need to re-plan the menu," Nora stated dryly, launching me into fresh peals of laughter which were so uncontrollable, I was unable to utter a word for some five minutes.

Alice shook her head ruefully, eyes twinkling, and remarked to her mother, "Sometimes I just don't know what to think about her."

Nora smiled back at her daughter, looked over at me, my tears running, still on my laughing jag, and replied seriously, "Well, *I* think you got a good one this time."

Alice and Nora shared a small private moment, filled with the history of years past, of intertwined lives. Alice's grin grew even larger and she nodded acknowledgement.

More than anything *that* finally sobered me up, as it dawned on me through my near hysteria, that I had just received, in this moment of profound foolishness, the ultimate accolade from Alice's mother ... her approval.

Our friend Ronnie—a "postal person" as Alice likes to call her profession[†]—called the other evening to invite Alice and me over for dinner next week.

Actually it's a command performance.

Ronnie's widowed mother, Goldie, will be visiting from Arkansas, and Ronnie needs reinforcements. She wants Alice and me to meet her mother because we are "the most presentable" of all her friends—meaning we can converse about many things, we don't hang out in bars, we both have mothers of our own and are sensitive to the plight, we don't strobe out "Bull Dyke" in ten-foot letters when we walk into a room, we can be counted on not to say "fuck" in polite conversation, and last but not least, Alice is one of Ronnie's oldest and dearest friends.

Goldie's actually very sweet and funny. She's warm and cordial to Alice and me, and seems quite relaxed in our company. Ronnie is a bit nervous; however, likely just the natural tension of having her mother here rather than anything to do with us. Dinner is great as usual, Ronnie being the great cook that she is.

At one point in the evening, Goldie endears herself to me by telling an embarrassing story. This is the mark of true character by my standards; you've gotta be able to tell "dumbs" on yourself, or you fall short of the mark.

[†] Feminists introduce the politically correct term "mail carrier" in the early 1980s.

In her tale, she is late for a doctor's appointment in a large medical building in Little Rock, after driving in bad weather for an hour to get there. Goldie dashes into the elevator, flustered and hurried. As she steps out onto the doctor's floor, her keys slip from her hand, hit the metal elevator edge, slide through the gap, and fall six floors down the shaft to God-knows-where.

She flees into the doctor's office, and the building management is called to send over someone who knows something about the lower bowels of the building.

Before it is said and done, Goldie is mortified with embarrassment. The whole building is in an uproar. The elevator is shut down at last, service cut to half the building, all this at the end of the day when people are trying to go home.

She ultimately involves five maintenance people in her distress, each enlisting the aid of another, till they locate one able to access the small and dangerous crawl space in the pit of the elevator shaft, sift through whatever is down there, locate her keys, and restore them to her. It takes more than three hours to accomplish, the effort of multiple workers and the disruption of everyone in the building, leaving Goldie pretty much feeling like a penny waiting for change.

It must have been horrifying at the time, but it sure makes a good story now.

While Goldie and I clean the kitchen, Ronnie confides to Alice that she intends to have a serious discussion with her mother and "come out" to her after all these years. It has long weighed heavily on Ronnie that she lacked the courage to be forthright and proud and tell her mother she's a lesbian, no matter the consequence, and let the chips fall where they may.

Ronnie indeed has a bad case of nerves.

By week's end, Goldie has left to go home to Arkansas, and Alice and I return to Ronnie's to see how she survived and to get the scoop on the "lesbian declaration."

"Well, I was nervous as hell when I announced to Mother I had something to tell her," Ronnie explains. "I hoped she'd not be too upset, but I thought it was important at this stage of both our lives to be honest with each other."

"That was a good way to start," I comment encouragingly.

"Yeah, it leveled the playing field a bit, because after that she was nearly as tense as I was," Ronnie said, chuckling. "So I just came out with it. I said I was a lesbian—that is, a homosexual—and I've been one all my life. She was rather quiet for a minute, so I asked her if she understood, 'cause I wasn't really sure she'd ever heard of such a thing as a homosexual. It's Arkansas, you realize, in a really small town, and she's pretty naïve and sheltered."

"I hope you didn't have to explain it to her," remarks Alice.

"No, I didn't have to explain *that!* Explanations were to come later."

Ronnie scrubs her hand over her face and pauses to light a cigarette. "She thinks she's always known. She and my father had talked about it once, and that really upset me. I'd rather Dad hadn't known. I don't think he would have been too understanding about it, and he was probably very disappointed in me. That part was painful."

In truth, Ronnie doesn't keep her sexual orientation from anyone. She is an imposing woman, of ample physique, has done a tour in the Marines, and still retains a bit of "drill sergeant" in her demeanor. She's direct, honest, loyal, has a dry sense of humor, and holds strong opinions.

I can't describe her without remarking on her deep and abiding interest in politics and current events. She's extremely well informed in the doings of the government and the mis-doings of politicians. It's impressive, the scope of her knowledge of these things. She often loses me after a few minutes, when she quotes this senator, or that secretary, or some committee chair.

But regarding her sexual preference, anyone who understands there are multiple options would draw the correct conclusion about her within a few moments.

Ronnie continues talking about her mother. "But what turned my bowels to water was what my mother said next. It was after we'd pretty much talked it out and run through the highlights of my life, and Mother said, 'Ronnie, since we've been talking pretty frankly here, there's something I'd like to ask you now. It's something I don't understand and maybe you can help me. Actually, it's a *word* I don't understand.' "

"Oh, shit!" Alice blurts.

"Eeek!" is all I can manage.

"I started to really get nervous then as Mother continued to hedge around it.

" 'Yes, it's a word I've heard, and I don't have anyone to ask, or anyone I *would* ask; I'd be too embarrassed.' "

Ronnie rolled her eyes at us and went on, "Well, the sweat had broken out on my upper lip, and the wheels were spinning in my head, with a different word written on every wheel, each word more explicit than the last. I'm too bashful to explain some of those words to *anyone*, let alone my mother! I had wet rings under my armpits, and was squirming in my seat."

Alice and I exchange glances, sympathy springing up in our hearts.

"So then Mom pulled herself up, as if with great courage, and said, 'Now, Ronnie, you don't have to explain it to me if it's too awkward for you, but ... oh well, here goes: I know what the word *homosexual* means, but, but ... what does the word ... *heterosexual* mean?'

"Heterosexual? *Heterosexual!*" Ronnie's voice is shrill even in the re-telling of it, "Mom, that's you! YOU'RE a heterosexual. It's what YOU are!

" 'Oh, it is NOT!' Mother blurted. 'I most certainly am NOT.'

"She positively bristled with insult," said Ronnie. "Can you believe that?"

From the safe distance of an ordeal endured and a week past it, Ronnie can finally smile as Alice and I rock and sputter with laughter.

What can I say? It's 1978, and America is still blindfolded and closeted and common knowledge isn't nearly so common. Obviously.

DATELINE, 1978—A **thoroughbred** named **Affirmed** presents America with yet **another Triple Crown** winner one year after **Seattle Slew** earned the Triple in 1977. Even more astounding, **Affirmed beat his rival Alydar,** who came in second in all three races as **no horse has ever done** before, nor since.

Blackouts in New York City set off several days of arson and looting throughout the city. US President **Jimmy Carter** facilitates a **peace treaty** between President Anwar Sadat of **Egypt** and Premier Menachim Begin of **Israel** at Camp David. Nearly 1,000 **followers of Jim Jones commit mass suicide** in Jonestown, Guyana after cult members **murder Congressman Leo Ryan** of California.

The community of **Love Canal** near Niagara, NY is evacuated when hazardous waste dumps are uncovered and **declared unsafe for years to come. New York** is rescued from **financial crisis** by federal loan guarantee. *Mork and Mindy* **hits #3** in television popularity, right after *Three's Company* and *Laverne and Shirley*, with *Happy Days* coming in #4

tooth & nail

Late April 1978 and Alice and I are celebrating the first anniversary of living in our home. A minute after I take the first sip of the Cold Duck we popped for the occasion, I break a tooth on a peanut—a dry-roasted, salted Virginia, one from the very product line I've been selling for three years as fundraisers for schools and youth groups. Yeah, yeah, I've heard all the jokes: "A salesman for a nut house workin' for peanuts." In the lean times—and there have been a few this year—it's fair to say that Alice and I live on them. And irony of ironies, my newly broken tooth has me seeing gold, though not in the form of any kind of treasure.

A gold pendant—shaped like a streak of crooked lightning on a gold neck chain—dangles in front of my eyes as the dentist bends toward me. His blond chest hair peaks out above the V-top of his surgical scrubs, and his muscled forearm, also covered in fine blond fur, bears a heavy gold bracelet at the wrist. In one earlobe, a thin gold hoop.

"Looks like you need a root canal and crown, and actually, I'm afraid you need root canals in both teeth to each side of that one," he says. "You also need root canals in the two opposite teeth on the other side of your mouth."

I can't believe what I'm hearing. Five root canals! I've already had previous—supposedly permanent—root canals in three of these five teeth, and in one of these, a root canal has been done not once, but *twice* before!

"Well, the root canals will have to be done over as the nerves evidently were never totally deadened," he says. "The techniques have changed a lot since a decade ago. And the roots of your upper teeth are very, very long; they extend very high up in your jawbone."

Only thirty-seven years old, and I'm already long in the tooth.

"We have much better ways to do root canals now," my beach-boy, thirty-something dentist assures me. "I guarantee once we do them and cap them, you'll never have to worry about those teeth again."

"Right, Doc. That's what they told me when they did that one root canal for the *second time*," I reply with a hint of dejection in my voice. Seems as if I've lived my life in dental chairs, getting nothing but bad reports.

The fee he quotes to repair the defective teeth triggers my gag reflex and makes my eyes water. In order to afford his recommendations, we'll have to take out a second mortgage. (Apparently gold jewelry, cocaine, and surfboards don't come cheap.)

Root canals! Good Lord, not even the Suez Canal cost that much!

"Check with my girl out front, and we'll schedule the work as soon as possible," he instructs, despite my balking.

"Hold it. Not so fast," I protest. "What's the alternative? I'm not a bit sure I want to go through with all this. These teeth have been trouble for years. What if we just pull them and get it over with?"

"Well, it's your mouth. However, I'm sure we can fix these teeth so they'll never give you trouble again. But if you want to go that route, we *could* pull them," he says, pausing for a moment with obvious reluctance, "... and put in a bridge. You have a strong back tooth on either side we can hook the bridge to. But I don't recommend this way. Teeth can be saved; they don't have to be pulled."

But I'm just tired of it. I've been living a long time conscious of these bum teeth, babying them, only to be piercingly rocked from time to time by foods, liquid, or air that is either too hot or too cold. I am sick of being held hostage to them. And sick of the recurring ransom they require. To pull them will fall short of bankrupting us, and once done, I'll never have to hear this kind of bad news again. About these *particular* five molars, anyhow.

A week later, I leave Alice sitting in a crowded waiting room and follow a technician down the hall to the extraction room.

"Just relax now, the sodium pentothal acts quickly and will put you totally out. You won't feel a thing," the dentist promises as he pats my arm. The lightning-shaped coke spoon on his gold chain winks at me from a nest of pale chest hairs as he injects the shot.

"Nice necklace," is the last thing I remember saying.

Next thing I know, Alice, led by a dental technician, hustles in the door of the extraction room. "Hey, hey," she says. "How's it going?"

I am vaguely aware that I've been shouting. Incomprehensible and garbled, but definitely *shouting*.

Tears, big as horse turds, stream down my face while I weep huge, broken sobs like a two year old. My mouth is packed with great hunks of cotton gauze, which flare my lips out into a bizarre snarl.

And though I may not look it, I am very glad to see Alice. "They refu*th*ed to give me watah," I manage to wail through the gauze packing and hiccuping sobs. (*Th*uffering *Th*uccotathh. I sound exactly like Daffy Duck!)

"It's okay," Alice says, holding my shoulder, trying to comfort me.

"I need *th*om watah, and tho-*th th*ad-i*th*-tic ba*th*-turd*th* won't give me any," I holler around the bulky cotton in my mouth. I glare malevolently at the closed door, beyond which the sadistic bastards blithely ignore my pleas. "There MU*TH*-T be *th*om watah round here," I insist as I look around the room.

The counters along each wall are full of jars, bottles, instruments, and metal trays. But not a sink. Nor any drop to drink.

Once more the door opens, and a young man asks, "How's it going in here?"

"Pul-ee*th*e, I need *th*om watah, DES*TH*-perately!"

"Sorry, can't give you any just yet. The anesthetic needs to wear off a bit more, and then we'll give you water," he responds agreeably.

"Okay," I answer, lowering my voice, talking behind the side of my hand, as if to a fellow conspirator. "Then, how 'bout ju*th*t a *th*mall *th*ip of WINE?" I wheedle in the most winsome way I can manage, considering my gauze-packed sneer.

He smiles hugely and says, "Just a little longer and I promise we'll give you some." He then ducks back out and the door closes.

"What did I tell ya? *Th*ad-i*th*-tic ba*th*-turd*th*, all of 'em," I mutter to Alice, who deserves an Oscar for keeping a straight face.

Then I notice it—the spit basin!

Above it, a thin, curved, tubular faucet. Forming at the end of the faucet is a tiny drop—a tiny, single drop of cool, clear, water. As if in slow motion, that silvery little bead begins to extend, elongate, dangle, until—it traces a long, slow-motion trail through the air as it falls, falls, falls down past the rim of the mint-green porcelain bowl, dropping, dropping, through the flat metal ring … and down the drain of the spit basin.

I try to get close enough to peer down the drain hole, then twist in my chair to try to look *up* the thin faucet tube, checking if any more precious fluid is on its way.

"Okay. I *know* watah com*th* out of thi*th* machine. One of thee*th* knob*th* mu*th*t work!"

Before Alice can stop me, I twist, flip, and pound every button, switch, and toggle to be found on the console column of the dentist chair, all to no avail. I can't find any control that releases water, and fall back in the chair defeated.

Alice strokes my head and holds my hand as I attempt to rest. An errant thought occurs to me, stoned as I am, and I speak aloud, "A boll weevil."

"What?" Alice questions. "What did you say?"

"A boll weevil," I answer, pointing to my cotton-crammed mouth, with solemn certainty. "Thi*th* mu*th*t be what a boll weevil feel*th* like."

I'm not aware of her laughing because, right then, the technician enters the room. "Okay, we're gonna let you go home now. Stand still just a minute now. Are you steady?" he asks as he and Alice both help me up and to the door.

"I'm not *th*-tepping pa*th*t thi*th* door until I get *th*om WATAH! Thi*th* in*th*-tant! Pul-ee*th*e!"

"Okay. Okay," he replies, wheeling around and disappearing into another room.

I grouse. "It'*th* not a*th* if I wa*th*n't a*th*-king them EVEWY *th*ingle *th*-econd for *th*om." Of my darling deadpan Alice, I ask, "Did they think it wa*th* ju*th*t a pa*th*-ing fan*th*-y? *Th*ad-i*th*-tic, that*th* what." I am indeed thoroughly di*th*gu*th*ted … uh, disgusted.

The technician hurries back to the room with a cup of water and a straw.

Disdainfully I take it from him and, with the precious water now in my possession, I treat him to my most witheringly regal glare. Threading

159

the straw through a path in the cotton wadding in my mouth, I manage to get some water at long last.

"You better get somebody to recalibrate that dentist chair," Alice tells him as we leave the clinic.

⁂

Apparently I'm allergic to sodium pentothal. I get an "emergence reaction" that makes me weepy, angry, and belligerent. Some people even get combative. Alice said that while she sat in the waiting room for me that day, she could hear me shouting the moment I regained consciousness.

Two patients in the waiting room rushed up to the window, nervously canceled their appointments, and hurried out the door. I learned later that my alarmed surfer dentist brought Alice back to the recovery room to see if she could quiet me down before I started a stampede.

Why I supposed Alice was not able to get me water I don't know, but in my drugged state somehow I thought we were in it together.

On my follow-up visit to the dentist, I am of course compelled to extend profuse apologies to everyone in the clinic. Judging by their chuckles and grins, I'd been vastly entertaining. Like my English friend Tish says, "Just a figger of fun."

I wish I could say that was the end of it. But far from it. It turns out that two of the teeth requiring surgical excision were broken during the extraction! So, I have multiple stitches in my gums, too, and within a week of the surgery, I've also ended up with three dry sockets in the upper jaw.

If you've never experienced this, I can only say it is a painful condition that sometimes occurs after extractions, where the surface of the gum heals over before the open socket heals inside. This isn't supposed to happen in upper teeth where the wounds usually drain by gravity.

The month passes in a miasma of pain and a fog of drug-induced sleep. Today, all I really recall of this recovery time are sore gums and facial neuralgia, much of the pain brought on by slivers of jawbone working their way through my gums. And to add insult to injury, my new bridge needs constant adjustment; it rocks and rolls in my mouth like a raft in rough sea. Or, ever so attractively, just pops out when I speak, more often than not while in mid-sentence.

Alice cared for me through most it, tending the dogs, the bills, the house, and getting fluids and food into me at sufficient intervals. "I'm about to blow my hard-earned butch image," she mockingly complained. "If you breathe even a word of this to anyone, I'll have to resign from the club."

Schools were closing for summer, beginning my hiatus from my peanut job. In previous years, I supplemented my income by telemarketing or selling *Dollar Saver* ads or some such thing, so I began to look for temporary work.

Alice actually isn't doing so well herself. Her doctor, three months before my dental drama, halted the cortisone shots she had routinely received to keep her joints supple and the pain reduced enough for her to continue the work she performs at her job.

"I can't keep shooting you up," Dr. Fred told her. "You were just here two weeks ago, and it was barely over a month before that. It's always one joint or another, Alice, and I can't keep doing it like this or your adrenals will crap out and you'll develop Cushing's disease."

She has, in fact, started to show a puffy look about the face, a telltale sign of Cushing's. For years Alice had gone to Fred about every three to six months for "a fix," and he would inject cortisone into one of several arthritic spots, her thumbs or elbow or shoulder or hip or knee. But after seventeen years of this, the visits recently had become more and more frequent.

Dr. Fred has been Alice's orthopedist since her car accident. They have established more a friendship than professional relationship over this period, and he has seen her through some dark times and long years. Every time she limped into his office, Fred asked, "What have you been doing to my fusion now?" He felt a real proprietary claim on her fused ankle.

It's a fifty-minute drive on the freeway to and from his office, and Alice and I had the routine down to a science.

Immediately after Fred injected her, we'd jump in the car and head to a little mom-and-pop market nearby for a bag of ice to keep the inflammation down in the injected body part. From there we'd drive to the nearest fast food chain to load up on grub to satisfy the ravenous hunger that invariably set in, a side effect of the cortisone. By the time we'd get home, Alice was typically exhausted—as much from shoveling food into her face fast as she could as from the other after-effects of the medicine—and she'd fall into bed till the next morning.

During one such visit, Fred took hold of Alice's arm and began palpating her gnarled elbow joint. He then took his ballpoint out and marked a tiny circle on her skin at the site on her elbow where he planned to inject. While moving her arm this way and that, he, totally lost in diagnostic thought, absentmindedly stabbed his pen again and again at the pocket protector in the breast of his white lab coat till Alice finally asked, "How do you expect to hit that little spot on my elbow when you can't even find your pocket?"

Fred laughed so hard he was nearly undone and twice, before injecting, he had to sit back down to wheeze in laughter.

But on our last visit to Dr. Fred, he laid down the law. "Alice, I'm not shooting you with cortisone anymore and I'm putting you on three months' disability as of today. If you don't vastly improve after the respite, I'm gonna insist you put in for your Social Security."

Alice was somber and silent.

"You knew it might come to this, kiddo," he added quietly. He reminded her of the dire predictions she received from her doctors in the early years after her accident, when they told her that she'd likely never walk again. After she stubbornly proved them wrong, they then said she would be unable to work—but if she attempted it, she'd end up with a shortened working career due to long-term arthritic effects of the trauma.

"Yeah, I know," said Alice, ducking her head. "I was just hoping to outrun it."

Fred looked closely at her. "Well, you still might. Let's see how you do after a rest from nine-hour days and constant, fine-dexterity, motor activity."

Actually, Alice had already reduced her hours, starting at five in the morning and coming home six hours later around eleven. Her boss had been happy to do anything it took to accommodate Alice and keep her working, including this new work schedule, since she was the only technician who performed all the highly specialized computerized tests. She fit a full day's work into five or six hours—about all the consecutive time she could tolerate—but only if she went to work before everyone else, when she could have the run of the lab alone.

Extremely organized and working without interruptions, Alice could, with the sole use of all the equipment, manage several computer tests at once by staggering the timing of the various testing components and procedures. Even with the diminished hours, however, this critical exacting work requires the fine motor function of her arms, hands, fingers, and thumbs.

And she's just about lost all that.

So, in the midst of my dental fiasco, her three-month layoff on disability came to an end. Fred told Alice to "start the paperwork, kiddo. This isn't going to improve."

Even should she find other work that didn't require the use of her hands, she was no longer able to sustain the eight-hour days of a normal workweek.

This next trial of our life starts at the moment I no longer have any teeth left to grind.

The government has been systematically "cracking down" on Social Security claims, starting by taking away wheelchairs from people with broken backs and withdrawing Social Security from people who are bedfast. We're not surprised, therefore, when the initial application for Alice's Social Security comes back denied. Nearly all new claims are perfunctorily denied as a matter of course.

Thus it begins, and it will not end for fourteen months.

Alice hired a lawyer and filed an appeal. The lawyer will get one-quarter of any lump sum awarded, which would be the amount Alice should have received monthly to that point, if not for the denial. Provided, of course, she wins her case. Meanwhile, her income has stopped cold.

Well, when you're desperate there's always welfare, right?

What Alice finds out stuns us both. With no dependents—children or parents—she is not entitled to any general aid whatsoever. Here she is, a single woman who has worked all her life, contributing to society, to the community, funding the tax rolls for thirty years, and now that she is no longer able to work, she's entitled to no benefits. However, she likely would have been eligible if she were a drug addict, a boat person, or an amnestied illegal immigrant. In these years when generations of families are locked into the system, trapped in a cycle of both welfare dependency and poverty that exiles them from the world of work because of the structure of the programs, Alice is ineligible even for that much.[†]

The caseworker at Welfare researched for some sort of aid for Alice while her social security claim hung in limbo. We learned that there is a way that Alice can receive a meager subsistence—if she agrees to pay it back in total when—if—her social security benefits come through. As Alice's "landlord," I receive a $120 voucher for rent, which only covers a fraction of our $545-a-month mortgage. Since the mortgage is in my name under my GI bill, Alice is technically considered a renter, even though the property is jointly vested to us both.

Alice also receives a $48 voucher for groceries, insofar as they determine she needs to eat. The voucher barely puts a dent in our $200 month grocery bill. And she receives a meager $38 a month as an "allowance," which maybe covers gasoline, personals, and a little dog kibble, but couldn't even touch our other real-world expenses. Forget utilities. Forget taxes. Insurance. Phone. Garbage. Sewer.

Alice receives a grand total (and I use that term loosely) of $206 dole a month, which she is obligated to pay back, if and when she wins her appeal and is awarded the interim payment. Her take-home pay from her former job was $825 a month. This is quite a comedown for us.

And then there's the Social Security Administration, who is building their case for the defense. They send Alice for lab and X-rays and demand medical records from all the doctors she's seen since her accident seventeen years ago. She also has to retrieve hospital records and medical affidavits

---

[†] The Earned Income Tax Credit began in 1975, but was minimal and expanded multiple times in the 80s, 90s and in 2001 as an anti-poverty tool and incentive that helps people, provided they have children, get off welfare.

from Dr. Fred. Then, after she's done all that and sends it to them, they lose the records.

Fortunately, we kept copies of everything, so we re-submit.

Then her records are accidentally and mysteriously sent to some government offices in Maryland, and more time passes till the snafu is corrected and the records sent back. And just when you would think it could not get any more ridiculous, her records are misplaced for a *second* time. And, we re-submit *again*. But the real kicker is when they send Alice for a physical examination.

She shows up at the address they gave her and takes a seat in the clinic's waiting room, which appears not to have been cleaned in at least a decade. Turns out that the clinic is only used on rare occasions to perform flight physicals for the military. The sole office girl, apparently assigned there only on those specific occasions, tells Alice this, as she waits. Evidently there is no nearby government facility other than this to send Alice to, and she ends up being the only "patient" for the day.

Once in the examining room, Alice perches warily on a cracked leather table and surveys her surroundings. Everything is decrepit and has an abandoned air about it. The usual clinic paraphernalia of trays and jars is on the counters. One large glass jar with a metal lid holds a stack of 4" x 4" gauze pads—not sterile but supposedly clean—that bear a hint of grey and all their corners curl up.

Alice jumps off the table, walks over to one of the metal instrument trays, and lifts the lid. Inside, she sees a pair of forceps covered in an antiseptic solution so old it has formed a slimy, solid gel that is actually pulling away from the edges of the stainless steel container.

The doctor's arrival interrupts any further exploration. Donning a wrinkled lab coat hanging open over a crisp Air Force uniform, he proceeds to palpate and examine Alice's shoulder, neck, wrist, elbow, hip, knee, and ankle. All on the wrong side.

"Could you tell me why you are examining only my left side, Doctor?" asks Alice.

He reaches for the papers on the counter, leafs through them and hands them to her. *Rule out severe traumatic arthritis, all joints – LEFT SIDE.*

"That's very interesting, because all my injuries are on my *right* side. Ergo, the arthritis is on the *right* side. It's my *right* ankle that's fused. My trauma injuries were all right-sided," Alice points out.

"Well, that's the government for you," he says, with a shrug and a grin.

is it sisters?

"Yeah," she snarls. "I'm beginning to see how this works."

So we've been fighting a war of wills, the old waiting game. The government has played it for ages. They did it back in the fifties with the servicemen who suffered injuries from the hydrogen bomb tests out in the Nevada desert.

They did it in World War II with the WASPS and with the WAFS, the female flight instructors who *taught* the men to fly planes for combat, who *ferried* airplanes over hostile seas to Europe and Guam, *delivering* them to male pilots—all without military standing or benefits themselves until fifty years later when this status was, at last, justly awarded to what few women survivors remained.

They did it with the Vietnam vets who suffered the ill effects of Agent Orange.

Christ, they did it with the Native Americans for two hundred years!

And now they are doing it with Social Security Disability Insurance.

The idea is to stall long enough, to send you on wild goose chases, to lose paperwork behind the file cabinets, to stonewall, boondoggle, and generally fuck up until everybody dies, gives up, or fades away.

Once I recovered from my dental issues, I took extra jobs to try to hold it together, but I don't know when I have seen Alice so frustrated. She fumes and fusses impotently, which doesn't help her condition. She does her best not to give in to it, tries not to feel angry or vengeful or hopeless. People won't begin to "go postal" for another five years, but government tactics like this could make even your sainted aunt want to shoulder an Uzi and spray a few clips into the nearest federal building.

Finally, thirteen months later, the appointment date is set.

"Okay, Alice," her lawyer instructs, "this week I want you to concentrate on two things: the medical chain of events since the accident and the description of the pain, your limited movement, whatever you are experiencing. Next week, we'll do a Q&A rehearsal, so you are prepared for some of the questions the judge might ask you. You and Nancy might go over it in the meantime."

The reconstruction of the procedures and problems she's undergone since the accident is fairly easy. Harder is the description of the physical symptoms.

"Just concentrate on one area at a time," I say, "and try to describe how it feels."

"I ... I don't know if I can."

"What do you mean? You have a fine vocabulary, and you know medical terminology—plus this is not a new condition. You've dealt with this forever."

"I know. I know ... it's just not that easy."

"Why not?"

Alice takes a moment to get it clear. "Two reasons: the second one is that I'm not good at analyzing pain. It's painful, and I usually leave it at that."

"Okay, maybe I can help with that. What's the first reason?"

She looks at me long and hard. "Nancy, I spend much of every waking hour trying to keep the pain away."

I have long known she does something, has some method she has developed to deal with the chronic and increasing aches and pain, but this is fascinating, and I want to know more. "How do you do it? Do you know?"

"Well, I distract myself. I ... play little games in my head. I, uh ... wall it off. Bargain with it. Only allow so much in. When I have pain somewhere, I put my concentration elsewhere, in another place ... or something. I can't explain it."[†]

I try to absorb what she says. "So, I don't get it. What's the problem?"

[†] Some of these are now recognized techniques taught in pain management clinics today, but Alice had come up with them herself. Back in the seventies, other than drugs, there was no such thing as formal pain control and management methods, that I am aware of, unless it was in the big urban areas.

The expression on her face is one I've never seen before. She looks haggard; there is a weary set to her jaw. And in her eyes, the flicker of fear.

"To do this, I have to let the pain … in."

The magnitude of it hits me, makes my puny tooth travail look like Carnivale in Rio.

No wonder she's afraid! What if she can't control it again, rein it in, bank it down, whatever she does? What if it's like opening the lid of a box too full, and it won't all go back in again?

And she has to feel it—all of it—all at once. Till now, the only way she handles it is to pay strict attention only to the demand of whatever particular joint is hurting the worst at any given moment and deals with just that one area. If another area clamors for attention, she turns her focus on that one till she's pushed it down. And so it goes, pain after ache after hurt, through all the hours of every day. Just to keep it to where it is barely tolerable. Her energy is often sapped from the strain of it, and the pain breaks through. But this? This requires a full-body meltdown of her defense system.

I begin feeling scared for her.

"Okay, well look, let's take it one area at a time, slowly, and try to make the distinctions for it. We won't go on to another place till you feel okay about quieting the first one again. Where is it easier to start, at the bottom or top?"

"I don't know," she says, "let's just start, I guess."

"Okay, think about your shoulder and tell me what it feels like."

After a moment, she says, "It hurts."

"Oh, that's helpful. Can you put that into more descriptive language?"

She purses her lips ruefully. "Well, it does hurt. More every second for that matter." Tension crosses her face and she frowns.

"Okay, let's get some basic guideline questions, then. Worse when you move it? When you put pressure on it? Is it sharp? Dull? Stabbing? Aching? Throbbing? That kind of thing? What helps it go away? Heat, cold, massage, what?"

"A lot of drugs, a whole shitload of drugs." She grins, or I think it is a grin—maybe it's a grimace. "And I hate drugs."

And so it goes.

By the end of the month, when her appointment is set, she is once again taking drugs—pain pills, muscle relaxants, anti-inflammatories, sleepers. And she looks like hammered shit.

We meet the lawyer at the courthouse and follow her into the elevator, up a few floors, and to some chairs in the corridor.

"Okay, this is it, you guys," the lawyer says. "You wait here and I'll take the papers in to the judge and meet him. And Alice, I'll come out to get you when the judge is ready."

"Okay," Alice replies, looking steely. Girded up for battle.

The lawyer lightly touches Alice's shoulder, causing her to jump.

"Take it easy, Alice. Just keep your head clear, and tell it like it is," says her attorney. "It'll be fine. I have a good feeling." Then she enters the courtroom, leaving us to wait our turn.

"Hmphh!" Alice responds, which, knowing her, can mean any number of things.

I take her hand, and we sit quietly. Telepathically, I try to send calm, soothing signals through my hand into hers. In short time, I sense the tension in her shoulders relaxing, whether from my efforts or her own.

Suddenly, the courtroom doors burst open and the lawyer rushes out, this time moving in quick long strides. "Okay, come on, we're outta here," she snaps, walking rapidly to the elevator and slapping the button.

"What? What?" Alice sputters as we jump to our feet and join her. The lawyer bobs from foot to foot, impatiently. The elevator is taking such a bloody long time coming.

"What happened?" I ask.

"In a minute. I'll tell you in a minute."

We board the elevator, go down to the cafeteria floor, and find a table in a corner.

"That's it. It's all over. He signed the papers."

"He ... what? Did what?"

"The judge! He opened up the file and started to read, flipping pages back and forth rapidly. He muttered, 'This is ridiculous. A waste of time and money.' I wasn't sure what he meant, and that's when I started to get really nervous," says our lawyer. "Then, he pulled the verdict paper on top, wrote on it, signed it and stamped it, and gave it to me."

Alice's lawyer taps her pencil on the table with residual nerves, then stops, puts her pencil down, clasps her hands together, and shakes her head.

"He said, 'This case never should have come before me. It's patently valid. I have approved the social security with full interim payment, fourteen months' worth. I'm sorry this woman had to go through all this.' "

Alice and I can't keep our jaws closed. We sit wide-eyed and mouths agape. We must look like the village idiot and her cretin companion.

"So that's it, Alice," the lawyer says. "Social Security will send you your first monthly payment next month—the judge marked it 'expedite'—and the remainder of the interim will come to you in a few weeks. I'm sorry to have to take one-quarter of it. I don't feel as if I really did that much, but it's already in the paperwork … as is general aide, they'll get their money back off the top, too."

"That's all right," Alice replies. "You did a lot. You kept on their tail for all this time. I want to thank you for your help."

Alice's $450-a-month benefits begin the following month. Thank the Goddess! And out of the $6,300 interim back pay Alice is owed, the lawyer gets $1,575, and local government takes back the $2,884 they advanced in general aid. And Alice gets the remainder, $1,841 for fourteen months' back pay, which will come in handy to pay off some of the bills we accrued.

It's okay, though. We survived.

And Alice, over time, regains her pain control through her techniques and manages to get off all drugs but aspirin and a more effective anti-inflammatory for arthritis, which she now can afford to buy at $35 a month.

Oh, and three years later, her case came up for review. One look at the judge's comments on the case verdict, and the Social Security Administration never bothered her again about it. Whatever that judge wrote was sufficient unto the day for the evil thereof.

DATELINE, 1978—**Gold** reaches an all time high of $200 an ounce. The **US dollar plunges** to record low against many European currencies. The energy crisis and increase in fuel prices causes demand for economy cars, particularly **Japanese imports, which** accounts for half the US import market. After nearly 30 years, **Volkswagen stops producing the Beetle,** having manufactured 20 million cars. **Oil tanker Amoco Cadiz runs aground** causing a slick 18 miles wide and 80 miles long, polluting 200 miles of Brittany coastline.

The US stops production of the neutron bomb, which is designed to kill people without destroying buildings and infrastructure. The first **Susan B. Anthony dollar is** minted on December 13th.

World's population estimated at 4.4 billion. Serial killer David Berkowitz, aka the Son of Sam, is sentenced to 25 years to life in prison. Sid Vicious, former bass guitarist for the defunct Sex Pistols, arrested in New York and charged with the **stabbing murder** of his girlfriend, Nancy Spungen.

Pol Pot's regime is overthrown, but not before he executes, starves, or works to death 1.5 to 2 million Cambodian people in his four-year reign. The **Shah of Iran,** a US-supported dictator, flees in exile and the Ayatollah Khomeni and his forces seize control. **Three Mile Island,** a Pennsylvania nuclear power plant, suffers a partial meltdown and releases giant clouds of radioactive steam.

the paper route

My dental travail and the denial of Alice's social security coincide in late April of 1978. Within a matter of weeks our money situation has grown fairly desperate as we wait out Alice's protracted case with the Social Security Administration. So, I look for every way I can possibly earn enough to keep the mortgage paid and the dogs fed. We're barely hanging on.

Before the year is out, I will be holding down four jobs: my primary job selling promotional peanuts to schools in the morning, auto fleet sales in the afternoon (the fill-in summer hiatus job that I end up extending through spring), and a job performing in-home insurance physicals in the evenings, sometimes until eleven o'clock. The first moonlighting job I take on, at the beginning of June, is in the very earliest of hours: a paper route—a position I find in, well, the paper.

"**O**kay, well if you're interested, be here at three-thirty tomorrow morning, and I'll take you around and show you the ropes," the route supervisor tells me over the phone.

I've just answered the paper's ad to deliver newspapers and got the lowdown on the job. Even with Alice's physical problems, she can still drive the car for the few brief hours while I throw the papers. Simple, right?

Throwing. That means hitting ... except I can't hit my own butt with both hands, not even if my hands were magnets and my ass was high-carbon steel. But I am about to become a thirty-seven-year-old, female newspaper boy, without even this simple qualification.

"Tuesday's inserts are furniture stores and such, Thursdays are the grocery inserts, and Sundays are the coupons, magazines, TV guide, and store ads," says the route supervisor as he drives me through the dark streets into a residential neighborhood. "Sundays are the biggest bunch. Insert your papers before you leave the warehouse, then fold the paper in thirds, put a rubber band around it, and it's ready to go. You can fold 'em in the car as you go along if you have the inserts already stuffed," he instructs. "On rainy days, slide the folded paper into the plastic bag, twirl it, and make a simple tie.

"Once a month, you slip the bill under the rubber band," he says, turning into the dark street of a middle-class neighborhood. "The newspaper supplies you with the bills in your route box. You stamp them with your address. The customer sends the check to you, and you pay the paper. If the customer doesn't pay, you gotta go collect or you lose it, cause the paper charges you for it anyway."

"Okay, I got it. Sounds simple enough," I say.

"So, you get the route printout, and you just throw the papers the same way every day." He sends two papers flying, one behind the other, out his driver's window as he speaks. *Plop! Plop!* The papers fall neatly, well up into two side-by-side driveways.

"Any changes in the route, you get a green card in your route box, so check it every day." *Plop! Plop!* Two more papers in adjacent drives. He expertly slings another paper over the top of the car. The paper's flight ends with a *plop!* into a driveway on my side of the car.

"So part of every route is driving ...." *Plop! Plop!* We turn a corner, down another darkened street within the housing tract. He continues his tutoring, grabbing hold of another paper, and tossing it over the car. *Plop!* It lands smoothly on a porch.

"... And part of the route, you park at a parking entrance to the apartment complex and walk your papers in." *Plop!* Over the car. *Plop!* Over the car. *Plop!*

He throws the papers with an effortless ease, each dropping precisely where I imagine the paper's perfect placement.

I *know* where the papers should land. However, actually *throwing* them anywhere close will border on a Vatican-sanctioned miracle. Suddenly I feel a little queasy about this whole thing.

"Okay, you can help me carry some. I'll deliver five papers in each of these two buildings ..." *Plop!*—he throws one up a stairwell. *Plop!*—drops one on a doorstep. *Plop!*—flips one over a hedge onto a patio.

" ... And when I'm done, we go back to the car, drive around to the next entrance into the complex, and walk the next batch in." *Plop!* Another paper lands on a doorstep.

"Okay, here's a fun one," he says. "It goes up to the third floor." He hefts the paper, and it lofts straight up, up, up, and with a *Plop!* drops over the rail onto a *third-floor balcony* ... right in front of a sliding glass patio door.

He walks away, never missing a beat, continuing his instruction. "So, basically, that's it. Every route has about one hundred to one hundred thirty drops and it takes about—"

He stops mid-sentence, realizing that he has left me behind, still standing where he left me, stunned and staring up at that third-floor balcony.

"Something wrong?" He beckons to me, grinning.

Gulp. "Are there many like that?"

"What? You mean those balcony ones? I've got two on my route. Forget it, you can take the stairs or the elevator up. It just takes time, is all. Anyway, a route usually takes you about an hour and a half, maybe two hours to do. So, you want the job?"

The next morning, in what can only be labeled as very, very high up in the butt crack of dawn, Alice and I arrive at the warehouse to load up ole Scarlet, Alice's classic 1964-½ Mustang convertible, sadly in need of new upholstery, rag-top, and paint job.

Stocked with our route list, a trusty *Thomas Guide* map book, and one hundred thirty copies of the *Orange County Register* to deliver, off we go into the cold, dark morn. I fold and rubber-band the papers while Alice drives. There's a sizable pile at my feet by the time Alice brakes the car in front a ranch-style house—our first delivery. It has the typical target choices—driveway, front path, or doorstep—all about thirty feet from the car.

Paper in hand, I steady my arm out the car window, test the paper's weight, and plot the trajectory. Allowing for the wind factor, I snap my wrist and send the paper flying. It lands with a *plop!* —six whole feet away from the car.

Determined, I open the car door, step out, and walk the six feet, pick up the paper, and give it another underhanded throw. *Plop!* Better this time, but still a critical ten feet away from the house. Walk to it, bend down, pick it up, and toss it onto the doormat. *Plop! ... Okay, we're off to a good start.*

Onto the next house. Toss. *Plop!* Open the car door. Pick up the paper. Toss again. *Plop!* Walk ten more feet. Pick up the paper. Toss again. *Plop!* And another success! After three plops. *Riiiight!*

Lord, whatever made me think I could do this?

For my first over-the-car toss, Alice brings the car to a complete stop while I take careful aim: arm straight out the window, parallel to the ground, paper weighing in my hand. I heave the thing up over the car, and bang my forearm smartly on the doorframe. The paper arcs and comes to land ... *Plop!* Yes, over the car! And into the gutter at the bottom of the customer's driveway.

Open the car door. Walk around the car. Pick up the paper in the street. Underhand toss. It sails twenty feet up the path ... where it hooks into a box hedge. Walk across the lawn, wrestle with the bush to retrieve the paper, then sprint up the path, and let it fall from my hand to the front doorstep. *Plop!*

Wonder how many over-the-car tosses are on the route. My inner arm aches and already an ugly purple bruise is spreading.

We carry on, wending our way through the development, where we are to deliver about twenty-five papers. Toss, stop, *Plop!* Get out, walk, toss again. *Plop!* And on and on it goes. Count it a victory if the news lands on a dry, solid place anywhere on the property. My new rule is to stay away from anything green, on account of dew and moisture; I go instead for the driveways and pathways. Hitting a doorstep is total wishful thinking.

Alice and I are onward to an apartment complex of about two hundred units housed in multiple buildings, where there are thirty-four papers to deliver on foot. A major driveway boxes the entire complex, with several walkways that lead inside. These walkways act as our staging areas. At the first opening, I grab an armful of papers, eight total, walk into the complex, and deliver the papers in that area. Then I head to the next outlet and the driveway where Alice is waiting for me. Grab six more papers, wander around another cluster of buildings, toss the papers, then out again through yet another walkway to the next rendezvous with the car, where I pick up eight more papers.

Footpaths meander throughout the complex, faintly lit in the night by an artistic placement of outdoor lights. Elephant-ear plants and birds-of paradise cast ominous waving shadows across the lawns and buildings. I trot around the path, tossing papers on doormats.

Then, loft one up a stairwell.

Plop! ... Ca-thunk! ... thunk! ... thunkthunk! ... thunk.

End-over-end, back down the stairs, the paper tumbles. This particular throw requires a sideways flat toss, to drop the paper evenly on a top stair step (or nearly on, rocking at the edge.)

Merely twenty or so such demoralizing tosses on our route, each an exercise in humiliation. By the tenth or twelfth stairwell throw, it's just pure comedy. Laughing hysterically, I watch yet another newspaper propel end-over-end down a flight of steps, *ca-thunking!* all the way. I'm giggling and teary-eyed in the purest panic reaction.

Once back in the car, Alice and I head into another neighborhood tract. We loop cul-de-sacs and crisscross streets with names like Teresa Marie Terrace and Kim Court. Developers of California's bedroom communities often confer honor on the women in their families by naming streets after them, bequeathing all of us such thoroughfares as Beatrice Boulevard, Peggy Place, Stacey Street, Lois Lane. Clark Kent. (Okay, just kidding about that last one!)

There are a few retail businesses on the route where the goal is to toss the paper close enough to be obvious that it belongs to the building without it colliding into a plate-glass store front, and not so far away that it tempts passersby.

Our route ends with three more apartment complexes and a few scattered and sundry houses. One hundred and thirty newspapers delivered!

An hour-and-a-half job done in *only* three hours! Oh, Lord!

Both of us are exhausted from the strain, and I still have to shower and go to work at the nut company—my "real job," not this goofy gig.

Three-thirty in the morning comes early. And it's dark. And surprisingly chilly, even in early June in Southern California. But we are off to try it again.

And again.

And again.

And again.

Morning after morning piles up in our life, like newspapers on a vacationer's doorstep. As the mornings go by I get better at it. Then I get downright good. The challenge is to throw the newspaper in the same spot every day, whether at the head of the path, at the top of the drive, or on the doormat. To toss one up a flight of stairs with a solid landing at the top, or one step down. And I manage to accomplish it, more times than not.

Who'da thunk it? Me, the original non-jock, the super-klutz at sports? I've never dunked a basket, I can't remember the bat ever actually connecting with the ball, and nobody ever asked me to play catch with them. Hell, the only way I ever returned a volleyball was to cram it back in the sports closet. And here I am, aiming at something—and making it.

I feel like I'm Woody Allen winning the Heisman Trophy.

Within two months, we assume a second route, and when an awkward driving route is split up, we get a part of the split, which together increases our deliveries to three hundred papers. It takes us about three and a half to four hours to deliver all of them.

We hear other carriers laughing about their petty pranks, trading stories as they stuff their inserts; how they make the newspaper stick on the back windshield of the customers' cars on a dewy morning. Or skid the paper under the car, so the customer will have to hunt for it. Or toss a few up on the roof. (In the first difficult weeks of our route, I actually did toss a paper hard enough that it landed on the roof of a house and was perversely thrilled to be able to do it. But it hadn't been for spite, and I left them a replacement.)

I labor to do a steady, consistent, and anonymous job. Meaning, delivering newspapers in a seamless manner that renders the carrier behind the task as virtually non-existent. However, let a paper go missing, and suddenly the carrier comes into full focus, and the customer is abruptly conscious that the daily paper doesn't just magically appear at his doorstep every morning. Which, for some reason, makes them doubly pissed.

Now I don't say it applies to everyone who takes a morning paper, but there are definitely some confirmed type A personalities in the bunch. People who fanatically begin their day with a succession of rituals: brush, bathe, shave, etcetera—obsessive in the pattern of their procedures and in the order of their routine. The coffee gets made at a particular point in the morning rigor; likewise, the paper must arrive at the prescribed time, or the whole damn day is wrecked.

is it sisters?

Woe to the newspaper carrier who arrives late on her appointed rounds. Mostly we are blameless, especially on those mornings when the trucks are long in bringing the freshly printed papers to the warehouse, getting us off to a late start. On such days there'll be no fewer than five customers on the route pacing in irritation out in front of their houses, slippers flip-flopping in indignant rhythm, bathrobes flapping in the breeze.

There's little forgiveness in people for whom a good day or a bad one hinges on there being no disruption in their morning regimen.

At the other end of the spectrum, we have two different elderly customers on the route. Each one has written me a note stating that they can't bend down to pick up the paper from the driveway. For them, I take special measures to place their papers on the arm of their mailboxes. Their little notes of appreciation make the small effort worthwhile.

Then comes the billing process. Our routine consists of labeling the return payment envelopes with our address, then placing them in a stack according to the order of our route. Each bill is slipped under the newspaper's rubber band for the appropriate household.

In this sort of billing system, the newspaper charges the carrier for the number of households delivered, whether the checks come in from the customers or not. We lose money every month with a few forgetful customers who move without canceling, while we blithely deliver free papers to the new tenants.

And we are cheated every month by a few deadbeats who possess mean, shriveled spirits. Honestly, anyone who would stiff a "paperboy" must have the soul of a decayed walnut.

Aside from those few minor hindrances, I get to hear the birds wake up and watch the world renew itself every morning (sleepy though I am) while in the company of the woman I love. And an astonishing thing happens with this silliest of all jobs ... I start to like it. Despite the ridiculous hours, the mornings we are made late, and the occasional deadbeat, I like it. There is a whole world out here in the still of night, a world I never really knew before. Oh, I've worked graveyard shifts many times, but never outdoors. Never spent these three hours to dawn, day after day, watching the world wake up, seeing the mystical transition from dark to light, being present every morning for the sunrise.

It is a cumulative life experience I've never known, and it subtly affects me, renews my connection to the earth. In the middle of concrete streets and city lights, I have tapped into a primal mystery, to a basic underlying force of nature.

Best of all, I have, in the course of all this, renewed confidence in myself and my ability to cope with life's vicissitudes.

I attain a tranquil sense of peace and contentment, though not on any conscious level right now. I'm just too tired. One morning, in fact, Alice whipped the car around a corner—and got an unexpected surprise. I'd been quietly dozing for the two blocks between tosses, paper in my hand at the ready, and when the car corners ... I don't. I just toppled into her lap, nice as you please. Another time she makes a sudden stop for a kitty causing me to surface from my stupor and, on autopilot, throw a paper ... into the wrong yard.

Observations on the world of the night:

... It belongs to cats. There is no doubt. And it requires an ever-vigilant driving eye to avoid the prowling felines. Also, not all cats' eyes glow the same color in your headlights. They vary in shades of green, gold, orange, aqua, and blue, in that fluorescent quality that reflects out of a dark night in the beam from your car.

... Women kissing their scantily clad men goodbye at the doorway, then jumping in their cars and leaving. This seems a major shift in societal mores to me. No longer, apparently, is he the overnight visitor; no longer is she the breakfast cook. Probably he isn't either.

... A couple locked in a passionate goodbye kiss. She in office attire and he naked, but for the cowboy Stetson cupped over his vital parts.

... And what is increasingly becoming a somewhat shocking tally, the extraordinary number of men and women alike who start the day with a can of beer.

… Runners, joggers, walkers, and other early morning jocks. The modern fitness craze is just getting underway and avoiding its early morning participants becomes every bit the challenge of trying not to hit cats.

And of course, there is the Great Gas Shortage in the midst of all of this. For months, we are victims of the gasoline companies' scam—the artificial tightening of gas supplies in order to drive up prices.

Near as we can figure out, it is occurring nowhere in the nation to the extraordinary extent it is happening in California (and nowhere in California except LA and Orange Country, the mecca of the automobile.)

Never-ending lines of cars form at gas pumps night and day. It takes well over an hour's wait anywhere to get a tank of gas. Sometimes an hour in line stretches to two hours, three hours—and once, even four.

Authorities declare odd-even rationing in order to control the growing public anger, which often flares in the long lines at the pump. If your license plate ends with an odd number, you're allowed to buy gas on odd-number days of the month, even license plate numbers on even days. No need to police it. The impatient public, lining up twenty to fifty cars deep at the pumps will likely stone anyone with the wrong plate trying to get in line on the wrong day.

Fortunately, the license plate on Alice's Mustang is odd and my VW Fastback is even, so nearly every day, Alice spends an hour or two sitting at a gas station to keep the cars filled for us to drive the route and for me to get to and from my other three jobs, not to mention our other transportation needs.

Complicating matters further, there's the very real fear that our gas may be stolen. It's occurring everywhere, so Alice and I are ever vigilant. It is the rare make-and-model that is manufactured with any kind of gas tank security in the 1970s. The fuel door on the average car has no interior lock and is accessed by simply flipping the door open. And the gas cap itself is just your basic twist variety. There are no such things yet as locking fuel doors with inside car releases. Subsequently, in these days of midnight gas siphoning, key-locking gas caps are at a premium, selling between $20 and $30, when they can be found.[†] We never are able to find any, let alone afford the coin.

[†] These gas caps screwed in like today's, but had a key lock in the middle of the cap that shot out two bolts or bars under the cap and locked the cap in. You couldn't pull or twist out the cap without the key.

In the insanity of this so-called gas crisis, stations everywhere are closed or have only one or two pumps working, and an underground intelligence network springs up. They track which stations have recently been supplied by gasoline tankers and predict where gas will be available for sale. Nowhere is the underground more active than among the newspaper carriers, and each morning we share information on where gas is available.

It's simple, really: No gas, no paper delivery. No work, no pay. We are a brotherhood (plus two token lesbians) formed out of crisis and necessity.

We've been at it about seven months when we have The Morning From Hell. In the dark before dawn, a late-model car, making a turn, slams into another. These are the days before cell phones, so Alice must drive to a pay phone to call for help while I stay at the scene with the drivers.

The driver who caused the accident is a Vietnamese woman with almost no English, or what English she does know is shocked right out of her. Neither driver seems hurt, but I am stunned by her response, which is to drop down into that flat-footed squat, a body position more easily attainable to native-born Asians, which rests the backs of the thighs tightly against the calves—a near impossible posture that requires great flexibility and makes my knees ache at the mere sight of it. In this position, this business-dressed woman rests her arms on her knees, hides her face in her arms, and begins a low pitched, droning moan, which voices her shock, fear, and despair, a moan resonating with memories revived— of sudden violence, crashes, damage, in a homeland left behind.

And only twenty minutes later, we turn onto a wide street in the pre-dawn to discover a man staggering along the side of the road, muttering to himself, and clutching his arm. His bloody arm. Alice again stops at a pay phone and puts in another call to the local police station for help.

Forty minutes after this, I toss a paper up to the doorway of Pep Boys Auto Store, then direct Alice to stop as she is about to pull away.

"Wait! There's something wrong with this picture."

Shattered glass is strewn along the pavement, and an entire panel of plate glass is missing—the window in front of the cash register. And Alice places another call to the police station. The dispatcher now has us on a first name basis, and we are beginning to feel a little bit like Captain America.

On another perfectly ordinary morning, just after dawn, I take an armload of papers from the car for delivery to an apartment complex with one hundred sixty units.

"See ya at the next stop," telling Alice.

Toss, *Plop!* Toss, *Plop!* Walk the path around a building and flat toss a paper up a stairwell. *Plop!* Perfect landing. Flick one right, *Plop!* One left, *Plop!* One up onto a third-floor balcony. (Yes, I would have you know, I also make—every day—two successful *third-floor balcony* tosses, therein endangering a glass patio door. Proudly counting this skill among my list of lifetime accomplishments. But the real tribute should be for the first time I mustered the courage even to try it. Too bad they don't give out medals for such valor.)

Heading around the corner and along the path—one more paper to go and out to the car for more. From behind me, come several command-ing male voices, which I take no notice of and continue walking briskly toward my delivery drop.

— "Hold it!"

— "Stop where you are, sir."

— "Sir!"

— "SIR!"

— "Stop where you are and put your hands in the air!"

And then, it dawns on me: The "sir" that all these disembodied voices are addressing is *me*! I come to a halt, put my hands in the air, slowly, since I am holding a potential weapon—a Thursday morning paper heavy with shopping inserts. Turning around, slow and easy, I count no fewer than five guns trained on me by plain-clothed as well as uniformed policemen.

Once my profile reveals I am not a "sir," the officers all come up from their crouched positions behind bushes and trees, holster their guns, and start a chorus of stumbling apologies.

—"Sorry, we thought you were the guy we were looking for."

—"Our report said he's wearing jeans and a light colored sweatshirt."

—"Sorry, we didn't mean to scare you."

—"He just broke into an apartment and got away with some money and credit cards."

When I have enough breath to speak: "This is my route. I'm just the paperboy. I'm here every morning."

—"Yeah, Okay, Okay."

—"Go ahead on."

—"Sorry."

Upon my return to the car, and telling Alice about the episode, the full import of what just happened hits me: I just came close to being gunned down by our Boys in Blue.

Alice, likewise, has a hair-raising incident. On a Sunday morning well into dawn, after we had thrown most of our papers, Alice has a call of nature. We pull up to a gas station and park the car right by the women's restroom. She walks out to the front of the station to get the key. I occupy the time reading the Sunday supplement and moments later Alice comes along, accompanied by the gas attendant who is chattering away as he unlocks the door for her. In a little while she comes out and slides into the car.

"Well, that was exciting," she says. "I almost got myself killed."

"What do you mean?"

"Just that! I damn near got shot."

"How? Who? What?"

"That dopey gas station owner. Seems he came to work, opened up his bay doors, and went into the office and started to count his cash just as I entered the door, wearing this knit cap and sweatshirt. Next thing I know, he has a gun in his shaky hand, and it's aimed at me. 'Stop right there!' he shouted at me."

"Jesus, Alice!"

"I raised my hands and said, 'Whoa, fella. I just came in for the key to the ladies room.'"

"My God, you coulda been shot!" I'm horrified.

"No shit, Sherlock! That's what I'm tellin' ya! He was so rattled, I thought the gun was gonna go off by accident anyway. 'Ohmigod, Ohmigod,' he was saying, 'I almost shot you, I almost shot you.'

"I say, 'Well, that's a goddamn dumb thing to do—open up before you count your cash.'

" 'That's how I do every morning,' he said.

" 'Yeah, well *this* morning, you almost killed me. I suggest you vary your procedure a bit.'

" 'Oh, I'm sure sorry, lady. Ohmigod, I'm sure sorry.'

" 'Well, just don't let it happen again,' I told him. Alice scrubs her face with her hand, in dazed wonder. "Shit! Scared me so bad, I almost didn't have to use the damn bathroom anymore. Helluva note, to get killed for a pee."

The culminating effect of the paper route was unexpected and sur-prising—a legacy of inestimable value. The quiet repetitive nature of throwing papers morning after morning in the gray light of pre-dawn had seeped into my psyche and was restorative.

For at its end, I discovered a new confidence because of this simple mundane job, which was undertaken in total ineptitude and incompe-tence. Amazingly, I developed hand-eye skill, the ability to throw those papers straight out for a distance of up to thirty feet and over the car the same, and put them in the same spot day after day in each yard, driveway, and doorstep. My happy customers and their tips proved it.

More important, I gained a new assurance that no matter what befell me, no matter where I would land, I could always, if I had to, make a living for myself delivering newspapers. This knowledge healed some fundamental insecurity, allayed some underlying fear, forevermore. I've taken care of myself since the age of fifteen, yet not without self-doubt, never with a true sense of my ability to always do so.

Also, I reaped the satisfaction of doing work for the work's sake, even at this most insignificant job, menial, mediocre, and unskilled. Of doing the work well. To find within its mind-numbing monotony, a measure of worth and challenge. To give the lowliest labor the dignity of its doing. A very Zen thing.

Emerging from this triumphant as if from a knightly quest, a hero's journey. We delivered three hundred papers a day, seven days a week, for twelve months and fifteen days.

And in so doing, we saved our house.

Together, Alice and I weathered one of our hardest, most trying times together, and emerged victorious, albeit exhausted. We came through undefeated before adversity, combined in our strength ... and still in love.

Y'know, it just don't get much better that.

DATELINE, 1979—Iranian militants seize the US Embassy in Teheran and take 66 **American hostages;** the militants demand the return of the exiled Shah from the US. As the **American media** begins counting off days of captivity, the militants release 13 black and women hostages; **President Jimmy Carter** deports illegal Iranian students, freezes Iranian assets, and bars oil imports from Iran.

Soviet forces invade Afghanistan. Margaret Thatcher becomes England's new Conservative Prime Minister. President Carter and Soviet leader Leonid Brezhnev sign the SALT II controlled-arms agreement. The Sandinistas government takes over in Nicaragua, prompting the US-supported dictator Anastasio Somoza to flee the country.

Mother Teresa of Calcutta awarded the Nobel Peace Prize. US **inflation** hits highest level in 33 years as OPEC doubles price of oil.

Sally Field wins the Oscar for Best Actress in *Norma Rae*. *Kramer vs. Kramer* wins Oscars for Best Picture and Best Director; the controversial film depicts a single father (**Dustin Hoffman**, Best Actor) raising his children after his wife (**Meryl Streep**, Best Supporting Actress) leaves him. Television news magazine *60 Minutes* takes #1 slot. **Neilson's** rating system ranks *Dallas* and *Dukes of Hazard* in the top ten television shows.

northward bound

It's the end of the first quarter of the year—1979—and Alice and I are still plugging along with our newspaper route every morning. Alice's Social Security case has recently been resolved, but now her sixty-eight-year-old mother Nora has taken ill, prompting Alice to drive up to Northern California to care for her while I stay behind and hold down the fort.

Nora's health is declining. She requires additional care, more than what we can possibly provide from this end of the state, so far away in Orange County. It quickly becomes obvious to Alice and me that more change is on the horizon. It's only a matter of time before we decide to put our house on the market, try for a quick sale, and move up to Humboldt County to be closer to her.

This will be a big change, for me especially, never before having lived in such a tiny settlement, where the nearest town is as small as Eureka. (Its population just twenty-five thousand.) Nora actually lives twenty-six miles south of Eureka, in the tiny rural community of Bluffside, the population a scant seven hundred. But I love the area, and I'm up for it. The sweeping beauty and towering grandeur of the redwood country is unsurpassed. And we'll be living about five miles from the ocean, which means temperate climate. It tends to get its fair share of rainfall there, too, much like the weather of Portland, Oregon, though not quite as wet as Seattle.

This is all fine by me, as I am beginning to find the relentless sunshine of Southern California unendingly boring—it wearies the soul.

We don't have much of a household, but we do have more than can be accommodated in Nora's tiny mobile home of just 800 square feet. We figure, for the immediate time, Alice and I—and our brood of three dogs and a cat—can move into "the cabeen" (cabin, with a French accent)—an old, 14 x 16 foot motor court cabin on the property. But until we figure out our permanent situation up there, our household items will have to be packed up and stored away.

Our house attracts a buyer by the end of April, and it's looking like escrow will close in the next sixty days, about the same time the school year comes to an end and I go on summer break with my job at the nut house. But until then, I'll still be working that job as well as delivering papers every morning. With Alice now getting her social security, I have given up the two other jobs in my working day.

But Nora is once again back in the hospital, and the sense of immediacy to get up north as soon as possible has Alice and me under a great deal of pressure.

By the Fourth of July weekend, Alice decides to move in advance of me and heads up north with Brandy, our Great Dane. Rion-kitty and our other dogs, Cherub and Patrick, stay behind with me to bring up later when the loose ends are tied up with the sale of the house, which is dragging on. The Gas Shortage remains in full swing, and the odd and even gas-available days are still a prominent feature in how most people go about planning their transportation needs.

Alice fully stocked her Mustang with water, food, and supplies, in case, along the 700 mile trip, she gets stuck somewhere without gas and is unable to get any for a day or so, but discovers her survival gear is totally unnecessary immediately beyond Los Angeles.

By the time she gets to Bakersfield, just over the mountain pass from Los Angeles into the San Joachin Valley, gas is plentiful at every pump. Station attendants just laugh when she asks how the shortage is affecting them. All the more evidence the entire gas panic is bogus, aimed primarily in Los Angeles, the most car-dependent area of the country, and staged by none other than the gas companies to drive up rates to meet OPEC demands.

When Alice arrives in Humboldt County, Nora is in the hospital in Eureka with pneumonia and diabetic complications. But what Alice finds most disconcerting is her mother's apparent overnight dementia and disorientation, when she had neither the previous month. Whether it is the result of the hospitalization itself, which can often be a confusing experience for the elderly, or (as is more likely) the result of the drugs she was given, Nora is now talking nonsense much of the time, having vivid and horrifying nightmares, and awaking with the residual dream shadows seeming more true to her than reality. Meanwhile, I continue the final stages of packing up the house and holding down the paper route myself, but every bit concerned at the level of worry I hear in Alice's voice during our daily phone calls. She's been traveling back and forth to the hospital, twenty-five miles each way, twice a day. And Nora's dementia is not improving. Her needs seem to change from minute to minute. Increasingly, I grow anxious for our house to close escrow so I can get up there to help take up some of the slack.

Nora's release from the hospital throws Alice into a twenty-four hour, care-giving regimen. She set up a bed and portable commode in the living room for Nora, which allows Alice to at least doze off in the reclining chair while monitoring whether Nora awakes and wanders around. Although Nora is out of it in many ways, she is still Alice's mother, and very much contentious about taking instructions from Alice. Much of the time, Alice's attempts at Nora's personal care are met with resistance. Showers become a hellish effort.

Sometimes Nora forgets she's just eaten and demands to be fed once more, or conversely, refuses to eat, claiming she's just finished a meal and is being forced to eat again. Skipped meals are a no-no for an insulin-dependent diabetic, and the daily diabetic routine of testing and shots itself becomes a struggle and often leaves Nora or Alice in tears.

Nora has also begun to hallucinate, talking to non-existent people, imagining she is supposed to be elsewhere, often trying to escape from Alice's watchfulness to go off who-knows-where. She still smokes and has to be monitored with it, so Alice confiscates all matches and lighters to ensure that her mother doesn't set herself alight while Alice's attention is on some laundry or kitchen duty.

For me, time continues to drag on forever. Escrow passed the eighty-day mark today and Alice sounds utterly exhausted and very stressed on the phone. I'm frantic to be up there with her.

And Nora is back in the hospital yet again, after only a week at home. She is diagnosed with congestive heart failure, and her dementia is still in force. No one can explain the sudden onset. At least the hospitalization will provide a few days rest for Alice, who is wiped out from being ever vigilant with Nora at home, and from the necessary round-the-clock care. Alice is tired and troubled.

But not this night. Tonight Alice calls me laughing.

"You're gonna love it up here," she says, chuckling. "I've got a Humboldt County story to tell you, and you're gonna love it."

It has to do with Skylab, America's first Earth-orbiting space station, which had been launched back in 1973. Skylab was home to three sets of three-man astronaut crews, proving that humans could survive in space under proper conditions for at least three months' duration. It's equipped with the most varied experimental hardware ever on a single spacecraft, and has supplied scientists with the first recordings of solar activity above the atmosphere. In its six years of orbiting the planet, it sent back a grand total of a hundred and seventy-five thousand solar pictures that provided valuable information on Earth's resources and environmental conditions.

Orbiting 300 miles above Earth, its orbit began to decay prematurely, five years after the last manned crew, due to especially high sunspot activity. The seventy-seven ton space station is coming down now, and NASA has been issuing projections for possible re-entry times and places.

Anxiety in some folks following the story isn't alleviated by the reports, since it is very likely the space station will only partially burn up in the atmosphere as it falls through. Knowing the damage even baseball-sized meteors can cause, let alone something this big, has created a world of tension among some worrywarts who have been monitoring the situation.

Finally, on this day, July 11, 1979, Skylab has come down.

"So there I am, leaving the hospital tonight," Alice says with more life in her voice than I've heard in a while, "and as I walk out the front door, the news rack catches my eye. The local newspaper has a banner headline in huge print."

Dead air.

"Yeah, so what did it say?"

"It says, 'SKYLAB ... MISSES ... EUREKA!' "

I burst out laughing. It is one of those comical things that gets funnier the more you think about it. We laugh till we're giddy, blowing noses and mopping eyes.

Skylab has come down in several large chunks in an uninhabited area of Australia and the Indian Ocean. Skylab has, indeed, missed Eureka—by the narrow margin of 8,000 miles!

Finally ... escrow closes. Wasting no time, I supervise the moving crew, throw my suitcase in the trunk, pack a lunch and thermos, place Rion-kitty in his carrier, load him along with Patrick and Cherub in the car, and blaze on up to Humboldt.

Twelve hours later, I'm weary but so very glad to see Alice. The dogs bounce all over her in excitement. She lets Rion out of his carrier and launches into a stern talk with him about not being pissed with all this, stating emphatically that she is putting trust in him to stay put and come back to his new house when he is done exploring his new environment. (Being the bright kitty that he is, within a half hour he returns.)

Alice's eyes are so deeply ringed with dark circles she looks like a raccoon, and she declares she is simply dead on her feet.

I kiss Nora on the cheek, and she responds affectionately, saying quite lucidly, "Well, glad you finally made it. We've been waiting."

I look questioningly at Alice and she shrugs.

"Can you handle it for an hour or two?" She asks, clearly about to fall down with exhaustion. "I really do need to sleep."

"Go ahead, Alice. I'm okay, now that I'm here. I'm pretty wired up. I need to unwind a bit anyhow."

"Fine. There's some food left from dinner. We've both eaten, but Beanie might need some fluids. She's a bit dehydrated. "Beanie" is Nora's nickname—from *Beanie and Cecil*, the TV cartoon. Alice and her half brother had saddled Nora with it many years ago and the moniker stuck.

I chat with Nora as I feed the dogs, heat up something for myself, and make her a cup of tea. Her hands are shaking badly, so I transfer the hot liquid from a cup and saucer into a tall mug that she can manage more easily. After a while, Nora drifts off to sleep, and I kick back in the recliner and whisper a small prayer of thanks to the Powers that Be.

Home at last.

The next days go by in a haze. The movers arrive and stuff all our things into the "cabeen." Alice and I take turns sleeping in Nora's bedroom as we spell each other in the living room with her care. For the next five nights, in the recliner that sits next to Nora, Alice or I pull guard duty all through the night.

I take over the bathing chore on my second day there, finding it easiest to climb in the shower in my underwear right along with Nora, speedily scrubbing down her front side, then spinning her around to wash her back while she holds onto the bar and lets me have at her. She is strong enough to stand through it all, but any effort to wash herself without help is too much. By the end of her showers, she is breathless, but clean. And she tolerates my intrusion on her person easier than her daughter's.

In fact, only three days into my arrival and her trust in me is put to the supreme test. After making breakfast for us all, and sitting down to the meal, I realize Nora isn't eating her English muffin.

"Nora, would you prefer toast to the muffin?" I ask. She shakes her head, picks it up, and puts it down again. Something about this puzzles me.

"Nora, why aren't you eating your muffin?"

"There's ants on it," she says.

I stand up, walk around the table, and pick up the muffin halves, turning over both pieces and examine them carefully. I put my hand on her shoulder. "Nora, there aren't any ants on the muffin. You must be having floaters in your eyes or something. I wouldn't let you eat anything that has ants on it. You need to trust me. The muffin is okay to eat."

Alice holds her breath as her mother picks up the muffin, inspects it carefully, gives a slight shrug, and proceeds to bite into it. Alice's face expresses deep gratitude as we exchange a look between us.

That night it's my turn to stand vigil, and as I help Nora onto the bedside commode, she looks beyond me and exclaims, "Well, hello, Emory. What are you doing here?"

Emory is her brother—dead twenty years.

I turn to look, the hair rising on the back of my neck, and the room is empty. At least to my eyes it is.

The next day another startling thing happens when her friend, Amelia, stops by. For half an hour, Nora had been visiting with her best friend, Mattie, and talking nonsense and smoking an imaginary cigarette all the way down to butting it out in an imaginary ashtray. Mattie's eyes are filled with such sadness that her best friend has been brought to these straits.

But when Amelia arrives, I serve the three some hot tea, and Nora suddenly seems her old self, as if a switch has been turned on. She holds a normal conversation with her two friends, and her trembling ceases entirely!

I serve her tea in a cup and saucer, something impossible for these last four days since I've arrived. Alice lights a cigarette for her, and Nora holds it between her fingers as she lifts her cup daintily with the same hand, without a tremor.

Throughout the rest of the evening, she is completely lucid and normal and still free from the shakes. She seems unaware she has ever been any different, and even her sense of humor is back.

"I don't know how it is!" she remarks.

"What?" I ask.

"Those strings," she points to the blue-green carpeted floor. "Where the hell do they come from? It seems I'm always picking up little threads and strings on this floor."

Sure enough, three white threads, a few inches apart from each other, lie on the floor in soft curves.

"It's so weird," she says as I bend to pick up the threads. "Every day for years I've found a white string or two on this floor. It always makes me think that somewhere something is unraveling. Probably me." For the first time in weeks, Nora is laughing.

The next morning, Alice reports that apart from the one time she needed to use the portable commode, her mother slept soundly through the night.

Nora is still clear-headed and not trembling, though she doesn't care to eat anything, saying that her stomach is upset. She looks quite pale and delicate, and seems restless and fidgety, but can't tell us what is wrong. Not pain, not shortness of breath. Just queasiness.

And … something else, something she can't identify or explain.

Finally she asks Alice to call the doctor. She thinks maybe she needs to see him.

While dialing the doctor from the phone in the kitchen doorway, Alice keeps a watchful eye on her mother lying on the bed. Then it happens.

Nora abruptly retches. I'm sitting next to her and quickly react, turning her shoulders swiftly, moving her on her side so she won't choke if she vomits.

She instead gives a huge sigh, and I feel her flesh go rigid under my hands, her body growing heavy and limp, I turn her on her back just in time to see her eyes slowly become fixed and dilated.

"Aw, Godammit!" Alice slams the phone on the hook and rushes to Nora's side. "Aw, Beanie. Aw, Beanie, Godammit."

Alice takes my place beside her mother. Softly, she strokes her mother's face.

Nora is gone.

Alice clasps Nora's hand, and finally, after several minutes, I close Nora's eyes and we sit in silence. Alice looks up with tears tracking her cheeks. "I'm glad it's over," she says. "She didn't want to be like this."

"No, she certainly didn't," I agree. I had seen Nora's fierce independence matched only in one other—her daughter.

"It's so odd though," Alice says. "I feel … really happy. Isn't that weird? Light. Like everything is okay now. Like … like it's entirely *inappropriate* to feel sad."

I hadn't wanted to say anything, but I feel the same thing myself. Almost bubbly. Like something wonderful has just happened. As if we've just been given good news.

Alice stands up and hugs me. We hold on for a long time, each feeling this strange conflict between this undeniable lightness and serenity and Nora lying lifeless on the bed.

It seems as though a kind of Grace has just settled upon us.

Family arrives. Neighbors come. Friends bring food. And a car drives up and three friends of Nora's emerge from it, all Pythian Sisters in the same Supreme Temple. They are in dresses, wearing hats, and carrying a variety of dishes. The street is full of cars, and rather than walk the long fence line to the driveway, they all three, while balancing their condolence pies and casseroles, throw one stocking-clad leg after the other over the low fence, and stride in sturdy heels across the yard to the house. It just tickles me to see this.

The funeral service, however, is a farce.

Nora was an irregular churchgoer, but she had faith, and was fairly practical, straightforward, and unassuming about religion. She believed that one's relationship with God is a private matter, and therefore didn't much tolerate any sort of piety or proselytizing.

Nora's regular minister is out at Church Camp, this being the middle of summer, so another local preacher has been prevailed upon to officiate.

"I didn't know Nora," the preacher begins, "but I'm assured she was a good Christian woman, and I know she would have wanted everyone here today to know Jesus as she did."

I feel Alice stiffen beside me at his impertinence, and I put my hand on her arm.

"If you don't know Jesus yet, know Him as your personal savior," he intones, "Nora would like it to be upon this occasion that you find His consolation, that you take the opportunity of her passing into His hands, to find Jesus in your own heart."

Alice is building a head of steam, outraged at what she feels is an effrontery that this preacher is turning her mother's memorial service into a pathetic attempt to guilt-trip a few more converts into the fold. I fear Alice is going to rise up in all *her* glory and beat the man bloody with his own Bible, in front of all of Nora's grieving friends.

And that's when I see them … all over the carpet. All over that chapel's burgundy carpet. I elbow Alice sharply and point to the floor.

Strings!

White strings—thin, curled, and twisted—scattered all over the carpet in the funeral parlor. Nora's damned strings!

We each look sidelong at the other for a long minute, and then my new fear is that Alice and I will disgrace ourselves by bursting into hoots and howls. I can see out of the corner of my eye the color rising above her neck as she fights to keep the laughter from rioting out, and I offer up a private little thanks to Nora, wherever she is, for sending us what is, yet again, a small, timely manifestation of Grace.

Not to mention sparing that pompous Bible-thumping minister the kind of Bible-beating he would never live down.

mattie and duke

As we process getting past the funeral and try to get things sorted out—closing the loose ends of Nora's affairs and moving our things from the small cabeen into the larger mobile home—Nora's best friend Mattie gives us her quiet support. She often stops by on her way to buy groceries, asking if she can pick up anything for us. On more than a few of those first nights after losing Nora, Mattie is generous enough to invite us to her home for dinner. And so another meaningful friendship begins.

When Nora died, Mattie was the first to arrive on the scene. Just as the ambulance pulled up, she was already rushing down the street and was up to the door before the paramedics even got out the stretcher. Before the EMTs took Nora away, Alice and I prevailed upon them to allow Mattie a minute alone with her friend.

Mattie was devastated.

She lives just down the way from Nora's mobile home at the end of the lane in a traditional, saltbox-style house that's more than a century old. Behind the house stands her large equipment barn, which edges along the fence line of a sprawling ranch property owned by one of the area's long-established families—pillars in the community. On it sits a two-story "ranch" house (a mansion really, with eyebrow windows which charm me at first sight), and serves as the primary focal point from the front window of Nora's mobile home, even though Mattie's far less assuming house is in the forefront.

Mattie had become Alice's mainstay in dealing with Nora's illness through those long several weeks before I could get up here and set up the household. During those weeks, Mattie was Alice's resource for all things needed in the community and a much-appreciated helping hand in Nora's final days. But it's in the aftermath of Nora's death that we come to know more about Mattie, particularly on the nights we dine with her. We learn, for instance, that she's long been divorced, her ex-husband a kind of a local character, living over in the next small town and now remarried. Mattie has two daughters by him: Melanie, who is married to Greg and has a son named Brian; and Giselle, a divorcee whose ex still lives in town and owns a local garage. They have an adolescent son named Paul, whom Giselle is raising.

I actually met Mattie when Alice and I took our first trip up north here to visit Alice's folks back in 1977. I remembered her then as friendly, neighborly, and possessing a southern accent and a sweet, little giggle. She also struck me as tall. Later I learned that she would have been even taller, but for a slightly crooked back due to childhood polio.

And then there's Duke, Mattie's significant other.

Duke had become the county "catch" a dozen years before, back in the late 1960s, when his wife of thirty years died. He was then as he is now: a lean, tall, handsome cowboy with a Gary Cooper-like charm. Every eligible woman in the community set her sights on him. And for a few years there, he gave them all a spin as he took first one out, and then another, enjoying his bachelorhood after all those married years. Having ten or twelve women vying for you must be quite an ego builder.

I wouldn't know.

So after a few years of playing the field, and a few small scandals and catfights, Mattie won the "Duke" prize, and the two established a companionable relationship, now about ten years along. She cooks him three meals a day; he buys all the groceries.

He lives in a trailer up on his little ranch a scant mile away. But three times a day his old, beat-up Ford—with his border collie Buster and his German shepherd Sarge churning around excitedly in the pickup bed—rolls down the lane and pulls into her drive to the back door. A few nights a week that truck stays parked in Mattie's yard overnight. Duke has his own bedroom in her house.

He gets a pension from his twenty years as a sheriff in the Bay Area. Soon after his wife died, he retired from yet another twenty years on the

State's payroll—his second career— as a heavy equipment operator for the highway department. He owns his own backhoe and road grader, among other pieces of equipment, up on his ten-acre spread. He keeps three horses, a few steers, and a couple of goats up there as well.

Duke is quite active with the rodeo crowd in town; the Cattlemen's Association of Humboldt County hosts a great rodeo locally in July every year.

For years, Duke has trained all the cutting horses used on every ranch within thirty miles around. Nearly every wrangler in the county, during his growing years, has come under Duke's sway. He's taught every young, aspiring cowboy who wished to learn, how to rope, dog, hog-tie, and ride cattle.

"I can't keep a burn barrel more 'n two months around here," Mattie often gripes. "Duke rides Samson down here ever' chance he gets, and practices his ropin' on my steel drums, draggin' them up field and down furrow. They're so durn bunged up after a few weeks, I have to go get new ones again. I got a standing order down to the feed store for 'em. You'd think after all these years a-doin' it, he wouldn't need to be out there th'owing ropes around a barrel day and night."

Duke is now nearing seventy-five and not showing too many signs of slowing down. He's up at dawn every morning, feeding and watering the livestock. And he keeps busy on the ranch the rest of the day, repairing the equipment and cultivating the feed. If not on his ranch, he's typically found in town at the feed store or stock auction yard, chawing with his cronies.

So nearly any evening that we are invited over to Mattie's, Duke, too, is at the table. He is a gentleman of the old school, never a coarse word falls from his lips; he's soft spoken and mannerly; his comportment around women is deferential, courtly, and gallant. And when he is truly tickled, he giggles with the truest "tee-hee" of anyone I've ever known. No wonder he'd once been considered the catch of the decade.

And Mattie feeds him well, too.

She's a great cook, Betty Crocker-style—stick-to-your-ribs, down-home cookin' with plenty of variety, and all of it larruping good. She gets bored easily, so she serves the most inventive menu of any cook whose table I've been privileged to sit at. She has an adventuresome palate and uses always the freshest ingredients, much of which she grows in her own garden.

As for Duke, music is his creative outlet. He plays drums and sax-ophone in a little band that sometimes gets booked for the dances at the local Moose Lodge or Grange Hall, which in his courting days got him out of some tight scrapes with the competing women, conveniently removing him from some of the more interesting catfights. While the ladies battled over him on the sidelines, he played on the bandstand, act-ing more innocent than he had a right to be.

Inevitably, Mattie became a fixture in our lives, and we in hers. She showed me how to can food with a hot water bath and pressure cooker, how to make jelly and jam and various pickles, and how to keep a country kitchen. She taught me to loosen my city-bred life like a too-tight belt. She helped me mold to the rhythms of the country, and adjust my tempo to the transit of the seasons.

Eventually we planted to compliment each other's garden. I'd plant zucchini one year, and she'd plant beans. I'd plant garlic, and she'd plant onions. And what we didn't grow, she knew where to order from local growers. We bought lugs of peaches and canned them together, making a Saturday project out of it. Nothing prettier than jars of perfect peach halves swimming in golden nectar and all lined up in the sunlight.

Every year we'd order the more elegant, small-seeded blackberries—one lug of marionberries and one lug of olallieberries—and split them between us. We mix the two types of blackberries to freeze. Mattie taught me that the best way to freeze fresh berries is to leave them unwashed, spread out in a single layer on cookie sheets. Bag them once they are frozen, and you always have the makings for a berry pie in your freezer. You clean and rinse the berries while they are still frozen, but never before; otherwise they'll end up mushy.

Mattie also knows where to go to pick the best local Himalaya black-berries. She scorns the bushes located too close to roads for being dusted with the exhaust fumes of passing cars, and leads us instead to virgin creek-bed brambles and pasture hedgerows, where we pick in the close company of curious cows chewing their cuds. There, Alice and Mattie and I pick the native Himalayas till our hands sting from prickles and stay blue-stained for a good week. From the literal fruits of our labor, we make jam, grinding the small, sweet berries first through a food mill to remove the worst of the big seeds.

Until you've feasted on homemade Himalaya blackberry jam daubed on Mattie's baking powder biscuits, well, you just haven't lived, I tell you!

My homemade pear butter is Mattie's favorite. I use pears picked from her friend's tree when they are ripe. And you should know those pears don't have the shelf life of store-bought, which go from days of being brick hard directly to inedible mush within a minute and a half. Tree-ripened pears are juicy enough to run down your arm to your elbow when you bite into them, and are as sweet as the lightest honey. You have to eat them over the sink. Everybody should have a pear tree in her life.

But practicing the secrets of down-home cooking isn't Mattie's greatest attribute. She is also full of stories—of her growing up years in Arkansas or of the people in our area. She recounts tales that make up local lore anywhere folks grow up and spend their whole lives together. Not gossip, exactly. Just stories. History.

One story she tells us is about the time she crossed the lane one evening to take some freshly canned pickles to a neighbor (who, by the time we moved into the area, no longer lived there.) As Mattie approached the porch, she caught a glimpse of the couple through the window in the living room. They were both nearly naked; he had her panties on his head and was darting back and forth, chasing her around the furniture amid her giggles. Mattie, not wishing to bring notice to herself, backed away quietly and went home.

Next midday, she once again took the pickles across the lane. This time, over coffee and muffins, her slightly embarrassed friend confessed they had been playing "Hens and Rooster" the night before. Mattie thinks such goins-on are just funny as all get out. She's a bit naïve when it comes to sex play—for her, the term is an oxymoron.

Mattie says as little as she cares about all that sex stuff, though, she thinks both her daughters seem to have gotten their fair share. She despaired over those two girls, Melanie and Giselle, in their younger years, for they each defied custom and convention and embarked on active sex lives before marriage, don't you see? Mattie had thought them both wild and libertine.

Well, maybe … but nothing suggests they were exactly what I'd call Olympic material.

And religion has changed them both since their younger days, causing each to pull in her horniness, and adopt a somewhat pious attitude about it. Mattie is none too keen on their zealous new piety, but gives reluctant credit for the sexual reform it seems to have brought about.

Mattie is always slightly puzzled about all things sexual. She once told me that her mother died when she was very young, so on the second day of her honeymoon, she called home to her daddy, weeping into the phone and begging him to let her come home. Nobody had told Mattie that her husband would want to do "that." Her daddy told her to stay where she was, said it would get better, and "that" was what a wife and husband did.

She never said if ever it did get better, except perhaps on one night of wild abandon.

Mattie confided in me one long day while canning beans together that she and Duke came home from a party after she had a little too much to drink.

She said, "I don't know what it was. Something happened there; I felt real funny. And Duke said, 'That's all right, darlin'. You're supposed to feel that. It's good.'"

"Well, yeah," I replied, to be encouraging. "It is good, isn't it? It sounds as if you had an orgasm."

"Well, I don't know what it was," she said. "But I told him not to do that again."

"You did?" I was stunned.

"Yes, I didn't like it. Not at all."

"Why not? What didn't you like?"

"I was out of control. It just felt like I was out of myself. I don't want to feel that way ever again."

Now what do you say to that?

❧

One night past midnight, very soon after Alice and I settled into the mobile home, Mattie called us on the phone concerned something was wrong 'cause our lights were on so late. Country folk aren't used to such habits.

I'm a natural night owl and love to indulge it when I don't have to get up at the crack of breakfast. Alice often retires late, too, and newly menopausal at forty-five, she sometimes surfaces with night sweats, unable to get back to sleep, and toddles out to the living room, turns on a light, and reads for an hour or two. Lights go on and off through the night at our house like ships signaling at sea.

So we were amused when Mattie told us that she herself never turned the lights on in the night. Instead, she and Duke relied on a bedside flashlight for navigating through her darkened house. We learned not to fear that burglars had broken in down there whenever we saw flashlight beams snaking eerily through the rooms. And Mattie grew accustomed to our illuminated vigils in the wee small hours.

Late one night Mattie awoke to a call of nature. Led by the pinpoint ray of her trusty flashlight, she made her way down the hallway to the bathroom located in the shadowed heart of her silent, old, country house.

Shuffling in the gloom to the familiar spot, she hiked up her nightgown and began to lower herself onto the toilet seat ... only to come to rest instead on Duke's bare lap. Unseen in the deep shadows, he had fallen asleep on the pot more than an hour before she arrived.

Mattie screamed in alarm, shot straight up in the air, and went flying forward, right over the high rail of their old-timey, claw-foot bathtub and down into its deep belly.

Duke in turn startled awake and leapt up instinctively, pajama bottoms wrapped around his ankles. Dopey and clumsy and blind in the dark, he tripped inside his pant legs, lost his balance, and followed Mattie over the rim of the tub, landing on top of her.

The shrill siren of Mattie's scream filled the air, but Duke couldn't quite place the sound, blinking in the blackness, half asleep. No clue where he was or how he got there, he was in that peculiar state of shock where sensory input registers only a single sense at a time. With his bare ass against the ice-cold porcelain tub, conscious first of his own body—the hard, cold surface against his back and butt and—Ohmigod!—underneath him something warm, soft, and squishy. Something fleshy and writhing!

Duke bellowed in mortal fear and went wild trying to pull away from the thing beneath him.

Mattie, all the while, hadn't stopped shrieking like a maniacal banshee since she'd sat down on *something alive* ... and it jumped in the tub right after her. On top of her now, squirming and leveraging against her. Chilly and boney and howling!

Mattie and Duke—each fighting in the pitch dark to escape an unknown horror, yelling and grunting with effort. An advantage of one, a hindrance to the other. Nobody getting anywhere fast.

In the icy chill of a too-tight tub, their long, boney limbs entangled. Soft flesh knocked and bruised. Knobby knees fought lethal elbows. Fast and frantic and brief.

Individual terrors mounted to an inevitable crescendo until … they pee'd … each of them.

Hotly.

Lavishly.

Uncontrollably.

Peed all over themselves and each other in that antique tub—the final flourish of a bizarre fandango.

Both flashlights were found later where they'd rolled beneath the tub. His was turned off; he'd flicked the switch when he sat down—saving the batteries, dontcha know? Hers was still on, but the tiny beam shone impotently, glass face resting flush against the wall.

This tale comes directly from Mattie; she loves telling a good story, even if it means telling on herself. And despite this episode, both she and Duke never altered their midnight ramblings by flashlight; constitutionally unable, it would seem, to waste good electricity once lights had been shut off for the night.

Nancy's Pear Butter
(Or Pear Honey)

4 cups peeled, crushed fresh pears
2½ cups sugar
¼ teaspoon salt
Juice of one lemon

Combine all ingredients and cook slowly in heavy saucepan over low to medium heat, stirring to keep from sticking for approx15-20 minutes until spreading consistency. It is honey colored if cooked no longer than necessary for right consistency, otherwise it darkens.

Pour into hot sterilized jars and lids. Boiling water bath for 5 minutes. Remove and let seal. Makes 2½ pints.

Mattie's Salad Dressing

2/3 cup catsup
1 cup oil
1 clove garlic
Juice of 2 lemons
3/4 cup sugar
2 teaspoon salt
1/4 teaspoon paprika
1/2 cup vinegar
1 chopped onion

Mix all ingredients together and put in jar and refrigerate. Lasts three weeks refrigerated.

Mattie's Cottage Cheese Drops

1/2 cup butter
1/2 cup brown sugar
1 cup creamed cottage cheese
1-1/2 cups uncooked oatmeal
1-1/4 cups flour
1 egg
1 teaspoon vanilla extract
1/2 teaspoon baking soda
1/2 teaspoon baking powder
3/4 cup chopped nuts (optional)

Beat butter and sugar till fluffy. Add cottage cheese, mix well. Stir in oatmeal and dry ingredients. Add egg and vanilla extract. Drop by teaspoon on greased baking sheet.

Bake at 375 degrees approximately 15 minutes.

Mattie's Easy Sweet Pickles

(Also makes nice salt pickle by leaving out sugar)

This is a great recipe for start of season, when cucumbers are just coming on, or end of season, when they are sparse and you're just sick of the whole damn pickling production anyway, but can't bring yourself to let them go to waste.

Pack cucumbers (slices or chunks) into quart jar and add:

1 cup vinegar

1 tablespoon of salt (kosher or un-iodized)

½ teaspoon alum

1 tablespoon pickling spices

Fill jar with cold water and seal tightly. Leave six weeks. Anytime thereafter can be eaten as salt pickle.

OR: Drain pickles into saucepan. Rinse pickles. Wash jar. Add 1 cup sugar to juice and heat to dissolve sugar. Pour back over pickles and refrigerate. They are ready to eat 24 hours later.

May be made one jar at a time, as needed. Need not be canned and sealed if kept refrigerated.

Mattie's Lemon Meringue Pie

Makes a 10-inch pie
1 cup sugar
4 eggs, separated
3+ tablespoons flour
4 tablespoons juice fresh lemon
1 tablespoon cornstarch
1 teaspoon grated lemon rind
2/3 cup milk or water
1 tablespoon butter

Mix sugar and flour. Add liquid, butter, 4 beaten egg yolks, and lemon juice and rind. Cook in double boiler over hot water till thickened. Stir constantly for about 20 minutes. (You can shorten cooking time by using saucepan over low direct heat, but constant stirring is essential.)

Turn into baked pastry shell. Top with meringue, and take topping a little overtop crust to keep it from sliding. Bake at 325 degrees for 15 minutes till golden.

MERINGUE

Beat the four cold egg whites till stiff enough to keep a peak. Add ¼ cup sugar and ¼ teaspoon cream of tartar.

DATELINE, 1980—US breaks ties with Iran. Iraqi troops invade Iran, sparking an eight-year war between Iran and Iraq. A race riot in Miami protests police brutality. Mount St. Helens erupts in Washington State, causing 26 deaths and $2.7 billion in damage. FBI's undercover operation "Abscam" (for Arab scam) implicates, for accepting bribes, over 30 public officials including a senator and seven congressmen.

Coca Cola Co, the world's largest user of sugar, switches to high-fructose corn syrup when world sugar prices soar to 24 cents per pound, up 60 percent from 1979. Atlanta's $70 million Hartsfield International Airport opens with 138 passenger gates, 44 more than Chicago's O'Hare Airport. The Federal Hourly Minimum Wage is set at $3.10 an hour. In Murchison Falls National Park, Uganda, park authorities report that only 1,400 elephants are left out of the estimated count of 14,300 in 1973. No rhinos are known to remain in the park.

Production begins on the first commercial Magnetic Resonance Imaging scanner. Banks led by J.P. Morgan make massive bailout loans of $1 billion to the Hunt brothers who allegedly tried to corner the silver market. The US Supreme Court rules that "live human-made microorganism is patentable matter." Genentech, Biogen and others rush to commercialize biotechnology.

Robert Redford establishes the Sundance Resort and Institute in Provo, Utah, to support independent filmmaking and playwriting. The Planetary Society is founded as a space advocacy group, dedicated to the exploration of Mars and the Solar System, the search for Near-Earth Objects (NEOs), and the search for extraterrestrial life. Carl Sagan dramatizes the mysteries of the universe in his 13-part TV series *Cosmos*, making famous the phrase "billions and billions of stars and galaxies." Mothers Against Drunk Driving (MADD) is founded in Irving, Texas. Actress Mae West dies in Hollywood at age 87.

humboldt harmony

Many of our friends vacation with us over the years, driving up the coast to stay a few days in our funky cabeen, partake of our hospitality, and explore the grandeur of the redwoods and the solitude of the north coast beaches. Some even make a regular yearly visit of it. And still others come to abide permanently in Humboldt County, finding it hauntingly unforgettable.

Shortly before Alice inherited Nora's property, our friend HoneyBear—the business partner of Josie, since a few years after our early days at the clinic—relocated in Eureka and opened a custom jewelry shop in Old Town. Josie stayed back in Long Beach with her boyfriend, Russ, running the original jewelry shop there, but within a year or so, she too joined the "Great Northern Trek" to Humboldt.

HoneyBear's parents live in Oregon, in a town just over the California border. They're elderly, and like Alice with her mother, HoneyBear's trips up the coast had become more and more frequent, so he decided to move on up, to a comparatively large town to be nearer to them.

Sometimes in the busy summer season our guests arrive on each other's heels, and I worry that we'll have to stack 'em like cordwood in the living room. We've already had more than one near miss, with ex-lovers leaving just as former lovers were arriving. The nightmare of every dream hostess.

The nearest town is pretty much shut down by seven at night. For some of our friends it's their first real visit to the country, their introduction to small-town atmosphere, and it's hard to predict how they will react. I can tell you for the most part that I'm a lousy judge of it—the ones I think will settle in and be comfortable are often edgy and mildly anxious when faced with the silent, dark, country nights with nowhere to go and nothing to do. And the ones I fear will want to leave in a day and a half, out of sheer boredom, nestle in like they have come home at last and are reluctant to leave when the time comes.

Ronnie and her life partner Tess are prime examples. Ronnie grew up in a small town in Arkansas and was happy to leave it for Los Angeles. Tess, too, is well accustomed to the bustle of a busy city, having lived most of her life in both Boston and Los Angeles. They're pretty much party people at this stage, working hard all week and pubbing on the weekends. Disco is big these days, and Tess likes to get her aerobics activity on the dance floor. And Ronnie is used to twenty-four hour supermarkets and restaurants and fast food conveniences. So the first time they visit, I thought that within two days it would be agony for them. But they both relaxed and became regulars after that. In time, they also relocate for good up here, becoming permanent fixtures in Humboldt County.

It just goes to show, you never can tell.

Another friend, Justine, the professional singer, also visits with some regularity. On her first visit, she arrived late at night, driving the twelve-hour trip from Los Angeles in a record ten-and three-quarter hours. She owns a little olive-green Karman Ghia that she's christened 'Fern', and she flat tears up the road with it.

When she pulled into our driveway, we welcomed her into our home and, in between her yawns, shoved some food into her. Then we walked her out to the cabeen to introduce her to its amenities, including a portable potty chair (with chemicals), two barber chairs, an upright freezer, and a washer and dryer. She crashed on the bed before Alice and I barely traveled the fifty feet back to the house.

About seven the next morning, Justy awoke to the sound of a mighty machine roaring nearby—very nearby. She told us later that she opened her eyes, looked blearily around her strange accommodations—the washer, dryer, freezer, barber chairs slowly coming into focus. Much perplexed, she asked herself, "How the hell did I come to fall asleep in an appliance store?"

As the noise grew louder, she rolled out of bed and opened the door to a huge road grader, the wheels so massive they dwarfed the doorframe Justy was standing in, and they were backing, backing, straight toward her. (*And the highwayman came riding, riding....*)

It was Duke, decked out in an orange hard hat and sitting up high on the monster machine, backing it up to get a good long run at our driveway. The little lane that runs along our property is an unpaved gravel road, and twice a year Duke revs up his road grader, rides it down from the ranch, and re-grades the gravel. Afterwards, he finishes the job off by smoothing down Mattie's drive as well as ours.

Justy commented dryly that she hadn't realized there was this much excitement to be had up here in our little boondock corner of the world.

On that same visit a day or so later, Justy joined us at Mattie's for dinner, along with Duke, of course. We all tucked into Miss Mattie's food, scarfing the meal like orphan waifs. Duke had planned to head out and rehearse with his band after dinner, but knowing Justy's musical background, Mattie asked her if she would please play something for us. So the five of us ended up trooping into their small music room, where, along with a piano, Duke kept his drum set and sax. Justy took a seat at the upright and began rippling through a few chords, finally launching into a version of *Don't Fence Me In*.

Duke joined in as if answering a mating call, setting a rhythm with brushes and cymbals. But as Justy got into a groove, Duke abandoned the drums in favor of his sax, excited to play with a professional who knows her way around a tune. After a few honks, he left off again to brush the high hats, then blat once more on the sax as Justy reprised the chorus. Duke literally didn't know whether to blow, beat, or go blind.

Justy then segued nicely into Mattie's favorite tune, "Little Brown Jug," giving it that kind of Glen Miller swing treatment. My only regret was that Justy's back was to Duke, so she never saw him manage every now and again, in his frenzied musical excitement, a one-handed cymbal riff while simultaneously tooting the sax.

Mattie's smile was as wide as Texas, watching the show of both Justy, who was hamming it up for all she was worth, and Duke, his face gone red and sweaty with the effort to perform his plural musical feats.

As for Alice and I, well, we just had the best old time watching Justy charm those two with her impresario impression, and as she ended the song with a flourish, I motioned her to stop, afraid Duke might succumb to apoplexy if he attempted yet a third song.

Thereafter, on subsequent visits, Justy never fails to head down the lane to Mattie's for a cup of coffee with those two. She does that at least once on every trip she makes up to Humboldt, with or without Alice and me. She even sends them postcards whenever she travels.

On one particular trip to Europe, Justy sent them several cards. Alice and I learned of this when Mattie returned from a walk to the post office, rounded into our yard, and trotted up our front steps.

"Hi, neighbor, how's it going?" I asked on opening the door.

"Fine, fine. I had to hurry to check the mail myself today, and get there ahead of Duke."

"Oh?" inquired Alice. She knew it was Duke's habit to pick up his mail, as well as Mattie's, on his way to her house for lunch every day. The postmistress of our little town of seven hundred souls never hesitated to give Mattie's mail to Duke, of course. Everyone knew they were together.

"Why'd you get there before him to get the mail?" asked Alice.

"Well, Justy's in Paris, isn't she?"

"Yes," said Alice, curious where this was leading.

"Well, she sent us one of them naked French postcards a day or two ago."

I started to choke and sputter; Alice looked horrified. For a moment our imaginations ran darkly wild.

"Naked French postcards?" Alice managed to squeak out.

We exchanged looks that said, "Surely not! Justy wouldn't, would she?" But knowing Justy, as ornery as she is, you can never be totally certain about anything.

"Anyway, I decided I'd better pick up the mail myself while she's over there in Europe," Miss Mattie continued, "in case she sends anymore of them naked women French postcards, 'cause Duke brought that one home and studied it all during lunch, and durn if it didn't give him notions."

"Well, I guess we can't have that." I said, trying to rub the amusement off my face.

Mattie wrinkled up her nose, eyes twinkling. "I hid it, but I'll show it to you when you come down for dinner tomorrow night. After Duke has gone home, that is."

"It's a d-d-deal," Alice stammered with some trepidation.

The next night, Alice and I held our breath all through dinner, and true to her word Mattie produced the dreaded French postcard, just as soon as Duke left for the evening, his truck still pulling out of her driveway.

It was a museum card from the Louvre, of Canova's famous sculpture, *The Three Graces*.

Well, the marble women *were* naked ... and voluptuous, for that matter.

And it was a *postcard*. From *France*.

When we later told Justy, she howled with laughter and evermore made it a point to scandalize the postmistress of our little town every time she went to Paris by sending more postcards of naked women—Renoir's *Nude in Sunlight*, Ingres's *La Grande Odalisque*, Manet's *Olympia*.

Mattie is embarrassed by the pranks, but bears it well, provided she alleviates the other concern anyway—Duke with his notions. She made us swear we would tell her when Justy is traveling, particularly abroad, so she can make certain to pick up the mail herself.

She knows she can't stop Justy from teasing her by sending the "French postcards," and no doubt her mail is now the talk of Bluffside (and I think Mattie secretly enjoys the notoriety), but at least she can circumvent the "horny Duke problem" by intercepting them.

On another one of her visits, Justy went with us to Mattie's for dinner, and Duke and Mattie regaled us with the latest local gossip of the courting young people right across the lane from them. The family who lives there has three daughters, and their oldest, a girl of twenty, is dating one of the brothers who owns the local market-slash-hardware store just around the corner.

He's about twenty-eight, hard working, and his family has money. A good catch. The girl works at the store part-time, and often he walks her home the short block after her shift, where they stand outside her gate in the dusk, and talk and kiss and pet. Once in a while, maybe a brief dry hump or two in the twilight.

Meanwhile, in the kitchen window across the street, night after night, Duke and Mattie eat their dinner, forks sometimes poised midair and mouths open, watching the scene through the window like it's a soft-porn movie.

"We keep the kitchen light turned out 'cause we don't want to embarrass them," Mattie confided with a whisper.

Justy laughed till tears streamed, rocking back and forth. Mattie and Duke beamed at her delight, but completely missed the joke. Once Justy had her breath back she burst into the Beatles' song: *"Why don't we do it in the road ...."* An impromptu performance that left Mattie giggling and Duke tee-heeing. Not being up on music more current than Lawrence Welk, they both naively assumed our talented Justy was making the song up on the spot.

DATELINE, 1980—**Ronald Reagan** is elected by a landslide as President of the United States, and Republicans take control of both Houses for the second time in 50 years. **Supreme Court upholds** limits of federal aid for abortion. **Small pox** is eradicated. **John Lennon is shot** dead in New York City. *Dallas* takes #1 over *60 Minutes*. M*A*S*H continues in top Five, and *Love Boat* ranks in at #4.

WHHM Television in Washington, DC becomes the **first African American** public-broadcasting TV station. **Steve McQueen**, film actor, dies in Juarez, Mexico, at age 50.

In California, a class-action suit against Proctor & Gamble for all women injured using the recalled tampon brand Rely, linked to **toxic shock syndrome**. California state officials place the entire Santa Clara Valley **under quarantine** due to a **Mediterranean fruit fly invasion.**

Jesse Owens, the 1936 US Olympic-gold medal winner for track and field dies at age 67. *The Empire Strikes Back* is released and becomes the highest grossing film of the year. Comedian **Richard Pryor** sets himself on fire and nearly dies while freebasing.

philadelphia freedom

Alice and I have now lived in Humboldt Country for fourteen months, and the time just seems right. It is early October 1980, and we are flying to the East Coast, where Alice has never been, and where seven years have passed since I've last been back to see my family in Philadelphia. A lot has happened in that time—the most significant, of course, are the five years Alice and I have been living together as a couple. There has been no great reveal to my family of our relationship, nor do I anticipate one with this trip. They know we live together, and some may draw their own conclusions, and others probably won't give it a thought. I will not back away if asked, but I plan to play it casually and see what happens. And I may not be as calm about this as I would like to be.

We'll be staying with my sister Lynn in South Jersey, across the river from Philly. We'll visit and sightsee and immerse ourselves in the full vibrant display of color that autumn brings, where seasons really do change, that is if the elemental spirits of fall oblige us and if we time it just right. In any event, we will definitely experience the alien country of the East Coast, and the quirky and eccentric natures of a particular group of Easterners that are my family.

K nowing how different the East Coast is from the West, how different small-town life is to big city life, I supply Alice—who has never been east of the Mississippi—with "The Rules," a list of do's, don'ts, and bewares as long as a politician's speech.

Rule: In the Northeast, make only the very briefest of eye contact when passing strangers.

216

Rule: Keep your antenna up, and stay tuned in public at all times.

Rule: For safety in the city, walk with purpose (I know this one will not be easy for her, considering her syncopated limp.) Rule: Remain conscious of the whereabouts of your wallet, purse, etc., and keep bags and packages tucked up under your arm or clutched tightly in your hand.

Rule: The observation of personal space is different on the East Coast. People stand closer than those on the West Coast, though they remain more remote. Remember, elevator behavior originated in the Northeast ... everyone stares straight ahead, faces front, and keeps from touching anybody. This applies to subway behavior, too, where you jostle as the train does, but with restraint, to keep from bouncing off people as much as possible. Bounces and brushes must remain impersonal and unacknowledged—it is threatening if your fellow jostler seems too aware of having touched you, even accidentally.

Rule: Above all, ignore even the slightest bit of rudeness. Anticipate brusque, terse communication from anyone in public service—and from almost everyone else as well. (I envision Alice, in her direct way, grousing and snapping all up and down the East Coast as she encounters what she might interpret as inhospitable, ill-mannered, and belligerent city folk.) Actually, most of this is not rudeness, I tell her. It's more a communication and behavioral style, just very different from other parts of the country. Easterners tend to be more outspoken. They get right to the point, convey displeasure more readily, and seldom mitigate their opinions or complaints with what passes for manners in other parts of the country. What is said, then, often comes off flat and absolute and opinionated and lands with a shock on the sensibilities of people from other areas.

Rule: By contrast, expect more formal manners from people you do know. Count on more conformity to rules, less relaxed hospitality, and much less casual house etiquette. No *Mi casa es su casa* to be found here. No *Y'all come back now, ya here?* And certainly no *Help yourself to anything you see.*

Rule: Ask permission to get a drink of water or to use bathrooms—every time in a passing visit, not just the first time.

And plan to be hosted to death, offered lists of beverages, plied with endless food suggestions. The host who fails to provide what you require is remiss and won't go to heaven. And somehow, *you* will be considered crass should you request what they have failed to anticipate.

I tell Alice about how horrified my mother was that time when she hosted my sister's wedding rehearsal dinner, and a young guest brazenly opened the freezer for more ice. A very serious faux pas on the impolite guest's part, who failed to seek permission to breach the privacy of my mother's freezer. It was a closed door after all, and worse, the guest called attention to my mother's lack of adequately anticipating and providing enough ice. On the East Coast, it is embarrassingly rude to run out of ice (or anything else for that matter), but equally boorish to point it out.[†]

Alice's shitty airplane karma is in full force today. The plane is crowded, stuffy, barely pressurized, and she is fighting throughout the flight her usual battle with the flight attendant just to get a lousy glass of water. Suddenly, while descending for a landing, as if in answer to Alice's ongoing pleas, fluid jets out of a seam in the bulkhead beside her and hits her straight in the head. The flight attendant, answering our summons, merely "tsk-tsks" and mutters something about "condensation" before she scurries away, saying she'll report it. Then a long, steady stream of some unknown liquid arcs out the bulkhead right onto Alice. A passenger in the seat behind her takes pity and shoves his blanket onto her shoulder to help absorb the mystery liquid.

We can only speculate what it is, perhaps a precious fluid vital to remaining airborne has dangerously emptied from some broken thinga-mabob. Or maybe it is some grim effluvia from a plumbing conduit. Only one thing for sure, condensation it is *not*. Not in that volume, not with that force, and not with that persistence and staying power. Something, somewhere is leaking. Badly.

On the ground, we de-plane for a one-hour layover before the next leg of our journey, and Alice collars the stewardess and displays the extent of

---

[†] Or, at least, that's how it is in 1980. Young people everywhere will gradually grow less formal, less well trained in the old manners, less concerned than the old guard. And much of the social grease will be lost in the years to follow.

the soaking she'd suffered. Chagrined, the attendant sees to it that we get our seats changed for the remainder of the trip. But once back in the air, Alice keeps a leery eye on the overhead and interior walls until we land.

Philadelphia turns out to be a delightful surprise. First, in the warm reception my family has given Alice. We've been living together now for five years, yet we certainly aren't "out" to anyone in the family. But my family has immediately fallen in love with Alice, with her wry wit and quiet charm, making her feel very welcome and making me proud.

And second, in the seven-plus years since I've last visited, and in the seventeen years since I last lived here, the changes that have occurred in the city itself are extensive and amazing. Heavy reclamation in the center of town has restored and enhanced Philadelphia's colonial beauty and architecture, jump-started perhaps by the country's bicentennial four years earlier and later the gentrification of some previously pretty scummy areas has made the lovely old historic city look respectable again. The streets and sidewalks are clean and uncluttered, thanks to community service programs that put misdemeanor offenders to work in the city's sanitation regime.

From my sister Lynn's house in New Jersey, where we are staying, the ride on the speedline into Philadelphia, which I'd never used before now, is clean, efficient, and rapid. Along the way, Alice and I enjoy the view of the passing countryside—thoroughly and utterly. It is East Coast scenery at its colorful best, with the maple, oak, and sycamore trees just beginning their autumn turn of russet, yellow, and orange against a backdrop of old, red-brick and gray-stone buildings, all of this laced by mile after mile of black telephone poles and wires.

Alice is unprepared then for the train's sudden dive into a tunnel, traveling under the Delaware River to the other side. I see signs of controlled panic on her face and pat her hand reassuringly, telling her above the shriek of the subway train that everything is all right. The train clatters and lights flash outside the windows in the darkness of the tunnel. Then, just as suddenly as we entered the tunnel, we whoosh into an underground station and come to a smooth stop. People pour out of the train, with Alice and I trickling out last, barely making it through the door ahead of the incoming push of commuters.

We haven't got our city tempo yet. Alice is still shaken from her sudden claustrophobic experience, so we dawdle along, country-slow, into the city bustle.

Before exiting the station, we stop to puzzle out a curious oddity: a bill changer machine. We push in a dollar bill, which is sucked up instantly into a currency slot built right into a wall, and out drop coins, the exact change, into a metal cup. We then feed the coins for the exact fare into another machine in the wall and press the appropriate buttons to select the destination. And a ticket tongues out of the wall and into our hands.

Amazing! Walls that take bills and give coins and tickets!

Such marvels would become commonplace in a year or so in similar machines, even in remote areas like our little Humboldt County. ATM's would appear everywhere, but for now, this is a new and wondrous experience, and our first encounter with this aspect of progress.

All this juxtaposed against the stale subway smells of dampness, urine, dirt, people, ozone, and electricity, a scent curiously evocative for me. But I see Alice's nose crinkle and know she is right now filing this new and vile aroma in her olfactory memory as "subway."

We emerge from the underground into the gray light of the city, beneath the upward swoop of skyscrapers. Moving sideways at the top of the stairs, enough to let the mass of people behind us go by, Alice and I gawk like a couple of corn-fed yokels.

Conservatively dressed businessmen walk the downtown streets in suits, ties, and shiny leather shoes; women in career suits, dark hose, and tennis shoes (their high heels carried in totes.) The din of traffic and voices, motion, sound, stink, and crush—all the features of cosmopolitan life. And people carrying ... *things*! In contrast to California, where people dress significantly more casual and rarely walk, never missing an opportunity to sheath themselves with the metal casing of an automobile, here in my birth city, people seem oddly vulnerable, striding along with arms, shoulders, and hands burdened with bags, newspapers, umbrellas, parcels, books, radios, clothing, babies.

"'Scuse me, lady. Can you spare a cigarette?" asks a young man with stringy hair and torn khakis, beaming disarmingly at Alice. And before I can stop her, Alice pulls a pack of Marlboros out of her pocket and shakes a ciggie out at him.

"Thank ya, lady, 'n bless ya. 'Av ya got a match?" He studies her surreptitiously, gauging how far he can push this. His gap-toothed grin widens.

"Umm. Umm." He puffs on the light she gives him. "You bin so kind, can I ... could ya ... have ya got any change ya can spare?"

As I tug on her sleeve, Alice dips her hand into her pocket and pulls out the coins the subway wall had given her and drops it into his dirty hand.

"Come on." I tug her away just as I catch the avaricious gleam in the eyes of four or five other nearby panhandlers about to converge on her. I have a vision of them cutting her away as easy as cattle horses cull out a branding calf and not letting her go till she is stripped of everything on her person.

"Don't do that!" I reprimand. "Alice, I can't believe it! Your first ten seconds in the city and already marked as a 'touch' by the street people. You gotta guard yourself and get tough, or we'll never get out of here alive!"

She smiles rather vacantly at my over-reaction, her eyes and attention torn involuntarily from me by the constant kinetic flow around us.

"I'm flat serious now," I warn. "Just say, 'No, sorry, sorry' when they approach you, and above all keep moving. Don't stop!"

My city paranoia is operating at high gear, knowing now that I need to be vigilant for us both, to protect myself and an unheeding Alice from all the city vices and evils I have half forgotten.

In 1980, the homeless in the streets live mostly within urban areas. Sadly, it will take only a few years until this shame spreads throughout the nation in city, town, and hamlet, pretty much beginning with Reagan's reduction of social welfare funding, especially the closing nationwide of most inpatient mental facilities. My guard is down after too many years of country ease and small-town safety. But right now I am as taut as a cello string and hyper-alert in overcompensation.

We are rubes, all right ... hayseeds, out of our element, babes in the woods, innocents abroad, lambs at the slaughter, marks, and (only a matter of time) hapless victims, unless I take great care.

Coming to this huge habitation, we'd left a total population of just seven hundred in our immediate town, ten thousand in the town three miles away, and another twenty-six thousand souls residing in the big town of Eureka thirty minutes north. Our entire county boasts a mere one hundred nineteen thousand citizens, in nearly the same amount of land as half the size of New Hampshire, twice the size of Delaware, or three and a half times the size of Rhode Island.

Now here we are in a city of 4.5 million … most of them evidently right here on Market Street with us.

A perfect opportunity for Alice to test the Don't-Make-Eye-Contact rule. As we walk south, then west on Walnut Street, she directly focuses her eyes and full attention on oncoming people. They walk toward her and quickly dart across the street, edge far around her, or shoot back hostile stares as they pass her. Alice locks her eyes on theirs as she conducts her experiment, and of course, they feel challenged, threatened, or anxious by the frankness of her gaze; they correspondingly bristle, shy, or flee.

This truly amuses Alice! It is true then, the no eye-contact rule!

She has proven it by empirical study and the evidence is in. The scientific researcher in her is already considering the next investigation in the lineup. I begin to regret the list of rules I have drummed into her. This already promises to be a long trip.

We do the usual sights of Colonial Philadelphia—Betsy Ross House (Alice loves the fountain out front with the bronze cats circling around it, very lifelike in their poses), the Philadelphia Museum of Art, Independence Hall, Carpenter's Hall, and the anachronistic Ben Franklin "home."

Franklin's original dwelling has not survived the passage of time. So the city has, with no accurate drawings or paintings to work from, erected on the actual site shiny aluminum girders to delineate the frame and mark the elevation of the second-story roofline of the historic structure that once stood there. Happily, Franklin's print shop, along with the nation's first post office still stands and can be visited. But of his house, only this skeletal metal shell. Cleverly effective.

Alice became very distressed about the setup for the Liberty Bell. This is all new since I had left the city to live elsewhere. Back then, the Liberty Bell was still housed in Independence Hall, but with the revamping of the downtown area, a special building had been built to display just the Bell, out in the new concourse area.

Our attention is drawn to a recorded message broadcast inside the new glass building that now houses the Liberty Bell. Not sure if it is malfunctioning, or perhaps there is a setting somewhere, but we can't seem to locate any such thing, so the recording continues to loop through four foreign languages before Alice gives up in disgust. We move on, never hearing the speech in our own native English.

Not to deprive any foreign visitor of the experience of knowing about one of our country's favorite symbols, but clearly this is not the way to go about it. There should be separate headphones, with a selection board for the language of choice. Alice's opinion is that English is the official language of the land, and therefore English is what should be coming through the loudspeakers.

But she gets over her snit soon enough with a tour of Christ Church and the adjacent graveyard with its fascinating and poignant grave markers, many dating back to the 1600s. We amble through the lovely churchyard reading epitaphs and marveling at how the simple carved words connect us to people who lived and breathed in this city so long ago.

Next, we tour the wonderland that is the old Wanamaker's Department Store, which proves to be one of the highlights of our trip, with its open atrium situated at its center and the daily concerts performed from a pipe organ several floors up. The store, immortalized in several vintage movies, will cease to exist come the dawn of the twenty-first century, though the building still stands. But for now, we relish another great American pastime: shopping, as it was done in its large department store glory days.

Here, Alice, the investigative (and mischievous) spirit that she is, decides to test out elevator behavior, too. By shifting closer and closer to a woman in the store's elevator, Alice makes the poor thing so uncomfortable that she backs off clear to the wall. And when Alice turns to her, makes eye contact and nods to her, the woman becomes twittery and jumpy and hastily gets off at the next floor, pushing out past Alice.

"Alice, stop it," I plead.

"What?"

"Just cut it out. Promise me you won't go testing all the rules, or you'll get us in some real trouble. Or alienate my family if you go flouting the conventions I've told you about. Now, promise!"

is it sisters?

"Okay," she says, petulantly, digging the toe of her shoe into the department store carpet.

"Now, I mean it!"

"O-KAY!"

I mean, jeesh … sometimes!

On another day, Dad tags along with us. He's an amateur historian and a proud Philadelphian, and enjoys filling Alice in on the historic significance of the landmark sites we are visiting.

They stroll ahead of me at the entrance to the famously photographed Elfreth's Alley, the city's oldest, continuously occupied residential street since colonial times. I snap a great shot of the two of them, walking ahead of me, side by side. It will become one of my favorite pictures.

We ride the subway once again, much to Alice's reluctance, but it's the quickest way to get to where we are heading: the Franklin Institute, which houses a mechanical museum complete with a walk-through human heart (so massive it occupies two floors) and a full-sized, 350-ton, coal-fired, steam locomotive running *indoors* on tracks.

The subway to the Institute rumbles and sways, hisses and squeals, and, at every curve, screeches that particular metallic scream that only subway trains can do. We look out windows filled with the blackness of subterranean depths, interrupted by the flash of tunnel lights as we streak past.

And then it happens: the lights in our car blink off and on, once, and a minute later, again. Alice's steel grip on a nearby seat handle betrays her anxiety, and as the lights flicker off and on a third time, her knuckles turn bone white.

"W-what is it?" she asks.

"What's what?"

"There it is again. What's happening?" Her voice rises in panic.

"Oh," says my father. "Well, you see, as the cars ride over the inter-connections of alternate tracks, where the tracks can be switched to go in new directions, it causes a momentary break in the electrical contact ..."

He's off on one of his pedantic discourses, this time explaining the minute functional intricacies of a modern-day subway system, but stops in mid-sentence when he turns in Alice's direction and sees that she is pale and trembling, eyes darting, sweat broken out on her upper lip.

"Alice? ... Alice?"

She turns her panicked eyes on him.

"There's nothing wrong. Everything's all right. Don't be alarmed. It's normal for the lights to go off and on like that."

She tries to relax as she registers his assurances. But she is visibly relieved by the time we get off one stop later and head out of this glorified, underground mole burrow and up into daylight.

We spend yet another day with my father out in the Dutch Country. This time, we borrow my sister's car, giving Alice the opportunity to drive the picturesque countryside dotted with patchwork fields of beans, oats, corn, and other feed and money crops.

We are lucky to see quite a few horse-drawn, black buggies—sporting incongruous rear license plates and dangling reflectors—as we drive through the Amish settlements of Bird-in-Hand, Intercourse, Blue Ball, as well as a few others with less suggestive names.

In the fields, we witness bearded Amish and Mennonite farmers wearing their traditional flat black hats. With leather horse reins draped over their shoulders, they drive teams of workhorses and mules pulling harvesters and threshers in the un-mechanized farming methods of yesteryear, setting them apart from "the English" neighboring farms—modern, motorized, and equipment-rich. Amish and Mennonite children in plain garb—blue dresses for the girls under full black aprons, black stockinged, and soft black caps covering their hair and the boys wearing blue band-collared shirts, black pants with suspenders, straight-cut black coats without lapels, and black hats. The youngsters walk the country roads coming home from their study classes.

Then we see the most amazing sight: a horse-drawn, black buggy pulled up to a drive-in teller window at a local bank, itself a square, redbrick building with a carport overhang. A long shot of this paradoxical scene would not infringe on the privacy of the typically camera-shy Mennonite farmer since its focus would not have been personal. It would instead have juxtaposed two contrasting symbols. It is a delightful image, and alas, a missed photo opportunity that I will have to re-visit only in the memory of it.

The fields are redolent with cow and horse dung, perfume to my nose after subway and car exhaust. It is indeed a glorious day, made all the more so when we stop to eat at a marvelous Pennsylvania Dutch restaurant that serves the superb, hearty, plain foods of the area in generous family style.

The broad, plank table is laden with ham, stewed chicken, corn, snap beans, potatoes, and, of course, the seven sweets and seven sours historically served at the typical local's dinner. Pepper hash (a peppery vinegar slaw of finely chopped cabbage), chow-chow and piccalilli (relishes), bread-and-butter pickles and dills, apple butter (a thick apple sauce, brown with cinnamon and spices), oxford beets (a heated, sweet, pickled beet in a thickened sauce), and spiced apple rings ... that sort of thing.

We pass the food around with the others sitting at our table, perfect strangers sharing in the repast. Desserts include stewed mixed fruit, bread pudding with raisins, and shoofly pie (a molasses pie with a crumb topping), along with plentiful hot, aromatic coffee.

We thoroughly enjoy our meal, and it is a pleasure to watch my father "set to" with a trencherman's appetite. He says it's been years since he's been in the Dutch Country and tasted the area's particular delicacies.

As we leave the restaurant afterward, Alice is especially enchanted by an elaborate birdhouse, a Purple Martin birdhouse to be exact, situated on a sturdy pole outside the restaurant. It is a veritable multi-storied, apartment compound for the sociable and very beneficial North American swallows that call it home.

At a local flea market we delight in the special character of things found on this coast: painted Toleware, Dutch crafts and manufacture, various handwork and quilts, pot holders and aprons and bonnets. Dad finds a print of an old steam engine and buys it to put in his office at the admissions office of Children's Hospital in Philadelphia, where he has worked for almost thirty years.

On the way home, as Alice drives us down the four-lane highway, I am once again treated to an example of my father's renowned indecisiveness.

"Dad, what road do we need to take to get back?"

"Well, we can take the 322 till it runs into Highway 202, or we can take 340, which is the Old Philadelphia Pike over to Highway 30 and come in on that, or…"

"Dad!" We are in traffic and swiftly sailing along past whatever turnoffs might eventually get us home.

"Well, if you care to, we could drop down and take the 3, which brings you into Philadelphia a bit lower down than—"

"Dad! Right now! Which road?!" I speak sharply, angrily. I know if I don't pin him down, we'll wind up driving clean off into some other state.

"Oh, sorry, I forget. Let's see where are we, now? Did we just pass Highway 340?"

"Yes!"

"Oh, well we probably should have taken that."

We backtrack and get on the right road, and though everything seems okay after my outburst, I'm feeling sorry that I spoke so impatiently to him. It wouldn't have killed me to apologize to him, but I don't and I'll later wish I had.

❈

We split up our two-week trip by renting a car, leaving Philadelphia and New Jersey, and driving up through New England for the changing of the fall colors and to fulfill Alice's long-held desire to see Cape Cod. We figure this is a great way to manage our trip, give my family a break, and allow everyone to resume a normal life for three or four days before we impose on them again. And it gives us time alone to regroup and assimilate some of our experiences before we continue on to the next leg of our journey.

new england in leaf

Heading up to Cape Cod, we drive the scenic route much of the way, sticking to the road that parallels the Delaware River. The leaves haven't turned yet. It's October 19th, and I'm panicked, despairing that we have traveled so far, all the way back East for Alice's one trip of a lifetime, and here we are—too damned early for the changing of the colors. I'll just have to open a vein if she misses it.

Nevertheless, the rolling eastern Pennsylvania countryside stuns with its wet, green, and shiny beauty. A look decidedly darker than the golden appearance of California, punctuating the fact that the East Coast lies farther from the sun as we orbit. The landscape's muted wash has much to do with this different quality of light as well as the density of the wooded country. Maybe the darker tones of the land owe some of its character to the underlying slate and granite, as if the bedrock informs coloration to the soil and on into the foliage and tree trunks. The outcroppings of rock are many, black and glittery, streaked of orange iron oxide, overall affording an impression of subdued gray, umber, and emerald green.

We drive the winding road in and out of quaint towns and villages occupied by storefronts, inns, and homes of colonial shape and heritage, nearly all built well before 1950, and many others two hundred years older than that. Houses of brick and native stone, where wood serves only as ornamentation of shutter and porch. And everywhere coach lanterns, hitching posts, and marble stoops.

The Delaware Water Gap (where the Delaware River cuts through a large ridge of the Appalachian Mountains) displays the water here much cleaner than at its harbored mouth, flowing below us in a deep, brushy, tree-filled gorge. A far cry from the wide, industrial river it becomes just a hundred miles beyond. It is little wonder this very spot inspired the likes of Elizabeth F. Ellet, the first writer to record the lives of women during the American Revolutionary War, to pen "this wild scene, resolved that none but Heaven shall look upon its beauty."

Then, quick as a minute, we enter the state of New York, and here the rolling hills begin at last to show the colors of fall—maybe we aren't too early after all.

Alice can't get over the rapidity with which we left one state and entered another, a remarkable surprise for a native West Coaster who all her life is used to traveling up road and down, back and forth, hour upon hour without ever once leaving the state.

The trip from Los Angeles to our home in Humboldt County, for example, is 700 miles and takes twelve hours of fairly non-stop driving to navigate, provided one only breaks off for pit-and-potty stops and dines on the go from packed ice-chest lunches. And there's still plenty of California on both ends. Top to bottom, California is nearly 900 miles long traveling the fastest, flattest inland highway I-5 through the fertile San Joaquin Valley. That trip makes for a seventeen-hour intensive drive, and much longer should you decide to take the scenic route, navigating winding mountain roads and the serpentine Pacific Coast Highway.

The same distance on the East Coast would take you from New York to Atlanta, and you'd cross maybe nine state lines in the process. (Similarly, the length of California is almost the distance from Chicago to Dallas. And against our biggest mainland state, it's also about the same distance from Port Arthur to El Paso—Texas itself as wide as California is long.)

In two hours of driving the Eastern Coast states, you can easily cross at least one state line. And you'll feel, in much of the Northeast, that you're almost always within civilization, each vista boasting at least one house, barn, or church steeple. Notice the density of place names on a map of the East compared to the West and this becomes evident.

Never the open break of Montana, the sky like an overturned bowl about you, or the flat prairie grasslands of Kansas, which are not so damned flat when you actually navigate them. Never the rocky jutting of the Utah Redlands, with their backdrop of purple mountains' majesty;

never the scrub, wind-scarred expanse of west Texas, the rounded golden hills of California's canyon country, or the reaching redwood forested northland of our home.

Much of the East is a civilized land, a long inhabited country, a world tamed. Not the cultivated, cobbled feel of Europe or Britain, not so claimed or conquered; this is still the New World, after all. Oh, there's wilderness left to it yet, for sure, amid the orchards and rolling pastures, and planted squares of winter rye. Those great mountain ridges, which roughly seam the East's north to its south, form a rugged backbone and are vast and formidable. There are still many places unpopulated within these mountains, areas of pristine undergrowth and thicket; woods of pines, balsam, hemlock, and spruce; antique stands of hardwood trees: various oaks, hickories, maples, ash, elm, cherry, walnut, birch, sycamore and beech, concealing sequestered brooks or springs; places where the pixies may not be routed out, nor fairies yet gone to ground.

My friend Sonny once remarked on his first trip to the East Coast how shocked he was to find so many trees here, under the impression that the Eastern states timbered off the trees a hundred years ago, nothing left but cleared farms and concrete. Even more, he was astounded to find large refuges of trees *inside* the cities, having seen in films and photographs only urban views of block, glass, and steel skylines, and none of the woodsy, urban environs or harvestable timberlands of the whole countryside that lies beyond the cities.

Our misperceptions are largely dictated by movies and TV. People on the Pacific may think of the coastal cities of the east as vast concrete wastelands of wall-to-wall buildings, save for a few gap-toothed breaks filled with the rubble of demolished tenements. Likewise, people on the Atlantic Coast are sometimes guilty of assuming all Californians live on convoluted ribbons of highways (when they don't have skateboards attached to their heels and surfboards under their arms.)

In Upper New York we find exactly what I've been dying to show Alice on this trip, and all through Vermont and New Hampshire it continues—*the color*. I've often tried to describe this experience, but words alone are hopelessly inadequate. The colors captivate Alice. Me, too. We pause and pull over time after time. And she glories in it—leaves in full array of maroon, scarlet, magenta, trees of orange, sienna, russet, gold, yellow … and green, too. There is nothing like witnessing this firsthand. Film is simply incapable of capturing this gift of glory—a feast of the senses—before the gray-white winter. The smell of cold in the air fills our noses, odors of wood fires in hearths, and leaf mold, wet, cold-rotting vegetation (not that funky, soggy, tropical smell of warmer climes.) Even an occasional whiff of burning leaves in outlying places, where that is still permitted.

In Massachusetts, we drive a long stretch of the Cape before turning back to find a place to stay the night, eventually deciding on a room at a Ramada Inn and promising ourselves to do the whole Cape the next day. But for now, we seek rest and sustenance.

The temperature has sunk merely to the low-fifties outside, mind you, but these East Coasters go about their business covered in worsteds and woolens, in cashmeres and angora, in thermals and ragg, in all the dark colors of a dying forest; whites and pastels packed in moth flakes immediately following Labor Day, and not resurrected till Memorial Day. All the colors at the close of the year—drabs, navy, brown, hunter greens, grays, and black, much often expressed in mixtures of tartan, herringbone, and tweed. It's fashion finger crossing, a haberdashery amulet against the killing cold to come.

This time of year, pilot lights are lit, gas is turned on, heaters are filled with newly delivered oil, and thermostats are set. Heat arrives smelling of six months of accumulated dust and long-sitting condensation in pipes. This is all done by the calendar, with total disregard for actual weather conditions. Subsequently, by October 1st, every house, restaurant, hotel, and office is heated and heated and heated—as if to get a jump on it, laying up warmth enough to forestall the coming cold, the feared freeze. As if the tundra were at the doorstep, and the snow load even now creaking the attic joists. As if the permafrost has already crept right up to the hay-mulched roses on its hoary toes. Verily, these people heat their indoors with a vengeance.

In every home forced air heat crawls up the walls and blankets the ceilings like smoke, so each time you stand up, the hot air fills your ears and nose and mouth like cotton batting, suffocating, making the survivor in you want to drop to the cooler floor and crawl out to the safety of the clean, open air.

So on this perfectly tolerable fall evening of forty-eight degrees, storm windows are latched, storms doors installed, the heat blasting. And Alice and I are dying.

We drop our suitcases on the beds in our room. It screams "generic American motel anywhere in the country": clean, tidy, boringly nondescript. We draw open the drapes, find the window latches, release the catches to open the casements, and let in the air—clean, cool, second-story, Cape Cod air. The unbroken sea air breezes across the dunes, the treetops, the roofs and smoky chimneys, absorbing their flavors, and wafting delectably into our stuffy little room. We drink it in like draughts of ale. Smoky, salty, fresh, and deliciously cool. Behind us, the drapes luff like sails into the middle of the room. Divine!

Alice reaches for me then, as I do her, and we stand in the cooling breezes and hug each other, rocking quietly, reveling in the solid comfort of each other, just hugging and caressing. Here we actually are … in old Cape Cod. Patti Page's warm voice singing, on the jukebox that plays in my head, that signature song's first line: *If you're fond of sand dunes and salty air ….*

"Hungry?" Alice asks, still clutched in our embrace.

"Starving."

"Me, too," she says, breaking away at last. So, with the nippy air breezing through the curtains, flapping like flags, I snatch up my purse and a jacket and leave with Alice to hunt up some dinner.

We find a popular eatery with passable food, served on plank tables surrounded by captain's chairs; a restaurant whose most salient feature is an open fireplace large enough to roast a moose in, which is, of course, blazing—blasting heat out into a room already over eighty degrees. Grates in the floors and ceilings discharge gas-heated air as well. I shed my jacket immediately upon entering.

After dinner, we ride back to the motel with car windows open, hair tossing about our heads in glorious cool abandon. Back at our room, Alice turns the key in the lock, opens the door and stops, steps back in the hall, and double checks the number on the door. She then moves cautiously into the room, hesitating. Tense. Looking all around.

"What's wrong?" I ask anxiously, following close behind.

She doesn't answer as she continues her check of the room, darting to the bags on the beds, opening, looking in, and satisfying herself that everything is intact. By now I've caught up with her and begin searching, too, for signs of theft, breaking and entering, intruders. In our absence, the windows *have been closed*. They are now latched, drapes primly drawn, radiator going full blast, the layers of heat in the room brushing our knees, neck, faces.

Either there has been a cold-sensitive would-be-thief with fingers too chilblained by the room's raw air to properly rob us, or … I could hear it now, how it must have happened:

"Desk clerk, there's something wrong with the heat up here on the second floor. Cold air is whooshing down the hall chilling me to the bone. I had to stuff my pillow under the door against the draft. Please come up and see if somebody punched a hole in a wall or something."

Then would have followed a systematic search for the source of the unleashed, impertinent air. The bellboy must have fought his way up the open hall, coming to our room—the room of the fresh-air freaks—and after plowing through a wall of wind, grabbed onto a snapping, twisting curtain tail, found the window crank and shut it, deafened by the sudden silence. Windows re-bolted, heater reset to top speed and temperature. Thermal sanctity restored.

Probably happened like that.

The next day, we drive up the Cape, admiring the area's cottages and homes, so distinctive they set their own architectural style—low square frames, steep pitched roofs, central chimneys, and front doors flanked by shuttered windows and dormers—looking like they've been painted into the landscape, so perfectly do they reside here. The Cape is comprised of fifteen separate towns and the two islands of Martha's Vineyard and Nantucket, each possessing its own unique character. Dunes are famous along the whole of the Cape, and we content ourselves with what can be seen by car, since Alice's fused ankle dictates that she can't walk well in sand. We stop at cranberry bogs aglow with a color that—like the changing of the leaves—can *never* truly be duplicated on film. It is simply not reproducible. The bogs are flooded this time of year, magenta crops of cranberries soon to be harvested floating on the water, a surface of geometric square ponds of berries in that jewel of a hue I always think of as "blue blood."

In Provincetown, we dine on lobster rolls, made up of chunked lobster meat in a buttery sauce that is ladled generously onto freshly baked dinner rolls the size of hamburger buns. Afterwards, we stroll away the afternoon, ambling though the narrow streets, empty now of all but the bravest winter-hardy tourists, not afraid to chance the temperatures rapidly falling into the low-fifties and high-forties (*brrrr!*). We wander in and out of myriad shops not yet closed for the season, admiring this East Coast art colony and noting the distinctions from similar shops and galleries back home in California.

We find galleries filled with paintings and photos of the Atlantic in its many moods, a more capricious and dramatic ocean than the Pacific, its colors grayer, greener, blacker, stormier. Even the smell of the Atlantic differs, a bitter beneath the tang, a tinny-ness to the salt. Pacific lobster is no match whatsoever for the Maine variety in size, let alone taste. Likewise, the oysters are milder in the West and the clams clammier in the East. But you can't get better crab than those pulled out of the Pacific. I find it fascinating, the sometimes indefinable chemistry that affects the taste of things, whether seafood from various oceans or crops grown in different soils.

Later, we head back by way of Plymouth to see the area's famous namesake rock. Big mistake! Alice is once again incensed, this time because the national treasure must be protected against vandals, souvenir-seekers, and defacement. The iron gratings that surrounds the Roman Doric portico that houses Plymouth Rock—which is no bigger than a common chest of drawers—may permit a view of the historic landmark, but denies access. Plymouth Rock had once been much larger, we were told, but years of people chipping away at it had reduced it to its present size. The rock is no more than a legend anyway, but still, it is the principle of the thing.

And then there is the issue of the nearby statues. Alice is miffed all over again with such depictions as a looming Pilgrim father in his buckled shoes and square collar and very large, distinctive hat, juxtaposed against the "Red Man," lowly and less than life-sized. "Typical!" she says, disgusted.

So much for historic sites. I'm not exactly batting a thousand with them. So far, Alice is more impressed with the cemeteries and the bronze cats at the fountain outside the Betsy Ross House than most anything representational of Colonial American history.

But she does love New England. Loves the huge stands of maples and the tales of abundant winter sugaring. Loves the coastal towns that have managed to maintain enough of the original nineteenth-century characteristics indicative of whaling and tall ships and the seagoing trade that she'd only read about in books—all now made real. Loves the sights and sounds, smells and textures in this country, home of Alcott's *Little Woman*'s irrepressible and intrepid Jo March, and Hawthorne's enduring Hester Prynne of *The Scarlet Letter* (whom John Updike called an epitome of female predicaments), and Melville's tortured and obsessed Ahab in his dark pursuit of the white whale, *Moby Dick.* New Englanders, all. Not to mention the historical figures of Pocahontas, Paul Revere, Henry Hudson, and Cotton Mather, and the poets, Emily Dickinson, Amy Lowell, and Robert Frost. All of these characters—fictional and real—are recast in the actual settings for Alice. I love seeing her make all these connections.

We readers carry so much of the world envisioned in books inside our own heads, unaware of their impression on us till we see firsthand their homelands. When that happens, there is often a great joy in discovering the reality that has already been so precisely drawn in our minds. We are able to visit the actual places underscored by the descriptions and lives of generations of people, once written and now made real. This evocative richness is a special pleasure for the literate traveler.

The days pass all too fast, and time approaches to hit the road again, back to New Jersey, Philadelphia, and my family. Our mid-afternoon departure down the Massachusetts Turnpike will have us pulling in very late to my sister's place in South Jersey.

Toll roads and turnpikes are an unsettling and disturbing experience for Alice, what with their endless sterile miles absent of gas stations, billboards, rest areas, inns, motels, and truck stops. Instead there are inbound and outbound tickets, tollbooths, and charges ... fees ... COST! The true meaning of "freeway" strikes her like a thunderclap. Gives her a new appreciation for the wild and woolly roads of the West and all their clutter, broad expanses, reckless comings and goings ... freewheeling and truly "free" ways.

After an hour's drive, we exit at a Howard Johnson's for coffee and a bite. Here, we find a little dog standing on the walkway to the restaurant. He is a mixed breed, reminiscent of Benji, with a gray and brown coat, layered in orange clay, dirt, and road grime. The poor thing is drenched from the steady drizzle of rain from the last hour.

After questioning the waitress in the diner about him, we learn he's been abandoned on the highway—as many dogs and cats are—by people who, we can only hope, will spend eternity in a special ring of Hell for their callous and cruel transgression.

We put the little dog in the car and take him with us, planning to find a home for him after we get back to my sister's in New Jersey. But by the time we pull into her driveway late at night, we are madly in love with him, and start making arrangements to fly him home with us.

Ludlow (named after the Massachusetts town where we found him) is about to begin a new life adventure as a California pooch—an immigrant, like so many of us in the golden land of milk and honey. But first, another week in Philadelphia.

family matters

Today we visit my mother, who lives alone in a comfortable two-bedroom apartment. She and my father are separated again, since about a year ago. They were married for fifteen years, then separated for fifteen years, then due to health issues cohabitated for about six years after that. But old bitterness and resentments resurrected, especially on Mother's part, and they are split once again. My sisters and I take pains not to add any fuel to the fire.

Mother has multiple health problems; she contracted spinal meningitis when she was forty-five and spent more than two weeks in a coma—survived it, but was left with profound deafness due to nerve damage. Then two years after that, she suffered a massive heart attack. But with a history of mental illness, she has always been a difficult person: her infirmities merely serve to ramp that aspect of her personality up a notch. She refuses to learn sign language, and the hearing aides that augment her hearing do little more than amplify the non-specific jumble of sound she is barely able to detect.

As a result, although she owns a phone, she finds it too distressing to answer, not knowing who is on the other end without a protracted guessing game. Mind you, this is a couple decades before LCD screens and caller ID, so Mother uses the phone only for outgoing calls in which the person called must listen to one of her hour-long harangues while contributing little. And she refuses to give out her phone number to anyone—not even to any of us, her own family. But her deafness isn't the only reason she does this. Even aging and in poor health, she manages to control and manipulate the whole family. Well done!

Mother and I have a long history of dissention and struggle. Naturally, I am anxious about this visit, seeing her for the first time in seven years. In the seventeen years since I'd left for good, I've kept my visits few and far between. Our exchanged letters and her one-way monthly phone calls kept us in touch, but my exile had been deliberate; my long-ago departure was in fact an act of rebellion and declaration of independence.

Still, for women (and sometimes men), "mother" is our primary relationship. Nothing matches her—not lover, husband, sibling, or child—in significance and influence. Until we reconcile, remedy, redress, and forgive our mother for any wrongs (and perhaps she forgives us), we are never truly grown up, never completely become our own person.

And in this separating, we come to see her in her human form instead of the archetype, the power figure. We see her as a woman going through life just like us, with all the fears and doubts, joys, passions, sorrows, insecurities, triumphs, stupidity, and radiance inherent in ourselves. She's just twenty years or so ahead of us on the Great Conveyor Belt of Life. By often-painful process, we come to recognize her impact on us, realize how much of ourselves we owe to her, how very like her we are. (God help us!) And finally, in light of this distilled truth, we come to understand how we are very different, too. We must acknowledge all this to ourselves, even if we do not—or cannot—admit it to her.

So today, I consider that I'm past all that, believing myself to be in power of my own life, out from under my mother's sway at my advanced age of thirty-nine, only twenty years behind my fifty-nine-year-old mother. But then again, I haven't yet seen her.

Plus, this is the first time that she'll be meeting Alice.

And we—my sister Lynn, Alice, and I—arrive late, late, late. We ran into unexpected road conditions creating a traffic jam at the bridge to Philadelphia, and because of our mother's phone situation, were unable to call her.

Lynn is beside herself with anxiety, knowing how such a thing can set our mother off on a diatribe. "She's going to be so upset, and she'll probably make a scene about it. Alice, you should be prepared. There's no telling how she can be when things like this happen. Sometimes she launches into a tirade for hours about it."

"Don't worry. I can handle it." Alice says. And I knew she could. She could always handle anything and often de-fused a situation in her quiet humorous way.

However, all these factors add to my growing tension. And sure enough, there's Mother sitting in the window, her forehead furrowed with worry and agitation.

Suddenly, my heart goes out to her. I know her concern is genuine for her four daughters and their welfare—for me the oldest, for Lynn, Ann, and Mae as well. I see her afresh, as a small, aging woman in poor health and coping as best she can with life.

In this moment, all my fears evaporate, all my doubts about my ability to deal with her dissolve. I am now in full realization of the truth of it. I really *am* my own person in control of my own destiny. Yes, this woman is my mother, but she exerts no supernatural power over me ... and I love her.

When she recognizes us in the car, her worry turns to genuine joy, and I greet her with a kiss and warm hug as I had never done, not since I was a little girl. She holds me close and returns the warmth, tears springing up in both our eyes.

Mother greets Lynn affectionately, too, and I introduce Alice. For her part, Alice manages to charm my mother in an instant. Well, she has a bit of help with that.

Catching Mother's eye, she speaks very slowly and distinctly to allow for my mother's deafness. "I want you to meet your granddog."

"My *what*? What did you say?"

"Your granddog." And with that, Alice gently tugs Ludlow forward on his leash. Up until this moment, he was completely unnoticed in the turmoil, quietly content to stand behind Alice in his naturally unassuming way. This orphan dog we found on a Massachusetts highway has made a total transformation after being thrice bathed and primped to a fare-thee well.

Our new little doggie shines those round, brown eyes up at my mother, and, in a flash, she is done in. Positively magical in this moment, the mutt is like a Disney character emitting sparkly stars all around and invoking gooey, sentimental music out of nowhere. Well, he captivated me from the get-go, didn't he? Enough to want to fly him 3,000 miles home to California with us.

"Oh, my! Oh, my, my. How sweet! Whose dog is he? What did you say, again?" she asks Alice.

Alice once more repeats for her, "Meet your granddog."

"Grand ... dog?" My mother is starting to bubble up as she finally gets it. "Did you say my granddog?" And she is off—laughing so hard, I catch her arm as she staggers with mirth. When she subsides and catches her breath, Mother leans over and pets Ludlow's head. "I've never had a granddog before, little boy. You can come and sit right by me."

Beaming, Mother pulls Alice to her in a quick hug, and, with that, accepts her into the fold. Alice has met and conquered my mother with one sentence (though oft repeated), relieved the tension due to our lateness, and gained total acceptance on the wave of a laugh. The woman I love is every bit as beguiling as any granddog.

While Lynn puts the coffee on, we all sit around the dining table—my mother's throne room. In Mother's house, I don't recall a party ever held anywhere but here. The dinner table is the center of all entertainment, all hospitality. I remember all those occasions of Mother holding court at table and, growing up, Lynn and I were the serving wenches, scullery maids, and (by our lights) Cinderellas—always in the kitchen, never at the ball.

We laugh about it now, but we both felt very put-upon in our teens. And we weren't silent about it then, either, after the company had gone. Mother put up with a lot of guff from us.

"I remember you telling me, Nancy, that you and Alice have a traditional Christmas dinner of oyster stew and baloney sandwiches," Mother says. "I always thought that was so original."

"Well, it happened on our first Christmas that we were living together. I had a hankering for oyster stew, and I was stubbornly insistent about not cooking a huge Christmas Day dinner. You can always do that on the following weekend."

Alice chimes in: "Christmas Day is a time to play with all your new books and toys, not slave in a kitchen. You should spend all day in your warm jammies, along with a roaring fire and a snifter of brandy and faithful dog by your side."

Bear in mind every statement has to be repeated at least once for Mother to hear it. It wears on everyone's nerves, Mother's included, even in convivial circumstances.

"And the baloney sandwiches," I continue, "were just 'cause that's all we happened to have in the house. So it became custom after that."

"Well, in your honor, and since we won't be able to spend Christmas together, I planned your traditional Christmas as our lunch. Today we're having oyster stew and baloney sandwiches," as she leads me into the kitchen to assemble the lunch.

Alice and I genuinely appreciate her thoughtfulness, and the stew is excellent, made with Chesapeake oysters and cream. "I always use the oyster liquor and real butter," Mother tells me, stirring the fragrant stew. "And I bring the cream just barely to a boil, even though you're not supposed to, because it curdles ever so slightly and thickens it. I like it that way."

To go with it, Mother sets out some Trenton Oyster Crackers, a small round hardtack cracker, which you crumble up in your palms like walnuts and drop in the soup. They are hard as walnuts, too, and unlike the usual crackers that grow soggy immediately, they maintain their crunch and give real body to the stew. The best!

And, true to her word, our chowder and crackers come accompanied by a pile of baloney sandwiches stacked on a cut glass serving plate. And here is where I notice another difference between the two coasts. Cold cuts east of the Mississippi taste totally different. Do different meat packers supply the Eastern states than the Western? The baloney is noticeably tastier here somehow, and we have it with white American cheese slices on good, fresh, white bread, with mayo, mustard, and lettuce. Very WASP. Very East Coast. Very Merry Christmas!

For our final weekend here, Lynn invites the remaining family members to her house for a group visit. Dad is present, and so are my youngest sister Mae and her husband Joe, along with their two young kids. Lynn's significant other, Carl, and her two pre-teen daughters, Sharon and Claire are here. Alice and I went to see my other sister Ann on a separate visit, so she is absent. As is Mother, who never attends anything that Dad does, counting several family weddings (their long-standing animosity.) And anyway wherever Mother is included, it becomes a "Mother event," with everyone shouting so she can hear, forced into repeating inane comments over and over (the kind of asides that don't warrant saying once, but end up being shouted multiple times till everyone's eyes are rolling.)

After we all eat and spend a few hours all together, the kids go upstairs to play, and brother-in-law Joe pulls out a couple of joints.

This is novel. I like grass now and then, but never imagined smoking reefer with my family. Dad abstains, but has no objections. Mae also abstains, saying marijuana makes her paranoid, so she sticks to her Seagram's Seven and 7-Up instead. Lynn meanwhile is lighting candles all over the downstairs, burning sticks of incense, locking all the doors and windows, and drawing the curtains.

Okay, so the whole damned family is paranoid. But Mother has the degree on the wall, so the rest of us are pikers by comparison. (Well, on second thought, maybe we don't seem so benign compared to *your* family.)

The guys are now the audience, giggling hysterically, while we women entertain. First we discuss Lynn's habit of bringing out the best for company, and the rest of the time subjecting her family to lesser quality.

"Okay, Lynn," says Mae, preparing to prove her point. "What kind of toilet paper do you normally use? Not the good stuff you have in the bathrooms right now, I bet."

"No," Carl pipes up, supporting the allegation. He names a brand that sells by the pound with the wiping surface of fine sandpaper.

"See!" Mae cries in triumph. "See! Now why would you make everybody closest to you, the people you love the most, use that crappy stuff and trot out the expensive stuff only for company? You're just putting on the dog and showing off, that's all."

"No, that's not it," Lynn defends. "I'm not putting on the dog for anybody. It's actually just that I'm cheap."

We all laugh as if this is high comedy. Tears running. Stoned.

"I like the kind of toilet paper that has those little puffy cushions on it, myself," Dad adds, his fingers and thumbs pushing together as if squishing tiny paper pads. He has a contact high.

"It comes from Mother," I say, and everybody groans and giggles.

"Oh, God," says Mae, "it always comes down to that. It all comes from Mother. How come I was exempt?"

"You're fourteen years younger than I am," I answer. "You missed a lot. But you have your own kind of crazy, so don't get haughty."

"Yeah," Joe comments. "You won't buy anything but brand names."

"Of course," Mae crows, "the best! I buy the best. Best Foods, Kellogs, Gold Medal, and Charmin."

"It's the same thing in reverse, Mae," Lynn points out. "It's just your rebellion *against* it. I copied Mother's cheap ways and you defied her by always using all brand names. Which aren't always the 'best,' I might add, just the most expensive."

"I like to squeeze those fat little pillows on bubble wrap," Dad says, his fingers making little pushing gestures.

"Oh, I like to pop them, too," Joe agrees.

"No, I don't pop them. I just squish them," Dad clarifies. Oh yeah, definite contact high.

"Mother always used to send us to the neighborhood store for a stick of butter when company came," I say, getting back to the topic at hand. "Not a pound, mind you, but a single, solitary, chintzy stick."

"Oh, that's why you won't eat anything but butter now!" Alice exclaims.

"Besides," says Lynn, "Nancy and I remember when margarine first came out. The dairy industry tried to keep their foothold by regulating against it having the appearance of anything like butter. So, it was sold in a plastic bag, white like Crisco, with a yellow dot of food coloring in it, and you had to pop the yellow dot from outside of the bag and massage the stuff inside to mix the coloring all through the margarine, then squeeze the mixed-up goo out into a container to keep."

"Eww! Really? I didn't know that. Really?" This is news to Mae. "You mean it came all white in a bag and you had to mix the color into it?"

"Oh, I don't think I'll eat margarine ever again," says Joe.

"I remember that," Dad says. "I liked to squeeze that little button of yellow food dye, too." No wonder he abstained; he could get high on the atmosphere in the room.

"Remember when we were tossing the bag between us and it burst, and half-mixed margarine splattered everywhere?" I ask. Everyone howls with laughter, commenting on the fine, greasy mess that must have been.

Then Lynn dives into a confessional jag. "I used to sneak into the kitchen and eat things I wasn't supposed to. I'd slice the thinnest slivers off the birthday cake and eat one every time I went into the kitchen."

"That was you?" I ask, laughing. "The cake mysteriously got smaller and smaller by the hour, and no one would admit to eating it."

"It was me," Lynn confesses. "I even sneakily baked the Peppermill tarts one day when everyone was out, and for some reason I used the red serving tray instead of a baking sheet. The paint came off the tray and left two perfect triangles of bare metal where the tarts had baked."

"Oh, God! So, *that's* what happened to that tray." I'm beside myself with laughter.

"And I played billy hell scraping the paint off the bottom of the tarts before I could eat them, too."

"Those tarts had a real nice puff pastry to them," Dad adds.

The day has come to a happy end, and everyone is sober now, the high dissipated, and Mae rounds up her sleepy kids for the ride home. We had a grand time: bellies full, cheeks and sides aching from laughter, a feeling of family bonding and general conviviality. Dad prepares for his exit, standing by the front door in his overcoat. When I approach to say goodbye, he holds me in a long hug.

"You take care of yourself, my Big Girl," he says. "Be happy if you can."

He then turns to Alice, looking her straight in the eye, and shaking her hand, holding it at length in his grip. "Thank you, Alice, for being my daughter's ... uh ..."

The pause gets lengthy. The corners of Alice's mouth slowly begin curling up.

" ... uh ...."

Her smile grows bigger.

"...uh ... her friend," Dad concludes, smiling warmly, and shaking her hand again. Alice's grin is now as wide as a jackass eating briar bushes.

So there it is, my father has acknowledged Alice and I as friends and lovers, giving us his approval. And his blessing.

DATELINE, 1980—Six US embassy aide **hostages** escape from Iran with Canada's help. **Soviets invade** Afghanistan, prompting President Carter to embargo grain and high tech exports to the USSR. **Carter also approves** arms sale to China and **boycotts Olympics** in Moscow. **Congress approves** the Crude Oil Windfall Profit Tax.

President Carter signs a measure that requires four million men, ages 19 and 20, to **register for the draft**. A **secret attempt to rescue** hostages by US forces ends in failure with a helicopter crash in the desert that kills eight servicemen.

CNN, the 24-hour Cable News Network, goes on the air. The deposed **Shah of Iran, 60, dies** of cancer, the last of his dynasty that ruled Iran since 1921. The *Voyager I* **passes close** to Saturn during her three-year, 1.3-billion-mile journey, making new discoveries on the planet's moons and rings.

Major **US banks raise** their prime lending rate to 21.5 percent, a new record high. The US **economy continues to suffer** from rising inflation and high unemployment. Inflation continues in the US as **prices rise 12.4 percent**.

US **personal bankruptcies** number 367,000—up from 209,500 the previous year. US **gas prices** soar to $1.22 a gallon. **Rollerblade, Inc.**—founded by Canadian hockey player Scott Olsen, 20—markets an inline street skate that will become wildly popular. **Pacman** becomes the bestselling arcade game of all time.

home sweet humboldt

*Eureka's Old Town occupies a grid twelve blocks long and four blocks wide.
Situated along Humboldt Bay, the town, from the mid-1800s through the turn
of the century, was the largest city in the state, north of San Francisco. It was
upright, bustling, and (mostly) respectable. But nestled amongst its reputable
businesses and shops, it also contained the underbelly of the county and was home
to a hundred or more taverns, brothels, flop houses, and dens of iniquity. In those
bygone years, Eureka claimed twenty-four houses of ill repute as well as an inde-
terminate number of independent floozies—seven ladies of the night to every male
resident. Much of their patronage, it must be noted, was from the hundreds of
transients off the many and varied ships that utilized the harbor: gold miners,
loggers, lumberjacks and dairymen, migrants and new settlers.*

*By 1980, gentrification had introduced propriety to the area, forcing what
seedier human elements that survived into a few small pockets farther along the
wharf. The original Victorian buildings are preserved in many cases, and where
upscale offices, restaurants, and shops occupy the converted spaces, there are still
small alcoves and cribs where the historic population of scarlet women once plied
their trade.*

I t's been nearly a year and a half since Alice and I moved up here to
Humboldt County, and we've settled well into the lifestyle and pace
of the area, taking advantage of all it has to offer. Buying season
tickets to the Ferndale Little Theater will become an annual tradition for
us, and over the years we will be treated to a series of performances that

rival those offered on the stages of Broadway, Philadelphia, and L.A. And because it is a helluva lot less hassle to get to the theater here, we attend more often than we had in Southern California. There's no hour-and-a-half drives in eight-lane traffic, no big parking fees, no long drives home.

We also have a multitude of other entertainment options. In addition to possessing one of the finest music curricula in California with talent from around the world, Humboldt State University showcases dance troupes and jazz combos, comedians, and big-name singers and musicians on the college circuit tour. And the community Humboldt Light Opera Company is simply great, too, tapping into the local talents of students and residents alike.

The Christmas play put on by the independent Commedia Dell'Arte School will become another yearly event for us. Near as we know, it is the only school of "physical theatre" in America to offer an MFA, billing itself as "a theater of place featuring history and stories of Humboldt County."

Traditional Christmas festivities of the community include the Monday Club's annual Christmas Craft Sale, the annual Hospice Light-Up-A-Life Tree Lighting Ceremony, the Ferndale Christmas Tree Lighting Ceremony (of the tallest living Christmas tree in the nation), and an all-day Christmas Music Concert held at the Fortuna Veteran's Hall. The day-long concert offers a continuous performance schedule of holiday music played by all the local bands and performed by all the local choirs and choral groups. The groups change every forty-five minutes throughout the day. You can come anytime during that day and stay as long as you want—for free. The entire thing is recorded by a local radio station for broadcast on Christmas Day.

Now approaching our second Christmas in our new community, we decide to see firsthand what the all-day concert is all about. Our timing is just right, arriving at the concert hall at noontime just as the Ferndale High School choir is finishing their program, and the next group is about to go on. Spectators are coming and going, since many families and friends often stay just to root for their particular singing group or band. But many others, like Alice and me, tarry to hear several groups and ignite the Christmas spirit.

The Veteran's Hall, where the concert is held, is long and narrow inside, with polished wooden floors and folding chairs. And colder than an ice floe. The event organizers pay no rent for the use of the building, provided no heat is used. Otherwise, the in-and-out traffic all day would have run the heating bill higher than the whole winter season put together.

The chill factor is compounded by the fact that it is, by Pacific Coast standards, especially cold outdoors this year, with temperatures dipping into the low forties. But this damned tall-ceilinged, un-insulated, wood building sits on a high foundation that traps frigid air beneath it all winter, and stays so cold inside you could hang meat. The most anyone can tolerate the building is about an hour, then their feet grow numb clear up to mid-calf. That pretty much guarantees a rotation of audience, with empty seats available during performance rotations. †

The Scotia Band, named after a nearby town, is up next. It draws its thirty-member brass band from workers of the town's century-old lumber mill. Their uniforms are all red and gold, and they do a fine job on some of the more popular Christmas pieces. Once finished with their program, they pack up their instruments as the next group, the College of the Redwoods Choir, filters in. The audience, in the interim, visits with each other, catching up on news and exchanging pleasantries up and down the rows of folding chairs.

With the next musical group finally in place, the conductor makes a few last minute checks. It appears that something is going on, some hitch, involving several whispered conferences and milling about among the members at the rear of the choir. Catching the eye of the conductor, one of the singers at the back rank raises his hands and shrugs a silent message, "I don't know."

"We've got a little problem, folks," the conductor announces with a turn to the audience. "Our first number starts off with a four-bar introduction of chimes and ends with another eight bars. The chimes are here, but the Scotia Band must have gotten off accidentally with the mallet that's used to play them."

The audience laughs and chatters, happy to have the hold up explained.

"So, here's what we need, folks: a shoe or a boot that has a leather heel, 'cause the chimes mallet is a little, hard-leather hammer."

---

† Today the concert is held in the comfort of the River Lodge, a large convention space built since on the levee of the Eel River, with large airy windows offering the great view, excellent acoustics ... plus, it is *heated*!

The audience falls to.

Enthusiastically, people begin stripping off and passing forward their shoes and boots. The chimes master, as he receives each one, gives a few experimental taps. *Dint-dint-dint ... Tonk-tonk-tonk.* He shakes his head, rejecting loafer and high heel, wing-tip, steel-tip, and brogan. Footwear flows overhead, hand to hand, through the audience like some bizarre boot brigade.

One at a time, he tests the footwear for tympanic suitability, and one by one, this exacting chimes master finds them wanting. *Tin-tin-tin. Dunk-dunk-donk.* Finally—*ding, ding, dong, dong.* Beaming broadly, he holds up a woman's tall zipper boot with a fat, three-inch heel.

Applause and rolling laughter erupts throughout the auditorium, and the audience re-ties, re-buckles, and re-zips. Within moments, the river of exchanged leather goods dries up and the shuffling and grunting dies away.

The conductor raises his hands, signaling the focus of the choir and audience. With a steady look to the chimes master, who is holding the woman's boot high above a rack of hanging chimes, the conductor gives the downbeat, and with it the chimes master brings the heel of the boot smartly down, bonging along the rack of pipes and pure tones chime forth.

Ding, ding, ding, dong. Ding, ding, ding, dong. Ding, ding, dong, dong, Di-ing, Di-ing.

"*The Bells of ...Saint Mary's . . .*" the choir sings the familiar song, doing a rather credible job of it with beautiful inflection and harmony all the way to the end of the song.

"*... Ring out for you ... and ... me.*"

The chimes master again taps each pipe with expertise, slow and measured, as if it's always accomplished using a woman's high-heeled, zipper boot.

Ding, ding, ding, dong. Ding, ding, ding, dong. Ding. Dong. Di-ing. Do-ong. Di-i-innngg.

He finishes the bell-like finale, boot still upraised as the sweet reverberations slowly die away.

With a roar, the audience jumps to its feet and thunderous applause fills the icy hall. Of course, half the thunder is friendly laughter, and the audience keeps it up through two bows from the choir and three bows from the blushing chimes master.

The conductor retrieves the boot and holds it up as the audience sits again. The stalwart boot itself gets a solid round of applause—and another ripple of laughter.

"And to whom do we owe the honor?" he asks the audience. A woman near the back raises her hand as everyone titters. I wonder if her poor toes are frostbitten, considering how cold my well-shod feet are.

The conductor walks down the aisle to the end of her row and bows deeply toward the lady benefactor, proffering the performance boot across his bent forearm as if it were a fine bottle of wine. Everyone giggles and claps in appreciation of the gallantry and the acknowledgement. And once again, hand to hand along the row, the honored boot is passed back to its rightful owner.

Now that's something you don't see in a concert hall every day.

⚜

Mattie is breathless with excitement. She just hurried up the street and knocked at our door, full of the news: "We just had a robbery at Henry & Carla's, and wait till you hear what happened," she says, sitting down at the table to sugar the coffee I offer her.

Henry & Carla's is a small market on Highway 36, about three miles away. Like many of the small, family-owned markets in our area, it's a combination general store cum post office cum gas pump. In later years, it would also include a video rental.

"Henry & Carla's got robbed?" Alice asks.

"When?" I query.

"A half hour ago. Didn't you hear the sirens?"

"Yeah," I say, "but we just assumed it was an accident."

Highway 36 is an east-west, two-lane road through the redwoods and farmland, and mountains further on. It is narrow and serpentine, treacherous in spots, and even the native-born have been known to crack up on one of the big trees at the road's edge or plummet over the side on a turn. More than a few have lost their lives over the years due to speed or inattention on that road.

"Well, wait till you hear," Mattie says, sipping her coffee. "These three guys came into the market and messed around as if they were shopping till a lull came and no one else was there. Then they held it up, got all the money from the register, and dashed out and jumped into an old, red Trans Am and peeled out, heading east toward Bridgeville."

"Did they have guns?" Alice asks.

"Evidently. But here's the great part. Henry immediately got on the phone and called down the road to Mark and Hannah's to warn them."

Now I know you're gonna think I made up these names, but in our county people take credit for their businesses. No "Wash & Fluff" for us; it's Miller's Laundromat, if you please. Not the "Booze Shop," but Harvey's Liquors. We like to know the person with whom we were trading, and the merchants aren't ashamed to specify.

Mark and Hannah's is another little local mercantile store on the highway, about three miles farther along.

"Henry hollered into the phone, telling Mark he'd just been robbed by three guys in a rusty, red Trans Am headed their way," continues Mattie. "And Mark took it from there. He yelled to the two customers in the store to get some help and firepower. One of them grabbed his rifle from the rack in his truck. The other guy lived right across the road and sprinted home as Mark made two other calls."

As it happens, there had been a cutback at Mill A, so a lot of loggers were sitting home watching daytime TV when the robbery happened.

"My God, what did they think they were doing?" I ask. "Is this vigilante justice or what?" I'm a little scared to hear the outcome of this tale.

"Well, they were protecting their own, I think." Mattie helps herself to a homemade butter cookie and some more coffee. "Anyway, in the three-four minutes it took that Trans Am to speed up to Mark and Hannah's—which, I might add, they also intended to rob—there were five or six pickup trucks making a barrier across the road and about ten guys taking cover behind them with rifles and shotguns locked, loaded, and leveled.

"The Trans Am came screeching up, skidding nearly sideways, and thinking fast, those crooks made it a full turn around and sped back the way they had come."

"Holy cow!" Alice bursts out. "It's the goddamm Wild West!"

"What happened then?" I'm spellbound.

Mattie shrugs. "The same thing in reverse. Henry, back at the first store, had already called a few of the millworkers living nearby after he warned Mark, and they were gathering to hurry down to Mark and Hannah's in case they needed help. So when they got Hannah's call that the thieves were headed back thata-way again, they set up a roadblock right there, and that Trans Am came roaring around the bend to the same durn scene from the opposite direction—pickup trucks and good ole boys with their trusty rifles and shotguns aimed right at 'em."

"Well, did anyone ever call the police, or did they just string 'em up on a redwood tree or something?" I ask.

"No, nothin' like that, now. The boys back at Mark and Hannah's had immediately jumped into their trucks and floored it to follow right behind the Trans Am when it took off, hell bent for leather. So when them robbers came to the roadblock at Henry & Carla's, they was in a squeeze being chased from behind and they know'd they'd had it. They opened their doors and fell out onto their bellies with their hands behind their heads. That's when somebody called the sheriff to come mop it all up."

Mattie obviously enjoys the tale, and for that matter, we enjoy her telling of it.

"So, if it all just happened, how'd you know about it so fast?" I ask her, still new to small town dispatch and the speed with which news travels.

"Well, Carla's sister, Janie, called Mona over in Rohnerville, and she called Gladys, and Gladys called me," Mattie explains, naming names I'd mostly heard but not met.

"I imagine by now the news is clear up to McKinleyville and heading up to Crescent City." Mattie giggles. "And those good ole boys down at the stores prob'ly already poured down a snootful and are gonna tell each other the story—and anyone else they can corral—over and over tonight till they're all too drunk to pr'nounce they own names."

Mattie stands up and walks her cup to the kitchen. "Well, I'd better git on home. I have a few more phone calls to make m'self."

Mattie heads home to make sure the jungle telegraph is well covered for her share of it, and Alice and I remain sitting where she left us, amused by and utterly astounded at the high drama of small town life.

And now, I'm telling the story to you. Exactly how it happened.

DATELINE, 1981—The day of **Reagan's inauguration**, mere minutes after he is sworn in, 52 hostages, held in Teheran for 14 months, are **suddenly and improbably freed** under a US-Iran agreement. They return to the US five days later. In March, **President Reagan is shot** by John Hinckley and wounded, along with the Press Secretary and two guards. **Another gunman wounds Pope John Paul II** six weeks later.

The first DeLorean DMC-12 rolls of the assembly line. **Space Shuttle *Columbia*** with **NASA** astronauts **John Young** and **Robert Crippen** orbits and returns to Earth. It is the **first time** a manned reusable spacecraft has returned from orbit. **Prince Charles** of Wales marries **Lady Dianna** Spencer at St. Paul's Cathedral in London. **MTV** (Music Television) is launched on cable television.

General Synod of the **Church of England** votes to admit women to holy orders. Luke and Laura marry on the US soap opera *General Hospital* and ranks as the highest-rated hour in daytime television history. **President Ronald Reagan** signs the **top secret** National Security Decision Directive 17 (NSDD-17), authorizing the **Central Intelligence Agency** to recruit and support **Contra** rebels in **Nicaragua**. The first American **test-tube baby, Elizabeth Jordan Carr**, is born in **Norfolk, Virginia**.

President Reagan fires 13,000 striking air traffic controllers from their jobs. **Chris Everet (Lloyd)** wins Wimbledon for third time (also in '76 and '74.) **Reagan nominates** Sandra Day O'Connor, 51, as first woman to sit on Supreme Court. A walkway in lobby of Hyatt Regency Hotel in Kansas City collapses killing 110 and injuring 188. The illness that will come to be known as **AIDS is identified. Henry Fonda and Katharine Hepburn** win Oscars for *On Golden Pond*.

the sundowner and the
missionary

T he night is as long as a tax audit and every bit as grueling. I am working the graveyard shift—eleven to seven—at Cordoba Convalescent Hospital where eighty-four patients reside, most of them elderly. Four nurse's aides—I am one of them—make rounds every two hours. Loosely supervised by one sole RN, we assist some to the bathroom, put bedpans under others, and change gowns and linens on the rest. We take vitals, rub backs and feet, and generally calm, coax, and care for all the patients.

Very little sleeping gets done in this sort of place. Many residents exhibit what is referred to as sundowner's syndrome, a phenomenon where senile people become more alert and agitated after dark, wander about, chat it up, and stay awake any way they can. Perhaps subconsciously they fear death will steal over them in the dark, in the night, in their sleep, so they have to keep their eyes peeled for it. No one knows for sure why this happens, but it's a fact of life in every nursing home in the world. Even the fearless, the blind, the deaf, and demented, sleep light or fitfully, with us nurse's aides traipsing up and down the halls every couple of hours, flipping lights off and on.

To make matters worse, Signey is trying to escape again. Her room is closest to the nurses' station, the better to watch her night and day. However, the RN on duty is seldom at her desk any night, too busy dispensing medications from one patient's room to the next.

Signey is a small, sweet, Finnish woman with an air of elegance about her. She periodically seems to forget the four other languages she speaks fluently and reverts to her mother tongue exclusively. At such times, for whatever reason, she will take a notion to get all dolled up and slip away out the door.

The convalescent home fronts a busy street that borders a magnificent stand of redwood trees leading into the city's largest park, ending four short blocks away near the zoo. The park is typical of the Pacific Northwest, with few expanses of lawn. It is virtually a forest, made up predominantly of redwoods and furnished with a few benches and the odd picnic table barely discernible in the canopied darkness.

When Signey escapes, day or night, she heads directly for those trees. More than once in the primal deep of those woods she's been found—lost, cold, frightened, and alone for hours. The thick cover of branches, which doesn't begin till nearly forty feet up the trunks of redwoods, keeps sunlight from the forest floor, and the trees are so large in girth, so dense, so concealing, a tiny, confused, panicky woman can easily remain undiscovered for a long time despite a frantic search to find her.

Locking exit doors from the inside of institutions such as this one is both illegal and dangerous. And alarm doors are not yet installed. To bolt Signey up in her room when she lapses into these fugue states disturbs her greatly, of course, and the rare time or two it was tried, she cried and pounded the door in bafflement and fear. Certainly no one wishes to jacket-restrain her to a chair or a bed. Still, her attempted (and occasionally successful) escapes occur with dismaying regularity.

Between rounds, we have ten or fifteen minutes left to chart our cases before starting all over again. Signey has stayed with us in the dayroom, chattering to us in Finnish, her old face wide with smiles, drawing pictures in the air with her expressive hands. Her face isn't actually wrinkled. Her skin has that look of fine crepe common to the very old and very fair. At eighty-four, she's actually quite lovely.

"Okay, Signey, back to your room now. And, why don't you lie down and go to sleep?" I suggest. She trills something in Finnish and waves me away as she retires to her room.

But when I pass by again, I see Signey beginning to dress herself with care, searching her closet for just the right blouse or dress or suit and its complimentary accessories of costume jewelry, scarves, and belt.

She brushes her fine, white hair and curls it under with her fingers into a smooth, silky pageboy, reminiscent of the whiskey-voiced actress June Allyson, who was popular in the 1950s.

Signey pats powder onto her aged face and neck from an old-fashioned powder box, overlaid with decorative bits of mirror. Carefully inspecting her work in a hand mirror, she applies apple-red lipstick, smacking her lips together to blot. She tucks a hankie in her purse, then reaches toward her shoe bag for just the right pair of shoes to match her smart outfit. The bag is empty!

I confiscated all her shoes earlier and locked them in the drug room of the nurses' station, hoping this time to keep her busy searching her room and, consequently, safe within the facility. And it works.

Signey spends the night frustrated and puzzled—but out of danger—hunting every inch of her room for her shoes. Eventually, with the breaking dawn, she succumbs to an exhausted sleep. It never occurred to her to help herself to another person's shoes for her forbidden—and failed—outing. And by her standards, still operating amid her delusions, her slippers were simply unsuitable for outdoor wear and a horrid match to boot.

Curled up now on her bed asleep, Signey still wears the pink suit she had picked out many hours earlier, complete with an ivory blouse, a printed, silk scarf abloom with pale, pink camellias, pearl earrings and matching pearl bracelet. Beneath this elegant ensemble, she wears a slip, lace undies, and silk stockings. Fuzzy red slippers? Dear heavens, no! They would never do.

Maybe when Signey wakes up she'll be normally responsive again, speaking English again and content to stay put. My shift, however, is over, so I leave her as she is: beautiful and sleeping soundly, in the competent hands of the arriving day shift now.

The ground fog on this cool, crisp November morn is slow to lift. My near solitude on the road for the thirty-minute drive leaves me free to appreciate Humboldt's tree-covered hills and mountain ridges, one behind the other, fading to softer, paler blue as they recede into the distance. The mountains close to home display smoky ruffles of fog at their bases—the overnight exhalations of the tall trees, with their vaporous breaths renewing the atmosphere—and everywhere wispy, white tendrils of mist rise up against the blue-green skyline of the woods.

My commune with nature ends when I pull into the driveway, take the keys out of the ignition, and notice, as I walk the steps of the house and enter, that every light is ablaze.

In the living room sits Alice, rigid in her chair. On the floor at her feet sits Giselle, Mattie's thirty-nine-year-old daughter, drinking a cup of coffee, her legs crossed tailor-fashion.

Something alerts me that this is not a neighborly stop-over-for-an-early-morning cup-of-coffee. Mmh-mmh, this has all the appearance of the end of an up-all-night-cup-of-coffee. The realization of it sharpens me right up.

That, and the fact that at seven-thirty in the morning my Alice is wearing a hat—her navy Greek fisherman's cap—tugged tight and low on her head so it domes up in the center, a far cry from its usual jauntiness. The band of the hat is jammed down so hard it makes Alice's ears flare out. Overall, she looks a bit like Elmer Fudd.

Her hollow, owl-like eyes betray that she's pulled an all-nighter. So … a long night for us both, then. Yeah, as long as a six-pack pee, with the same sudden, empty sensation at the end of it.

But hey, I'm a cool kinda gal. I give them both a breezy "Good morning" and flash a bright, stiff smile. Alice's greeting seems subdued and evasive. Giselle, entirely at ease, wears an odd expression that puzzles me for a moment.

Cats. Cats come to mind. Paw-licking, face-rubbing cats. Smugly contented. *Shit!*

I excuse myself to the bedroom to change out my uniform. Hmm. The bed hasn't been slept in. Or maybe it was slept in and re-made? More hmm. Or maybe it was re-made, though far from slept in? Uh-oh. Time to fall back and re-group.

I've never had any reason to doubt my lover's faithfulness. But neither have Alice and I sworn a blood pact of sexual fidelity. Our relationship was forged on the anvil of the seventies, with all that decade's ornate scrollwork of open marriages, consenting adults, wife swapping,

threesomes, group gropes, and other middle-class adaptations of the sixties free-love flower children. In comparison, we are almost square.

By now, in 1981, we are fairly long lasting, nine years all told, six of
them living together—monogamous, harmonious, and settled. Content
as two ticks on a terrier. Just lesbian, that's all.

Once past my initial surprise of finding the Alice-Giselle tableau, I
begin to feel a little less muddled, and a bit less panicked, and remind
myself the jury is still out on whether anything even happened.

As I change my clothes, I remember how in our first months together,
still so new to each other, we had played What If? You know—*what if* one
of us feels an incredible attraction to someone else and wants to have an
affair? *What if* an old lover comes back wanting to be lovers again? Worse
yet, *what if* that old lover is a man? *What if* a friend you care for deeply,
but have never slept with, is having a hard time and comforting them is
liable to lead to sex? Is there ever a good reason for a mercy fuck?

The answer sensible people come up with is this: it is folly to stay
with someone if you wish to be elsewhere. Folly and demeaning, and it
kills love faster than hammering an ant. If a wish to be elsewhere crops
up, your partner must be told at the soonest. It's really rotten to keep her
in the dark, left to torture herself, wondering if she's imagining things.
She will feel it. She will know.

Oh, and having sex just to ease someone when they are hurting is
never mercy. It's more like introducing famine after fire and flood. Oh
sure, let's just have sex together, with all the baggage *that* brings, and see
if we can compound that pain, complicate those problems. Yeah, riiiiight!

Anyway, I take pains to look nice, and that half-pisses me off. I put
on a crisp blouse and slacks instead of my usual after-work scuzzies. Slip
a fast comb through my hair, a dash of perfume, a dab of lipstick. Give
the competition a run for her money, I suppose.

The competition, by the way, is an attractive, diminutive woman
who married young and divorced, then became a teller at a local bank to
support herself and her son. About six years ago, she also got religion.
Not the old-timey religion of her mother (a matter of great confusion
and sorrow to Miss Mattie), but a more literal, fundamentalist, separa-
tist sect, which runs a compound on some prime ocean real estate here
in the county. The compound hires out the young boys of its congregation to local farms to buck hay in the summer and to pick the fields in

the fall. The older boys work throughout the year in two church-owned businesses specializing in pest extermination. The girls labor within the multiple barracks and common halls, performing laundry, garden, and kitchen duties. All work for no pay, work just for the love of the Lord— and the benefit of the Church.

Giselle had moved herself and her son into the compound, and there she cooked and cleaned and her son was indentured. That would be the polite word. (There are no slaves anymore, right?) When Giselle's son turned eighteen, the church elders expediently shipped the boy off to Guatemala to serve a branch of the sect there—a deliberate ploy, calculated so college wouldn't entice him away from their influence.

His mother meanwhile signed on for a foreign mission, a mission she had to *pay the church* to work in, costing her a healthy chunk of her savings for the privilege. Giselle only recently returned after contracting a tropical illness in the Far East and is now staying at her mother's home down the lane. Mattie has long been angry with her daughter for abdicating "real life" for this cult-like religion, for involving her grandson, whom she loves and misses terribly. And she is angry for Giselle's inability to take charge of her own life and "grab hold."

And now, here is Giselle sitting in my living room at seven-thirty in the morning.

I saunter into the kitchen, pour myself a cup of coffee, and stroll back in the living room to join the two women. Totally composed. Completely relaxed. Don't ever let 'em see you sweat.

"Good to see you, Giselle. How are you doing?" I ask.

"I wasn't so good last night, but I'm better now," she replies, sending Alice a look so warm, so luscious, it's almost wet.

Cute! Cute as a cocked pistol. The game's on.

It doesn't take a psychic to read Alice. In *total silence*, her mere expression broadcasts, "Aw, shit!"

"Last night?" I ask innocently, remembering to keep the conversation going and wanting to see just how far Giselle the missionary intends to play this.

Breaking off her lingering gaze at Alice (whose eyes are directed elsewhere, anywhere), Giselle says, "Yes, I really needed to talk to someone,

259

so I came up to talk to Alice, and she offered me a glass of wine, and well, one thing led to another, and I'm afraid I got a little drunk. " She milks the pause for all it is worth. "And anyway, I'm still here."

"Aww, rat-shit!" Alice's reaction noiselessly booms into the atmosphere of our private, inner speaking.

This time when Giselle slides a sidelong glance from where she sits, practically cuddled at Alice's feet, she meets head-on one of Alice's frosty, take-this-further-at-your-own-risk stares. Giselle at least has the grace to blush, drop her eyes, and dissemble a little.

"I ... uh ...."

Alice and I both wait.

"I'm ... uh, afraid I kept Alice up all night with my foolishness, uh, and I should probably go now." Giselle floats up from her cross-legged position with no more effort than any lighter-than-air-filled object and takes her empty cup out to the kitchen.

"Oh, don't rush off just 'cause I'm home," I call out to her, not able to resist reading my line. I shoot Alice a wicked look, and her gaze is still a little icy around the edges.

"Don't you start, either," she telegraphs emphatically, but aloud, she simply says, "It's been a long night." Suddenly I'm contrite knowing that whatever happened here had to have been an ordeal.

"Well, Mom will be up now and looking for me," says Giselle from the kitchen. "So I need to get home, I guess. Thanks for the hospitality, the wine, and everything." She says the last part slightly breathy. Seems she can't resist one last move, but it's wasted. Alice only nods. Ever the gracious host, I stand up to see Giselle out.

She sidles her pretty, petite self down the steps and off down the street. What's that? Did her tail just twitch? Yes, I think it did. Satisfied as a cream-filled feline to have rounded out her evening by starting a little fuss in the home camp, maybe?

Ah, but she doesn't know us. Doesn't know what we have. And will never be so lucky.

"Lord, what was that all about?" I ask, turning from the door.

Alice looks up, weariness evident in her face, "You'll never believe the night I've had," she says, knowing full well that I would believe it. Totally.

It seems Giselle had arrived on our doorstep about eleven-thirty last night. She'd clearly had a drink or three already. She was so upset and confused, she told Alice, and wondered if she could come in and have a glass of wine and just talk? Alice, to be social, joined her in a glass.

Giselle proceeded to complain that her life was a mess, her religious quest not working. Cambodia was a good experience for a while; she had been serving the Lord, carrying the Word to the heathen and all, but then she caught dengue fever, and had to come back, and oh, Alice was so good to let her talk like this, and she'd just have some more wine if she could.

Alice rubs a hand over her weary face. "I thought she was gonna say she had decided to leave the mission and wasn't sure what she was going to do next. She drank several full goblets of wine and the tears were flowing. Then after the sniffles passed—I couldn't believe it!"

Alice, perplexed, throws her palms up, "She got sort of simpering and coy. Flirting! I thought I was mis-reading it. I only had one glass of wine myself, and I can tell you, after that I never took another drop! I knew I needed my wits about me with this one."

She groans at the memory of her night, and this whole business starts to tickle the fool out of me. But I try to smother it till I can get the full story.

"Before I knew it, she was standing up over me and running her fingers through my hair." Alice mimes petting gestures in the air, and continues, "... saying how soft and fine my hair is. What a marvelous color it has. How it gleams in the light and feels warm to the touch.

"Oh, God!" Alice wails after a brief pause. "I knew then I hadn't imagined it. And I recognized this game, too. How many times before, I wondered, has old straight-arrow Giselle waked up to find herself in a *woman's* bed, after a night she daren't think about? Nor remember! On the one hand, I was coolly wondering just how many 'sexual accidents' Giselle had chalked up in her life, and in the next moment, realized she'd tagged *me* for another hit-and-run! I totally panicked!"

She gulps. White rims of remembered terror show in her eyes. "I fought her off all night."

Alice the unflappable. Alice the unruffled.

A woman normally possessed of a tranquility that rivals even the Buddha himself. Calm, cool, and collected Ole Alice is truly shook up!

I almost choke on my swallowed laughter, but manage to croak out, "What did you do?"

"All I could think of to do—I made coffee and quoted scripture."

Well, that does it! Great guffaws blast out of me.

Alice had gone through a strong religious phase as a young person, studying for two years at a Bible college. The phase passed as Alice continued to explore broader spiritual concepts. But she still manages to impress many a scripture-spouting Christian with her phenomenal store of chapter-and-verse and fight-fire-with-fire rebuttals. But this, with Giselle? Truly rare!

"It isn't funny," Alice complains, a bit irked.

"I know," I say with a rasp in my voice when I can stifle my laughter well enough to speak. "It's not funny. So, what happened next?"

"Well, she wouldn't leave my hair alone again after I brought in the coffee, so I got up and put my hat on."

Her Greek fisherman's hat. That explains it. And she yanked it on so tight, crammed it down so hard, her ears stuck out like open car doors. Ever so attractive. And romantic!

"Uhh. Then what?" I squeak, my eyes spurting tears fashioned by my contained laughter.

"Well, Giselle got even less subtle about it, said she was kind of tired and could she go lie down? I said, 'No, no, no,' that she'd just have to go home. 'Oh, please don't make me go home,' she begged, and started to cry again, 'I'll be good, I'll be good.' "

With splayed fingers, Alice reaches up and firms the hat on the dome of her head, as if to reassure herself, probably just like she did when Giselle reached that particular moment in the drama. "And then she talked again about Jesus, and how she wishes He'd fill up more of her life and take away the longings and stuff."

Alice looks at me, distress apparent in her eyes. "It was that way all night long. She didn't drink any coffee till just before you got home, but this is the third pot I've swilled down." Her voice is steeped with strain. "It was a good excuse for a while to stand up and be busy, till she caught on and ambled out to the kitchen to corner me there. I'd grab a cup and head for my chair so fast, I had to tack into the wind!"

Strangled noises escape my throat as I try to hold back another burst of laughter. Alice, meanwhile, rubs the back of her neck and valiantly soldiers on. "She'd plop at my feet and take up the Jesus thing again. It was back and forth like that for hours. I was so tired, but I didn't dare go to our room and leave her to sleep it off on the floor or anything. She'd have been in our bed in a New York minute."

As Alice speaks, her panic of reliving the night begins to dissipate. But I'm nearly busting a gut.

"I could have just demanded that she leave. But there's Miss Mattie to think of. If Giselle went staggering home in the middle of the night after putting the finishing touches on her drunk at my house, waking everybody up, there's no telling what mischief it would cause. Besides, I just wasn't up to the fuss to get her to finally go. It seemed more reasonable to tough it out till morning, and then you'd be here. Giselle would talk herself sober, and Mattie would get up and be watching up the street for her to come home."

With her story finished, Alice slumps as if finally purged, relieved to have it told.

"So you warded her off all night, sitting under your hat, quoting the Bible, and leaping up every fifteen minutes for coffee?" I can't stop myself. As soon as the words fall out of my mouth, I collapse weakly, in hiccupping hoots.

"Well, it worked," Alice defends. "And it isn't a damn bit funny, you know. You weren't here to protect me and wouldn't be back till morning, and she knew it!" Her mouth twists wryly. "It's been a long time since I've had to face anything like this. I've forgotten how to get out of these scrapes. God protect me from straight women," she says, holding a cautionary finger in the air. "... who know not what they do!"

"There you go, getting preachy," I say, relenting a bit since I've finally caught my breath. "Besides, I was a straight woman once, and I'm glad you weren't protected from me."

"You were different."

"How different could I have been? I was straight—I was even married."

"You were responsible for your actions. You didn't try to hide from your own self."

"Oh, I can't take credit for that," I say with a shrug. "If I'd known how to—even a bit—I might have done. Besides, how do you know?"

"I remember what you said, foolish person." With that, Alice thumbs the brim of her hat up, pushing it off her ears, stands up and heads for the bathroom to empty some of that coffee, leaving me to ponder. Alice can be truly exasperating sometimes.

She's barely turned the doorknob again when I call out to her. "Okay. I give up. What did I say?"

She returns to find me where she left me—sitting on the floor, in the very place Giselle had been earlier. Back in her chair, capturing me in a quiet, level look, she begins softly, "What you told me was: 'I've never done this before, nor wanted to. I'm gonna have a whole lot of soul-searching to do about this. But I can't—and I don't want to—think about it now.'" Her lips curl in a small smile of remembrance. "You said, 'What I want now, is for you to take me to bed.'"

Alice's eyes are clear, direct, and very warm, gazing at me. Reaching me to my core, as only she can.

"I said all that?" I flush at the sudden memory of our first time together—the initial touch of Alice's body, her *woman's* body against me, the hot, pliant, silky feel of her—a guarantee to fluster me. And suddenly I'm the one who is very warm, aroused at the memory, leaning against the chair there at her feet, stroking the ropy, blue-vein pattern on the back of her hand.

She has the nicest hands—solid, substantial, dependable hands. And in everything she does she uses them with a grace and competence and economy of motion that is pure pleasure to watch. And even more so … to feel.

"Well, uh…." I clear my suddenly thick, gravelly throat. "That was some helluva speech I made back then."

Alice catches my sexy thought, and her slightly wicked smile lets me know it. She adjusts her hat again, this time to a more rakish angle. "Well, it was a pretty speech, and you took your sweet time soul-searching, too. Kept me waiting three years while you did it." Her voice now more softened, deepened. "But the wait was worth it, lady." She lifts my hand, draws it to her lips, and kisses my palm.

Abruptly, Alice pulls back and peers at me. "Wait a minute, what did you think when you walked in here this morning?"

I tilt my head up to better see her. "Well, I admit, it didn't look good for you. It was obvious this was no typical drop-in-for-morning-coffee visit going on." I suddenly find some interesting lint on my slacks and start inspecting it. "And I found I had a little more soul-searching to do when I went in to change my clothes."

"About what?" she asks, her eyes narrowing.

"About what I would do if it really was what it looked like."

"And?" Her tone is a little ominous, and it's all I can do not to squirm under her pointed stare.

"Well, I wasn't willing to worry until you told me to." I take my hand back and hug my knees. "But," I continue slowly, pulling my eyes away from her, "if it was what it looked like, I knew I couldn't do a damn thing about it. I'd just have to wait it out."

Alice is mute, not broadcasting in her silent language, just looking at me. Inscrutable as a Chinese cat.

I take a deep breath and continue. "There's nothing for it, Alice. I'm hopelessly in love with you, and I'd probably have to take about anything you'd dish out, so be kind."

My head ducks to cover my complete vulnerability. Bad enough to blab it out, worse to let it show all over the place. Don't kid yourself. Loving someone so much that you are helpless doesn't get any easier just because you've been doing it for years.

When I can't take the quiet any longer, I look up at her.

Her smoky-blue eyes are deep enough to fall in. She is utterly still, with a serene centeredness that I find so safe and stabilizing. So enviable.

When she has my total attention, she says it. "I love you, lady."

The light in the room seems to dim just then, and I am momentarily unaware of anything except an intense, deep, emerald light flowing from her eyes into mine. It had happened once before, this beam of *green, green light*, many years ago, in a similar circumstance. A phenomenon I have, until now, always doubted.

Time stands still in this moment. When it restarts, there is a tiny, buzzing inside me. I feel slightly vibratory. Then the room brightens, what with full daylight streaming in the windows and the lamps still on everywhere. The moment now gone ... or maybe it never happened.

I get up and start turning off the lights. Unplug the coffeepot. Let the dogs in. Put the cat out. Lock the door. The phone rings and Alice picks up. It's Miss Mattie.

"How'd Mattie sound?" I ask Alice when she hangs up the phone.

"Very concerned that Giselle had imposed on me. Bent out of shape about Giselle's drinking," says Alice as she clears the coffee cups. "She thinks it's hypocritical."

"If she only knew the half of it!"

"No, I wouldn't wish that on Mattie. She'd probably die of heart failure!" Alice says, following me back to the bedroom. "Anyway, in the confusion, I forgot to ask, how was your night?"

"Interesting! But not as interesting as yours!" I answer, laughing. "Signey tried to escape again. I hid her shoes and it worked to keep her there. Looks as if you and I both learned a lesson from Gandhi."

"How's that?"

"Passive resistance. Don't you love it?"

"I wouldn't exactly call mine passive, popping up and down all night." Her humor regained, Alice finds some perspective about the whole episode.

"Gandhi and his homespun, Signey and her shoes, Giselle and your hat—funny, it's all clothing."

"And I can't wait to get out of mine," she says. "I be weary."

"Well, I shouldn't wonder. No rest, you know, for the weary. Or is it wicked?"

"Wasted."

"Wanton?" I wisecrack. With that, she fraps me on the head. I giggle and turn into her arms. "Or maybe *wantin'*. Just how weary are you?" I nuzzle her a bit, softly lipping along the base of her neck, taking my time. I don't know if it is working on her, but my nipples start to tighten. I trace the contours of her collarbone lightly with my tongue, and she draws a quick breath.

"Umm, pretty weary," she whispers.

"Well, you ee-wee-sistible woman," I tease her in my best Elmer Fudd voice. "Why don't you just wee-move that wee-dicullous hat and take me to bed."

The navy cap sails across the room, snags on a spoke of the hat rack, and swings like a pendulum. But I am no longer noticing.

DATELINE, 1982—The British win over Argentina in the Faulklands War. **Israel attacks** the Palestine Liberation Organization (PLO) and invades Lebanon. **John Hinckley** is found not guilty by reason of insanity for shooting President Ronald Reagan. **Alexander Haig** resigns as Secretary of State.

Meryl Streep takes Oscar for Best Actress in *Sophie's Choice.* **Jessica Lange** gets Best Supporting for *Tootsie,* a film that depicts a man posing as a woman to get a role in a soap opera. **Microsoft introduces MS-DOS** designed for the IBM personal computer (PC), which allows other manufacturers to produce clones. **Compaq announces** first IBM-compatible PC, released four months later at $2,995. **Compact discs players** (CDs) are introduced.

Princess Grace of Monaco, formerly known as the American actress Grace Kelly, dies in car accident at age 52. **Carl Ripken** is named the American League's Rookie of the Year. **Soviet leader Leonid Brezhnev** dies at age 75, and is succeeded by Yuri Andropov. **Barney B. Clark** lives 112 days after receiving the first artificial human heart implant.

Half a million New Yorkers demonstrate in favor of a nuclear freeze. **Unemployment tops 10 percent,** the highest since the Great Depression. **Federal budget deficit** exceeds $100 billion a year for first time ever. **Equal Rights Amendment fails** to make deadline to pass, and thereby falls three states short of ratification.

the pact

It's a full moon in May 1982. Up until late this afternoon, Alice had received no advanced warnings that she was about to suffer a heart attack, at least none that she will ever tell me about. And it comes, of course, at the most inopportune time.

We are both home when Mattie's call comes in. Duke has fallen out the patio door and she needs my help. The workmen were rebuilding the porch yesterday, but Duke forgot that there was nothing left of it when he opened the door onto thin air moments ago. He cut himself badly and injured who knows what? So, I leave Alice to go off with them, attending to Duke's wounds in the backseat of Mattie's car while she madly drives the thirty miles to Eureka. We are to meet Duke's doctor in the ER of St. Joseph's hospital, where he is dividing his time on weekend emergency call between there and Redwood Memorial, the much smaller sister hospital in Fortuna—the very hospital where I happen to work as a ward clerk.

There are multiple emergencies at St. Joseph's, more than one might expect for this small community of 26,000 people. The waiting room is crammed full of patients in various stages of illness and injury. We are seen perfunctorily, but we are at least given, while we wait, some gauze to hold against Duke's wound. More than an hour and a half passes before he is seen, and when he finally is examined, his doctor seems quite rushed, having just received a call down to Redwood Memorial—located just three miles from where we just came from—to handle an emergency admission there. After giving Duke a quick look over, the doctor orders him to stay overnight in the hospital for observation.

Since so much time has passed, I call Alice to tell her the outcome but get no answer, so I call Mattie's younger daughter, Melanie.

"I've been trying for the last hour to find you there at St. Joseph's, Nancy," she says, her voice filled with tension. "But all they could tell me was Duke hadn't been admitted. Alice was taken by ambulance to Redwood Memorial. She's had a heart attack. She called the ambulance herself."

My Alice is in the hospital! And here I am, thirty miles away from her without a car, stuck at a *different* hospital. Duke is being admitted into his room right now, and Mattie can't leave him since he is too addled to go through the admission process by himself. This can't be happening!

Frantic, I place a call to my friend Christine who lives in Eureka, and when she answers the phone, I do all but command her to drop everything and get me down there. By the time she is driving me back towards Fortuna, night has already fallen, the light of the full moon shining brightly on the river as we drive along it. I say little to Christine as we travel the interminable distance. I'm lost in a fog of fear, unthinking—not daring to think.

When we finally arrive at Redwood Memorial, I learn that Alice has been admitted directly to Intensive Care, in a small isolation room of that unit, since—in what's turning out to be a typical full moon—the main ICU is crammed full to its capacity of five beds.

I dash from the information office to the Intensive Care room and stand at the foot of her bed. An IV is running into her arm. She is hooked up to oxygen via clear, plastic prongs inserted up into her nostrils. Electrodes attached at various points on her body report the results of her heart rhythm on the monitor's glowing green screen. It also shows real-time readings of her blood pressure, pulse, and respiration. An active, moving line traces her EKG. She looks dreadful, her color pasty. She's clearly still in pain.

"You scared me to death," I blurt out, bursting into tears, holding onto the bottom bedrail for support.

Meanwhile, a nurse monitors Alice's heart rate—no doubt for agitation at my very presence. But Alice pats the nurse's hand to let her know it is all right.

"I know, I'm sorry," answers Alice. "I couldn't help it. Scared myself, too."

She tells me the heart attack hit her while she was in her chair, right after she'd lit a cigarette. The pain so solid and paralyzing, she was absolutely unable to move. When it eased up about five minutes later, the cigarette had burned down to her knuckles and she was able to get up and make her way into the kitchen to call the ambulance. She immediately retrieved her jacket, went to the porch, and sat on the steps to wait.

Naturally, to calm herself she lit another cigarette.

I vow on the spot to have two more phones installed in our home: one at her chair and another at her bedside. Phones are still hooked to walls in these days—no portables or cells, and, in most rural households, one phone suffices—unless life and death relies on the few footsteps it takes to reach an outside line.

The cigarette issue will be something to deal with later.

For now, however, I stay in the ICU room with Alice, still standing at the foot of her bed while the nurses administer dose after dose of morphine, Lidocaine, and other drugs. The cardiac monitor next to Alice keeps showing erratic spikes with increasing regularity, subsequently triggering increased concern, activity, and watchfulness on the part of the ICU staff. The nurses dose Alice with a good deal of morphine over the course of the next four hours. That Alice does not die tonight will later be attributed to this fact. The morphine relaxes her heart enough to sustain the massive anterior and lateral right-sided infarct that has been occurring. In other words, the morphine is the one thing that prevents Alice from completely blowing a hole in her heart.

Soon the doctor arrives—the same one, of course, who had seen Duke (and me) up at St. Joseph's earlier today, and he does a double take.

"Didn't I just see you in the ER at St. Joe's?" he asks me, taking his stethoscope out of his pocket.

"You did. I was up there with my neighbor."

"Hmmph," he mutters along with a muffled comment that ends with "full moon" as he proceeds to examine Alice. He asks her about her pain, and then listens to her heart and reads the nurses' medication notes. The doctor obtains a printout of a full electrocardiograph on tape from the machine Alice is hooked up to and reads it and marks it without comment. He leaves orders and heads back up to Eureka. Alice is once again left in the care of the nurses, who will ultimately save her life.

Three or four nurses cycle in and out of her room throughout the evening. The furrows between Alice's brows crinkle and deepen from time to time, the only indication she gives of any discomfort. Each time I see her grimace like this, the monitor's green screen mirrors her discomfort with an erratic series of jagged activity of the bright lines continually tracking the quality of her heartbeat—activity that doesn't bode well. And each time, a nurse, observing the changes on an outside monitor, enters the room and offers Alice another shot for her pain. The charge nurse tonight is a highly competent man named Patrick. I've noticed him before in the hospital, but never worked with him.

Alice continues to have these episodes that sketch the irregular intervals and spikes on the view screen. Though the monitor is capable of sounding alarms, these have been muted off—and the observable irregularities seem somehow more ominous for the silence. I know just enough about the look of trouble on a monitor to terrify me.

When the nurses roll in a crash cart, Patrick takes me aside.

"We're having difficulty," he says. "Alice keeps throwing PVCs (premature ventricular contractions.) Her heart wants to fibrillate. If it gets worse, we may have to use the paddles and defib her. Shock her heart while it's caught in a flutter to make it resume its normal pumping rhythm."

"I want to be here, Patrick."

"You can be here. But *only* if you promise me that you will leave *immediately* and without protest if I tell you to go." Patrick looks at me intently, his face grave.

"I will go when you ask, if *you* promise *me* that as soon as you can safely leave her, you'll come out and tell me what's going on." I return the grave, intent look.

We have a bargain.

Alice is alert but obviously tired, helpless against the ravages of her body.

"Don't you go anywhere," I order her from the foot of her bed.

"I won't ... if I can help it." Her reply does little to calm my fears.

"I won't let you go," I say, knowing that we are both about to go in for the fight of her life.

Soon, another series of wrongly formed spikes begins to jump wildly across the monitor, but this latest episode doesn't stop, and Patrick turns to me with an abrupt demand.

"Nancy, go!"

As I leave the room, I turn to see him with paddles in hand, raised, and poised over Alice. She's looking up at him, fully conscious, beating on her own chest, urging, "You'd better do it!"

I am left with this lingering horrific image as the door to her room closes behind me. I lean my back against the wall and slide down, meeting my butt to my heels, dropping my face down on my bent knees in the hospital hall.

Bear with me as I try to put into words how it was, what I understood was happening in that moment so many years ago. You must suspend any disbelief and hear me out. But I tell you true, how I knew it to be.

I rode the winds of my fear as I traced our subtle connection to each other, then latched onto her trailing spirit tails and refused to part with her. I was in a place of rushing motion and howling darkness. And there was tremendous risk. Risk, if she stayed here when she should have gone. Risk, that she'd leave when she might have stayed. I held on.

I don't mean to imply she had no power in the matter. If my strength and determination to keep her here had any part in her staying, it was with her complete consent. She could have overridden any hold placed on her. Hers was the ultimate voice—or penultimate, actually. There is some Voice higher than that as well, some Influence. Even so, I only know that sometimes we are given a choice. To go or stay. In such moments, this human exercise of will is often shaded with conflict when what it requires is a clear and decided mind. The conflict is caused by the need to escape pain. Add that with the fear of dying, the regret to leave, the wish to stay in the lives of those whom we love ... and the compelling lure of the beyond.

What are the unseen mystical possibilities? What if Alice was ambivalent while I clutched her here? What if I held her despite the total breakdown of her body? What if my holding consigned her to a body that was unresponsive? Trapped her. Comatose. Could any of this happen? What if you could catch and hold someone in the space between the worlds? Maybe this is how some ghosts are made. Did I have such power to hold her? To a certain extent, I believed so.

I had seen the poignant, delicate dance between the caregiver and dying person, a slow minuet of strength and helplessness, as the stronger invests their labor into the keeping of the mortally ill person. I've witnessed the intention, the will of the loving provider, the refusal to give up on behalf of their beloved. Watched the slow irrevocable decline, despite the care. And I have seen the alternative: the ease with which a terminally ill person dies after the spouse, child, parent, lover, finally gives up struggling to keep them here. And when permission to go actually is given ... the departing one often slips away effortlessly.

While the battle with illness is still enjoined, the dying person's effort is so great, so exhausting. Like a bug on a pin, the dying beat against the cotton batting of their ebbing life, pinned by the body's betrayal, helpless to fly, unable to crawl away. Till finally there is no choice left but to die, capitulate, give it up, take the only door out that opens.

Sometimes it is not a beloved person but pain that acts as the pin that holds us here. Pain is a great deterrent to death. It requires so much of our consciousness. It demands consideration, the focus of attention to this body, this place, this realm. When pain is relieved, people can let go, loosen the grip of mind and will and relinquish control. Pain thwarts the easy transition from here to ... *There.*

If pain persists—and death is to be the answer—one must transcend the pain to glimpse the outpost edges of life. Rise above it to see the destination, to find the Door of Veils. If pain is not appeased by any other means, this transcendence must be accomplished by the most difficult and seemingly unnatural act ... that of total surrender to it, of giving in to the pain, embracing it, bathing in the icy flame of it. With that end to resistance, pain lets go and is no longer perceived. And death can come, if death awaits.

This is some of what I was understanding as I sat on the floor against the wall in that hospital hallway, clutching her essence and filling the shrieking void with screams of my own—no, no, no, no!

Alice, I understood, was effectively harnessed to the starting block while deciding whether to enter the raceway. Her surrender to death would have to come after she rejected being kept here. And after she wrenched herself from my grip, from my need. My pull to keep her was the initial force Alice would need to escape, if, indeed, she consented to go.

I didn't intend to make it an easy choice for her. In the reality that underlies our awareness in this life and informs it all, I had a grip on her in the black void and planned to keep her here or make her drag me along with her.

On this particular day, Alice made the decision to stay ... and endured the outcome of that decision, both hers and mine, which was to awaken to pain, to exhaustion, to fear, to anxiety, to the prospect, if not the likelihood of diminished capacity, of rehabilitation—months of it—and all, ultimately, to no avail. It meant coming again to that same precipice in some future time, imminent or distant, to face again the terrifying edge of the worlds. In an hour—a day—a week—a year—or longer—but inevitably, again.

Christine waited with me in the hallway that night, witness to my reactions. She told me later that she'd never seen me so angry. Angry? How odd to have that drama so totally mis-read. Anger? But that's what my fear, my battle, must have looked like. I'm sure I looked fierce.

As the drama of the evening unfolds in this hallway, various friends begin to arrive. Christine must have made some calls. Good friends Marcus and Lily, with whom we play cribbage one night a month, have come. They are active retirees, and hospice volunteers with Alice and me, trained in the same class, and they live on a seven-acre hillside in Bobcat Gulch, just before Fortuna. And Mattie is here after leaving Duke up at St. Joseph's, checking in to find out about Alice and then staying. I acknowledge them, but I cannot afford to lose my concentration.

Time has become irrelevant in this instance. It is only the present moment that counts—it's all *now* until it is *then*. I will learn later that Alice's ordeal with the crash cart lasts more than an hour. When the door to her room opens, Patrick steps out. He scans the room at eye level, then catches sight of me at his feet, huddled on the floor. He squats down to talk to me, as if confronting the patient's family on the hospital floor is the most ordinary thing to do.

He tells me that they had finally regulated Alice's heart activity after zapping her on *three* separate occasions. But it had been touch-and-go, and he is uncertain now that her heart will stay regular and stable. Alice is resting, he says, but I can look in on her, if I wish. I am then expected to leave her to rest and trust her to their care.

But Patrick says something else, something interesting. He confesses that he just had the most unnerving experience of his career. "What usually happens when a patient goes into fibrillation that requires the paddles, they just pass out. Alice never did. I have *never* had to do that on someone who was conscious, when the heart begins to flutter like that, they *always* pass out.

"I was waiting for her to lose consciousness so I could apply the shock," he adds, marveling. "She was eyeball to eyeball with me. She said, 'You'd better come on! Come on!' She began beating on her chest, and I had to knock her hands away to get the paddles in place and zap her. Of course, with the shock, she did black out then."

Patrick's eyebrows raise and he shrugs in wonder. "I've never seen anything like it. Someone staying conscious like that with their heart fibrillating so badly."

I realize with his comment how hard Alice fought to stay here, afraid to give over to the darkness, afraid she'd slide away unless she maintained control.

When I enter the room, her eyes are open, and she locks on mine with attention and follows me as I move to the bedside next to her. She is still home in there.

"Hello, love," I say softly. "Glad you're still here. Please stay."

She closes her eyes and I hope that means she agrees. She appears exhausted, but gamely hanging on. I touch her head and lightly brush her sweat-damp hair off her forehead with my fingertips. Since her fused ankle makes it very hard for Alice to keep her leg cocked up without help, I assist by holding up her leg while a nurse catheterizes her.

Alice is so totally spent.

I have never seen her so tired. My own heart freezes in fear at the sight of it. I whisper to her that I'm right outside the door, that she can ask for me anytime and that I'll peep in and check on her periodically. I hope it comforts her. By now it is three in the morning, and Room 2, a little four-bed unit right across the hall, is not in use, so I ask at the nurse's station if I can camp out in there for the night. They tell me I can, without hesitation, since they all know and work with me. Professional privilege, I guess you could say. But instead of resting, I wear a rut across the hallway from Room 2 to the doorway of Alice's room, wandering back and forth, just barely opening the door a crack, peeking in on her as she dozes fitfully, unable to sleep myself.

The next morning Dr. Tustin, another doctor in the medical group, comes in and performs a Swans-Gantz application, which requires running a balloon up Alice's brachial artery in her arm. It is from him that I learn the extent of Alice's heart attack, the extent of the damage.

To her, he says, "Alice, you have smoked your last cigarette. The next forty-eight to seventy-two hours will tell the tale—they are critical. If you survive them, you have smoked your last cigarette. And," he continues laconically, "if you don't survive ... then, I repeat ... you have *still* smoked your *last* cigarette."

Well, that's clear enough.

Alice is forty-eight years old and she has smoked a pack and a half a day for thirty-two years. And I, too, am a smoker, having smoked a pack a day for twenty-six of my forty-one years.

That same morning, while I make a request for a couple days leave, Alice is moved to a vacated bed in ICU proper, one directly in the line of sight with the nurses' station. Her new room enables me to slide in through a utility door, where linen carts and supplies are kept, and poke my head through a curtain to check on her without letting light in or drawing attention to the fact that I am there. I do this practically every fifteen minutes throughout the day.

As the night before, I catch Alice awake more often than not. But she must be a little better because tonight it's not unusual to find her looking up and acknowledging me with her eyes.

On this second evening, Josie leaves HoneyBear to man the jewelry shop alone and comes to spend the next couple of days camping out with me in Room 2. This allows me to take a break and go home to feed the dogs while Josie takes over and spells me at those times. She also alternates the fifteen-minute checks with me and steals a look at Alice. I use the hospital shower for two days, not willing to be away for the length of time that it would take to go home.

I am convinced that my vigilance is important to the outcome of this calamity. Alice almost slipped away once, and I know it's arguable, but I greatly fear to risk her being alone again, without me to stand sentry before that fearsome final path. Mostly, her incapacitating exhaustion alarms me. As Alice improves, I begin to extend the time I check on her, actually pulling up a chair and sitting at her bedside, particularly at meals so I can help because she's too tired to eat. The exertion is never appreciated until you, or someone you love, have to expend heroic effort for such a mundane act. Her arm trembles as she lifts the fork to her mouth, and chewing her food seems to use up all her strength.

But Alice continues to improve daily. She is now on a beta blocker and her blood pressure is stable and her cholesterol levels are fine. Also her blood sugars are totally normal, which I will find significant five years later, when she tests positive for diabetes, which in retrospect, the doctors will determine was the undetected underlying cause of *this* heart attack.

So, after the two-week standard hospitalization in those days, Alice is finally released to go home once the discharge nurse Zandra McColl comes in to give Alice her brochures and instructions. I am pleased because Zandra is one of my favorite nurses at the hospital, but if I'd known everything she was going to include in her topics I might not have been so relaxed about it.

She greets us with "Hey, Nancy. Hi, Alice. Glad to meet you. We've got a lot to cover and I have a lot of handouts and stuff to give you, so we'll get started."

Zandra opens her case and takes out a large packet. She reviews the cardiac diet recommendations from the American Heart Association with Alice and tells us about the Redwoods Aerobics Program, the monitored exercise program at the Fireman's Pavilion in the park.

"I put your name on the list as a recommended participant, and I want you to promise me you'll show up within the week," she says. "You need to get some good cardiac strength back, and this program has nurses on duty and a hot-line to the hospital, so if anyone gets into trouble there's immediate help."

"Sounds good to me," Alice agrees. "It's a little scary thinking about exercising this soon after all that pain, but I'll sign on. It sounds as if it's the safest way to go right now. I have an exercise bike at home, but that's not too appealing at the moment."

"Mm-hmm," Zandra acknowledges. "It's primarily a walking program down there, but there are also stationary bikes and rowing machines. And while we're on the topic of apprehension about exerting yourself, I want you to know within three or four weeks it will be safe to resume your normal sexual activity without needing to be afraid. Whenever you can climb a flight of stairs fairly easily, you're good to go."

Zandra is very matter of fact, very comfortable. Alice breaks into a grin, but I blush about fourteen shades of pink-to-purple. So if Zandra has any doubts how things are with Alice and me, one look at my face will have given the game away.

"Well," Alice begins, " ... I have been wondering about that."

That is odd, because I haven't given it the least thought. Shows you how scared I was with this whole thing. Had I thought about sex at all, I would have written off that part of my life without hesitation, just so long as Alice is still alive. Clearly she isn't ready to be past that stage of *her* life, however.

"No need to worry. Your heart is stronger than you think. Just take it slow and easy for the first few weeks after you resume activity—that's usually better for women anyway, isn't it?" Zandra says, laughing, with Alice and me joining in. "The first time you have an orgasm will feel a little strange because you're going to be divided between going with it and watching yourself cautiously at the same time. It'll be all right, though. Within another month, you'll be fully sexual again and enjoying your usual routine."

Alice is in a mood to joke, "And if my usual routine is swinging from the chandeliers, would you still say that?"

Zandra laughs easily. "Well, I might caution you a bit on being that strenuous for a while. But at the same time, I'd probably want to know who did your ceiling reinforcements for you." It is probably a quip she's made a thousand times before to the same wise-ass comment. Still, it's hard to top that.

She has more to say about Alice resuming all levels of activity, of not turning into a "cardiac cripple," and assuring her that her strength would return, and with the exercise program and diet management she'll probably wind up healthier than she's ever been.

"Of course, you will not go back to smoking," Zandra continues, her voice sounding a stern warning. "How about you, Nancy? You smoke, too, don't you?"

"Not any more." I say. "I quit last week."

"You did?" Alice turns to me surprised.

"Well, I knew you would have a harder time if I was still smoking, so after you passed the worst of it, and I wasn't so wrought up about you, I decided to quit and try to be done with my withdrawal by the time you got home."

Alice studies me, a bit stunned. Her eyes are shining and soft with love.

Zandra clears her throat and Alice and I are both startled. We seem to have forgotten that she's still here. "Well, that makes it easier, Alice. But you are *not* to smoke or you'll be right back here. I can guarantee—smoking is the worst thing you can do after a heart attack. Nicotine constricts the blood vessels and puts a huge strain on the heart. Try sucking on sour lemon or sour apple drops when you have the craving. I'm told that helps."

"Licorice helps, too," I say. "I looked it up in my herbals."

"No booze, either," Zandra reminds. "I'm sure your doctor will let you know when you can resume any drinking. Keep up your stool softeners for a while. You don't want to be straining."

Parenthetically, I learn that an enema is never given to anyone who has recently suffered a heart attack. Doctors debate whether or not it's because of an actual nerve connection or merely some inciting ingredient in the enema solution. I suspect the anus may have a link with one of those mystical meridians in Eastern medicine. I don't know if our Western medicine has ever attempted to explain it, but they do acknowledge it: stimulation to that area can have a definite deleterious effect on a recent heart patient. And that leaves us open to a whole raft of snide and *smartass* comments to be made about this *un-holy* connection—heart to asshole and vice-versa—but I'll refrain from more and leave it to you to make them. (Don't say I never gave ya nuthin'.)

Zandra tells Alice that she can almost expect to have one or two more hospitalizations within the next six months. "It nearly always happens, so I'm cautioning you."

"Why? What for?" I ask, alarmed.

"Well, most people have some kind of pain episode—gas, indigestion—which mimics the feeling of a heart problem, and it is scary enough to send them to the ER. And sometimes it does turn out to be real. So err on the side of caution, and get it checked out if you have any similar symptoms or any of the standard signs we've just gone over."

Zandra was right—about two months later Alice has a suspicious chest pain that sends us back to the ER. After her blood is drawn for cardiac enzymes, she is admitted to a room in the ward. Here, she is installed with a telemetry device, a remote EKG-type gadget that attaches to the chest and monitors from the nurses station. We await the results from Alice's enzyme tests as her blood is taken and analyzed at various intervals throughout the next seventy-two hours. Eventually, Alice's chest pain dissipates (very likely a case of heartburn and gas), and she is feeling calmer that this is probably a false alarm.

She's still a bit worried though. Her doctor had given her permission to add a glass of wine with dinner, and since she's wound up back at the hospital, she's afraid he will rescind the privilege. Alice is really not that much of a drinker these days—she imbibed more than her share in her misspent youth. Still, that allowable glass of wine looms large for her, especially now, in view of the fact that she no longer smokes. She's been strictly compliant—not easy after a thirty-year, pack-and-a-half-a-day habit—but all these restrictions are taking a psychological toll.

No one seems to better understand this than our friend Justy. Ornery as ever, she arrives on her first visit since Alice's brush with death, showing up stating she has "come to cheer Alice up." She's here with us at the hospital today, appearing just after the nurses give Alice permission to take a shower.

"There, that'll do it," says Rachel, the floor nurse, as she removes the tape from the telemetry device from Alice's chest. "Don't be long in the shower now. And if you get into any difficulty, have Nancy buzz us. We'll be standing by. I'll come back and attach the telemetry again when you're clean."

Rachel places the device on the bedside table, and Alice and I head for the shower, leaving Justy on her own for a while.

"I'll be just fine," Justy assures us, before crinkling her nose in a dramatic show of fake disgust. "And since you're about two days overdue for your morning shower, I'd consider it a great personal favor if you proceed without delay."

"Very funny, Justine," responds Alice, as she continues toward the bathroom, moving a little slower than usual perhaps, but otherwise she seems okay. "You behave yourself and don't get into any trouble while I tend to this."

"Trouble? Me?" Justy asks innocently.

"Just park it, and watch some scintillating daytime TV for a few minutes. And don't terrorize the natives, will you?"

I stand by in the bathroom just outside the shower while Alice scrubs and sluices. She is nearly finished when Debby the charge nurse bursts through the bathroom door in a panic.

"Are you all right, Alice? Are you having chest pains? What's wrong?" she demands, breathless.

"I'm fine," Alice answers. "Why? What's going on?"

Debby opens the shower door and presses her stethoscope against Alice's wet chest, water still issuing from the showerhead. Alice, naked, reaches for the faucet and turns it off before the nurse gets thoroughly soaked herself. Debby removes the prongs from her ears and gives Alice a critical once-over.

"Okay, you look to be all right. Are you ready to get out?"

"Yeah. What's this all about?" Alice steps into the towel I hold out for her and she dries off her front while I pat down her back.

"I don't know. I can't say," says Debby. "We just got some very strange, very alarming readings on your telemetry."

Uh-oh. Justy.

Now Rachel bursts into the bathroom. "I have the crash cart. Do I need to call a Code Blue?"

"No, everything seems to be okay," says Debby, calmer now as she reviews her assessment. "She's not fibrillating. Pulse is rock steady. Must have been a glitch in the monitor. It's a false alarm. Call off the dogs."

Debby looks down at herself. She has a sodden streak on one arm and shoulder of her uniform top. "Well, I didn't get too wet."

"Sorry 'bout that." says Alice, handing her a towel.

Debby dabs at herself, smiling. "All in the line of duty." She gives Alice another appraising look as Alice puts on a clean hospital gown, then pats her on the back and leaves.

Meanwhile, Justy sits demurely back in the room, intently focused on a truly boring and inane game show in the vast offering of daytime television's boring and inane game shows. The telemetry monitor is on the bed table and so pointedly disregarded by Justine that it seems to have a glow around it. She, herself, is busily manifesting a halo, somewhat askew, which blinks in and out—visible only to Alice and me.

Rachel picks the telemetry device off the table and leaves the room behind Debby. "I'll go get a new one of these, and be right back. There's evidently something faulty with this one."

"Ju-u-usty!" Alice demands when the three of us are left alone.

"What?"

"Don't 'what' me. What did you do?"

"Well, I didn't think I *did* anything till the nurse came rushing in. I got bored and was just wandering around the room. I picked up the little monitor and looked it over. I held it up against me to see if I could feel anything from it, and then ... I just held it up to the TV. I guess it sent a funny signal through it. Sorry."

We thought it best not to tell the nurses, lest they throw us all out on our ears.

Later that same day, the doctor discharges Alice—no heart attack. And he allows Alice to continue drinking that one glass of wine every night with dinner. The next day, Justy presents Alice with a large, stemmed goblet and declares it to be the perfect vessel for Alice's glass of wine with dinner. It holds about 10 ounces.

"Now, remember, just one glass with dinner, Alice," Justy teases with mock sternness. "One glass is all you're allowed—doctor's orders. One glass. One fucking *big* glass."

One night about four months after Alice's heart attack, we finish eating dinner—lemon chicken and gingered broccoli with bean sprouts. Before Alice's heart attack I bought a wok, and since the American Heart Association approves most Chinese food, we'd been eating Chinese just about every night since.

We'd gone whole hog into it, learning to use chopsticks, setting the table with new Asian-style dishes, chopstick holders, a new teapot filled with green tea. We also purchased a new butcher knife and an authentic Chinese cleaver.

The hardest thing about cooking Chinese food, we found, is the time it takes to chop the ingredients, and Alice truly does elevate it to an art form. She spends an hour every afternoon sitting at the table, chopping the vegetables perfectly for the evening's menu. She slices the celery precisely on an angle, every piece the same size. She angle-cuts the carrots, too, turning them a quarter turn with every chop. Ditto the onions, mushrooms, bean sprouts, bok choy, whatever; all the ingredients beautifully prepared for cooking in typical Alice fashion. No matter what Alice does, she makes the effort count for herself, with a Zen-like focus, taking pride and pleasure in the endeavor. In this case, creating precise and uniform pieces.

With this same exactitude, she will stack clean dishes in the drainer as she washes them, till they resemble a tower of precariously balanced pieces in a tableware sculpture, cantilevered and engineered. I refuse to unload a drainer after she's stacked it. One misstep, one prematurely removed piece, and the walls of Jericho come tumbling down. Like a game of chinaware pickup sticks, this is. And I decline to play. That's all right, because she seems to enjoy the dismantling as much as the assembly. I don't know if she does things this way to relieve the boredom, or because she is so in the moment that her focus is always sharper on what she is doing than mine would be. Even when she's multitasking—washing dishes and talking to me and mindful of the animals and listening to the news in the background—she is centered on the project at hand and can be building an architectural dishware delight at the sink in the midst of everything else. Or chopping veggies Chinese-style, perfectly, as if styling them for a glossy magazine photo shoot.

After all the cutting, Alice fills each wedge of a multi-section Tupperware container with a different chopped ingredient. By the time I get home from work, all I need to do is start the rice, marinate the meat, and wok away. Dinner is usually ready within twenty minutes.

Tonight, however, I have to attend to a housebound patient, and subsequently get to my own home way behind schedule. We eat so late that by the time we finish it's already time for bed. Alice showers, I clean the kitchen, and she lets the dogs out while I take my turn getting clean. She's in bed when I come out of the bathroom. She has the TV on, but mutes it as I crawl into bed. I roll to her and put my head on her shoulder and she pulls me close.

"Sorry I was so late tonight. Thanks for having the rice cooked and the veggies ready," I say, snuggling into her shoulder. "You feeling all right?"

"Yeah, I'm fine. Had a good walk at RAP tonight." That's the Redwoods Aerobic Program she goes to three times a week. "But I had a conversation with Loreena Fitz while we walked, and she said something that bothered me, and I want to talk to you about it."

"Oh? What was that?" I pull back to look at her.

"Well, she's recovered from her hip replacement pretty well, but her son is ill, you know. Terminally ill with cancer."

"I remember."

"Anyway, she was upset because last night he told her he knew he was close to the end, and he didn't want her holding on to him and trying to keep him here when it was time for him to go. She said she'd been thinking about it all day, and she didn't know if she could do that—just let him go. Not after she and his wife have been fighting desperately to keep him alive. Anyway, it made me think."

"What about?"

"We have to make a pact, you and I." She turns on her side to face me, and I feel a chill.

"Are you all right? Why are you bringing this up now?" I'm a little panicked.

"Don't be upset—I'm fine. I told you why, it was Loreena who got me thinking. I'm more than fine. I'm feeling better than I have in a long time. I've lost weight. I'm eating healthy, thanks to you and the wok. I'm not smoking. And I'm getting exercise. All my tests are good. It's the perfect time for us to talk about this."

"Okay." I feel reassured, and in fact she does look great. Her color is good, her stamina has very much improved, and she is more energetic than she's been for months, maybe years. "Okay, shoot. What about it, this pact."

She takes my hand and curls it into her chest. "When I had the heart attack, I know you did something to hold onto me. Something ... intense."

"Yeah. Yes I did. How do you know?"

Alice brings my hand to her mouth and kisses it. "I felt you. And I ... I had a choice. To go or stay. I don't remember a lot about those few days in the hospital, but I do know that first night there was a point after I was pounding on my chest and Patrick zapped me ... I didn't want to, but I could have died then. You were holding me here, very strong, very ... determined. And it helped me. It helped keep me here because I was going to have to fight to stay. And I really wanted to stay. There were ... winds? Something? Motion ... that I could have gone with. That I resisted."

When she pauses, her eyes focus on something far away, and at the same she seems to find her center somewhere deep inside herself.

"I'm glad you stayed," I whisper, not far from tears.

This brings her attention back from wherever she was, and she looks at me, then touches my face and kisses me again. "I wouldn't have missed it for the world. I want to be here as long as I can with you, lady. I love you, you know."

"I know."

She sighs and locks her eyes with mine. "The thing is, I'll never want to go. I'll never want to leave you. But it just might come to that, sometime. It just might be that I get ... too tired, too sick, or something could happen that would mean I'd be here in a condition I wouldn't want to live with. You know?"

"Yes, I do. I do know. I knew it that night. I knew there was a risk to holding you back ... if you needed to go." This is hard! This is hard to talk about. Discussing the potential need to give my True Love permission to leave this life. My crushing dread at the thought of living on without her. Something must be showing. I evidently make some movement away from this subject, because Alice pursues the topic relentlessly.

"Nancy, you have to promise me." She's very serious, her eyes commanding and no-nonsense. "There may come a time when you have to let go. When I'll *need* you to let me go. Because ... even if I must, I won't want to leave you, and if you make it harder, if you keep me ... well, I'm afraid of that." She's quietly beseeching me now, and I comprehend it all too well.

It's my turn now to be reassuring. I take her hand and grip it hard.

285

"Alice, I do understand. I really do. I know it could happen that way. And I don't know if I'll have the courage to face it, to live here without you." I shudder, trying to shake off the very thought. "But I promise you, I won't hold you if you *need* to go. And if you get stuck here somehow, I swear to you, I'll pull the plug, Alice."

She takes a deep breath and appears to relax. This isn't an easy conversation for her, either. She has a lot of courage, this woman of mine. I've never met anyone as brave.

This is not the first time we've been here. We've talked about these issues before, back a few years ago when we both attended a hospice volunteer class. The topics of death and dying sparked some serious personal discussions between us, causing us to draw up advance directives for health care. We both have been pretty specific in our stipulations.

We also have promised each other, if circumstances ever come to that, we will help each other get out of here if necessary. Neither of us has any problem with that. The will to live. The will to die. Quality of life issues. We are both pretty clear about all these things, and fortunately, in complete accord with each other. That isn't always so between people who love each other. We are lucky.

"You have to remember your vow to me, too," I continue. "I expect you to do the same thing for me, if anything should happen."

Alice listens intently and then draws me into her arms. "You know I will," she whispers. And I do know it.

But I also know she will not have to.

I am very conscious that I can never relax my guard, that I need to be careful, take care of myself. Because I know deep in my heart of hearts, with a calm and abiding certainty, that I will need to be here for her. Somewhere in the book that underwrites this life, I had signed on to be the one to survive.

I know this, and perhaps she does, too.

But not now, not yet. We don't need to think about this any more tonight.

For this moment, we are both alive, both healthy, and both very much in love with each other. Sleep will be postponed for a while. For now, we are called to more important matters. Communication of another sort, one in a more tactile language.

Szechuan Peppersalt

2 tablespoons Szechuan peppercorns
1 tablespoon salt

Heat a small frying pan or saucepan over medium-low heat for
one minute. Add peppercorns and stir continuously in dry pan
for about three minutes. Do not burn. Remove and let cool.
Grind peppercorns into a coarse powder with a mortar and pes-
tle, or grinder. Add salt, mix well. Store in tight container. Use
for flavor and garnish.

Chicken With Lemon Sauce

3/4 pound boned chicken breasts, cut into small thin pieces, 2" by 1-1/2"

Marinade
1/4 teaspoon salt
2 teaspoon rice wine or dry sherry
1 teaspoon soy sauce
1 egg yolk
1/8 teaspoon pepper or Szechuan pepper

Lemon Sauce
1/4 cup sugar
1/4 cup chicken broth
2 tablespoons water
1/4 teaspoon salt
2 teaspoon cornstarch
1 teaspoon sesame oil
Juice of 1 lemon (about ¼ cup)
6 tablespoon cornstarch
2 tablespoon all-purpose flour
1/2 cup (approximately) peanut oil or other wok oil
1 tablespoon vegetable oil (added to sauce at end for gloss)
1 sliced lemon, if desired.

Combine marinade in medium bowl and add chicken pieces, mixing well. Let stand 15 minutes. Combine ingredients for lemon sauce in small bowl, set aside. Mix flour and cornstarch in medium bowl. Dip chicken in flour mixture to coat. Heat oil in wok and fry chicken a few pieces at a time, turning for about a minute until done. Remove with slotted spoon and drain well on rack over wok. Remove all oil except 1 teaspoon, stirring lemon sauce into the hot oil and bringing to boil. Thin with 1 Tablespoon water at a time if too thick. Add 1 Tablespoon oil at end to make sauce glossy. Stir and pour over chicken pieces, and garnish with lemon. Serve immediately.

Scallops With Snow Peas

Scallops (bay or sea) enough for two—approximately 3/4 pound
1/2 cup peanut oil or other oil for wok cooking
1 garlic clove, crushed
3 scallions, chopped in 1" pieces
1/2 pound snow peas

Marinade
1-1/2 teaspoons rice wine
1/4 teaspoon salt
Pinch of Chinese five spice (a mix of ground cloves, star anise, cinnamon, fennel and Szechuan peppercorns)
1/2 teaspoon minced fresh ginger root
1-1/2 teaspoons cornstarch
1 teaspoon sesame oil

Seasoning Sauce
1 tablespoon chicken broth
3 tablespoon water
1/2 teaspoon cornstarch
3 tablespoons oyster sauce

Rinse scallops and pat dry. Combine marinade ingredients and add scallops, mixing well. Let stand for 20 minutes while mixing seasoning sauce in a separate bowl. Heat oil in wok, add garlic till golden, and remove from oil. Carefully add scallops and stir-fry until done. Bay scallops will cook in a minute or less; sea scallops are larger and denser and will take a bit longer. Do not overcook. Remove scallops, draining any oil back into wok. Add scallions and snow peas, stir-fry lightly and add seasoning sauce. Remove vegetables with slotted spoon, letting sauce drain back into wok (add a little water to sauce if needed.) Arrange vegetables in circle on plates. Return scallops to wok and stir-fry lightly and quickly in sauce till hot again. Serve scallops immediately, in center of vegetable circle. Sprinkle with Szechuan peppersalt.

DATELINE, 1983—**Challenger's maiden voyage** includes the first spacewalk of the 9-year-old space shuttle program. **Supreme Court declares** many state and abortion restrictions unconstitutional. **Sally Ride**, 32, is first woman astronaut crewmember in space. **Soviets shoot down** South Korean Boeing 747 jetliner that strayed into Soviet airspace, killing all 269 aboard, including 61 Americans; President Reagan strongly condemns the act.

Mary Lou Retton wins the Women's All-Around Gymnastics Gold medal for the US. **Alice Walker** wins the Pulitzer for *The Color Purple*. **Harvey Fierstein's** *Torch Song Trilogy* wins a Tony Award. **Beirut** is scene of terrorist suicide bombing that kills 237 US marines. **US invades Grenada** to overthrow Cuban-backed regime.

Linda Hunt wins Best Supporting Actress Oscar for *A Year Of Living Dangerously*, in which she plays a man. **Lotus develops** business spreadsheet program. **Inflation slows** with declining oil prices. **Congress admits internment** of Japanese citizens was unjust; they also bail out Social Security system. Reagan calls for funding of **Star Wars Program.**

is it sisters?

Alice and I routinely schedule a special trip for our houseguests. And amazingly, none of our friends ever refuse to go along, mostly being game types and good sports, all.

Our guest picks up and inspects various items I have set aside for today's picnic. "Whatcha got there? Brie and English crackers ... chardonnay ... chocolates ... sliced Asian pears? Wow, fancy! Where are we going?"

"We're taking you on our favorite outing today." I am gleeful—about to have some fun now. "We're taking you to our dump!"

Blank stare.

"You'll love it. It's an ideal picnic spot." I pay no attention to the reaction—the stillness, the wide-eyed shock, the attempt to be polite and offer no objection, to display no overt disapproval—I anticipate and enjoy it. It's a benign prank I love to pull on all first-time houseguests.

"Uh ... If you say so," comes the hesitant reply.

We lead off in Alice's Ranchero (which we loaded with trash the night before in anticipation of this trip), with our mystified guests following behind in their car. How I wish to be a bug on their windshield and listen to their comments as we caravan the two lanes that make up Highway 36.

I imagine the conversation probably goes something like: "Well, I knew it! I knew moving up here in this forsaken wilderness would make

291

'em nuts sooner or later. We'll humor them a while and get the hell outta here as soon as we can."

Headlights are required as we drive in and out of the groves, through places so darkly forested the road is in a constant state of dampness. In a matter of moments, however, the darkness gives way to open sunlight, and we're riding parallel to the shining Van Duzen River. We cruise into small valleys lined with farmhouses, barns, and meadows dotted black and white, and tan with Guernsey and Jersey cows. At one point, we cross an arched concrete bridge built in the 1920s when the clean lines of art deco was in vogue and make a sharp left into the woods, which leads us to a clearing up a short, ramped road ... to several rusty-green dumpsters of immense capacity, similar to those found in any cosmopolitan area of the country. Aside from that, and the sign that reads Refuse Center, nothing distinguishes this area from the surrounding trees and countryside.

As we back up to unload our haul, our guests park their car and stand outside, open-mouthed with amazement.

"This is your dump?" one asks, greatly relieved and looking around the redwoods and Douglas fir for a clear spot along the river's edge.

"Yeah, isn't it great?"

"I never would have believed it! So where do we have our picnic?"

"We'll go back a bit the way we came and find a place in the trees."

After Alice and I rid our trash, we resume guiding our guests, retracing a quarter mile to a small road that takes us through the darkness of towering redwoods to a clear slope down by the river's edge. Known as Swimmers Delight, this lovely, state-protected grove is part of the local park system and offers a natural swimming hole, an easy-on-your-feet sandy beach, and plenty of room for sunbathing.

In summertime, only a few families and kids typically occupy it. That is to say, no more than maybe twenty people at a time can be found here in the busiest season—typically locals and vacationers camping overnight in the groves. At other times of the year, especially weekdays, it is a good bet that you'll be alone. At the most, one or two other people may be strolling the river's edge.

Opposite this idyllic spot, on the other side of the river, stands a solid red wall, a cliff of native stone and clay, which rises up a hundred feet to a tree-lined top. From the narrow crevices of the bluff's rocky face grow the ornamental, curling branches of Manzanita as well as red-branched

Madrone of a respectable size that have taken a rather precarious hold, seemingly growing from the very stone itself.

Silhouetted against the red of the cliff, a hawk swoops down and flies parallel to the riverbed, no doubt searching for steelhead (an ocean-going rainbow trout that returns to fresh water to spawn) or one of the half-pounders that make these waters their home. Whenever Alice and I come here, we never fail to see at least one of the indigenous Cooper's or Red-tailed hawks making a grand show like this.

In the clearing's sunniest area, we lay out our spread on a redwood picnic table the size of a Buick. While lunching, we watch the fish jump and the birds soar, enjoying the peaceful rush and gurgle of the river over shallows, which lie just beyond the swimming hole.

Sometimes if you are quiet enough, still enough, and the day grows late enough, you might see deer come down to water. Other times, the soft sand at the river's edge might bear the overnight prints of raccoon, possum, skunk, and, not infrequently, mountain lion. Alice and I always bring along bird and mammal guides on our excursions to this area to identify the wide array of wild life present.

Houseguests already caught before in our little trip-to-the-dump joke often demand a reprise. A couple of our return guests balked when we reminded them that they had already seen the dump: "Whatcha mean, we've already seen the dump? No law against going again, is there?" So, as a matter of course, nearly every visitor, whether first time or returning, is treated to a trip to the dump. And once they return home, they regale their citified listeners with tales of happy picnicking at one of the wonderful Humboldt County waste disposal sites.

With or without guests, it is our habit to stop, Alice and I, in the groves or along the river. Even in paradise, the chafe of everyday life erodes your awareness. In the midst of nature's glory or the middle of concrete and crime, nothing so heals the human heart as the moment taken, the detail noted—the tints of sunset, the glisten of rain. To be mindful attunes us to life, speaks to the spirit, and quiets the wearying racket within.

Nowhere in my experience are the spiritual benefits of nature greater than when near water, whether it be placid, turbulent, flowing, or falling. It stills and restores us. It is our kin; 80 percent of our own bodies are made up of it. Proximity to water produces harmonic change within us—the same way striking a tuning fork sets off a kindred vibration in another fork close by—causing us to resonate to its life-giving essence.

The hour or so spent lounging alongside the riverbank after the dump is as reviving as a good nap or a day off. As welcome as an answered prayer.

⚜

Once a month, Alice and I gather up all our unburnable trash. Cuttings and brush and paper products we set afire in the burn barrel, and when this gets full up with ashes, we load it also in the Ranchero to go to the dump. This being 1983, burning trash in a 55-gallon drum in the backyard is still allowed. The only requirements in our rural community are that residents obtain a yearly burning permit from the local volunteer fire department and observe the permissive burn days. (That is, days officially designated safe to burn in open-air containers with wire-mesh lids to catch sparks.)

On this day, the back of the Ranchero is piled high, tarped over, and lashed down. We just cleaned out a shed full of unusable junk—old umbrella staves, boxes of magazines—surely, we never actually *saved* any of that stuff. And off we go then, with our picnic basket of sandwiches and a thermos of coffee on our way to the dump.

It's only a 3-mile trip, but the dramatic changes in scenery seem to delightfully prolong the journey. Within minutes, the two-lane highway leaves even the marginal civilization we live in and enters a vast land of farms, forest, and wilderness, overshadowed by looming hills and paralleled by the winding Van Duzen River.

Highway 36 comes to an abrupt and complete stop on the right bank of the river, then makes a by-God, 90-degree, true right-angle turn onto the single-lane bridge, spanning nearly 500 feet across the flowing waters. Once you negotiate that right angle from the road to the bridge, you are committed—there's simply no turning back on a corner like that. People driving from the opposite direction on this single-lane bridge are obliged to back up to accommodate you. This bridge is negotiated like this every livelong day, dawn to dark, even by logging trucks traversing in both directions. This time, however, the bridge is clear, delivering us a mere hundred yards from the turnoff into the dump. †

We spot old Harold in his usual place. A metal salvager, he spends his days intercepting people bearing salvageable "treasure" as they back up to the dumpsters. He has a cozy, little set-up in the shade on a couple of broken-down chairs and a rickety table. Harold has witnessed our comings and goings often enough to know we never discard anything remotely good in the salvage department.

On this day a buddy of his joins him, an obvious newcomer to the business. We never learn his name, but our lives are richer ever after for his contribution.

His pal is as lean, sinewy, and small as Harold is lumpy, dumpy, and broad. When we pull up to unload, the little fellow springs up from his perch on a teetering off-balance chair and jogs briskly over to the back of our truck. "Ladies," he says, as he touches the dirty brim of his cap. "Here, let me help you with that." And he bounds to the back of the truck to open the tailgate.

I glance over at Harold long enough to catch him staring at the ground, his expression long-suffering.

Alice and I step back, having long since learned to shelve our lesbian self-sufficiency when an offer of male brawn comes our way.

The little guy vaults up into the truck bed and starts hauling stuff to the tailgate and pitching it with gusto into the giant maw of the dumpster below. "Harold," he hollers, "come help."

Harold sits like a great, knobby Idaho Russet, with as much animation and expression.

Conversely, his spry little friend is a spinning ball of energy in the back of the Ranchero, lifting this and tossing that.

The burn barrel is back there too, full of ashes, heavy and wet from the last rain. At home Alice and I wrestled it up into the truck bed by means of leverage and brute force.

---

† A decade later, the historic bridge will be no more. Abandoned initially, then torn down after being replaced by a sleek concrete, contemporary job, with bold, concave sides. A safer bridge, sure. But will lack the charm and sterling character of its predecessor. The new one is two lanes wide with easy access into the banked curve of the river. Where's the sport in that?

The ashes of modern paper products with toxic plastic coatings and inks are unusable for gardening (only wood stove ashes are beneficial potash.) So whenever the burn barrel gets midway full (or fuller, if we procrastinate), we heave, haul, and nearly hemorrhage, getting the damn thing out to the dump and emptied.

The poor little guy braces behind the 55-gallon drum, his shoulder to it, wind-milling on the edges of his shoes, trying to inch it out. When he reaches the seam of the tailgate, he stops to catch his breath, and wipes his sweaty forehead with a dingy, red, cowboy kerchief. Finally, he turns toward old Harold lounging in the shade.

"Harold, f'God's sake, c'mon and help."

Harold, who moves only to brush away the peskiest of flies, continues to sit still as a stump, indisposed to heft his bulk for the likes of our load, there being little profit in trash and ashes. Chivalry is an unknown—or long dead—concept to this old coot.

Still puffing and mopping his damp face, the little fellow, in his quick, bird-like way, glances a time or two at Alice and me. It's quite evident he is mulling something over, struggling to piece a puzzle together.

He leaps down from the truck, braces the bottom of the massive drum against the tailgate and tips its mouth forward over the dumpster. He quickly digs his heels in and throws his welterweight backwards against it, like a cowboy bulldogging a steer, holding onto the rim of the barrel for dear life as he and the barrel teeter at the brink, over the void below.

Alice lunges and grabs hold of the barrel to steady it, lest the little guy be carried over by his own enthusiasm. Together they shake it till the barrel gives up its heavy ashy load.

He then hops back into the truck, and begins heaving up the now-empty burn barrel, arms wrapped around it, and grunting with the effort. Once up there he resumes his mental puzzle, eyeing us back and forth again while rolling the barrel on the bottom rim, and tucking it back against the cab. His curiosity crests over the top.

Clearing his throat for attention, he asks us, "Is it Sisters?"

Alice glances at him from the end of the tailgate and says in her usual taciturn style, "Nope."

He nods, and a moment later asks, "Is it Sistrin-laws?"

Alice, never looking up, shakes her head. "Nope."

Not Sisters? Not "Sistrin-laws"? Uh-oh! What's left?

His brow furrows in vertical lines, mouth working in concentration as he vigorously brooms out the truck bed. And a look of an epiphany crosses his face.

Triumphantly, he hollers, "Harold, come here! Come over here and help these Widda-wimmen!"

Widda-wimmen? Widda-wimmen? Oh! Widow-women.

Harold just stares his piggy stare till our helper turns back to secure the empty steel drum and latch the tailgate. He tips his cap, receives our sincere thanks, and trots back to scold lazy, old Harold.

"Whatsamatter with ya, Harold? Couldn't ya come help over there?"

Harold only stares at the ground, shaking his head in resigned hopelessness.

We barely make it back into the truck before bursting. We hoot up the highway, guffaw through the groves, and laugh all through lunch.

"Is it Sisters?" we mock, sputtering into our coffee. "Sisterin-laws?" we utter, strangling on our food. "Widda-wimmen?" we whimper, weeping into our hankies.

We've now added another favorite story to our repertoire to tell and re-tell to our friends.

And many times since, whenever we meet women together, strong and assured, women with a certain look in their eyes, one of us inevitably will pose the question to the other, the question that asks it all, "Is it Sisters?"

DATELINE, 1984—The century-old Bell Telephone, known as "Ma Bell," breaks up in adherence to antitrust laws. **Apple Computers** introduces the Macintosh in an iconic commercial called *1984* during the Super Bowl. (It shows nationally only this one time because the estate of George Orwell challenges it.) **Reagan orders Marines** withdrawn from Beirut international peacekeeping force; also relieves the Sixth Fleet. **Andropov, 69, dies** and Konstantin Cherneko replaces him.

Soviets boycott and withdraw from 1984 summer Olympics in Los Angeles. **Scott Hamilton** wins the Olympic gold medal for figure skating.

A deadly F5 tornado nearly destroys the town of Barneveld, Wisconsin, killing nine people, injuring nearly 200, and causing over $25 million in damage. Vanessa Lynn Williams becomes the first Miss America to resign when she surrenders her crown, after nude photos of her appear in *Penthouse* magazine.

Bishop Desmond Tutu of South Africa is awarded the Nobel Peace Prize. **Unemployment falls,** inflation rate declines, economic growth accelerates, US dollar soars on international markets.

Rev. Jesse Jackson mounts first challenge by a black man for major party nomination. Democratic National Convention in San Francisco nominates **Walter Mondale** as presidential candidate and **Geraldine Ferraro** as his vice presidential running mate, the **first woman ever nominated** by a major party for high national office. **President Reagan** is re-elected with 59 percent of the vote.

Two Sikh bodyguards assassinate India's Prime Minister Indira Gandhi; her son succeeds her. **A Union Carbide plant** in India leaks toxic gas, killing 150,000 people. **The first MTV Music Awards** recognizes David Bowie for *China Girl* and Cyndi Lauper for *Girls Just Want To Have Fun*.

a summer bitter and sweet

Mattie has a new no-wax kitchen floor. She's spent weeks making the decision and now it's finally in.

"Well, it looks really nice," Alice says sincerely.

"I love the geometric pattern, Miss Mattie," I add. "It really compliments your open kitchen and makes the whole room look brand new."

"Yeah ... it does, I guess," Mattie says indifferently.

"You don't like it?" queries Alice.

Mattie's reply is lukewarm. "Oh, I love the pattern alright. It's just ...."

Long pause.

"What?" I prompt.

"I don't know ...."

Another pause.

"What?" Alice erupts.

"Okay. Listen," Mattie says dejectedly, proceeding to walk figure eights all over the kitchen.

"Listen to what?" Alice asks.

"Listen to the floor, of course!" Mattie huffs, irked at our failure to perceive the problem. We listen harder and there it is, barely audible, tiny, sucking noises with each step she takes.

"Hear it?"

"Yeah," I say. "It sounds a little bit like you have thin crepe soles on your shoes, only not nearly that loud. What's the problem?"

"The problem is it sounds like I'm walkin' on a sticky floor, that's the problem! And it's gonna drive me loony."

"Well, it could be your shoes," Alice suggests.

"No, it's not my shoes! I tried my whole dang shoe bag out on it, and some of them sound even worse than these."

Alice rubs her face to cover a smile fit for a clown. "Well then, it might be the no-wax finish on the flooring that makes it like that," she reasons. "It'll probably lessen in time as it wears off."

I can see Alice playing out the "whole dang shoe bag" scenario in her mind. Her crackup threatens to break through as she imagines Mattie: shoe bag beside her, dragged out from the closet, sitting on a kitchen chair to change footwear, then traipsing around and around in circles all over her kitchen, hearing the discouraging suction of her soles over and over, through the trial of every pair of shoes she owns.

"Well, if I'd a-known it'd sound like I'm stickin' to my floor every blessed time I cross the room, I'd a-traded this fancy no-wax shine for plain, old, dull linoleum," Mattie complains irritably. "I'm gonna be moppin' the durn thing till the-devil-take-it, tryin' to forever scrub the tacky off it."

Alice excuses herself, faking a need-to-pee before she loses it.

True to her word, Mattie washes her kitchen floor once, and some-times twice, every day from here on out. The no-wax flooring gleams relentlessly, just as advertised. It never lessens its shine, and likewise never loses—for Mattie, anyway—the sound of a floor gummy with spilled canning syrup. What the poor, tortured woman saves in floor wax, she ends up spending three times over in Pine-Sol and mop refills.

It happens in the course of all this that Mattie makes a more ominous discovery: a lump in her breast. Her doctor validates it is cancer, sends her home to pack a bag, and operates on her the very next morning.

Boom!—just like that.

We visit her in the hospital, and she is having a rough time dealing with the shock of it all: the radical mastectomy, the cancer, and the fact that she was hale and hearty one day, and the very next discovering an insidious killer residing within her body.

She is in pain, her arm swollen to twice its size from shoulder to wrist. Half her lymph nodes have been identified as cancerous and removed, leaving behind a scabbing and disfigured chest wall where once her breast had been. Radical mastectomies are truly radical in the 1980s, a virtual scraping of tissue down to the chest wall.

Paulette—an old friend and former rival for Mattie's Duke—has already put in a hospital visit. Mattie was little surprised to see her, especially when Paulette drew some booklets from her purse and proceeded to share her own experiences with breast cancer, mastectomy, and recovery.

Paulette is part of a volunteer organization that visits new victims of breast cancer in the hospitals and acts as peer counselors and friends to them—sometimes right to the end of their sadly shortened lives. Mattie never knew this about her friend in all the twenty years of their acquaintance. But she knows now, and Mattie finds her visit consoling as well as encouraging.

Fourth of July weekend, Justy pops into town just in time to help us hatch a plan to welcome Mattie home from the hospital in grand, old style. On the day of her discharge, Alice and I take turns checking the window for signs of Melanie's car while Justy gathers the props and gets us all ready.

At last Melanie's car turns into the lane, cruises past our house and pulls into Mattie's yard. We watch Mattie climb slowly out of the passenger seat, still favoring her tender, swollen arm. She and her daughter slowly make for the back door of the house.

This is our cue—we're on!

We steal out of the front door and position ourselves in the middle of the lane, lined up three abreast like marching militia. Each of us has a ketchup-stained, white hanky tied around her forehead. Alice holds a kazoo to her mouth, her cane carried back on her shoulder, and an American flag draping behind.

I begin to beat my drum—an old, ceramic pot—enthusiastically (if not altogether rhythmically) with a large serving spoon. And Justy, her keyboard propped across her arm on the highest volume in flute mode, launches spiritedly into a fine piping version of Yankee Doodle Dandy.

The three of us proceed to limp, drum, kazoo, and fife our way jauntily down the lane to Mattie's house.

We don't go far before Mattie and Melanie come right back out onto the front porch to see what all the racket is about. They catch sight of us marching down the street, in all our "wounded," limping, Fourth-of-July glory.

As we march, doors and windows open at neighboring houses, and soon there are quite a few spectators to our small (if not spectacular) parade.

We make a somewhat less-than-smart military right turn into Mattie's gate, pausing in her front yard to finish Yankee Doodle for its fifth and final rendition, and end with dramatic ruffles and broad flourishes.

Then one by one, we each make a leg, to take a bow before our audience of Mattie and Melanie. Applause breaks out all over the street from the onlookers, and Melanie and Mattie are undone.

"You girls!" is all Melanie can say.

Mattie, however, is a little more droll. "This used to be such a nice, quiet neighborhood," she says with mock regret.

A delegation of fools will cheer you up every time.

Mattie's recovery takes a long while, especially within the effected armpit where her lymph nodes have been extracted. She is experiencing swelling all the way down her arm that is painfully slow to reduce. Additionally, the post-surgery chemotherapy she's now on has her spending a good bit of time hanging over the toilet, day after day.

And that isn't all of it.

One afternoon my phone rings. "Nancy, can you come down?" Mattie sounds so stuffed up and noisily liquid in her head that I am instantly alarmed.

"I'll be right there."

I sprint down the street, and she opens the door to me—eyes puffy, tears streaming, a towel loosely draped over her head.

"What? What?" I gasp, out of breath from both fear and the frantic run.

She pulls the towel off her head to reveal clumps of missing hair, some sliding off and falling away on the floor, even as the towel drags lightly across her head.

"Oh, Mattie," I say, taking her into a hug as she whimpers in my arms.

I have been through this with three other friends. I'd hoped never to have to do this again—to comfort a woman whose hair is falling out from the effects of chemotherapy. More than any other side effect of cancer, this one hits women with an emotional jolt that wounds them to their core.

The loss of your hair is a primal indignity to your femininity and body image like almost no other disfigurement. Even knowing it will grow back is small consolation for a woman who is watching her tresses slide inexorably off her skull. It would seem to be a minor loss against some others—breast removal, hysterectomy, radiation burns, and the like—but the impact is often shattering and devastating. Visceral. The final blow.

But Mattie recovers. Her course of chemo eventually ends, and stubble reforms in a faint hair pattern on her little baldhead. Her chest scars over silkily and her distended arm girth is now somewhat reduced, her range of motion gets better, and the pain dissipates. Her energy returns and with it her good spirits. We are elated that she's gonna make it after all.

My mother, meanwhile, is planning a trip out to California. My sister Lynn and her significant other, Carl, are bringing her out on vacation, flying from Philly to San Francisco, where they'll spend a few days, then rent a car and drive up to Humboldt to spend four or five more days with us. My mother has been on a plane only one other time in her life, when she and my father flew to Texas to visit Don and me in San Antonio.

Our little town of seven hundred is very rustic, and I have some reservations about how my mother—queen of all things proper—will find it. Plus, we are still living in this tiny, 800 square foot mobile home, and I have to do some serious thinking about accommodations.

The cabeen is fine for most of our guests, roughing it without a sink or shower of their own and only a portable toilet on site. But it won't do for my elderly mother, who will have to stumble across the pitch-black yard in the night, or walk back and forth on the uneven ground to come in for showering. And for that matter, it isn't set up to accommodate Lynn and Carl, either.

There is no hotel or motel until three miles into the next town of ten thousand, and the bed and breakfasts in the region, while delightful and well booked, are farther away than that. None of this will do.

And then it occurs to me: the little tenant house across the street is currently vacant.

I make arrangements to see the inside, and it is, by all standards … a dump! Little more than 400 square feet, it is like a cheap, run-down motel suite with a kitchenette. But for a little vacation cottage, it might pass muster with some sprucing up—minimal furnishings, curtains, and the basics. It has old, peeling linoleum floors and clapboard walls, but I think it can be gussied up to a shabby charm. It's the most viable of all options, so I rent it for a week.

After giving the place a thorough scrubbing, I borrow a twin bed for Mother from Mattie and move it into the living room. Then I haul the double bed from the cabeen into the single bedroom for Lynn and Carl, add some end tables, a couple of chairs, curtains, throw rugs, bedspreads, and it is ready to go. Now to prepare the family.

"Make sure Mother brings some suitable clothing," I tell Lynn on the phone. "This is a gravelly dirt road we live on. She'll need tennis shoes or something flat and casual."

"I've told her but you know Mother."

I *do* know my mother. She is rigid when it comes to matters of dress and decorum. She never wears a skirt without a slip, nor a pantsuit unless she has a full-length pant liner underneath, doesn't leave the house ungirdled, and never goes without stockings. Her shoes and bag match, and umbrella besides.

She always manages to dress stylishly, often on a non-existent budget. In her middle years, when she was slender and vivacious, she was quite a knockout. As a younger woman, she conceded to changes in fashion and ditched the hat and gloves, but that's about as far as she ever felt it proper to go.

These days she declares that by the time she puts her teeth in, sets in her hearing aides, has her battery pack affixed, places her bifocals on her nose, gets all those clothes on, and is finally all together, she is altogether too damn tired to go anywhere. No wonder.

"Well, do your best," I tell Lynn. "Be sure she has some warm things. You, too. San Francisco is often very cold and damp in summer. She'll be more comfortable in sweats, but I suppose that's unlikely."

"Dream on," Lynn says.

"Yeah, well, she'll need sweaters, and maybe a scarf or even a muffler, especially if you intend to be on the bridges or take a boat tour of the Bay, even if it is August." The North Coast of California is considerably cooler than summertime in Philly. Cooler than summertime most anywhere. And Humboldt County is strictly casual. "She'll be overdressed anywhere here in what she wears to the grocery store back home," and I then explain the living arrangements to Lynn, confiding my bit of nervousness about them.

"I'm sure it'll be okay, Nancy. We'll manage fine. It's just for a few days."

"Well, do me a favor and prepare her for it. I really am concerned that she not be trying to walk across this dirt and gravel road in two-inch heels. She needs sneakers, loafers, anything like that."

Mother's health is always a concern these days. Since her heart attack, she is often short of breath and very slow in her movements. I give Lynn credit for tackling a trip of this enormity with her, considering the planes and flight schedules. She's made arrangements for a wheelchair at the airports so Mother won't have to walk far, and she's allowed a day or so at each end of the trip for resting, if need be.

And, of course, there's Mother's deafness. The thought of having to scream at her above the airplane roar makes me cringe for Lynn's sake.

I needn't have worried, though. They do just fine.

And Mother's stamina increases with her excitement to be in San Francisco. She even manages the cable cars, and they ride from the end of one line to another while she absorbs it all and assimilates the feel of The City.

But as I thought she might, Mother does get cold in the misty chill of summer in San Francisco, prompting Lynn to buy her a grey, hooded sweatshirt for their boat trip on the Bay. Mother is tiny—just five foot two inches—and round. She's also dark complexioned, so when she huddles up against the damp chill into her sweatshirt and peers out from under the hood, she could easily pass for an Ewok.

Days later, when my family arrives in Humboldt, Alice and I greet them in our driveway. While Carl pulls the car up in the drive, my mother, in the back, appears exhausted, her fingers in a death grip on the headrest of Lynn's seat.

"How was your trip?" I ask her before she even has a chance to emerge from the car.

"Oh my! The roads were so winding. I was absolutely petrified for the last two hours up here." Apparently Mother has white-knuckled it for the last leg of their five-hour drive to us.

Now, the north-south roads in California are for the most part fairly straight and tame, unless you take Highway 1, which wends along the jagged edge of the coast. But it's our east-west roads that cut through all the mountain ridges—the Cascades, the Trinitys, the Sierra Nevadas, Sierra Madres, the San Gabriels—these are the killers. They often scare the fool out of me, and unless I'm doing the driving, I'm apt to be carsick myself with the constant whipping back and forth of the wheel on the hairpin turns.

Most roads in Philadelphia and through mid and South Jersey are fairly unchallenging as far as straightness goes. Traffic is another matter.

But the good news is Mother finds the cottage delightful. She says it reminds her of the cabins she'd stayed at in her youth, up in the Pocono Mountains in Pennsylvania and down in Rancaucus in South Jersey. She declares it like summer camp.

And her concession to flat shoes? Jellies, those cheap and trendy plastic sandals that all the kids are wearing these days. But I'll settle for it.

For our first California supper together, I serve fried chicken, potato salad, slaw, and corn on the cob. When I hold my eaten-off ear of corn at each end for our golden retriever, Sadie, to nibble the kernels I've missed, Mother laughs so hard she almost can't catch her breath.

In her deafness, she is limited in her pleasures. For her, food is a profound delight, though she eats remarkably little portions. Lynn has despaired for years, taking her to many different functions and events, only to have her minimize the outing in praise of the food.

"So, how was your excursion to Longwood Gardens, Mother?"

"Oh, wonderful! We had such a nice lunch. I had fresh trout with string beans and a lovely rice dish. The rolls were hot and fresh, and we had strawberry shortcake for dessert."

"Well, how were the gardens? Did you enjoy the flowers?

"Oh, they were beautiful. Just beautiful. Very lovely. You know, there's nothing like Jersey strawberries. I'm sure those strawberries came from Jersey. They were so flavorful."

We do quite a bit of eating out at the local restaurants during our visit. We breakfast at the Samoa Cookhouse one morning, a great experience at any meal. It is one of the oldest operating cookhouses in the country, and the last facility of its type to be continuously serving meals. In its heyday, four to five hundred mill workers and lumbermen ate three meals a day here.

It opened to the public in the late 1960s, serving food in several large rooms as well as a selection of meeting rooms and private party rooms. In all of the serving areas, the food is hot, tasty, informal, and it keeps coming. You're seated at long slab tables, and the food is served family style, passed around among all the diners at the table.

Breakfast—consisting of juice, coffee, thick toast from homemade bread, oatmeal, scrambled eggs, bacon, ham, sausage, home fried potatoes, flapjacks, and dishes of stewed prunes and baked apples—is one price and the same for everybody. Mother pronounces it the best breakfast she's ever eaten.

However, much later, on the last day of the visit, at dinner in a nice restaurant in Eureka, Mother puts her fork down with a clatter and says, "Oh, I must say. This is awful. I haven't had a cooked vegetable since I came to California. They are all raw. Everything is just raw!"

Coming from a tradition of boiling the bejesus out of everything till it's mush in your mouth, I guess California cuisine was too nouveau, too outré, and too ... well, just too uncooked for her.

Today, we—Mother, Lynn, Carl, Alice, and I—are off to the fair. Humboldt every year holds a wonderful county fair in the beautiful old Victorian village of Ferndale, smack in the middle of flat dairy land that edges the ocean. And with a history of horseracing here dating back almost 150 years, the horse races are a big adjunct to the fair. The Fair has the beauty of being neither too large, nor too little. You can make it all around the exhibits in about half a day and go to the racetrack in the afternoon. Perfect!

The livestock exhibitions and auctions—and 4H Club promotions—run the gamut of steers and cows, horses, sheep, goats, pigs, rabbits, chickens, and turkeys. We wander in and out of the open barns that smell of hay and alfalfa and warm beasts who stand placidly chewing feed or muddling about in their pens, some alert to the people passing, some blithely indifferent. There is a subdued quiet overall, despite all the critters and people, just the murmur of onlookers and the susurrus of straw under foot and hoof, punctured now and again by a random moo or a plaintive bleat. Today the show is the hand-raised calves, adorable in their shades of soft golden tan and smooth black and whites. The goat varieties are wonderfully patterned, too, in their markings, with ears either erect or in large lops. One breed has hardly any ears at all.

The poultry house exhibits an incredible variety of chickens in all colors, some with great swirls of white feathers on their feet like ruffles, and around their heads like hats, elegantly ridiculous, looking hardly like chickens at all. It's a treat for Mom and Lynn and Carl to see some of the livestock on display, the real heartbeat of any county fair. This is pretty much a new experience for them, and they have a great time looking at all the animals up close, and listening to the entrants talk about their prized critters.

Several local garden clubs competing with each other have filled a large garden house with showy masses of vibrant fuchsias, spiky heather, frilly tuberous begonias as well as orchids and peonies and African violets. None of these are hugely fragrant, but all are delicate and take expert handling. The cool and quiet interior makes for a calm relief from the many fairgoers and dusty animal sheds.

Naturally, the commercial vendors have a venue, too. In a huge display hall that is noisier and more bustling than the barns, we find an array of booths offering everything from fancy knives, the latest kitchen gadgets, jewelry, batik and tie dye, sports equipment, and portrait art. Health and safety brochures are handed out by volunteer firemen, blood pressures administered by medicos from the local hospitals, and foresters from the area's lumber companies discuss sustainable yield charts and display timber samples and redwood burl plants, as well as your usual information from the representatives from the fishing and dairy industries.

In addition, there's a fairway of Ferris wheels and rides heralded by the tinkly, tinny, ersatz-calliope music that's part and parcel of every circus, fair, and penny arcade. Food booths roll out smells of charring meat, pop-corn, funnelcake, the cinnamon buns overriding it all with their sweet perfume. Hawkers with wheel games and quarter pitches (penny pitches in my youth), milk bottle and baseball throws, stalls of vendors sell-ing hats, scarves, sunglasses, and the requisite fortuneteller's booth. This year, they even offer helicopter rides.

Knowing in advance that we planned to come here, I decided to put my money where my mouth is and entered some of my pies in the judg-ing. I've been getting encouragement in the few years past for the pies I make for the Annual Hospice Rummage Sale and Kitchen. The compli-ments I've received from some very fine veteran pie bakers gives me the courage.

So I decide to try for a few categories, mostly to be able to show my mother how "country" I have become, how well adapted to my small town environment I am. One of the pies I've entered is from an old fam-ily recipe, my mother's Aunt Dolly's Lemon Sponge Pie. I also entered in the Chocolate Cream Pie and Pumpkin Pie categories. I baked all morn-ing and delivered the freshly made pies to the fairgrounds in time for the entry deadline two days ago, the same day my family arrived in the early afternoon.

So maybe I'm a wee-bit excited to get to the Great Hall. Most of the fair's judging takes place in this building, which includes entries for woodworking, quilts, sewing, fine stitchery, flower arranging, mounted and displayed collections, best grown vegetables, and baked goods. We admire the many beautiful quilts hanging on the walls, and the home-sewn bridal gowns complete with crystal beading, pearl bodices, eyelet trains. There are doll collections, button displays, framed needlepoint and cross stitch, woodworked furniture that has been sanded to satin fin-ishes, and the best examples of home-grown beets, corn, potatoes, onions, carrots, beans. One table displays a beautiful assortment of home can-ning, stacked in ranks of fruits, jellies, jams, pickles, beans, corn, and relishes—a rainbow of colors in glass jars.

And the baked goods—breads, rolls, cakes, muffins ... and pies. We wander around the display cases, oohing and aahing, tummies rumbling from the sight of all that delicious sweetness.

And there it is—Aunt Dolly's Lemon Sponge Pie, and alongside it ... a big blue ribbon.

I let out a yelp!

"What is it?" Lynn asks alarmed. "Are you all right?" Traveling with Mother tends to make her hyper-vigilant and overly health conscious.

I am tongue-tied and just point at the display case. Alice squeezes my shoulder, "You did it!"

"What?" Mother gets into the act. "What's the matter?"

Everyone finally settles down and follows my shaky pointing finger to the display—to the card that reads:

LEMON SPONGE PIE
Nancy Lehigh, Bluffside
First Place

"Aunt Dolly's Pie," I finally manage. "It took first place!"

"That's your pie?" Lynn squeals. "You won a blue ribbon for your pie?"

"Oh, my!" Mother finally gets it. "Aunt Dolly's Pie." And her eyes fill up with tears. "It's such a good pie. She would be so pleased to know her pie won a blue ribbon."

As flabbergasted as I am, that is high praise indeed coming from my mother, and I am so very glad I got up the gumption to enter this event.

"Nancy, you'd better come look at this." Alice is standing at the next case, bending over to get a better look at the bottom shelf.

"Oh, my God!" is all I can croak out.

The card reads:

CHOCOLATE CREAM PIE
Nancy Lehigh, Bluffside
First Place

"You did it again! Another blue ribbon!" Lynn is so excited she's actually bouncing. "How many more? Did you enter any more?"

It is beginning to register with me now, and I feel like I plunked down a gigantic bet on a long shot at the races and my horse came in first.

"One more," I say, "in the Pumpkin Pie category."

Everyone makes a fast, cursory survey of the cases.

"Here it is!" Carl shouts out, and we all join him in front of a case with a field of fourteen competing pumpkin pies on display.

The card reads:

PUMPKIN PIE
Nancy Lehigh, Bluffside
Third Place

"Ohhh, only a white ribbon. Just third place," Lynn says. Then she looks at me with the most peculiar expression, and we all burst out laughing.

"What? What's so funny?" Mother asks. The news hadn't registered in her hearing aid.

Lynn, still laughing, just points to the pie in the case, and Mother bends forward to read the card. "Oh, I'm sorry," she says. "Only third place. What a shame."

We all laugh that much harder, and I steer them to step outside, since we are making a proper spectacle of ourselves. We are still laughing loudly as we stand outside at the entrance to the Great Hall when a woman comes out from the building and approaches us.

"Excuse me," the woman says. "I'm sorry to bother you, but I wondered if everything was all right. I notice you folks are a bit excited, and I'm one of the staff monitors for the Hall."

"I'm so sorry," I apologize. "We were probably making a real racket. It's just that this is the first time I've ever submitted anything, and I entered three pies and took two blue ribbons and a white. I can't get over it."

Lynn speaks up. "I'm her sister, and this is her mother, and we're visiting from Philadelphia, and this is such a treat! It's just so wonderful!"

After Carl brings Mother up to speed in the conversation, she chimes in, saying to the woman, "It was my Aunt Dolly's recipe, and it's nearly a hundred years old. Imagine! My aunt's pie winning at a fair!"

Lynn leans in to me and speaks in a low voice, "You'd think Aunt Dolly resurrected and slaved over a hot oven herself." I smile broadly at that, aware my mother's praise has been more for the historical pie than for any of my doing and it tickles me, both her reaction and this, my own feeble bid for her approval and the half-realized turn it has taken. Ya gotta laugh when you catch yourself in something like that, don't you? Talk about your just desserts.

I turn and speak to the woman again, "I'm really sorry if we made a scene in there. We were just lost in the moment."

The woman chuckles at this. "I can't tell you how refreshing it is to have someone win and show some excitement. Frankly, it's mostly the same participants year after year, and the ribbons kinda swap around between one or two or three of the best bakers in the area. It's become almost an inside competition. And the winners are rather blasé about the whole thing. You've probably put a few noses out of joint today and have given some good cooks a run for their money."

The woman pats me on the shoulder, "It's wonderful to have some new interest in the event and some new blood in the game. Good for you! And I hope you'll enter again next year."

"You bet! I'm hooked now!" And I am.

From then on, I enter pies in every local fair for the next ten years. I will have some failures, even some embarrassments. But I also wind up with a drawer full of blue, red, and white ribbons.

Still, nothing will ever come close to that first glory, that first sweet taste of victory, as that very first first-place blue ribbon.

Aunt Dolly's Lemon Sponge Pie

3/4 cup butter
4 large eggs (or 5 small eggs), yolks and whites separated
1-1/2 cups sugar
1-1/2 cups milk
5 heaping teaspoons flour
Juice and grated rind of 2 large lemons

Cream butter. Add yolks and sugar to butter, and cream together. Add juice and grated lemon rind. Add all remaining ingredients, except egg whites. Beat egg whites till just stiff. Fold gently into lemon mixture. Pour in unbaked pie shell and bake at 350 degrees for 1 hour, till toothpick tested in the center of pie comes out clean. The top of the pie will be a medium dark brown.

DATELINE, 1986—**Supreme Court bans** racial bias in selection of trial juries. **Space shuttle** *Challenger* explodes in midair over Florida, **killing all seven astronauts** aboard. **US Navy repels** an attack by Libyan forces during maneuvers in Gulf of Sidra. US President Ronald **Reagan blames Libya** for two American deaths in a terrorist bombing of a West German disco, then **retaliates with air raids** over Tripoli and Benghazi. **Second Reagan-Gorbachev summit** is held in Reykjavik, Iceland, and ends in impasse over arms control and "Star Wars."

Congress approves broad revision of US tax structure, raising the bottom rates from 11 percent to 15 percent and lowering the top from 50 percent to 28 percent, eliminating many loopholes and raising corporate taxes. **Wall Street financier** Ivan Boesky is fined $100 million for illegal insider trading. A popular uprising overthrows Haitian president Jean-Claude **Duvalier,** prompting him to flee to France.

After a 20-year rule, Philippine dictator Ferdinand Marcos also flees his country, but not before moving billions of dollars in public funds to private US and Swiss bank accounts. **Union Carbide agrees** to settlement with gas-leak victims in India.

Halley's Comet returns to earth on its 76-year cycle around the sun. **Desmond Tutu** is elected archbishop in South Africa. A **Chernobyl nuclear reactor** in Soviet Union explodes and burns, **resulting in 31 deaths** within days, ultimately shortening thousands of lives, and requiring the indefinite evacuation of hundreds of square miles in the Ukraine.

Supreme Court reaffirms abortion rights. **Rehnquist is confirmed** as Chief Justice. **US House rejects** administration's "Star Wars" policy. Congress overrides President **Reagan's veto** of severe sanctions against South Africa.

The World Court rules that the US broke international law when it mined Nicaraguan harbors. President **Reagan denies** exchanging arms for hostages after a **secret initiative** to send arms to Iran is revealed; he later halts arms sales, **another indication** that funds are being diverted from arms sales to Nicaragua.

Democrats win the Senate majority. **IBM introduces** OS/2, which allows multitasking, running several programs simultaneously. **Larry McMurtry** wins the Pulitzer for *Lonesome Dove*.

miss mattie

We all felt like we dodged a bullet with Mattie's breast cancer two years ago, that is until we got the news that the cancer had metastasized to her lungs. Once again she undergoes surgery, a portion of her lung removed this time, and radiation is added to the protocol, plus another round of chemotherapy. Six months of treatment have passed since this bad news, and she has tolerated it all, but with considerable loss of strength and stamina.

Still, Mattie manages to bounce back some and resumes feeding Duke three times a day (much to his relief), and we once more anticipate that she'll want to bake a pie soon, and again, she does. And of course, her feet still stick to her no-wax floor, and she is mopping at the stubborn stickiness (and shine) up to two and three times a week now. The best indicator of her bounce back.

Then, without any specific event, she begins to spend more time on the couch, and then in her bed, and finally she is unable to do much of her daily activities at all. All within these last couple of months. Next, Giselle appears on the scene to care for her mother, and we know things aren't going to get better.

But surprisingly for a little while it does. Mattie goes grocery shopping with Giselle twice a week; Giselle drives her around to her various doctors; Giselle goes to church with her on Sunday, or that is to say, Giselle drops Mattie off at one church while Giselle attends another, then picks her up after their services.

Perhaps it is Mattie's last determined stand. Maybe it is the wide stubborn streak in her, which is fighting to keep the upper hand over her daughter. Perhaps her rally is due to Giselle's faithful ministrations, which go mostly unappreciated—an understatement since, by Mattie's lights, Giselle can do nothing right.

In any event, it is truly painful to watch. Mattie criticizes her daughter's housekeeping skills (which are to my untrained eye more than adequate.) But nothing is ever cleaned properly, put in the correct place, nor anything well done. Not the laundry, the grocery shopping, the bed making, nor the dusting or cleaning. Nothing is ever organized efficiently to hear Mattie's telling of it. And tell of it she does, to all her many visitors, both friends and relatives—more often than not in Giselle's very presence (if not, within her earshot.)

And the cooking ... well! The cooking is Mattie's fallback complaint if she can't find anything else to belittle Giselle with. Giselle makes meals as nutritionally sound as she knows how, but the food isn't down-home cooking. It is more California cuisine ... no gravies, pies, cakes, cobblers, no noodles and fricassee, no corn chowder, no black-eyed peas, grits, bacon, or hoecakes. Everything clean and light, steamed rather than stewed, broiled rather than smothered. Not to say Mattie would, or could, eat it even if Giselle managed otherwise; her appetite is so poor and her tolerance so limited. But it doesn't stop her from bitching about it, nonetheless.

Alice and I have dealt with enough patients and families in our hospice career to know Old Business being played out when we see it. It was obvious to us that Mattie is making her daughter pay for years of disappointment and inattention: her condemnation of Giselle's life spent within her fundamentalist church, which has left Mattie so embittered. Giselle is captive in it by her own guilt and sense of Christian duty, which she seeks to assuage by caring for her mother's needs.

And her mother is letting her have it ... in spades. To her everlasting credit, Giselle sticks it out, tolerating the abuse with minimal resistance.

But it's Duke who takes the brunt. He is adrift, floundering, and scared spitless with Mattie taken so low, and he wanders back and forth, in and out, throughout the day, just to be reassured, which of course, he seldom is. It grates on Giselle's nerves for many reasons, and she finally calls a halt to it and demands he stay away. Mattie is unable to claim the right to have him there, since she's lost the ability to manage the situation either for herself or for him.

In truth, the burden of Mattie's care is more than enough for Giselle to deal with. Still … it is a tiny, but definite, act of revenge on Giselle's part.

Like I say, painful to watch.

Mattie has a lot of support over these last months, from both old and new friends. She is part of a group who is also dealing with metastatic cancer, which meets weekly now at her home. I think she benefits from it even as two members lose their own fight and die.

Alice, during this time, is a mainstay for Mattie. The telephone is Mattie's lifeline to her. They speak three or four times a day, sometimes for just a moment or two, sometimes for an hour. I can't report what they say to each other. I just know it is quiet and intimate.

I work all day. Mattie's friends and family often visit in the evening, so I keep up with her progress through Alice. On Sunday mornings I take homemade soup down to her, relieving Giselle to attend church and the potluck after service.

It is the same soup every week because she likes it—just a clear-broth chicken soup with green onions and chopped bok choy, and rounds of carrots or kernels of corn. I sit with her while she eats and we chat. Mostly I listen to her recount Giselle's latest failures and shortcomings for the week. I let her rant hoping to dilute some of the venom, but it isn't to be. If a visitor or two stops by after church, Mattie will repeat the entire litany of Giselle's faults I've just heard for their benefit.

But sometimes Mattie will talk about other things. It must be hideously boring to have your attention focused unremittingly on the state of your health and its demands. I know it's hard to get away from—the needs of the body are so great. But, God! You must live for a moment of distraction. Maybe that's what some of the Giselle stuff is about. Distraction.

Mattie begins to take on the look of one terminally ill. Her bones sharpen in her face, her color pallid, her eyes sunken, making her look much older than her sixty-nine years. She is often short of breath, and sleeps with nasal prongs feeding compressed air. She uses a bedside commode now, but is visibly weaker and exhausted by even this exertion.

After church, one or two of her closest friends take to coming alternately, so I keep my visits shorter, leaving soon after another arrives. Sometimes all the soup I brought stays on the stove for others to eat. Mattie's appetite is sporadic, sated with mere mouthfuls.

And one such time, after one friend stops by, Mattie quietly passes away, mere moments after I left her to go back up the street, just minutes before Giselle arrives home from church.

I hear Alice speaking on the phone in the next room, but I don't know to whom. I'm barely finished dressing for Mattie's funeral when I hear her boots a-stomping.

"Get ready fast. We have to go pick Duke up from the ranch," she barks out. She executes a rigid, practically military, about-face, her resolute, staccato stride making a statement of its own, down the hall, out the back door, and then the immediate roar of the Ranchero firing up. It is obvious something has happened, and her jaws are locked over it. "They don't want to let Duke go to Mattie's funeral because they were 'living in sin,'" reports Alice as I hurriedly climb in. Irritated, she rips out of the driveway a little fast, scattering gravel.

"Who're they?" I ask.

"Mattie's self-righteous daughters, Melanie and Giselle." Uh-oh. A lightning bolt crackles in the storm cloud over Alice's head. "They think it's been scandalous, and this is their way to redeem it." She pauses while she negotiates a turn of the wheel. "It's also a shitty way to publicize their disapproval of their mother." Oh yeah, Alice is definitely pissed.

"So what's the plan?" I ask.

"We're gonna go pick up Duke and take him if he wants to go."

O-o-o-kay.

At Duke's place, Alice pulls up right next to Melanie's husband's pickup, where it is parked alongside Duke's trailer. She gets out, stopping to chin-chuck Sarge and Buster, who quiet their barking once they recognize her. She takes the stairs to the trailer and knocks three times. I get out and follow behind, just as Greg, Melanie's husband, comes to the door. He doesn't open the screen.

"I want to speak to Duke," Alice says without preamble.

"Well," Greg drawls slowly, "he's been pretty upset here."

"That's all right. He'll see me," Alice replies calmly, looking Greg straight in the eye.

Greg hesitates, then steps back, and a moment later Duke comes to the door. Duke graciously opens the screen door, and Alice takes hold of it, figuring to have the advantage if she needs to go in after Greg, I guess. Duke is pale and pinched, looking as though he might crumble at any second. He's dressed for the funeral, wearing a clean Western shirt, khakis, and his good boots.

"Duke, do you want to go to Mattie's funeral?" Alice gently asks. "I'm here to take you, if you want to go."

Duke looks down at his boots, then nods his head in a single emphatic "yes."

"Okay then, go get your hat and jacket."

Duke turns away to do just that, and Greg comes back to the door and launches into his song and dance. "Duke has been pretty upset, and Melanie and Giselle think it will be best if he stays here till the services are over. I plan to be here with him and keep him company while that's all going on."

Alice treats him to a steely eye, to her don't-screw-with-me bearing. "Greg. There's no point in arguing this. Duke wants to go. And I'm here to take him." If her speech gets any more clipped, it will have to be tapped out by telegraph key.

For a long moment, the two of them are deadlocked in the doorway. Alice is coiled tight, her rattles buzzing. Emotions play over Greg's face like a light show: uncertainty, irritation, vexation at being forced to deal with (and unable, for once, to avoid) the kind of issue he usually relegates to his wife. Then, his own never-absent anger, which flares and darkens, and I shift my stance behind Alice, ready for anything.

Duke chooses that minute to come back to the door—wearing a suede jacket and the new Stetson hat that Mattie gave him for Christmas five months ago. Greg's expression falls, faintly wistful at the desire, the missed opportunity, to smash Alice's face in.

Or lose his life trying.

Whether lost in his own turmoil, or simply missing the drama in the doorway, Duke walks out the door unseeing, past Greg and Alice, and down the stairs. I go ahead of him to open the passenger side of the Ranchero for him. Alice stares Greg down one long, last minute, then turns and follows Duke.

Duke slides into the car, and I next to him. With Alice at the wheel, Duke receives a little warm flanking, something he appears to need right now. All of us are quiet on the ride into town till Duke speaks quietly.

"They say I shouldn't go to the funeral, that it isn't proper for me to be there."

"That's pure bullshit, Duke!" Alice spits out. Duke gives a little tee-hee at that, and the tension in him eases a little.

I affirm it. "You have every right in the world to be there, Duke. Mattie would want you there."

At the funeral parlor Duke draws himself up, some of the steel coming back into him, and enters, taking his hat off as he does. The director of the funeral home moves quickly to greet Duke warmly—he's known him for years. The director shakes his hand and speaks quietly to him for some time, and Duke nods now and again as he does.

We are still early, and the room is lined with empty chairs against the walls. Mattie's casket is in the middle of the room. When the funeral director finishes delivering his conciliatory words, Alice and I gather Duke up and walk over to the casket, one of us on each of his arms. Mattie is laid out in her prettiest blue dress, one I've seen her wear to church. But there is a gauzy cloud of pouffy, cream-colored netting rising all above her, making her palely visible through it. I wonder who chose that option. She doesn't need to be hidden; no trauma shows in her face. I guess it is to make us mindful she has gone beyond the veil.

Duke, Alice, and I stand at the casket. Duke weeps silently, tears streaking his face, dripping off his nose, and we just stand, each of us lost in our own memory of her. After some time, Duke shifts, an indication that it's time to walk him back toward the wall, where we seat him about six chairs in from the doorway. I give him a hanky from my pocket, and he daubs his eyes and blows his nose delicately. I squeeze his arm and move a bit away, giving him space to grieve.

In that next moment, Melanie and Giselle enter the room. Melanie walks over, nodding and smiling at us as if nothing is awry. She speaks softly, coaxingly, to Duke, "Why don't you come with me, Duke, to the little private room right over there. You can be nice and quiet in there, and you won't have to see anybody or anything."

Nice try.

"No, Melanie, Duke is just fine here with us." Alice's tone is a hair sharp; her challenge much less pointed than it was with Greg, but iron-clad just the same. "He's all right; he's just sad," she finishes. Alice doesn't exercise her power often, but she is absolutely formidable when she chooses, and it takes a brave soul to go up against her. Of course, Melanie fears a scene even more than she fears Alice. And besides, she really is dispirited by her own grief.

Duke covers his face with his hand. Melanie touches his shoulder and turns without further word, walking back over to her sister, recognizing defeat. In that instant Greg arrives, and the three of them hold a whispered confab about it all.

People now start to drift in, every one of them stopping to talk to Duke, who makes to stand whenever a woman comes up to him, but every woman uses his rising gesture as an excuse to pat his shoulder to keep him seated, rubbing his arm, touching his hand. People extend their condolences to Mattie's daughters and Greg, too, of course. But not one of those who come to pay their respects fails to find Duke and speak to him with sympathy and kindness.

After the funeral, the church hosts a luncheon, and Duke is treated as one of Mattie's family by everyone in attendance, deferred to with attentions given to one closest to the departed, and in deepest mourning. All the church members are kind and tolerant. Well, nearly all.

Arlene O'Connell, the matriarch of the congregation and chief benefactor to the church, autocratically greets Duke, taking care to be sure she has the attention of the crowd as she does so. Ultimately she makes her way over to Alice and me and proclaims condescendingly, "Thank you both for taking such good care of *our Mattie*."

Response after response flits past unsaid, as Alice discards them one by one (there are some choice ones, too), before she finally allows herself to speak her thoughts aloud.

"Arlene, she was *our Mattie*, too."

"Yes, well, it was good of you, good of you," Arlene stammers, not quite expecting that, and hastily moves away.

Duke is ready to go soon after, plumb worn out with grief and the drain of the day. The faint stink of sanctimony lingers in our nostrils, and Alice and I are relieved to leave and see him home.

"You'll be all right, Duke? You have our phone number right there, don't you?" I ask him. He nods.

"You can call us anytime, day or night," adds Alice. "Come down if you need to. We'll be here."

He abruptly grabs Alice's hand, hard, and a huge sob bursts explosively from him. She quietly wraps around him and holds on for long moments until he is calm and ready to go inside.

So, we leave Duke and come home, both of us feeling our own deep sense of loss.

And nothing more is ever made of it as far as Mattie's family is concerned. Perhaps their responses on this day are due to the confusion and irrationality that grief sometimes triggers. At any rate, everyone goes on as usual, all of us still being neighbors and friends, as if none of it had ever happened.

Except, of course ... Mattie's gone.

DATELINE, 1987—President Reagan submits first trillion-dollar US budget to Congress as national debt rises steadily. **Stock market tops** 2,000 for first time. **Supreme Court rules** Rotary Clubs must admit women.

Iraqi missiles attack American ship in Persian Gulf, killing 37; Iraqi president, Saddam Hussein, apologizes. Prime Minister Margaret Thatcher wins third term.

Oliver North reveals in inquiry the approval of higher authority in Iran-Contra operations; former National Security Adviser **John Poindexter testifies** using profits from sale of arms to Iran to aid Contras. Secretary of State **George Schultz testifies** that he was deceived multiple times. Defense Secretary Caspar Weinberger testifies about official deception, intrigue. Chief of Staff **Donald Regan resigns. President Reagan says** that the Iran Foreign Policy went awry and ultimately was his responsibility.

the stroke

It is March 20th, 1987, and Alice sleeps next to me as I read. When she rolls over in bed toward me with more effort than it should take, I turn to look at her. What I see horrifies me: her face is contorted on one side, and her mouth is drooping. She speaks, saying, "I can't get my goddamn mouth to work." Except that's not what comes out. What I actually hear is garbled and unintelligible.

Alice rolls back over and tries to get up out of the waterbed—it's never been easy, always requiring a bit of a back roll to help loft yourself out. But she is awkwardly trying to shift herself out, and this time it isn't working. Besides, in my panic, I have hold of her shoulder and am telling her, "No, don't. Wait, let me help you."

We manage to get it together. She sits on the edge of the bed while I call 911. I tell the operator that I think Alice has had a small stroke. This seems to register with Alice, and she stops her struggle. When the EM techs arrive, they check her vitals, help her up, and she walks out to the ambulance under her own steam. As they drive her to the hospital six blocks away, I follow in my car, trying to stave off panic.

By the time Alice is in bed in the hospital room, I have recited her medical data to five separate people and am testy about it. "Yes, she has a history of a heart attack five years ago, none since. She has a fused right ankle, and her meds are in the chart, or damn well ought to be, since I've repeated this same information five times over in the last two hours."

"I'm sorry," the nurse apologizes. "I really am. I *will* consult the chart right now. I was just assigned to her and was trying to see if there was anything I needed to attend to at this exact moment."

"I'm sorry, too. I know you can't possibly have had time to find out what you need to know. It's just exhausting to have to tell this over and over, and I don't know what they would do if I didn't know all about her history. For sure, she can't tell you!" I feel the panic again, and my voice has risen, which alarms even me.

The nurse takes my arm. "Look," she says, "I'll be here with her for the next five minutes getting her settled and taking vitals. Run down to the cafeteria, and grab yourself a cup of coffee or something, and bring it back with you. You've been through a lot—take a little break."

I take her suggestion, but instead of getting coffee, I make a phone call to Caroline, who lives with us in our new three-bedroom home we all co-own, along with our three dogs and her two dogs. Once before, she was our roommate for a little while—years ago, just after I moved back to California for good to begin my new life with Alice. She's twenty years younger, and Alice, now fifty-two, calls her "the kid." Alice is more like mother than friend to Caroline, who, since the ambulance rushed from the house, has been waiting by the phone.

I tell her that my initial diagnosis—stroke—has been confirmed by the medicos. She's understandably shaken. I relay to her what I had just learned myself, that a stroke episode is a process rather than a single event. So, it wasn't necessary to admit her to ICU, there being little they can do, here in 1987, but observe her for a few days, with no specific medicines to override the stroke's effects. Also that more symptoms, more deficits, more changes, can come over the next seventy-two hours or so. It scares me to death for what might yet be. What I've seen so far has me terrified enough.

The next morning, I call the rest of our friends and family to tell them of this latest fearsome development. Josie first. She will come after work to be with me tonight. Next, I notify Sean and Rory, who just six months ago bought the mobile home and land that Alice inherited from Nora. (Alice and I moved into Fortuna at that time into the larger house with the dog run.) They were regular visitors before their permanent exodus up here to the redwood country. Like I said before, many friends who vacationed with us found Humboldt hauntingly unforgettable. Once they moved up here, however, their status elevated from good friend to family.

Sean and Rory are shocked and upset, volunteering to go on standby for anything I might need.

The doctor hasn't much to tell us, other than he has scheduled a CAT scan for later in the morning. She had a left-brain stroke, which controls her right side. It wasn't caused by a clot, but apparently the result of diabetic changes affecting the small hair-like feeder vessels to this particular area of the brain. Alice's diabetes is only *in this very moment* diagnosed. Until now, there had been no clinical indication of it. She seems to have no motor deficits: hands and feet work okay, swallowing okay, body functions are controlled. The extent of her aphasia—her speech and language difficulty—is not yet apparent. Her comprehension is uncertain also, because the immediate effects of a stroke often produce confusion and disorientation, so the verdict isn't yet in.

After the CAT scan is performed, the nurses bring Alice a lunch plate and my panic hits all over again. Alice—my fastidious Alice—dips her fingers in the mashed potatoes and begins to finger-feed herself, ravenously. It is obvious she is starving, but this is unthinkable!

"Alice, use your fork!" I command, wiping her fingers with the napkin and handing her a fork. She holds it awkwardly for the moment, and then seems to remember, and without further ado, begins feeding herself properly. And rapidly.

Friends check in by phone, and Josie comes late in the day after work to keep the vigil with me (as she has done on previous hospital occasions.) She is alone in the shop now, since Honeybear, at age fifty-three, passed away suddenly of a heart attack at Christmastime last year, seven months after Miss Mattie died. Josie will stay with me through the night and through the following several evenings, relieving me for a few hours while I go home, feed and check on dogs, shower, and take care of essentials.

On one of these subsequent late nights, we are witness to what I realize is another stroke, another episode, occurring while Alice sleeps.

"Jo," I say, "look at her hand." And we see her right hand go flaccid, slack, as only it can in a stroke, or paralysis ... or death.

"Is it another stroke?" she asks.

"I think so, or the continuation of the first one. Whatever. The effect is the same. I think it just got worse." However, the episode and the flaccidity are transitory, because moments later her hand looks normal again, and she even moves it in her sleep in a reasonably normal way.

The next day physical therapy technicians confirm what we saw, as Alice now has some slight residual weakness in her hand, which wasn't there before; but they predict this will improve. And it does.

Two nights later, late in the evening, as Josie and I keep vigil on either side of her bed, Alice is restless and uncomfortable. Maybe she's in pain, although when I ask her, she shakes her head no. I adjust pillows for her, and move the electric bed up and down. She's antsy and cranky, and after about an hour and a half of her twitchiness, and my ineffectual efforts to relieve her discomfort, I wail, "Oh Alice, I don't know what to do!" There's an air of despair in my voice while I choke back the tears. "What can I do?"

And then in the most touching of gestures, Alice reaches up and lays her hand on my cheek, her eyes telling me it is all right, there is nothing I can do, nothing I am leaving undone. Alice's thumb brushes away my tears. I swear it is the single most poignant act of love she has ever shown me, her most tender act in our life together, through fulsome years of her unceasing devotion and unrestrained affection for me.

I glance for a moment at Josie. She seems quite affected as she watches Alice reach outside her own needs, her body's demands, to comfort me.

Tears streak my face. I kiss the palm of Alice's hand and hold it in mine. My fears for her are ever grave, her condition uncertain, the outcome unresolved, but somehow she has gifted me yet again with her open heart, with her deep love for me, with the grace of her serenity.

As if some corner has been turned, Alice falls into a deep and restful sleep for the remainder of the night.

As one day leads to the next, Alice improves. Her thinking seems clearer, and she lets me know with her eyes and small bits of playfulness that she is still "in there." There is unspoken reassurance from her that I am not to put too much store in these superficial symptoms—underneath she is still here, unchanged at heart.

Her frustrations, however, have just begun. I'm told that while certain areas of the brain definitely control motor functions, breathing, and such, the medical community now suspects that memory and awareness are not relegated to just one area, but function globally throughout the brain. So, when any area is injured, new neural pathways have to be created, things relearned, or more often, re-accessed by way of another route.

We make so many connections and references to any given bit of data stored in our heads that most things are never lost, just inaccessible until a new road can be found to them. So, the job of Alice's speech therapist will be to help create these new bridges to the out-of-touch areas.

I come to understand this most clearly the day I bring Alice her portable radio. The noise of the hospital is very disturbing (her hearing has become hyper-sensitive, as we are to learn much later), and I think a radio and headphones may help. She reaches eagerly for the radio and attempts to turn it on. For five full minutes she pushes, turns, twists, probes every knob, button, and lever on that thing, trying to make it work.

"Do you want me to help?" I ask.

"No!"

Well, that is plain enough. Still, I have to sit on my hands to keep from ripping that radio away from her and just FIXING IT! She turns it over and examines the back, takes out the batteries, spends another ten minutes getting them back in.

Alice owns practically every hand and power tool known to man, and uses them expertly. She can completely take apart any car engine, pre-1965, and re-assemble it to run better than before. And she has just spent ten minutes trying to replace four batteries in a portable radio.

She turns the radio upside down and tries the buttons and knobs that way, to see if it changes the result. My spirits sink, and I feel profound sorrow as I watch this descent of an astonishingly intelligent woman, once a specialty technician performing complex computerized lab studies, whose daily work required advanced mathematical and analytical skills. A woman with a lifetime of reading that has broadened her comprehension of humanity and life. Whose head is full of information: history, engineering, medicine, philosophies, nuances of the highest thought ... this woman stymied; before my eyes, is reduced to being unable to figure out how to work a simple transistor radio.

I begin to understand she is running on some sort of formerly established pattern; intuitively I know she is remembering every single radio she's ever owned, and is reviewing systematically the working procedure for each of those devices. She has accessed her mental file labeled Radio, and is re-familiarizing herself with this topic, ruling out, by failure, each known model as she does.

We take so much for granted, relying on our brain to make complicated distinctions instantly and accurately. And amazingly, we experience so few stutters in the flow of information we call on.

I'm more aware of it in partnership with my computer; I often have to pause, delve deep in my head to access some simple functions of a software program I haven't used in a while. And the limitations of the computer itself have given me a growing appreciation for the effortless multitasking capacity of my own brain, the ease with which it performs most of the time, despite my many personal inadequacies.

Alice finally finds the proper mental pattern, and gets the radio turned on, tuned in, and playing. I kiss her goodnight and leave, the weight of what I've seen heavy in my heart. Will she have to do this every day, with every thing she touches? How affected is she by this catastrophic injury to her brain? How much can I stand to watch her go through? How will we both cope?

Speech and language and comprehension are the main problems, and the technicians with each visit bring new tests and diagnostic trials for her to perform. She does poorly, but we're assured that this is a normal finding at this stage, that there will be marked improvement as days go by. And each day does make a difference. The radio, for instance. I arrive the very next day to find her listening to it.

"Did you have any trouble making the radio work?" I ask.

She looks at me archly, as if to say, "What're you, nuts?" Aloud, she replies with some disdain, "Well, no!"

Foolish me. Obviously, the new bridge has been built to the file, "The Radio, How it Works" and she forgets there ever has been a problem.

The IV is removed, and Alice's oxygen is turned off. The nurse takes off the nasal prongs, and, noticing that Alice's nose is dry from the rubbing of the plastic tube and the arid airflow, offers a packet of Vaseline and instructs Alice to put some inside her nose.

I tear the little packet open with my teeth and run a thin ribbon of the lubricant on Alice's index finger. "Here you go."

She raises her finger to her face, draws back her lips, and almost has the Vaseline on her teeth when I glance at her and grab her hand. "No, love! Not your teeth, unless you think you're a showgirl or something. The Vaseline is for your nose."

I let go and she slowly raises her hand … again to her mouth. "Alice! No, not your teeth," I say, and hold her hand back. "It's not toothpaste! It's Vaseline for the dryness in your nose."

Yet again she raises her finger to her mouth, pulling back her lips to bare her teeth.

"Alice! No! Stick it up your nose."

"Hhhtick hhhit hhup yoor hhnose!" she answers sharply, jutting her greasy finger out to me.

I laugh too hard to do anything more about it and throw up my hands, tickled at her instantaneous feisty response. No doubt about it, this is still my Alice. She is "in there" all right. Once more she spreads her lips and raises her Vaseline-covered finger to her mouth … and stops short as though it finally registers, then moves her finger higher, applying the petroleum jelly to her nostrils, where it should be.

Alice has been in the hospital for just over two weeks and is set to come home tomorrow. (All hospital stays are much longer in this decade. Unlike decades to come, patients aren't kicked out in a day-and-a-half, still dragging their tubes behind them.) I rush home early from the hospital to clean up and organize the house. I'm a nervous wreck.

Alice has no real residual motor deficits, but I still want to get the shower set up with a stool and somehow need to figure out a way to rig a handle of some kind inside it—not easy in a shower surrounded by fiberglass.

Mainly I have to try to sort myself out, figure out what is wrong. Why am I so restive and anxious and frightened? Surely, the worst is past.

Alice has a full schedule of speech therapy due to begin two days from now, which will continue for some time, at three visits per week. Her diabetes, finally diagnosed, is to be controlled with diet and an oral agent, and she'll need routine finger sticks for testing. The good news is the mysterious and debilitating back pain, which she has experienced for the last six months, is miraculously gone. She reports no pain whatsoever—anywhere.

The gods are often good, even when they are unkind.

But what's wrong with me?

I finished the vacuuming when the phone rings—my youngest sister Mae, calling from Philly. She's heard from our sister Lynn that Alice had a stroke and is glad to know she is coming home with no more effects than the aphasia, which are considerable enough.

"So, how 'bout you? Are you okay?" she asks.

"Oh, I'm all right. Just tired. It's been a rough two weeks."

"I'm sure it has. Still … you don't sound happy about her coming home. What is it?"

"I'm happy—I'm very happy. I don't know what it is. I'm, I don't know … something. Scared. Anxious. It's probably just delayed reaction."

Mae isn't buying it. "Talk to me. There's something bothering you."

"Yeah, there is, but I don't know what. I can't put my finger on it."

"Well, is it her condition? Are you afraid she won't get better?"

"Of course, I am. But I know she will improve. How much, I don't know, but every day in the hospital there has been improvement—sometimes dramatic changes one day to the next. So I know even if she doesn't fully recover, she'll get better than she is right now."

Mae offers another possibility. "Maybe you're afraid she won't be who she is, who she's always been. Is she still in there?"

"Yes, thank God. She's there in her eyes. It's just hard for her to communicate what she wants to say, but she's in there all right. She acts things out for me, and I can read her amazingly well. She's who she's always been … it's just …."

I am getting close to it. I know we are at some kind of mile-marker in our life together. Things can either change significantly for the worse, or we can assimilate this event, this diminishment in her ability, and not be shaken, not be rocked, not take a different fork in the road.

"I think I'm afraid I won't handle this right, and that I could really blow it, and then, we'll never be the same." I start to cry.

Mae lets me cry for a while, and then says, "How would you blow it? What would you be doing that would make that happen?"

"If I handle things here, and take charge and do what needs to be done, I'm liable to upset a balance, which will make us both miserable. I'm apt to be my usual officious self and just control everything, till she gets angry with me—or gives in and lets it be, 'cause she's got enough to deal with, without fighting me for her autonomy."

"So, what can you do, then? I mean, *you will* have to take over and do everything, 'cause *she can't* do it. So, how do you know what to expect? All this is not just a state of mind. Right now she's incapable of handling anything but her own self—and maybe not even that," Mae says.

"I know! It's a tightrope. I only know that if I don't do this right, I'll lose my partner, my equal. I'll turn it into—into, you know—a Parent-Child situation instead of an Adult-Adult. And if that happens, she'll give up, I know she will; she's too independent a soul to let anyone take that away from her. And I'll die inside. I'll just die inside."

"So, this is it? This is what you're upset about?" she asks.

"Yeah. I think so. I feel as if I'm at the edge of a minefield and I have to discover a way to navigate it. I can't just march out like I usually do, confidently taking over. I need to have a clear idea how I mean to proceed, or it'll all blow up and there'll be no retracing the steps of it."

That's it! *I* simply have to learn a new way to be.

Alice has always been so strong a personality, she practically guaranteed that I'd never become too domineering without her reminding me of my boundaries. Very little negotiating was ever needed. My tendency to be controlling never extended to her, beyond what she didn't care to manage herself. I can organize and control the whole world if I want to, but in our home—in our relationship—there was clearly strength met with equal strength. You might say I controlled exactly as much as she allowed me to (which makes me smile weakly even to recognize the truth of this.) The balance of forces was always there; it kept us mutually independent, at the same time emotionally entwined.

It's different now. Alice is at a very weak place. She needs a lot of help, and for yet another time in our life, the burdens of everyday living have shifted between us—this time to my shoulders, and how much of any of it she will be able to resume is an unknown.

This loss of our customary burden sharing will weigh heavily on her, I know, as it would me if I were in the same position. And if I screw this up, if I am not sensitive to her, not aware that her limitations today may not be those of tomorrow, that she can improve or diminish the next day as well, we will have more problems to deal with, problems very different from the stroke itself. We will become different to each other. We can lose who we are together.

If I were to wound her spirit with heavy handedness, I could potentially lose her love. Or she might sooner die—no longer able to do things for herself (that quality of life issue again), especially if on top of that she is made to feel helpless. I now know what my problem is: in my heart this is a defining moment.

I have to learn to be in control without being controlling.

Yeah. A major concept for me.

I have to hold the reins so loosely in my hands that she can take up any line of them, or lay them back down at any time and not have to fight me for it. Not have to wrest the controls from my grasp. Her energy will allow for one or the other—being able to try something again, or wrenching it out of my grip— but not both.

And if ever once she has to sink back, too tired of dealing *with me,* even to attempt to resume an activity or responsibility, I will have taken a vital chunk out of her, one which can't be replaced.

"Thanks, Mae. I have a handle on it now, I think. It won't be easy. I'll have to be very vigilant that I don't overstep my bounds. And that's my natural tendency—just to step in and do; fix it; get it done. If I do, my worst fear will come to pass, and it has nothing to do with her stroke. It's that she'll no longer be fully who she is."

"Yes. I know it'll be okay. Just the awareness of the trap will let you avoid it. It'll be okay," Mae reassures me as she hangs up.

It is a revelation. And probably one which was a long time coming, in terms of my own life lessons. When you're a "take charge" kind of person, it's easy to ride roughshod over people, and I wonder how many of them in my life have just stepped back and let me gallop on by; and how much better for it would I be had I done otherwise? Oh well, we learn when we learn, don't we?

So, Alice comes home and settles in, and later this night I have a serious talk with her.

"You have the hardest job here, love, because you not only have to be patient with yourself till you are once again all well, but you have to be patient with me, too."

She cocks her head and looks at me, many questions in her clear blue eyes. We sit on the side of the bed, and she takes my hand to hold.

"Look, Alice, you know how I can get. Bossy sometimes, and know-it-all." She smiles broadly. "Well, I know I am. And mostly you just ignore me."

She nods and makes a humming noise that I know means words are coming, but it takes time. Finally she says, "Rave …on …uh, uh …uh, maniac."

I laugh out loud, and she joins me. I have heard her tell me that a few times in my life, always with great affection and a crooked smile. And it has always served to bring me down off whatever high horse I am perched on.

When I stop laughing I say, "The thing is I might botch this up from time to time, and I'm afraid about that." Again, her head cocks, her eyes twinkling. "I'm afraid if I take on any part of things that rightfully are yours, just because you are juggling everything right now, that I could be, I dunno, be too overbearing or something. And make you resentful. Or seem like I'm criticizing. Or just make you tired, and like it's not worth the effort to wrestle with me about it. And that scares me, Alice."

She sees how I am really serious about this, and her eyes are smoky warm, her mouth tender.

"I'm afraid we could lose what we have if I get too pushy. So, you have my permission to bop me on the head if I do anything stupid, anything that makes you feel as if I'm mothering, or smothering, or overstepping. Okay?"

She laughs and nods, bringing my hand up to kiss.

"I mean, I'm bound to fuss over you from time to time. I do that now, so you can expect it even more, but you need to let me know when I'm being a pain in the ass about it." Alice laughs again and hugs me with one arm as she sits beside me.

I get to the crux of it then and tell her she can take over, or give back, anything she wants at any time, and I will try my level best not to make that hard for her to do. That it may change from day to day what she can do or feels like doing, and I stand ready to adapt to that and help or not, as she wishes.

I tell her how afraid I am of losing her.

I ask her not to die.

She kisses my forehead when I say that and pets my face. "Please don't give up on me, I'm still learning," I finish. She kisses me tenderly and pulls me to her. Within minutes, we are in bed, lying like spoons and falling asleep.

Throughout the remainder of her stroke rehabilitation, she keeps her dignity. And I manage to keep from making a damned mess of everything.

Life conspires to give you what you need—not what you want, mind you—but what you need. Don't ever doubt it. Alice used to always say that. And now, once again, it rings true.

I was laid off at the mill just a month before her stroke. Kathleen and Sonny closed the mill and are trying to figure out how to pay a half million dollars debt they owe from circumstances beyond their control. In time, they'll re-open, and manufacture moldings and finished two-by-twos, gradually paying the debt off over the next five years. I'll be called back to the mill that September. In the meantime, between June and September, I work a temp job.

As life conspired, however, I am home throughout the spring, taking care of Alice after her discharge from the hospital as her true trial begins: rehabilitation.

The speech therapist comes to the house three times a week, and I arrange for a home health aide to come in and help Alice shower and shampoo. One thing less I have to do, and one thing she doesn't have to rely on me for. We are often accustomed to showering together, companionably (and frequently as foreplay), but seated on a shower stool and too tired to help herself is one indignity she doesn't need to share with me.

The therapy for aphasia is an extraordinary and revealing process. It begins with re-learning and reciting the alphabet, and repeatedly pronouncing various sounds: *m*'s, *ch*'s, *f*'s, *p*'s and *b*'s, and *th*'s.

I discover during this time that we all have "weak spots" in our early learning. Each of us has a hidden little faltering point when we recite the alphabet—a place where we had difficulty first learning it as a child. For many it is midway, around L, M, N, O, P. For others it is around the P, Q, R, S area. For some people it occurs around V, W, X, Y. Such "weak spots" resurface with aphasia. Fascinating!

Alice's is the M, N, O, area, where she tends to reverse them, or just get stuck for a second and has to really work to access the alphabet from this point forward. Like so much of this rehab process, once she works on it a few times, some new neural pathway is created to the information and she never loses it again.

As for the pronunciation, the stroke often affects the tongue and lips, which have to be exercised and any long-term deficit needs to be "talked around." Actually, one of the diagnostic signs that a stroke is happening is a tendency for the tongue to pull to one side or another, instead of midline, when the patient is asked to stick her tongue out. With time, this can go away.

The therapist uses a mirror to help aid in the pronunciation work; she makes the sound and the patient reproduces it while watching her own mouth in the mirror.

In these early days after her stroke, Alice has some trouble with "*th*'s."

"Okay, Alice," Lila says. "Time to work on the "*TH*" sound. Take the mirror and watch me first, then repeat the word looking at yourself. Okay ... thirty."

"Ss-sth-th-th-thirty," Alice follows, watching herself in the hand mirror.

"Good. Now ...Thursday"

"Ss-pth- th-th-Thursday," she repeats.

"Thigh," Lila says.

"Pth—pth—sth-the-the-thigh!"

"Good, try it again."

"Pth-th-th-thigh."

"One more time ... thigh."

"Sth-th-thigh," Alice struggles.

"Better. These "*th*'s" are hard for you, huh? But pretty soon it'll be easier, and you'll get your tongue around those "thighs" before you know it."

Talk about a pregnant pause!

Alice just busts a gut laughing. Me, too.

The comment was entirely inadvertent, since Lila is a sweet Christian woman who'd never dream of going there. Lila reddens with embarrassment, but joins in the laughter and that pretty much breaks the ice.

Every day after Lila leaves and speech therapy is done for the day, Alice gets up from the table and sits in her chair with relief, and I let in the dogs (banished for their distraction.) They mill around her, vying for attention, and she pets them vigorously, one by one, and speaks nonsense syllables to them. "Beedja-beedja, boodja, boo. Micka-micka-mocka," or something approximate. I recognize it as a release from the intense concentration, from the need to form real English words that make real English sense. Dogs don't demand such niceties. They're content with any sounds— it's all gibberish to them anyway.

Part of the therapy involves identifying flash-card type pictures and naming the activity or tool being used—a man digging in the garden and the word "shovel"; a woman in apron and a dress, bending over an oven rack and the word "baking." Many of the pictures are extremely gender-biased—they were developed at the outset of the discipline decades ago and never changed.

"Point to the tools a woman would use." Lila reads from her outline and shows Alice a sample field of simple line drawings: a pickax, shovel, an iron, spatula, screwdriver, skillet, knitting needles, and hammer.

Alice deliberately taps on the screwdriver, smirking all the while.

"Screwdriver," she says.

"Oh, this is your tool of preference?" Lila jokes.

"Yes. I hate …iron," answers Alice, pointing to the picture of the iron.

"Yeah, well, me, too. I hate ironing. These pictures are a bit outdated, aren't they?"

Alice takes her time. "You …could …say …that!" Even halting, her delivery is perfect, dry and sardonic.

"That's okay. We'll use them our way. Show me the tools your mother was apt to use, then."

Alice points to the hammer and pronounces it with another wicked grin.

"Yeah," I interject, "Nora probably chased Bud around with it, just trying to get his attention." To Lila I say, "Alice's mother was just as untraditional as Alice about such things. She was a better carpenter than Bud was. And she was a good cook, too."

Lila laughs. "Oh, the heck with it. I'll just read what it says on the page, and we'll do the best we can, then. I can't win."

The next step of the retraining is to remember strings of items. "Pick up the knob and put it on the door," Lila instructs, laying out separate little cards with pictures of various items. "Good," as Alice complies, and Lila replaces the knob picture on the table. "Now put the peas in the pot and the pot on the stove."

Alice picks up the stove picture, hesitates, then puts it back down and reaches for the pot picture and puts it on the stove.

"That's good, Alice, but you forgot something. What did you forget?"

Alice crinkles up her forehead, trying to remember the instruction, and then, "Oh-Oh, this, this," she says, and picks up the peas picture and puts it on the pot already lying on the stove picture.

"Yes, good, Alice. But now, let's try to do it in the right order of events. Okay, pick up the shovel, put it in the wheelbarrow and move them to the field."

And over time these instructions get more complex, till even I have to concentrate to keep up with it.

"Now, pick up the purse and put it on the bed. Take the rug and put it on the clothesline. Take the purse and put it in the basket, and take the basket and put it under the clothesline."

After a while, Alice gets very good at these convoluted quizzes. I'll be in the kitchen or in the next room paying bills, listening while they work at the table with the flashcard pictures, and wondering sometimes how she manages, as Lila varies the difficulty by creating absolutely illogical actions with the pictures.

"Put the shovel under the bed. Give the boot to the cat. Put the butter on the bush and the bush under the bridge."

Huh?

Often, when Alice can't find the word she wants, she substitutes some other word, one that is enough like it, or hints at it, so her speech is often puzzling to an outsider. She is brilliant at this, using inside references, literary allusions, or other leaps of linkage to convey her meaning. Even in my sorrow at her loss of freely expressed speech, I find her ingenuity delightful. The twists of her quirky mind are never more apparent than now, when she finds new byways in her brain to voice her thoughts.

When meaning *I'm going to use the computer,* she says, "I do Hal," making reference to the talking computer in Arthur C. Clarke's masterpiece, *Space Odyssey: 2001.* Or she'll use "clotting time," a lab test, when she means *blood.* And "writing implement" when she can't extract the simpler word *pencil.* Likewise she might say "eating utensil" when she forgets the word *fork.*

Stuck once for the words to convey *I'm going to bed, takin' the long trek down the hall,* she says instead, "Miles to go." From the Robert Frost poem, which ends, *"...and miles to go before I sleep."*

And of course, the all-purpose "It's good"—for *okay* or for *never mind* or *no more, I understand* and *that's enough, hush up about it,* and a myriad of other distinctions. Just "It's good, it's good."

Like "It's cool, man"—the beatnik, and later hippie expression in the early sixties—it covers damn near everything.

DATELINE, 1987—Third Reagan-Gorbachev summit in Washington, DC reaches agreement to dismantle medium-range missiles in Europe. A 5.9 earthquake in Los Angeles kills six, injures 100. Senate rejects Robert Bork for Supreme Court. Cher and Olympia Dukakis win Oscars for Best Actress and Supporting Actress in *Moonstruck*.

Aretha Franklin becomes the first woman inducted into the Rock and Roll Hall of Fame. The first supernova since 1604 is observed with the naked eye. American Motors acquires Chrysler. United Nations estimates the world population at 5 billion. Televangelist Pat Robertson announces his candidacy for the 1988 Republican presidential nomination. Construction begins on Channel Tunnel (the Chunnel), with the goal of linking England and France.

Stock market drops on October 19th, Black Monday, when the Dow Jones Industrial Average plunges 508.32 points, losing 22.6 percent of its total value. This fall far surpasses the one-day loss of 12.9 percent that began the great stock market crash of 1929 and foreshadowed the Great Depression. US budget reaches the trillion-dollar mark.

Klaus Barbie is convicted by a French court of Nazi war crimes and sentenced to life in prison. On a similar note, former Nazi deputy Rudolf Hess strangles himself at age 93 after having been in prison since 1941; he was the sole prisoner at the facility. In an attempt to re-populate their numbers, the last wild California Condor is taken into captivity, bringing the total to 27. *Les Misérables* is awarded eight Tony awards, including Best Musical.

her gift

As Alice's reading skills improve, my relief increases. Imagining my dear Alice not ever reading again has been the source of much trouble for me. She's never been without a book. From the moment I met her, I've always known her to carry one in the car and one in her back pocket. She's always had a book wherever she went. And both of us have wide nightstands by the bed, substantial pieces of furniture to easily hold towers of books—all in various stages of being read.

Since her stroke, however, we signed up for the national Books On Tape program from the Library of Congress, available not just to the blind, but anyone reading impaired. Every month, a listing of available titles arrives; the program provides a player, and cassettes travel back and forth in the mail to her. The beauty of the program is that it's government subsidized, so postage isn't necessary in either direction. That's pretty cool.

While not actually reading real books yet, Alice does read the newspaper every day. But she labors over it. Painstakingly, she explains how it is for her, and this is as another revelation for me.

Take this sentence in a newspaper article: *The two residents of Anaheim, John Smith and Jane Jones, both living on Main Street, reported hearing scuffling and shouting outside their homes after 8 P.M. last night.*

Most of us perform some sort of rapid scan and interpretation of words in our reading, such as: *two residents ... Anaheim ... John* (male) ... *Jane* (female) ... *Main Street* (oh yeah, between Thicket and Hedgerow) ... *hearing scuffling ... shouting ... last night.*

Alice has lost the ability to assess and associate specific words with certain attributes as she reads—such as identifying John and Joan as either male and female. Instead, she now must study each and every word with equal consideration, like a child beginning to read, pausing at every phrase to fully absorb its meaning. It's exhausting for her but she perseveres.

In any event, she is reading, and it eases me to see it.

"Okay. I drive now," Alice announces abruptly one day.

"Drive? You think you can drive?" I'm somewhat shocked, and a bit apprehensive.

"Well, yes," she answers dryly, very matter of fact.

"Are you sure? The idea scares me a little." It scares me a lot actually, because I still really don't know the extent of her abilities, or lack thereof. But I remember my vow not to obstruct her. "Okay, okay. We'll go to the other side of the highway and you can drive."

Without hesitation, she grabs her wallet and opens it. Teasingly, with an exaggerated emphasis, pulls out and shows me her driver's license, then chuckles at her own broad jibe and hugs me.

Yeah, I get the message—loud and clear.

Alice gets in the passenger side with me behind the wheel. The Ranchero and Scarlet the Mustang are gone now. We're in her Hyundai— the first new car she ever bought in her life. They just came out in the US, and are so novel, both for the fact that they are manufactured in Korea and because they are the lowest priced new car on the market now. When Sean and Rory bought Nora's mobile, Alice received a few thousand dollars as a down payment. But in order for her to maintain her MediCal benefits, Alice had to "spend down" her part of the money—and a down payment on anew car was acceptable for that process. She was very nervous about buying it and having car payments, but I was certain we could handle it all right. Before the few months leading up to her stroke, people often stopped and asked her about the Hyundai. She's fiercely proud of it.

So, now she's back in it, just not behind the wheel ... yet. I drive to an access road along the river, where we trade places. Now in charge of the wheel, Alice drives up and down the road with no problem.

"Do you want to try the highway?" I ask.

Without answering, she accelerates to the stop sign, obeys it, makes a right onto the ramp, and enters the highway, bringing us up to speed, using her mirrors to navigate lane changes.

There isn't much traffic, but she negotiates the road with the competence of a long-time driver, one with more than forty years experience on every kind of vehicle imaginable. She operated a tractor for her grandfather when she was just eight, and owned her first car by sixteen. Her memory of it all is apparently keen as ever.

She drives south on the highway for nearly an hour before she declares, "Go back now." She then takes the next exit, crosses the underpass, and pulls off the road. "I tired. You go," she says.

"Okay, love." We switch sides again, and as we do that, I realize how high-strung I am, and make an effort to shake it out. "Sorry, Alice. I realize I've been very tense and hyper-alert. I didn't mean to make you nervous," I say, again positioned behind the wheel.

"It's good," she says, using her catchall phrase with a pat to my leg.

"So, we know you can drive now. Are you confident to drive by yourself?"

"Yes." Her reply is emphatic.

"Okay. I just have one stipulation. I want you to carry a card with you that I'll type up—one for the car, and one you carry—a card, which says you've had a stroke, and it takes you a little longer to speak."

She raises an eyebrow.

"Alice, please! Just humor me with this. I've heard all kinds of stories about police officers hauling deaf people into jail and things like that. It'll make me feel better just knowing you have it with you. Please."

"It's good."

The card I create reads: *My name is Alice Joan Quincy. I suffered a stroke and now have aphasia. I hear and understand perfectly, but it takes me a few moments to answer because I have trouble finding the words. Please be patient.* Our home address and several phone numbers are on the bottom.

But I'm certain she never uses it.

343

Within the month, she's driving twice a week to the local college for her therapy and tooling around town at will. And one day she comes home with a story.

"I go market. Go to car. Lady ask, 'Where?' "

"A lady asked you for directions?" I ask.

She nods yes.

"What did you say?"

She pantomimes looking around, smiling, and shrugging her shoulders. I laugh because she is so damn charming about it. "What did the lady do?"

"Laugh. And ...." Alice pantomimes the lady shrugging, too. It seems there still isn't much she can't handle.

I might have known.

While Alice's motor skills seem intact, her mathematical ability is gone for the most part. She can add and subtract, if not asked directly to think about it, but any higher skills are lost, which are not so significant in terms of her daily life anyway.

But there are many paradoxes in this personal empirical brain study of mine. For example, Alice's ability to count money is unaffected. We practiced making change before she went out on her own for the first time. She patiently performed the tasks of giving and receiving the correct coins and differentiating the bills, and I can see she is just obliging me.

"You feel comfortable with handling this at a store, now?" I ask, already knowing she's fine. But I feel like I should ask it just the same.

"Yes. It's good."

"So, Alice—how come you can do this so easily, and it's more difficult to do figures in your head, or computations on a page?"

She thinks a minute, and shrugs. "I see better."

Yes, I guess that's so. Math is an abstract function, but it gets pretty damn concrete when it comes down to money.

One day I walked into the bedroom and thought I smelled cigarette smoke. It was a beautiful, late-fall day and the windows were open, so I didn't pay much attention. I idly assumed the workmen at the house next door were taking a smoke break.

Then, about two weeks later, I had occasion to open Alice's clothes cupboard. I never go into her things, but we were leaving for a doctor's appointment, and I was looking for her wallet to take. There on the floor of the cupboard was an open pack of Marlboros.

I was stunned.

Alice hadn't smoked in nearly six years, not since her heart attack. I decided to keep quiet about it till I had thought it out.

The next morning after breakfast, sitting at the table with her I broached the subject. "Alice, I need to ask you something. I went in your cupboard yesterday to bring you your wallet, and there was a pack of cigarettes in there. Are you smoking again?"

She ducked her head and wouldn't meet my eyes. "Little bit."

I made some decisions about how I might react before I approached her. I chose to be cool, the only thing I could do if I were to keep to my vow of not interfering in what is hers. Still…

"So, how much are you smoking?"

She glanced at me briefly and shrugged. "When done dinner. Morning. Nap. Just three. Could be four."

"You're smoking three or four cigarettes a day?"

She nodded.

"Well, Alice, you don't have to sneak them. If you're gonna smoke, you can smoke in front of me. You're a big girl." I smiled at her and touched her shoulder as I stood up and wrapped my arms around her from behind. "I wish you wouldn't smoke. You know it's not good for you. But it's not my decision. I won't try to stop you." I kissed her cheek and tightened the hug around the shoulders. "But I wish you wouldn't."

She patted my arms and I went about my business.

She never did smoke in front of me. But once in a while I could smell smoke on her, so I assumed she was indulging in those three or four cigarettes a day.

It was strange that she had begun to do this, but then again, if I had been as diligent about diet, exercise, and not smoking as she had these last six years, and still was dealing with all that she was—diabetes, stroke, heart attack, not to mention that mysterious back pain which had been there for six months till the stroke happened—I'd probably have figured the hell with it long ago and blissfully kicked over all the traces I could in wild abandon.

She no longer does her walking exercise three times a week at the Fireman's Pavilion as she had done for the last six years. Alice had become quite the program's grande dame after all that time. The medically monitored exercise program is for cardiac patients, hip and knee replacements, and basically anyone who benefits from a regular walking therapy, and Alice had been a fixture of it. She had taken a small amount of pride in her status—it had been her own province, an arena for her accomplishment, a place where she did not share the stage with me. A place all her own, and I wondered if she missed it.

Her days since the stroke had been occupied first with home visits from the speech therapist, which diminished to once a month at their office now. In between visits, she attended classes on computer therapy for writing and word identification and arrangement at College of the Redwoods. She was probably better at the tactile act of typing and visual task of reading than just plain speaking.

I think she just liked going to school, being on a campus surrounded by redwoods and green meadows where cattle grazed. And maybe this is a place she can call all her own. She drives there herself, of course, and negotiates it all just fine.

She also motors up to Eureka two days a week to work in the jewelry shop for a few hours, helping Josie to cast waxes for the gold. Alice learned to work the vulcanizer where the rubber cooks around finished molds, which Josie later uses for casting the gold and silver. I called Josie after Alice had been going up there a few times.

"Jo, I can't thank you enough for asking Alice to come up and help you," I told her. "She is so happy to be doing this. She came home and showed me the money you had paid her, and she was so proud of it, you'd have thought it was a million bucks. I never realized how much earning money meant to her."

"Yes, Alice thanked me, and put it in her wallet very carefully. I could tell she was really excited and feeling good about it." Josie's voice was warm.

"She gets her Social Security every month," I said. "And God knows she's earned that, but it goes right into the bank account, even though she has cash of her own from it every month, and I always ask if she needs any more. She usually tells me she still has some left over, but I cash out the same amount to give her every month anyway."

"Yeah, well, I guess it's not the same as going somewhere, doing a job, and getting paid for it."

"Evidently not." I add, "Look, Jo, no matter if you don't really need her anymore, or if she's not really helping you, please keep asking her to come up once or twice a week. I'd be willing to give you the money to pay her with. This really seems to mean something to her and I want her to have it."

"No, no. She really is helping me and I'm grateful for it. I need her to do this. It saves me a lot of time, and I'm happy to pay her for it. And besides, I really like having her here in the shop. She's good company." Josie said she found Alice's quiet presence a great comfort, strangely reminiscent of the days when HoneyBear was alive and working beside her. And they communicate just fine.

All that Alice needed us to know, she managed to convey with a few words, maybe a few simple gestures, and, of course, her direct blue eyes that always had a special way of saying it all.

For me, however, her speech was never tentative or awkward. I never lost the sound of her in my head, so whenever she spoke, I heard it the way she intended it.

As Christmas approached, Caroline offered to go shopping with Alice, but Alice said she was all right and wanted to do her own shopping. The Saturday before Christmas, she took off late in the morning, gaily waiving good-bye, and came back about three hours later, animated and bright, her cheeks rosy from the nip in the air. She bustled in the door, packages under her arms, bags dangling from her hands.

"I back," she declared, shaking the bags and pretending stealth toward the back bedroom, glancing back over her shoulder theatrically, pulling the packages against her as if they contained a great secret.

I could hear rustling and thumping as she tucked away the Christmas purchases, and for the first time in a long while, I felt the bubble of joy in me that her mischief always wrought. She dearly loved to play the fool for me and did it with such warm intelligence I was always delighted. It was one of our private games, and my favorite. Nothing was as good as coaxing a laugh out of her, unless she was the one being playful for my amusement.

When she emerged from the bedroom, she sat in her chair. I poured a cup of coffee for her. Graduated now from decaf to high octane, she sipped it with great relish.

"So, what'd you get?" I teased.

"Surprise," she answered haughtily. "Till Christmas," she added.

"Did you get everything you need, or do you have to go do some more?"

"It's good. I done. Little more."

"Okay, well, let me know if you need me to pick up anything."

She nodded. I had finished most of the gift buying for our mutual gift-giving, consulting her with catalogs, and she'd helped me make selections. But I knew her purchases today had been for me, chosen with her great love for me, and bought with money she'd earned at Josie's. Money she'd worked for ... and spent on me.

"Stockings?" She questioned.

"Whose?" I asked.

"You."

"I don't know. I think I'll take this one this year." I pointed to a long, knit stocking looped over one of the knobs of our bookcase.

She nodded, and I knew she'd even shopped for the odds-and-ends trinkets we stuff stockings with: pens, Post-it notes, pocketknives, a set of eyeglass screwdrivers, stuff like that.

An hour or more went by in companionable silence, the television filling the room with rumble as I thumbed through catalogs for last minute ideas.

"Oh!" Alice suddenly pushed herself up from the chair.

"Are you okay?" This was always my first question now, keeping the lid on my ever-ready panic.

"It's good, it's good," Alice reassured as she headed down the hall. I relaxed knowing whatever caused her to bounce up wasn't anything to do with her health. I heard clunking and rattling, and she came back down the hall with her hat and coat on and a bag in her hand. "I go, I go," she said, wagging the bag at me.

"Okay," I said, "come back soon."

She waved good-bye, revved up the car, and took off. About forty minutes later, she pulled up. and came in grinning.

"Everything okay?"

"It's good, it's good. I wrong. I fixed. Christmas—I tell." And staring pointedly at me, wearing that great grin of hers, she clutched the little bag to her belly with both hands, stuck her elbow out as if to hide it further, and made a show of sneaking it down the hall again.

"Okay." Charmed by her light-heartedness, I remained puzzled, but knew whatever Alice held in her hand had been satisfactorily remedied.

Christmas morning came with the usual warmth and sharing. Alice gave me a large, stuffed, white polar bear that played a Christmas carol repertoire consisting of eighteen tunes from a computerized insert in its belly. She also presented me with a small electric screwdriver with changeable heads that would really come in handy. And a six-pack of VHS blanks. And a very pretty scarf with a soft, swirling design.

My stocking she'd filled with ballpoint pens, a small address book, chewing gum, spiral tablet, an orange, some nuts, and a new coffee cup. Also, there was a pack of four wrought-iron house numbers wrapped in Christmas paper. She shopped well.

"I do wrong. Mistake," she said.

"You made a mistake? When? What about?"

She picked up the house numbers. They were flat wrought-iron, to be tacked up on the porch pillar. Numbers 1, 8, a 4, and a 5 ... 1845.

"Wrong. I get ...." She hesitated as she thought about it. "Number 6. I go back. Better now number 4."

"You had to take the numbers back and exchange one?" I asked.

"Yes. I say I tell you. Because ... I wrong. It's good."

So this was the mystery of the return trip to the store that day. She'd simply gone back, managed to convey her error to the clerk, and exchanged the wrong number for the right one. She never ceased to impress me with her courage, and her simple acceptance and ability to cope.

She never ceased to move me.

And for my part, I never failed on coming home to notice those wrought-iron house numbers, and experience the scope of her tender gift.

Her *greater* gift I had yet to fully realize here, at our last Christmas together. But in the months ahead, I would divine the mystical nature of her selfless generosity, and discern the final, full measure of her regard.

DATELINE, 1988—Vice President George Bush denies involvement in Iran-Contra scandal. **Congress rejects** President Reagan's request for Contras aid. Former National Security Adviser **Robert McFarlane** pleads guilty in Iran-Contra case. **U.S. Navy warships** and planes destroy two Iranian oil platforms and repel counterattacks from Iran. **U.S. Navy ship mistakes** an Iranian civilian airliner for a fighter jet and shoots it down, killing all 290 aboard.

Fires burn four million acres of forest in America, abetted by summer drought. **Toni Morrison** is awarded the Pulitzer for *Beloved*. **Computer security** becomes an issue when the first "worm" is introduced to thousands of computers on the Internet.

Governor Michael Dukakis and Senator Lloyd Bentsen are nominated at the Democratic National Convention. **Republicans nominate** George Bush and Dan Quayle. **Republicans are victorious** in 40 states. Attorney General **Edwin Meese resigns** amid accusations of financial misdealings.

Benazir **Bhutto is chosen** to lead Pakistan, first Islamic woman prime minister. **Terrorist bomb** on a Pan Am 747 explodes in flight over Lockerbie, **Scotland**, killing all 259 aboard and 11 people on the ground.

last

It is only now as I write this many years later that I can see that she had changed significantly. When I look at photos of that time back in 1988, it is obvious: her fragility, her frailty, her fading. But I never saw it then, never saw it in her face; never felt it.

I'm on the phone with my mother when Alice darts into the bedroom, sits on the bed next to me while tapping her chest and says, "Something wrong." Panicked, I scream into the phone to my deaf mother that I have to go, have to go.

"Can you walk?" I ask. Alice doesn't answer. Instead, she immediately stands up and starts down the hall to the front door and out to the car, with me hard on her heels, grabbing sweaters, my purse, car keys, as I hurry after her. I start the car and in seconds we are speeding toward the hospital.

"Can you tell me what it is?" I ask.

Alice struggles with words, and I see the effort it takes her. "Never mind, save it for the hospital." I press a little deeper on the gas and keep driving.

Mere minutes pass before I'm bursting into the ER, calling out for help. A nurse scurries up with a wheelchair, others open doors, get her on a bed, hook her up to oxygen and monitors. All this in a matter of moments.

—"Do you have chest pain?"

—"Show me where it hurts!"

The questions are flying.

I attempt to move things along and answer some of the more mundane questions. I rattle off medical history, current medications, the events that brought us here. Amid the chaos, I hear someone ask Alice about the names of her doctors.

"Give her time to respond," I interject, "she's aphasic—she had a stroke a year ago."

A year ago.

Today is March 10, 1988. Less ten days, it is exactly a year since she had the stroke.

Oh, God!

The truly bizarre thing is that just a month ago Caroline noticed we were coming up on the one-year anniversary. Jokingly, our housemate asked Alice how she wanted to celebrate it.

"Oh, I go hospital," Alice responded, calm as you please.

"Oh-ho-ho, no! Not the hospital!" Caroline protested. "You don't really want to go there, and visit the scene, do you?" Caroline laughed, and I did, too.

Alice just smiled and shrugged.

And here she is … in the hospital. God, this is too weird!

Alice is in no immediate distress except for severe shortness of breath. No pain, she manages to tell me. No pain at all. Not like before. Not like with the heart attack. She says this is different. Feels funny. The doctor orders tests, and they attach a telemetry to her. He determines that Alice need not go to the ICU. But she must be admitted to the medical unit until the cardiac enzyme test comes back from the lab.

Over the next few days, Alice undergoes a variety of tests and doctors' consultations. She seems to have had some cardiac episode, or just a sudden lessening of the heart's ability to pump.

One thing is certain, though: she's having difficulty breathing. Her lungs are battling fluids—a sure sign of congestive heart failure, the term assigned to describe the lungs' automatic watery response whenever the heart is compromised. And her condition worsens at night. Time and again, she bolts up out of her sleep and sits on the edge of her bed trying to catch her breath.

My nights are spent by her side, lying on an old, green, leather recliner, covered with a thin hospital blanket. I am here to keep her calm, to get help if she needs it. Just to be with her, go through it with her. The nightly breathing episodes are harrowing and exhausting for her. And I am just too petrified to be worried.

By day, they come and go—the nurses, the aides, the respiration therapists, the doctors. By night, we go it alone.

And I begin to fear where the journey will lead.

I leave Alice long enough in the day to go home and shower and change, pet the dogs, check in at the mill. I have left the crew at work to fend for themselves with no one in the office, and as day overtakes day, they try to manage without me.

The doctors can't offer much; at one point they want to send Alice to San Francisco to do more extensive cardiac workups. I am against it because I don't see how she'll even make the trip, since the least exertion seems to bring on episodes of her gasping for air, followed by extreme fatigue, which only ebbs after long periods of rest and quiet.

The doctors tell me there is one test to try first, which might help them determine what to do; it isn't invasive, and they can do it here.

"Do it, then!" My answer, of course, comes without hesitation.

The problem is Alice's heart muscle is not doing its job, which is producing the extreme congestion in the lungs. A portion of the heart muscle is atrophied and sluggish, unfed by the small vessels and the capillaries that supply blood to the heart. Diabetes is the culprit.

Diabetes has also been starving the small feeders to the nerves in Alice's legs, causing them to ache from neuropathy, for which she has been taking medication all this year. And in the same way, tiny hair-like bloodlines at one area in Alice's brain were starved, and, as we now know, caused her stroke last year. She never tested positive for diabetes prior to the stroke, but there is speculation now that six years ago her first heart attack may have been the result of undetected diabetes.

Every day, coming back from the short trip home, I bring stuff for Alice in the pockets of my sweater vest. Get Well greetings from our friends. A goody to tempt her. Something she's asked for, like her radio and earphones.

I kiss her hello, and as I assess how she is since my last departure, Alice focuses her attention on my pockets. She always delights in her finds—a note from a friend, a hanky, a comb.

And then it gets to be a joke. Anytime I leave the room, go to the toilet, check in at the nurses' station, get her a custard from the floor's kitchen, as soon as I come back to her room, she checks my pockets for surprises, presents.

"Now, Alice," I lecture, "the Pocket Fairy doesn't come *every time* I'm out of your sight, you know."

She gives me a look of tolerant forbearance. *Oh, ye, of little faith.* And then raises her eyebrows haughtily, looking away with a hint of disdain as if to say, *Well! That's how much you know about it!*

So, I elect to play her game, *with a twist,* and my next trip to the restroom includes a hurried visit to the hospital's tiny gift shop, which is so small it once acted as a broom closet in the hospital's main hall. Actually, it's *still* a broom closet, re-purposed with a movable counter, which extrudes into the hall and is staffed by a Pink Lady volunteer seated on a folding chair.

Not much stuff to choose from here. Just some greeting cards, gum, mints, toothbrushes, playing cards, a few stuffed toys. And a small display of tiny, cobalt, hand-blown glass bluebirds. Yes! That's it!

The volunteer finds a wad of tissue paper to wrap it in. In my pocket, it makes a small inconspicuous lump.

A few minutes after I get back to Alice's room, I make a point to lean over her, fluff her pillow, and nonchalantly arrange the tail of my vest so that it falls within her reach. She takes the bait! She makes a great show of reaching into my pocket to search for what she thought would be treasures unfound, clearly an attempt to tease me again with more pouting.

But this time, she gets a surprise. With a gasp, she discovers something in the very pocket she has stripped empty not an hour before. Pulling out the little tissue wad, she unwraps the glass bird, and laughs with utter delight. "See!" she says. She's positively beaming.

The Pocket Fairy *does come* to those who keep the faith.

The little bluebird holds a place of honor on her bed tray. It's there when she eats meals, and she strokes it absently in the night in her bad breathing times. She rearranges it on her table throughout the day and shows it to her nurses and therapists. The bluebird will be the last little joke we share together.

It isn't the last gift I give her, though. Being Easter season, I find a little fuzzy toy chick wearing a gingham bonnet. It is made to hang from its head with an elastic band and fastens around the overhead bar on the bed. Whenever she shifts positions in her bed, she can see it jostle and bounce.

Nearly two weeks have passed and Alice hasn't improved. Often now, when I come back from the restroom, a nurse is tending to her. She almost always is gasping for breath.

One late afternoon, during a shift change, a new nurse checks in on Alice as she naps. As unobtrusively as possible, the nurse takes her vitals and does it so well, Alice remains unstirred. The nurse pauses to examine Alice and turns to me before leaving the room. "She's very fragile." This is all she says to me before continuing her routine.

Very fragile. The words seem to contain some resonance. A distant knelling.

Two mornings later, I see that the urine in her bedside commode is scant and very dark— coffee-colored. As it is to be on this day, this fact is noted, but unexamined for portent. I am feeling removed right now, almost as if in a light trance.

Alice is exceptionally tired and lies back on the bed, closing her eyes. A pallor drains her face, then a strange, wide stripe of greyness passes diagonally across it, from her left jaw line to her opposite brow, followed by a pearly waxiness. Then slowly, slowly, color returns to her features.

I know what I have just seen. It has a name: The Shadow of Death.

As before ... noted, but not examined. Seen, observed, without emotional response, as I remain strangely above it, outside it.

Our friend Sean appears in the doorway, walking on his cane, here to visit Alice. He starts into the room, and something about it makes him hesitate. He looks at me intently, and without volition, I lower my eyes and shake my head.

He stands a moment looking at us, Alice and me, and indicates that he'll be back later and leaves quietly.

Moments later, I am dialing Caroline. "I think you better leave work and come," I say. I don't know why I do that. I seem to be on autopilot.

The nurses come and go. A technician tries to get a blood gas on Alice and gives up. Dr. Songer, her internist, enters next, and he examines her closely and speaks with her a moment before approaching me. "I'm going to move her down to ICU, I think, Nancy. She's going to need to be monitored more closely."

"Okay. When?"

"Right now. I'll get the nurses to help." Within moments, an army of medical staffers appear, and roll away her side table, unplug the electric bed, and wheel it out the door with her in it. They roll her backwards down the hall with her sitting upright in the bed, hands clutching the rails, eyes anxious and roaming.

"It's all right, Alice, they're just transferring you to another room." The sound of my own voice strikes me as strangely calm. And in the midst of keeping pace with Alice's moving bed, I notice that ridiculous, incongruous, little yellow Easter chick bouncing merrily from the bed's overhead bar, dangling just above Alice's head.

In ICU, Alice is once again hooked up to monitors that allow me to observe her heart rate. The EKG traces a jagged line across the screen as she rests. And I quietly drift into an odd, dream-like state, detached and ghostly. When Caroline arrives, she occupies another chair near Alice, and we just sit.

The next time Dr. Songer enters Alice's room, he asks to speak to us in the hall. "Well, her condition is very grave. The medicine I'm giving her helps her heart to pump stronger, but the problem is the med is only available in IV form. There is no oral equivalent. And without it ...." He hangs his head. "Her heart is not doing well at all—even with it. I'm sorry."

Caroline appears to be crumpling where she stands. I grab her, bracing my arm around her. "So, this is it?" I ask.

He pauses, then nods.

"Thank you for telling me," I say. "And thank you for doing all you have done."

"Are you all right?" he asks.

I shrug. "I've been very lucky to have known her," I tell him, with the only hint of passion I've felt all day. I move with Caroline back in the room.

"I'll check in frequently from my office," he says kindly. "Just ask the nurses if you want anything."

We walk back into the room, and Caroline drops into a chair. A nurse attends Alice, who is sitting on the edge of the bed because lying on her back makes her desperate for breath and panicked. Caroline and I swivel the over-bed table in front of Alice so she can lean over and lay her head on it. We crank it high, and place pillows on it. In this position, Alice seems to breathe marginally easier, though no position gives her nearly enough air. I grip her shoulder.

I won't hold her here anymore—her body isn't up to it. It is time. And I gave my word.

Our surroundings feel surreal. Time shifts on its axis. I speak to Alice calmly, from a highly focused place, acutely tuned in just to her. My voice seems to come from somewhere else other than me. "Alice, I don't want you to go. But it's all right. If you have to, it's all right. Do you hear me?"

She breathes with effort, forearms on the pillows on the over-bed table.

"Did you hear me, Alice?"

"Yes!" Her answer is resounding. Her breathing, hard and fast. She lowers her head onto her arms, and I sit down in a chair alongside the bed and hold the table with my hands and feet so it won't scoot away.

The vigil has begun.

Alice's purpling, bare feet are on the bottom crossbar of the tray table in front of her. Bent over, arms and head on the pillows, her eyes are closed, face pale. I sit myself at the short end of the table next to Alice. Caroline is here, too, ten feet away in a chair facing our direction. I touch Alice's shoulder and start to fuss about elevating her feet, which are swelling, the blue spidery veins clearly outlined against the backdrop of her mottled skin.

She waves me away, impatiently, then waves her hand in a softer, don't-do-that gesture. And then, another motion, which I clearly recognize—a signal that tells me to just be here. Stay here.

In my bizarrely altered state I seem to know that she can't touch me, can't have me touch her, if she is to go about the business of dying. There

357

is too much attachment, too great a bond to hold her here, making it hard to let go.

I sit back in the chair to go about my own business of trying to release my hold on her. Don't ask me how I know any of this, because it isn't clearly thought out. I am not thinking. I am simply *being*—in sync with Alice in a way that does not allow for thought.

Intuitively, I understand if I want to be part of her dying process, go with her as far as I can go, share this with her, I have to suspend all analytical thinking. There is no room for conjecture. Nor notions of the present, the future, or the impact of any of this. There will be time enough for all that later. I just have to *be* in this moment. Here. Now. Allow *this* to happen—without judgment, concern, consideration.

Just *be*.

I allow my body to relax, particularly mid-torso where the tension settles. Tears flow down my face, unheeded, disregarded. Idly, I mop them with a tissue, paying them no mind.

I begin to let go. Let go of her, as I promised myself, as I promised her. I will not do anything to hold her. I will let go of it—all ties, all links— and these seem to be located in my solar plexus. I begin to focus there, and feel something loosen ... tendrils, strings. Loosen. Release. Disconnect.

Alice, from time to time, raises her head, looking at Caroline, blink- ing at her surroundings. She never looks directly at me—never attempts to make a connection. But I know she is completely aware of my pres- ence. Knows I am going through this with her.

I try to make myself unobtrusive, benign, passive. Waiting. But here, right here with her.

It becomes clear to the nurses in the ICU that hers will be a con- scious dying and they stand by. Vigilant, should they be needed, but not interfering.

Time has no meaning, no reckoning. The event which is transpiring has no relationship to hours or minutes.

When Alice raises her head and shifts her position, I rouse from my fugue state enough to test myself, to ascertain that I am still as "unat- tached" to her as I can be. I make no attempt to reach for the "strings" of her unconsciously, by force of habit or any other means. I take pains not to rebind her from *there* back to me. Instead, I sink back into that same serene, dreamlike waking, trusting it to take me where I need to be. Close and alert, a heightened awareness even, but undirected, unengaged.

To witness. Just to bear witness.

Even so, actual time is passing and one of the nurses quietly approaches Alice, saying she seems a little restless and asks if she's in pain.

Without lifting from the pillow on the table, Alice shakes her head no.

"Alice, we have an order for morphine to give you, and I think you should take some," the nurse adds. "It will keep you relaxed. Why don't I give you half the dose?"

Alice lifts her head and focuses with effort on the nurse, then nods consent. A moment or so later, the nurse returns, gives Alice the shot and speaks to me, "That'll be better. She'll be more comfortable." I nod my understanding, and check the monitors to see that Alice's blood pressure has dropped to 90/50 where normal is 120/80, and her pulse rate is 64, and the normal is 80. Slowing down, then.

Tears continue to flow from my eyes, and I wipe them away without concern. My body is grieving even as I am still above it, still not centered on anything of this world but her. I withdraw again into that special space I share with Alice.

The nurse returns nearly an hour later. "I want to give you the second half of that shot now, Alice. You seem more restless again. We want you to be comfortable."

Alice nods, without lifting her head from the pillow. She holds onto the table before her. Her feet are blotchy and evil looking. Her respirations more labored and difficult. I'm glad she has agreed to the morphine. The monitors are down to 85/58 BP and pulse of 57. Respirations rapid at 28.

The nurse gives the second shot and stands a moment examining Alice bent over the bed table, head on her arms, lying on top of the pillow. Alice's breathing eases a bit and she relaxes slightly. Lightly, the nurse pats her shoulder, an expression of deep sadness on her face. I am oddly struck by that. And then she leaves as quietly as she came.

Next arrives Dr Songer—the ICU nurses had called him. He nods at me, and speaks to her. "Alice, it's Dr. Songer. Is there anything you need? Anything I can do for you?"

From her face-down position, Alice shakes her head no, and Dr. Songer walks back into the nurses' area.

I begin to be aware of an odd sense of movement, a gathering. Something is happening, something which feels like rising excitement. A rushing.

I look up, and the monitors are registering her dropping blood pressure, slowing pulse. The digital numbers are changing. P 57 ... 56 ... 55 ....

Dr. Songer and the nurses have moved into view and are standing by, on the other side of the bed. P 49 ... 48 ....

"I can't ... I can't ... I love you." Alice speaks clearly to me, but barely above a whisper.

And then ... she leaves.

Escapes from the top of her head, shooting forward from her crown as she is bent over the table. Leaves in a *Whoosh!* Goes forth in a burst of excitement and joy.

I feel myself drawn with her, pulled. I can see swirling ... what? Energy? Nebulous, gauzy, churning, and spiraling, moving away from her. A disturbance of the air, like a special effect in a movie.

And then, *she* detaches from *me*. Something trailing behind her, some unseen stalk, some cord comes away from me, strips away from my midriff area, pulls off my belly slightly left of center, a hand span above my navel. Peels away, just like silent Velcro, with that slow, ripping, unhooking quality.

She ... lets go ... of me.

I feel for it, feel with my hand for the hole in my gut, look down to the hole, which isn't really there .... I groan. Slump. My forehead sagging down to the table, next to the pillow and her arm.

She is gone.

The nurses and Dr. Songer move to her, begin to draw her away from the table, lay her back on the bed, lifting her legs up onto the mattress.

"She's going," Dr. Songer says, and I lift my head and see the numbers changing on the monitor ... P 43 ... 42... 40 .... Then the EKG flatlines. Her body finally registers what I know has *already* occurred.

Alice was gone—gone moments before her body actually died. A logical part of me registers this fact, validates what I have always suspected to be true. The body can still be functioning, maybe even be maintained at some level, but its occupant has vacated.

After a few moments, I stand up, and Dr. Songer comes around the bed and hugs me, holding on. Both nurses are weeping!

They both wrap their arms around Caroline and me in turn, hugging us, crying, expressing their condolences. I find myself in the odd position of comforting them, these three medical professionals, who should be somewhat inured to death.

More to the point, I am perfectly comfortable doing that because I have experienced a totally different thing than they have. I felt the joy, the release of her escape from here, and there is a brilliant euphoria that comes with that. Elation that I cannot explain to anyone else, an elation that Alice felt—and I shared.

The closest thing to it is the feeling in a room when a birth has just occurred, that splendid cheer the moment when a baby is born into this world. I know I will not feel this way for long. It will all come crashing down only too soon: the reality, the sense of loss, the comprehension that she's gone from this life. Gone—while I must stay.

But I am yet in the moment, a moment that has been exalted and joyful and transcendent.

Two ICU nurses and the busiest internist of the hospital, all are openly affected by Alice's death. As I hug them, I wonder how they can survive their jobs if it troubles them so powerfully when someone dies. Then at the same instant, I know this *doesn't* happen with every death.

There was something about Alice—some greatness in her. Something about the dignity of her passing, the near majesty of it, felt even by these nurses, this doctor, hardened to daily scenes like this, but responding at some deeper level to the death of this woman.

The nurse pulls away from me, sniffling. "Do you want to be alone with her for a little bit?" she asks me, wiping her nose on her tissue, and tucking it into her pocket.

"No," I answer. "I've been alone with her all along."

Caroline and I gather up her things, and I discover someone put the little glass bluebird on the table behind me. I hadn't known it was there, but when I turn to survey the area one last time, the light catches the deep blue of it, and I walk over and pick it up.

It was there for Alice to see right up to the end.

⚜

So what do I know about this now, two and a half decades later? What do I believe true?

I know I signed on to be the survivor. Somewhere in our years together I came to understand she would leave here before I did. There was inevitability about it, which I consented to, which I even abetted, knowing I had to be sure to stay alive and fit enough to see her through what would come.

And in that last year, small thoughts flitted across my mind:

"When Alice is gone, I will have to...."

"When Alice is no longer here, there will be...."

It drew me up sharp, such a thought. I'd hurriedly brush it away, and shake it off. But a part of me knew it was coming. And that it was getting close.

And I know her last year was a gift to me. A great gift.

Somehow. Some where. Some when. Alice made a deal with the Powers that Be that she would stay another year—just for me. She gave that year to me, gave me time to adjust, to accept the inevitable, to come to terms in my heart of hearts. She would tolerate, would yield to the lessening of her abilities that the stroke exacted, as long as she wasn't in pain, didn't get worse, didn't get too tired. The final evidential emblem of her love. Of this, I am convinced.

"Oh, I go hospital," she said a month before, when asked how she'd celebrate the one-year marker since the stroke. She knew. She planned it. She even indulged in the few daily cigarettes, knowing they would be of no consequence in the long run—and a tiny pleasure to be permitted.

Alice died one year and four days after her stroke.

And I know at the end, Alice took me with her as far as it was possible for me to go. That very strange, very present state I was in all day was my submission to the conditions of being allowed to consciously participate in her dying.

Through some subliminal instruction, I knew to be entirely *where she was*, not where I was, all that day, if I was to take part in the vast mystery of it. To share one last time, maybe the single most important experience with her.

And I know this to be true as well: wherever she has gone, she is also still here with me. With me always. And when my turn comes at long last, she'll be waiting as I step through into the next adventure.

postscript and
possibilities

There is a great truth. To the same full extent there was Joy, Sorrow takes its equal measure. And this is fitting. Never forget this—it brings a comfort all its own.

About ten years after Alice died, I started to write our story. The bulk of this account was penned from the perspective of sixteen years past her death. It was a hard journey, and only in more recent years have I become more comfortable with the loss. For the last eight years I've been refining this memoir, in addition to writing a supplemental one about the creatures and critters who passed through our lives and traveled beside us.

Oh, yeah, and I've been pretty busy living life.

This chronicle has been an attempt to fix the memory, to focus on her, and tune her in. After someone dies, remembrance gets fuzzy and grainy with constant handling. Or faint, for the very reason that it is not linked to the major events and highlights which you tend to recall most frequently. Small details get away, fade, and become irretrievable, if not sought after in the recesses of the mind. The larger portraits, by contrast, suffer from too much visiting, turning ordinary, dulled, familiar, without meaning.

In the final analysis, I'm afraid you'll have to take my word for it all, since Alice is unavailable for comment.

My love for her has not dimmed, my devotion is undiminished, my passion has not died. Present, still, is the spirit of her, the solid completeness of our shared life, the remembrance of that happiness, whose joyous ghost I've abided with through these years, and my heart has progressively been made lighter through this effort to revisit.

Lastly, I know with all the surety I possess, in this life or any other, that Alice remains—through all the vast stretches of time and the mysterious interstices of dimension—my *True Love*.

Over these many years, well-meaning people have asked me when I'm going to start dating again, or when I'm going to look for a new love. I always laugh a bit, and say I'm not interested, not looking, not trying to find.

And a few have asked me why not? Some sincerely want to know, earnestly want to understand, tenderly try to argue me out of my position. Or pity my unwillingness.

Sometimes I try to explain.

More often, I move the topic in another direction. It is like trying to describe Mozart to the deaf. Sex to a virgin. Chocolate to a Kalahari Bushman. There simply is no point of reference.

Like I said from the start, True Love—for all its demands and undeniability—defies description. What generally passes for love compares to True Love as silents are to modern movies—a faint intimation, a simulacrum, a tantalizing hint of what could be.

And I believe people actually know this.

If it's True Love, you already understand.

Or in your secret heart maybe you know it's not True Love by the ragged edges around your relationship, by a vague emptiness or "something missing," by a haunting yearning (often at the best of times), or the lack of total "fit."

But maybe you got most of it, most of what you think is possible, and you're happy and content with that. Otherwise, you might have to go on the hunt again, for something you are unconvinced actually exists anyway.

The truth is, I've had the unalloyed good fortune, the rare and precious luck to have had a True Love, and still do. Like the poet said, love can't die but, alas, lovers do.

The argument then goes, "But you can love again. All the more reason to find somebody new, if you've already been successful in love." Which tells me I am speaking with one who is deaf to Mozart, or they would know I have no incentive to look further, no nagging need to fulfill, no urge to complete. Not anything about this has changed just because Alice died.

Only those whose hearts have not been totally opened by True Love argue for finding another person to love, to live with. A True Lover left behind to continue on never speaks that way.

Don't misunderstand. Many True Lovers seek another companion, someone to love again. Of course, they do! Many people find it too lonely to live alone. Or need diversion from their memories. But they don't expect it to be like it was—this would set themselves up, as well as their new partner, for a miserable experience. Because anything less (and how can it not be less?) only serves to reinforce the inestimable loss of what once was. And often what they find again is "good enough."

So, good for them!

Since I enjoy and require solitude, it simply doesn't interest me to find someone to live with. I have friends and a social life and work, and I never even think of being alone, because in truth, I never am. I continue to live in the cloister of our love, even though my True Lover has moved on to another place.

I don't call on Alice as much as I once did when we were newly parted. I don't need to. I exist now with the assurance of her place in my life, in my deeper life, the one that underlies this journey of time and physicality.

And so I shrug off the well-meaning concern and continue on. I am content to accept the way things are and willing to accede to destiny, to the pattern I am meant to live. I live it well. I live it with an open heart. I live it, still, with Alice.

Each of us in our own way.

And ... no matter what you do about it, suddenly you are seventy-something, and it is a good twenty-five years since the love of your life died. In between has been filled with heights and depths and heartbreak and happiness. And if you are lucky, you have been able to claim that reality again that you lost—find her and fix her—in photos, in memories, in friends, or in a manuscript you've labored over, for the sheer sake of doing just that, claiming her again. Which means you've made it through.

You've not succumbed to the grief. You've learned how to carry it more tightly packed, learned how to shift it from time to time to relieve the burden, how to carry it resolutely, even. This constant encumbrance a part of you that speaks to the honor of it, like a battle scar or a war medal. You bear it with privilege and know that you will never be without it, for this sorrow is an earned and warranted treasure—a measure of the loss—and also the goad to your survival.

From time to time, the wind still blows through my heart, cold and biting and desolate. Mostly when this happens now, the image of Alice comes as well, unbidden, but oh so welcome—the soft shadows on her face, the golden glints in her hair, the look in her loving blue eyes. And with it the sultry, sweet voice of her, my True Love, as I first heard Alice saying, *I've been in love with you since the moment you walked into my lab....*

author bio

Nancy Lehigh resides in the home of her heart—coastal Northern California—"where the redwoods meet the sea." Believing she's had the luckiest of lives, and the best is yet to be. Visit her on her website/blog www.isitsisters.com.

Made in the USA
San Bernardino, CA
27 April 2014